"With *Daughter of the Dragon*, [ng different . . . a form of reclamation a n- erous storyteller; the Anna May he e es she was relegated to and turned to writ ty and wit."

—   *es*

"An incisive guide . . . *Daughter of the Dragon* offers a lively tour through Wong's world and filmography, and the film stills and portraits included throughout are a particular pleasure. Mr. Huang turns the spotlight back onto an important but largely forgotten film icon—one who shone brightly despite the bitter racial bias she faced throughout her long career."

—Julia Flynn Siler, *Wall Street Journal*

"*Daughter of the Dragon* gives us a sense of how difficult it was for Wong to operate amid the legal, cultural, political and social constraints that restricted the roles she could play in the movies and the choices she could make in her life. Yet Huang also lets us watch Anna May transcend those limits, sending witty letters to friends, welcoming reporters, posing for photographers and campaigning for war relief in China, all the while creating the character that still demands our attention." —Ann Fabian, *National Book Review*

"Deeply researched. . . . [Huang] presents a fulsome panorama of creative Berlin [and his] treatment of 1920s London, Wong's next stop, is equally detailed."

—Celia McGee, *AirMail*

"Exhaustive. . . . Huang uses popular, easily accessible prose, mixed with a professor's use of lengthy quotes from revealing sources and digressions into the influences of the day, to illuminate the main facts of the cinema idol's real-life exploits." —John Krich, *Nikkei Asia Review*

"This is the extraordinary story of the great Anna May Wong. . . . A hugely fascinating Hollywood story. And a timely, vital, complex, sad, moving, and triumphant American story. This beautifully written book is a marvel of cultural history and biography, and a loving celebration of an amazing woman."

—Paul Giamatti

"This is an epic read. Anna May Wong is brought to life and put into context amid America's racial and cinematic history as only a poet-historian can—

with wit, empathy, and wide-ranging erudition. Astutely researched yet also light-footed in its prose, this book absorbed and surprised me."

—Linda Rui Feng

"As with all of Yunte Huang's previous books, *Daughter of the Dragon* is another great work of resonant history. It reveals an America and Hollywood we know all too well and yet hardly."

—Wayne Wang, director of *The Joy Luck Club*

"Yunte Huang's superb biography of Hollywood's first Chinese American movie star . . . doubles as a reckoning with the country's attitudes about Asian people in Wong's day. . . . Tremendously elucidating and moving."

—Nell Beram, *Shelf Awareness*, starred review

"Huang's sympathetic treatment brings out the nuances of Wong's story, highlighting how she by turns acceded to and bristled against the stereotypes Hollywood asked her to play. . . . It's a fascinating—and long overdue—close-up of a Hollywood trailblazer."   —*Publishers Weekly*, starred review

"While Wong's life has recently been explored in historical fiction . . . most readers will find her real story even more engaging. Huang has created a page-turner nonfiction book with this biography by fleshing out the world in which Wong lived. Huang's lively, surprising, and all-encompassing biography of Anna May Wong should be on everyone's summer reading list."

—*Library Journal*, starred review

"[*Daughter of the Dragon*] capably tracks Wong's life and career, creating a tender, fair portrait of an important performer. . . . Huang illustrates details about Wong with passion and fervor, clearly delineating her struggles and achievements. When Wong succeeds, readers will rejoice, and when her circumstances limit her, readers will feel her sorrow."   —*Kirkus Reviews*

"In a deeply researched and far-reaching biography, professor and award-winning biographer Huang positions Wong's career achievements in America and abroad against the geopolitical challenges of the 1930s. . . . The result is a thorough, multilayered history of the too brief yet impactful life of a pioneering Chinese American woman artist facing racism and sexism in tumultuous times."   —*Booklist*

ALSO BY
YUNTE HUANG

*Inseparable: The Original Siamese Twins
and Their Rendezvous with American History*

*Charlie Chan: The Untold Story of the Honorable Detective
and His Rendezvous with American History*

DAUGHTER OF THE DRAGON

ANNA MAY WONG'S
RENDEZVOUS WITH
AMERICAN HISTORY

YUNTE HUANG

LIVERIGHT PUBLISHING CORPORATION
A Division of W. W. Norton & Company
INDEPENDENT PUBLISHERS SINCE 1923

FRONTISPIECE: Anna May Wong *(Courtesy of Everett Collection)*

For information about permission to reproduce selections from this book, write to Permissions, Liveright Publishing Corporation, a division of W. W. Norton & Company, Inc., 500 Fifth Avenue, New York, NY 10110

For information about special discounts for bulk purchases, please contact W. W. Norton Special Sales at specialsales@wwnorton.com or 800-233-4830

Manufacturing by Lakeside Book Company
Book design by Marysarah Quinn
Production manager: Lauren Abbate

ISBN 978-1-324-09513-2 pbk.

Liveright Publishing Corporation, 500 Fifth Avenue, New York, N.Y. 10110
www.wwnorton.com

W. W. Norton & Company Ltd., 15 Carlisle Street, London W1D 3BS

1 2 3 4 5 6 7 8 9 0

America I've given you all and now I'm nothing.

—ALLEN GINSBERG, "America"

What remains is solitude.

—MARLENE DIETRICH

Contents

LIST OF ILLUSTRATIONS

PREFACE

NOT A TYPICAL cradle-to-grave biography, *Daughter of the Dragon* examines the spectacular life and career of Anna May Wong, the Chinese American actress who once captivated the world with her enigmatic, almost tragic beauty. A screen siren far more complicated than her legendary celluloid image would suggest, she signed her publicity photos with the phrase "Orientally yours," suggesting a touch of both demureness and defiance. She is, dare I say, a study in inscrutability, a loaded English word that carries the historical weight of Chinese travails in America. Like Charlie Chan and the Siamese Twins, heroes of my two previous books, Wong speaks with a subversive voice that, while avowing the unbridled creative spirit of this great nation, cries out against America's bigotry and injustice toward those who simply *look* different.

I emphasize the word *look*, because who can forget Anna May Wong's signature bangs, her almond eyes radiant as if with cosmic rays, her willowy figure wrapped in a silky *qipao* (cheongsam) as if it were her second skin? For vintage shine, we need look no further than the now-defunct *Look* magazine, which crowned Wong as "The World's Most Beautiful Chinese Girl." Wong herself once famously said, "You can forgive a woman for a face that is not beautiful more easily than for a dress that isn't."[1] However, if mainstream America fell in love with Wong for her looks, that romance also became a taboo because of her looks. After all, she lived at a time when a Chinese would be deemed "too Chinese" to play such a role—a cultural absurdity plaguing both Hollywood and

Main Street USA, a racial attitude that imposed a virtual form of foot-binding on Wong throughout her career.

Born into the steam and starch of her father's laundry, Wong rose to global stardom. Such a rags-to-riches ascension may sound like an American cliché, but here's a spoiler alert: Wong had to go to Europe to be recognized as American, to Australia to be hailed as Chinese. Facing the "triple jeopardy" of race, gender, and age in Hollywood, "The World's Most Beautiful Chinese Girl" spent her twilight years nursing a drink in one hand, a cigarette in the other, running around a small shop in Santa Monica like an elderly maid with a Chinese feather duster. In other words, hers is not another Horatio Alger saga celebrating the American Dream. Instead, the Anna May Wong story is as much about her charm and drive as it is about how Hollywood as the world's grandest Dream Factory turned into a dystopia, or a "Dream Dump," as Nathanael West called it, for Wong and countless others like her; it is about those historical currents that molded, propelled, and frustrated her, and finally swept her up.

To write about Anna May Wong, then, is to write about the undulations of the American experience in the first half of the twentieth century. Wong came of age during the film industry's meteoric rise in which it grabbed the lion's share of the American imagination, a period when Hollywood became not just a place but a state of mind. Unlike so many of her "silent" generation, Wong survived film's transition from silence to sound, and later from silver screen to TV screen—a powerful testament to her talent and tenacity. More important, it was in the same period when America's Chinatowns remained exotic destinations, as distant and foreign as Shanghai or Tokyo, a time when Chinese immigrants were routinely detained on Angel Island in San Francisco Bay and denied entry into the country, while Japanese Americans were rounded up and sent to internment camps. A "star coolie," as it were, in Hollywood's Dream Factory, and endowed with a disarming appeal, she was not allowed to kiss or even be kissed by a white man, at least not on-screen, for fear of offending a misguided American sense of propriety. As a symbol of forbidden love, she embodied America's love and hate for the Orient, an inner war with itself in the crucible of race.

In her four-decade career, Wong appeared in more than sixty films, a dozen stage plays, several television series, and countless vaudeville shows. In the limited playing field allowed for a nonwhite actress of her time, always having to negotiate the binary stereotypes between the self-sacrificing Madame Butterfly and devious Dragon Lady, she carved out a distinct performative space for herself while blazing a trail for other Asian American artists. Compared to her costar Lon Chaney—dubbed "The Man of a Thousand Faces" for the myriad yellowface Chinese characters he had impersonated with the aid of adhesive tape—Wong was a woman of a hundred names who, figuratively speaking, died a thousand deaths. Like Sylvia Plath's Lady Lazarus, she did it so it felt like hell; she did it so it felt real. Each time, she would rise again, not to "eat man like air," in a vampirish way, but to show the world her undying commitment to her calling as an artist.[2]

Mind you, I am not quoting Plath in vain. Unknown to most, Anna May Wong was a remarkably gifted writer—articulate, stylish, and hilariously witty. The autobiographical pieces she published when she was living in self-exile in Europe, the serial articles commissioned by the *New York Herald Tribune* during her soul-searching China trip, and her voluminous correspondence with friends, especially Carl Van Vechten and his wife, Fania Marinoff, have provided me with a veritable goldmine of material. Whenever possible, I have tried to let Wong speak for herself or have reconstructed events based on her words. One of her favorite catchphrases was "and Confucius didn't say this," which always preceded her deadpans like a theatrical peal of a gong. As with her use of "Orientally yours," the droll expression was both self-mocking and brutally ribbing. Read together, her writings reflect a sharp mind acutely aware of its own place in a world that, on the one hand, is captivated by her and, on the other, looks askance at her. Between her satirical lines, between the parodically timid China doll and the intimidating Daughter of the Dragon, lies the alluring art of Anna May Wong, who continues to haunt us all.

With this book, I am also completing the trilogy I refer to as a "Rendezvous with America," a saga that explores the Asian American experience in the making of America. Beginning with *Charlie Chan* (2010), in which I traced the protagonist's evolution from rough-and-tumble Hawaii cop to fictional hero to Hollywood detective, I continued with *Inseparable* (2018), a book that charts the implausible rise of Chang and Eng Bunker, the original Siamese Twins, from subhuman, freak-show celebrities to slaveholding Southern gentry, married to two white sisters, who sired twenty-one children. In both books, I reexamined the tortured odyssey of controversial cultural icons, elevating and humanizing them through stories deeply embedded in the grand narrative of American history. Likewise, in this third installment, I illuminate Anna May Wong's spectacular rise from laundryman's daughter to global celebrity, against the broad backdrop of a world riven by racism, bigotry, and injustice. Whether it is Charlie Chan's resurrection from the graveyard of postmodern symbols, the Siamese Twins's powerful testimonial to what it means to be human, or Anna May's impeded rendezvous with America, my focus remains on this subversive genealogy of Asian icons, thus depicting the epic journey of Asian Americans in the nation's tumultuous history. As Confucius said—and he did say this—"Roads are made for journeys, not destinations."

DAUGHTER OF THE DRAGON

Young Anna May Wong *(Courtesy of Matteo Omied / Alamy Stock Photo)*

PROLOGUE

O N A HUMDRUM DAY in the mid 1910s under a crepuscular sky, the City of Angels spread out like a cut of nickelodeon reel. Having replaced gas lamps in 1882—the same year Congress halted Chinese immigration to America—the electric streetlights, the first in any thoroughfare of an American municipality, just came on. Like sleepers newly awake, rubbing sleep off their eyes, the lights blinked in the evening mist permeated with factory soot and Mojave sand. Pedestrians were as scarce as ghosts in this lull between day's-end rush and late-night prowling. Now and then, streetcars jangled, piercing the din of the city, which was in the final stages of a transformation from frontier town to a west-coast dystopia carved out of cacti and sand.

On a hilly street downtown, a Chinese girl, about nine, maybe ten, was climbing the steep sidewalk and hauling a bundle of laundry that appeared heavier than her small body. Fresh-faced, the child sported black bangs cut neatly above her big, bright eyes. Even as she strained under the weight of her load, she was agile like a bird, moving uphill in nimble steps. As she approached a plain frame house fronting the street, a gaggle of street urchins suddenly spilled out of a dim alley. Prancing and grimacing like a band of little griffins, they taunted her with a chant:

> *Chink, chink, Chinaman,*
> *Wash my pants.*
> *Put them into a boiler,*
> *And make them dance.*

She halted her steps, face flushed, round eyes flaring with anger. She turned and looked downhill, where a Chinese laundryman in a blue cotton shirt was watching her with the keen eyes of a father hawk. His hands were swollen from years of washing other people's soiled linen. Around his neck hung a police whistle, a must-have talisman for Chinese working outside the safety zone of Chinatown. Ever since the massacre of eighteen Chinese by white mobs in 1871, followed by two arsons in 1887 and 1892, the Chinese community in the city, facing unabated violence and harassment, had banded together and tried to live within the small plot of land sandwiched between the old Spanish Plaza and the railyard. When trips outside Chinatown became unavoidable, whether traveling to the docks or delivering laundry, these police whistles would prove indispensable.[1] And when the hoodlum boys saw the eagle-eyes of the elder Chinese man and his obligatory whistle, they beat a quick retreat while employing yet another popular, turn-of-the-century rhyme:

> *Ching Chong Chinaman sitting on a fence,*
> *Trying to make a dollar out of fifteen cents.*
> *Along came a choo-choo train,*
> *Knocked him in the cuckoo brain,*
> *And that was the end of the fifteen cents.*

As the hecklers all disappeared into the dark alley, their refrains still pierced the noisome night air. Wiping a tear off her cheek, the girl quickly pulled herself together and went up to the frame house. A white woman came to the door and took her delivery. To her delight, the woman gave her a penny tip.

After a curtsey with a sweet smile, the girl turned and scampered down the hill, the penny jangling against others in her coat pocket. Taken together, these coins would be enough for a ticket at the movie theater, evidence that the girl was dreaming something bigger: She planned to use the money not just to buy a ticket to a movie—or even, as the rhyme went, to make a dollar out of fifteen cents. She wanted to be a star, like those blonde actresses she saw on the silver screen: Pearl White, Alla Nazimova, Mary Pickford, and many other "picture personalities" displayed on lobby cards.

Entranced by these thoughts, the girl would invariably return to her father, who would be moping by the laundry baskets. Soon these two silhouettes would totter down another darkening street lined with faceless houses, windows dimly lighted, filled with stories of obscurity and anonymity. There would be another delivery to make, another hill to climb for her, a girl known at this point only as Anna.[2]

Chinese laundry, Los Angeles, early 1900s *(Courtesy of Seaver Center for Western History Research, Los Angeles County Museum of Natural History)*

PART ONE

FUN IN A CHINESE LAUNDRY

1

YEAR OF THE DRAGON

Anna May Wong, circa 1907 *(Courtesy of Mondadori Portfolio / Archivio GBB / Everett Collection)*

ANNA MAY WONG burst into the world at her father's laundry on the third day of 1905. On the Chinese lunar calendar, it was the tail end of the Year of the Dragon, a mythic animal symbolizing power, nobility, honor, and success. These great qualities might seem to bode well for the newborn, but aficionados of the Chinese zodiac would caution that she was a Wood Dragon, a person destined to be an introvert, a loner always in want of good relationships.[1]

The Wongs probably did not put too much stock into these horoscope readings. Their new brood was in fact a disappointment, especially for the father. Hailing from the rough mining camps in Northern California, Wong Sam

Sing was a laundryman with ambition. He had already had a son with his first wife in China, and now he was eager to extend further the Wong genealogical line in America with his second wife, Lee Gon Toy. Impacted by racist immigration restrictions, Sam Sing, like many Chinese American men during that harrowing time, had to juggle bits of life orbiting in parallel universes. On September 9, 1901, he married fifteen-year-old Gon Toy, daughter of a Chinese cigar factory owner, in San Francisco. After the wedding, the new couple, weary of anti-Chinese violence in rural America and lured by opportunities in Southern California, arrived in Los Angeles and set up their first home and laundry in Chinatown. A year later, and much to Sam Sing's chagrin, their firstborn, Lew Ying (Lulu), was a girl. And now, after moving to 351 South Flower Street—a short distance from Chinatown—he had hoped for a son. It seemed that Heaven was not ready to smile on him.[2]

Naturally, the birth of a Chinese laundryman's daughter would not be of any consequence to the world outside the nondescript Wong Laundry. On this midwinter day, the weather was almost perfect in the Los Angeles area: sunny, with a gentle northeasterly breeze at four miles an hour. The daytime temperature was seventy degrees, dipping to forty-eight degrees at night. The top story of the day came from the other side of the world: the fall of Port Arthur in China. After a bloody eight-month siege by Japanese troops, Russian Major General Anatoly Stessel, without consulting with the tsar or military command, made the shocking decision to surrender the Chinese port to the Japanese.[3] It signaled the imminent end of the Russo-Japanese War, which would result in the total humiliation of Russia and the rise of Japan as a global power. The news sent shock waves throughout the world, portending what Euro-America had dreaded as the "Yellow Peril."

In Washington, DC, President Theodore Roosevelt and the First Lady had held an annual New Year's Day reception at the White House on January 2, greeting foreign diplomats, Supreme Court justices, leading politicians, and other dignitaries. The first couple closed the ceremonial day by attending the comic opera *Love's Lottery*, performed by Madame Schumann-Heink and her company at the new National Theatre. Upon hearing the news about Port Arthur, the former Rough Rider, no stranger to international conflicts, continued to play his cards close to his vest, while also letting it be known that he would be willing to broker peace between Russia and Japan "when both belligerents jointly invite him to do so."[4] Nine months later, on September 5,

1905, Russia and Japan would gather in New Hampshire to sign the Treaty of Portsmouth, mediated by President Roosevelt himself.

The news of Japan's military victory lifted the spirit of the three thousand or so Japanese living in Los Angeles. Using racist lingo typical of the era, the *Los Angeles Times* described the response in the city: "The Japanese colony is in a state of subdued but infinite content. The little brown men of Los Angeles are not swaggering nor putting on airs in their rejoicings over the triumph of the Japanese army and the fall of Port Arthur, but their smiling countenances yesterday were not wholly to be accounted for on the score of New Year celebration." The next day, the same paper reported that geishas had been holding joyful receptions at entertainment resorts all evening. "In these places there was much feasting and jubilation," the *Times* observed.[5]

For the majority of Angelenos, the talk of the town on this fine midwinter day remained what had happened much closer to home: the Tournament of Roses Parade in Pasadena a day earlier. The annual festival, featuring parades, pageants, and chariot races, was usually held on New Year's Day. However, when January 1 falls on a Sunday, the event switches to Monday, January 2, because the founders of Pasadena did not want the festive hoopla to spook the horses hitched outside Sunday church services. Thus, having attracted seventy-five thousand people from the area and across the country, the seventeenth Rose Parade took place on the second day of 1905. A huge crowd descended on this "Crown of the Valley" via trains, electric streetcars, automobiles, carriages, motorcycles, bikes, or on foot. The interurban transportation lines were taxed to the breaking point. The Pacific Electric Company and the Santa Fe Railroad estimated that between 8 and 10 a.m., they had handled between twenty-two and twenty-five thousand passengers on their way to Pasadena. The *Los Angeles Herald* reported, "The exodus from Los Angeles commenced early in the morning and reached its greatest height at 9:30 o'clock, when the transit companies had difficulty in taking care of those who wished to be in Pasadena to witness the parade."[6]

Under the azure skies and against the purple hills, the eager throng crowded both sides of Colorado Boulevard and were treated to a spectacular extravaganza. Starting with the scurrying heralds and trumpeters, and quickly followed by the Police Marshal and aides, the parade featured floral floats of all sorts, marching bands both local and from out of town, equestrians, novelty acts, and the like.[7] Amidst a local carnival, an "exotic" item suddenly appeared that seemed more political than celebratory. As the *Herald* reported,

> As a crowning feature of the parade, following in the wake of the long line of heralds, pages, charioteers, fairies and damsels, came the "Yellow Peril." And as the expectant spectators caught a glimpse of a dazzling figure on horseback covered with a cloak of scarlet and crowned with the plumed helmet of a marshal, a shout of welcome and fellowship went up as they greeted the little Japanese with congratulations, while closely following their leader marched rank after rank of miniature warriors, dressed in a Japo-American costume, with the heavy rifle across each shoulder, a fitting representation of the sturdy little fighters of the Orient who have succeeded in bringing down the fame of the Slav.[8]

Not to be outdone, a natty company of fifty-eight Chinese American soldiers, trained by Captain Obanion of the US Army, also joined the parade. It was a regiment recruited from Chinatown by none other than Homer Lea—an eccentric five-foot-tall hunchback who was a Stanford graduate. It was Lea who had earlier gone to China to help restore the young emperor and, failing that, had now returned to the United States as a fugitive with a price on his head. At his command now was this small army of trainees meant to be sent to China to take charge of Chinese troops. Legginged, musketed, and grim, they "swung up the street like West Pointers, perfect alignment and cadence, rigid as German dragoons."[9]

The dual presence of Japanese and Chinese in the mix of this quintessentially American Rose Parade did not just provide the crowd some flavored amusement; it also provoked the editorial imagination of the city papers, characteristically sensational at the time. "The war between Russia and Japan has taught an object lesson to the great powers of the world," stated an article in the *Los Angeles Times* published soon after the parade. And the lesson was that the United States needed to build "bigger ships and bigger guns."[10]

In another piece, an editorial titled "The Immigration Evil," the author asserted: "The pouring of vast hordes of foreign immigrants upon our shores, year by year, is confessedly a serious evil, from the standpoint of American good citizenship." This may sound like the familiar xenophobic rhetoric that rises and falls throughout the history of this great democracy, but the editor was pointing his finger at one particular group of immigrants:

> It has never been, and should never be, the policy of the United States to exclude desirable immigrants. Some of our foremost citizens came to us from foreign lands, and others of their class will continue, let us hope, to come. There is ample room and need for them under the Banner of Stars. But the majority of immigrants, or at least a large proportion of them, are of a kind not needed nor desired in this country. They settle largely in the cities, becoming a charge upon public charity, and are responsible, to a great extent, for the crimes committed in the larger cities.[11]

It was the city dwellers he found most objectionable, the "huddled masses" who crowded into crime-ridden, poverty-stricken slums, who were labeled "the other half" by the Danish muckraker Jacob Riis in his 1890 runaway bestseller. In Los Angeles, it was the Chinese and Japanese, both showcased at the Rose Parade, who would best fit the bill for the *Times* editorial writer.

Especially for the Wongs, who had eschewed racial violence in remote rural areas and sought safety and communal connection in Chinatown, the editorial condemnation, with its familiar racist tinge, would certainly have hit home. Now that they had just added a new member to their household, with more children to come, the Wongs surely wished that the new Western-calendar year would be peaceful and prosperous. And perhaps in honor of the winter season, they named their second daughter Wong Liu Tsong, meaning "Yellow Frosted Willow."

2

CHINATOWN

Marchessault Street, Chinatown, Los Angeles, early 1900s *(Courtesy of Seaver Center for Western History Research, Los Angeles County Museum of Natural History)*

"CHINATOWN AS A SPECTACLE is disappointing," commented Jacob Riis in *How the Other Half Lives*. Granted that this Danish carpenter-turned-social-reformer, who was also a friend of Theodore Roosevelt, was referring to the ghetto on the Lower East Side of New York City, his overall assessment of Chinese lives in America, whether in New York, San Francisco, or Los Angeles, was one of rank condemnation—a curious comment at best for a man known for championing the lives of the immigrant poor. "The Chinese are in no sense a desirable element of the population, [and] they serve no useful purpose here," opined Riis. He further asserted that each Chinese person in America is "a homeless stranger among us."[1]

On the day of Anna May Wong's birth, January 3, Riis was, in fact, speaking in Los Angeles. Under the auspices of the Young Women's Christian Association, the statesman on immigrant pauperdom delivered a lecture in a packed Simpson Auditorium, just a few miles from the Wong Laundry. Illustrating his talk with photographic slides, Riis described an ambitious plan to transform urban slums "from darkness, dirt and despair to sunshine, cleanliness and joy, from physical and moral decay to bodily and mental health, from the haunts of robbers and cutthroats to recreation centers and playgrounds for children." He introduced a statistical fact that could have had some bearing on the new addition to the Wong family, claiming that twenty-five percent of children died annually because of the poor conditions under which they lived.[2] Although the protagonist of *Daughter of the Dragon* was able to beat the odds and grew up healthy, one of her future siblings would prove Riis's claim, falling victim to the hazardous and squalid living conditions that surrounded a turn-of-the-century Chinese laundry.

Except for some indirect references, Riis had nothing specific to say about Chinatown in his lecture. In his writings and speeches, the famed interpreter of slum life always claimed that he could not access the inner soul of New York's Chinatown, even though he had begun his journalism career by keeping a desk at the police headquarters on Mulberry Street—the heart of the city's Chinatown. Blaming it on Chinese inscrutability, he often resorted to clichés and stereotypes in his descriptions and condemnation of Chinatown life, portraying the Chinese as idolaters, opium addicts, inveterate gamblers, and, worst of all, corrupters of white souls. To get a true picture of Chinatown, or to better understand the early life of our future film star, we need to step away from Riis's pulpit and turn to the dusty pages of LA's storied past.

"THE FOUNDING of the city of Los Angeles," wrote Helen Hunt Jackson, a native of Amherst, Massachusetts, and one of the earliest mythmakers of Southern California, "is a tale for verse rather than for prose." Flipping through the nostalgia-filled pages of mission literature created by Jackson—who happened to be a childhood friend of Emily Dickinson—and other boosters of Los Angeles as the Lotusland, we are taken back to a supposed halcyon time marked by unspoiled nature. There we would presumably find a racial order characterized by beneficent dons lording over graceful, hardworking Indians, who "knelt dutifully before the Franciscans to receive the baptism of a superior culture, while in the background the angelus tolled from a swallow-guarded campanile, and a choir of friars intoned the *Te Deum*."[3] But reality is far more prosaic, if not brutal, and occasionally it throws us a curve ball.

Who would have thought that a Chinese explorer was actually one of the founders of the emerald city that rose from the desert and chaparral? Or, in a crude irony, that the birth of Chinatown was the result of a massacre of Chinese?

In 1781, when a party of twelve Spanish settlers founded the village of El Pueblo de Nuestra Senora la Reina de Los Angeles de Porciuncula, one of them was a Chinese man with the westernized moniker of Antonio Rodriguez. We do not know what his Chinese name was or where he originally came from, except that he was one of the many Chinese traders and craftsmen in the Philippines who had converted to Catholicism—hence his Christian name—so that they could continue their trade there. Most of the twelve heads of families were retired soldiers who continued to receive pay and rations from the Spanish government. Records show that Rodriguez, along with the others, received from Spain's royal treasury some material assistance toward settlement: "two each of oxen, mules, mares, sheep, goats, cows, as well as one calf, an ass, and a hoe."[4] Thus, Rodriguez became one of the earliest Chinese arriving in the New World via a detour, after a stopover in one of those nodes of the Chinese diaspora. Such a detour often leads to the erasure, or at least the obfuscation, of their Chinese origins. The so-called Siamese Twins, Chang and Eng Bunker, for instance, turned out to be Chinese in origin. Born in Siam of Chinese and Siamese parents, Chang and Eng arrived in the United States in 1829, two decades before the Gold Rush of 1850 would bring a large number of immigrants directly from China.[5]

When gold fever hit the American West, Los Angeles was still a sleepy pueblo built around the old Spanish Plaza (now part of the Los Angeles Plaza Historic District). The 1850 census lists only two Chinese men, both servants at the house of a Robert Haley. In 1854, when Joseph Newmark, a Prussian immigrant who would one day establish the oldest synagogue in Los Angeles, moved to the town, he reportedly brought a Chinese servant with him. As the city population quadrupled from 1,161 in 1850 to 4,385 in 1860, the Chinese population inched up only slightly to fourteen.[6]

The leader of this small cohort of Chinese was a laundryman who went by the name of John Tambolin—it seems that the early Chinese settlers, like the Bunker brothers, all chose to initiate or consummate their Americanization by anglicizing their names. Arriving in the embryonic town around 1856, Tambolin operated a washhouse with the help of two young Chinese men. Described in the local press as sort of a cultural go-between, he promoted Chinese culture and people in America. When he took a Chinese bride in 1862, the blissful occasion became the town's first Chinese wedding officiated by an American justice of the peace.[7]

The other Chinese who made overtures toward the non-Chinese population of Los Angeles in those early years was an herbalist named Chun Chick. In the summer of 1861, Chun moved down from San Francisco and opened a general store on Spring Street. A shrewd businessman who perhaps knew a thing or two about fengshui, Chun chose the location of his shop opposite the courthouse, thus avoiding the saloons and casinos of the infamous Calle de los Negros ("Negro Alley"), where the less reputable citizens and most of his fellow Chinese congregated. To entice Anglo patrons, Chun took the unusual step of running an ad in the English-language newspaper that simply announced: A CHINESE MERCHANT! In addition to stocking the general assortment of Chinese goods, Chun boasted "a fine display of preserves and other articles hitherto not obtainable in town."[8]

Thanks to the efforts by these two intrepid pioneers—Tambolin and Chun—the Chinese not only gained a toehold in what was still a rough frontier town but also increased their population by almost two thousand percent in the next decade. Before the 1871 massacre, 172 Chinese were recorded as Los Angeles residents, comprising approximately three percent of the general population. But historians believe that the 1870 census undercounted the Chinese, judging by the scale of the tragedy that befell the community in the following year. Excluded from meaningful interaction with mainstream society, most of the Chinese had no choice but to take up residence with so-called undesirables, living in a block to the south of the Spanish Plaza, in the middle of the vice district. As they went about their lives as laundrymen, shopkeepers, produce vendors, cooks, domestics, or common laborers, they faced enormous animosity from whites. As Carey McWilliams describes in his classic study of Southern California history, "The inevitable butt of a thousand jokes, the Chinese were heckled and harassed by old and young. By common consensus, youngsters were given free license to stone the Chinese, upset their vegetable carts and laundry wagons, and pull their queues [braids] for good measure."[9]

Increasingly, the daily harassment did not just happen on its own; it received an accelerant in the form of legislative acts and local ordinances specifically targeting the Chinese. Yet racism, even without the imprimatur of the law, had dogged the Chinese in California from the very beginning. The earliest example was the foreign miners' license tax, passed by the California legislature in 1850. It required a monthly payment of three dollars from every foreign miner who did not desire to become a citizen. Since a 1790 federal law had already declared "nonwhite persons" ineligible for citizenship, Chinese miners became the main target of the tax. In 1852, Tuolumne County passed a resolution banning all Chinese from the region's mines, a move soon followed by other counties and districts in the state. In 1870, San Francisco passed the Cubic Air Ordinance, requiring all lodging houses to contain at least five hundred cubic feet of air within its walls for each inhabitant. Since crowded lodging houses were the principal residences for the majority of Chinese in San Francisco, city officials enforced the ordinance only in Chinatown, arresting not the predominantly white landlords but their Chinese tenants. A subsequent law designed to humiliate the Chinese was the Queue Ordinance of 1873, which required all male prisoners to have their hair cut to within one inch of the scalp, a grim prospect dreaded by any Chinese man hoping to return to Manchu-ruled China, where the queue was mandated. Yet one more racist law intended to disrupt the normal lives of the Chinese was the Stick Ordinance, which prohibited the delivery of goods suspended from the ends of a pole, a convenient method of delivery commonly used by the Chinese. All in all, these laws were intended for two purposes: to exclude the Chinese from competitive employment sectors and to make life in California intolerable for them.[10]

No form of harassment, however, can compare to the bloody violence that broke out in 1871 in Los Angeles and other urban centers. On the night of October 24, a brawl between rival Chinese tongs in Los Angeles exploded into a race riot. After a police officer and a volunteer were caught in the crossfire, white mobs rampaged through the streets and tortured, shot, lynched, and burned eighteen Chinese. They also destroyed Chinese shops and terrorized the entire community.

The Los Angeles massacre represented but one incident in a chain of anti-Chinese violence: In the 1870s, thirty-one urban centers in California experienced burnings of Chinese stores and homes and expulsions of Chinese residents. Outside of California, a mob during an 1880 riot in Denver overwhelmed the police officers on duty and destroyed most of the buildings in Chinatown, in the process dragging a Chinese laundryman through the streets, kicking and beating him to death. In 1885 in Rock Springs, Wyoming, a mob of

150 disgruntled white miners, armed with Winchester rifles, stormed into the Chinese quarter, killing twenty-eight Chinese, wounding fifteen, and burning much of the district to the ground.[11]

In what became the crescendo of this anti-Chinese movement, Congress passed the Chinese Exclusion Act of 1882, which suspended labor immigration from China and reconfirmed the inadmissibility of Chinese for citizenship. Thus, the Chinese garnered the dubious distinction of being the first ethnic group in American history to be barred from entering the country, a special treatment that would later be inflicted upon other groups, based on nationality or religion, such as Jews in the 1930s and 1940s, Japanese during World War II, and Muslims in the era of Donald Trump.

In this sorrowful litany of historical facts, the Chinese often were perceived as helpless victims—passive, docile, weak, and unable to adapt or assimilate. The deeply flawed stereotype of a Chinese person as a sojourner—a transient worker who only wanted to make enough money to return to a life of ease in China—further skewed the truth and bolstered the racist rhetoric against an entire population. In reality, the Chinese community was resilient, proactive, and highly adaptive in an unfamiliar, hostile milieu. Even the 1871 Los Ange-

Chinese Massacre victims, Los Angeles, 1871 *(Courtesy of Security Public National Bank Collection / Los Angeles Public Library)*

les massacre did not deter the Chinese settlement. The routine of daily life was soon renewed with vigor: Merchants rebuilt their stores, laundries reopened their doors, and farmers once again began to visit Chinatown for trade and relaxation. Within weeks, Chinese merchants and other residents demanded that the city pay for property damaged in the riot. When the city council refused or dragged its feet, they sued.[12] Los Angeles County court records show that the Chinese won eleven of the thirteen civil suits they brought against non-Asians between 1869 and 1874.[13] In other words, the Chinese were themselves agents of change, not passive victims of abuse and discrimination. Facing violence, harassment, and institutionalized inequality, they looked within their own communities, forming associations and tongs when denied justice in courtrooms, building networks to the homeland when marginalized by mainstream US society, seeking alternative means of influencing local politics when denied citizenship and the right to vote.[14] After major events like the 1871 massacre, Chinatown residents responded to hostility and prejudice by drawing even closer together.

Such was the kind of Chinese community, constantly threatened and yet remarkably resilient, that Sam Sing and Gon Toy joined when the newlyweds arrived in Los Angeles in 1901. Bounded by busy Alameda Street on the west, and a noisy railroad yard and a soot-spewing gas plant on the east, Chinatown proper spread out along Apablasa and Marchessault Streets, hemmed in by Macy and Aliso Streets on the north and south, respectively. The former Negro Alley, today renamed Los Angeles Street, cut a tangent into the sounds and furies of Chinese life.

Most dwellings were wooden hovels jammed closely together, with tiny shuttered holes or no windows at all. Many residents had to cook in cramped quarters, with stoves or ovens wedged perilously between sleeping bunks. Even worse, many buildings had makeshift wooden porches in the rear, as well as wooden sheds, built of nothing more substantial than packing crates. Inside many of these flimsy additions were open brick fireplaces, posing a perpetual fire menace. A report of the Board of Fire Commissioners shows that from December 1, 1898, to November 30, 1899, fifteen alarms were called for various Apablasa Street structures. Another report states baldly, "There seems to be a separate housing standard for the Chinese. Comment on their bad living quarters brings forth a remark such as 'yes, conditions are bad, but they are Chinese.'"[15]

As more wooden buildings fell victim to fire and were replaced by more durable brick constructions around the time of Sam Sing and Gon Toy's arrival, Chinatown began to acquire its distinctive look, an appearance that would last until its demolition in 1933. As one visitor keenly noted, "One of the most striking points in viewing Chinatown is its bright color. The houses are for the most part of red brick, built flush with the street. . . . Here and there are wooden balconies ornamented profusely in brilliant hues, yellow, red, and green. Occasionally are window boxes filled with bright flowers. On holidays variegated lanterns are hung on all porches and doorways and gay pennants flutter thick in the air."[16]

Amid this riot of color appeared the exotically aromatic Marchessault Street, Chinatown's restaurant row. Showcasing roast ducks, BBQ pork, and other delicacies behind their windows, these dining spots, whether ornate lounges or seedy holes-in-the-wall, catered to both local residents and curiosity-seeking visitors. For the latter, there was a perfect "Chinese" dish to delight their palates: chop suey. An ingenious California creation literally meaning "odd ends," chop suey emerged from necessity at mining camps in the nineteenth century and soon spread across the nation. In addition to culinary adventures, visitors would also be treated, especially during Chinese holidays, to displays of fireworks, red packets, gifts, temple gods, and ceremonial rituals. As the twentieth century got underway, and when silent-era Hollywood became enamored with the so-called exotic charms of Chinatown, this neighborhood would experience a more profound change, a transformation that would seal the trajectory of the young girl known as Anna.

Yet, in 1905, the year Anna was born, Chinatown remained a dusty, noisy, if not smelly dot on the cityscape. By the end of the first decade of the century, most Los Angeles streets had been graded, graveled, or paved, some with sidewalks set in cement. But the roads in Chinatown would not be improved and modernized until the 1920s, and due to its status as private property owned by two pioneer families, the neighborhood had limited or no access to public utilities, such as heat, electricity, or sewer lines. What had helped create this disparity in the first place was the 1882 Chinese Exclusion Act—renewed in 1892 and made permanent in 1902—which wreaked havoc with Chinatown life. By preventing wives from coming to America and inhibiting family reunions of any sort, the law created an aging bachelor society among the Chinese. This, in turn, led to a sharp decline in the overall Chinese population in the United States: from 105,465 in 1880 to 89,863 in 1900 to 61,639 in 1920. In the immediate neighborhood of Chinatown in Lo Sang (Chinese immigrants' name for

Los Angeles), the 1900 census tallied 602 persons, of whom men accounted for 90 percent and women only 10 percent. In the words of an elderly Chinatown citizen, "America didn't have to kill any Chinese. The Exclusion Act assured none would be born."[17]

So, at a time when the Chinese population was shrinking, Sam Sing and Gon Toy were fortunate to have found each other and to be able to form a family that continued to grow. They were also fortunate in their choice of a business, a laundry that, as we will see, made it easier for them to gain a toehold in turn-of-the-century America.

3

THE LAUNDRYMAN

I wash your handkerchiefs soaked in grief
I wash your white shirts black with crime
Grease of greed, ashes of lust
In your house all the grime
Give me to wash, give me to wash
　　—WEN YIDUO,
　　　"A Laundryman's Song" (1925)[1]

ONCE AN ENDURING EMBLEM of Chinese life in America, the laundry occupies a unique place in the nation's Oriental imagination. A Dickensian curiosity shop of stereotypes, it is not only a crucible of cheap labor but also a storefront historical museum of Chinese immigration and American imagination.

Like the chop suey joint, or its distant cousins—the Greek gyro stand, the Jewish clothing store, or the more recent taco truck—the Chinese laundry was a ubiquitous fixture on the cultural landscape of America. In prelapsarian time, at least one such quaint emporium seems to have stood on every Main Street of small-town America—distinguished by a red sign printed with a "chopstick" font, and occasionally bejeweled with some hieroglyphic characters. "Sam Lee Laundry" and "Sing Lee Laundry" are said to have been two of the nation's most popular Chinese-laundry names. The owner and his immediate family, whose last name was most assuredly not Lee, were usually the only Chinese in town.[2] Indeed, as one sociologist quipped, "Each Chinese laundry is a Chinatown in every neighborhood."[3]

The year Anna May Wong arrived in the world, the *National Laundry Journal* ran a vignette titled "No Laundries in China," which ribbed Chinese laundrymen:

A Chinese laundryman, Los Angeles, early 1900s *(Courtesy of Seaver Center for Western History Research, Los Angeles County Museum of Natural History)*

"It's the funniest thing to me," said an old sea captain who for many years was in the China trade, as he settled himself comfortably in his chair and blew a few rings of smoke into the air, "that nine out of every ten Chinamen who come to this country open laundries and engage in a business which does not exist in their native land. As everyone knows, the Chinese at home wear soft cotton and woolen garments, according to the season, and there is not a pound of starch in all China. Stiffly starched clothes are unknown, and the Chinese men do not do the washing, as they do in this country. Neither is there any regular laundry in the Flowery Kingdom. Therefore it is more than passing strange that Chinamen should all come to America to engage in a trade so foreign to their home industries."[4]

We should, of course, take such a satirical piece with a generous grain of MSG. After all, the *National Laundry Journal* was the trade publication of an association controlled by white owners of machine laundries, who regarded Chinese hand laundries as competition. The idea that all Chinese could afford a seasonal change of clothing between soft cotton and warm wool was yet another American shibboleth. Even so, the fictional sea captain was correct about one thing: Before coming to America, Chinese men did *not* do laundry. In fact, the Chinese laundry was entirely a product of happenstance and necessity, an American-born enterprise that got its start in the mining camps during the gold rush.[5]

When those early Chinese argonauts arrived on the West Coast, they found not the fabled Gold Mountain of El Dorado but rather a swirling sea of discrimination and violence. Besides the Foreign Miners' Tax burning a hole in their pockets every year, the Chinese were also driven out of promising goldfields, so they could try their luck only in areas deserted by white miners. "No Chinaman's chance," a time-honored gem in the colossal compendium of American racist lingo, was born exactly in that context, referring to the slim chance that one's efforts would, to use another mining term, "pan out."

However, as Charlie Chan says, "Door of opportunity swing both ways." Out on the frontier, there was a shortage of women to do domestic chores like laundry and cooking. Miners would have to wash their own clothes or send them by clipper ship all the way to the Sandwich Islands (Hawaii) or even faraway Canton. Outsourcing was not a twentieth-century invention; nor was cheap Chinese labor. Laundry became a meal ticket for the Chinese men down on their luck in mining and eager for any opportunity to eke out a living. Learning on the go, Chinese men, who might have learned to plow the fields or hold an ink brush but had never "stooped" to washing clothes back home, started operating hand laundries to serve the same clientele who had just deprived them of any other means of survival.

The sporadic success of the Chinese laundry in mining camps would lead to the advent of shops in the cities. According to Paul C. P. Siu, a laundryman's son who did a trailblazing study on the subject for his PhD in sociology at the University of Chicago in the 1930s, the first urban Chinese laundry was established in the Gold Rush boomtown of San Francisco:

Early in the spring of 1851 one Wah Lee hung a sign over his door at Grant Avenue and Washington Street. It read: "Wash'ng and Iron'ng." Wah Lee, as it was told, was an unsuccessful gold miner turned laundryman. Where did Wah Lee learn the trade? No one knows. If he had been in a mining community, he might have had some experience with "wash'ng and iron'ng" before his return to San Francisco.

We do not know whether Wah Lee celebrated the grand opening with obligatory firecrackers to bring good luck and prosperity. As a pioneer, he was unable to monopolize the trade for long. Judging by the latter-day pattern of this immigrant economy, the Chinese laundryman tended to hire or partner with his clansmen. The helpers or partners, having learned the trade and saved enough funds, would often take off and open their own shops. Before long, variations of Wah Lee's signage popped up everywhere on the streets of San Francisco. In 1855, a British theater aficionado visiting the city reportedly was amused by the sign of "King Lee," which at first glance he mistook for the Elizabethan tragedy *King Lear*. It is reasonable to speculate that the sign had less to do with Shakespeare than with the possibility that the proud owner of "King Lee" was a blood relative of Wah Lee or simply a creative copycat. In this way, out of the cradle of necessity and by a twist of fate, the Chinese laundry began its sudsy saga in America.[6] As the Bard of Avon famously put it, "Double, double toil and trouble" (*Macbeth* 1.5).

Hailing from Northern California's mining region of Michigan Bluffs, laundryman Sam Sing had certainly followed the well-trodden path of his compatriots.[7] In Los Angeles, the laundryman stood at the very apex of Chinese professions. As we saw earlier, the trailblazer Tambolin had opened the first washhouse in town in the ancien régime of 1856. By 1860, ten of the fourteen "Chinamen" in Los Angeles were laundrymen. In 1872, according to the *Los Angeles Star*, eleven of the thirteen washhouses in the city were owned and operated by Chinese. The growth was exponential. By the time of Sam Sing's arrival, the 1900 census recorded fifty-seven heads of Chinese households as laundry owners, of whom one-third were Wongs.[8] Indeed, the Wong Kung Saw (association) was one of the two largest and most influential in Chinatown, the other being Louie Kung Saw. Deprived of cultural and civic ties to mainstream America, Chinese immigrants had to rely on these surname-based family associations or region-based district societies for almost everything, including job opportunities, emergency loans, arbitration of disputes, and frequently room and board, if one could call it that, at the association hall.[9] Over the years, the Wong clan, by dint of its numerical superiority and early entry into the niche business, had accumulated sufficient capital and knowledge to assist its members in opening their own shops. Thus, being a Wong had certainly provided Sam Sing with a decidedly economic advantage.

Upon his arrival in Los Angeles, and having paid a visit to the local chapter of the Wong Kung Saw, Sam Sing first set up his laundry on Marchessault Street, the crowded restaurant row. He soon moved his business and family to 351 South Flower Street, and his choice of new location, where his second daughter, Anna, would be born, is noteworthy. Flower Street was slightly at a remove from Chinatown, giving the Wong family easy access to everything in the Chinese community they would need—language, grocery, service, network, and so on—while avoiding the grime and overpopulation of the ethnic ghetto. Fong See, a prominent contemporary of Sam Sing and a future Chinese tycoon, had also chosen to live on the outskirts of Chinatown when he moved from Sacramento to Los Angeles in 1897. According to Fong's illustrious descendant, the bestselling author Lisa See, settling in Chinatown "would have been a step backward" for her aspiring Chinese progenitor and his Caucasian wife.[10]

Within shouting distance, though more than a stone's throw, from the racially monolithic Chinatown, Flower Street was a miniature melting pot. An amalgam of Germans, Mexicans, Japanese, and Eastern Europeans, the neighborhood was culturally diverse, prompting some historians to speculate on its influence on the future global star. In his pioneering biography, Graham Hodges maintains that the multiracial street instilled in Anna May Wong "an awareness of if not always a comfort with a diverse population." Such a view is reaffirmed by Karen J. Leong, who writes in her book *The China Mystique* that the neighborhood "rendered Wong and her siblings vulnerable to the challenges of being a minority among the increasingly diverse Los Angeles population."[11]

While the toxic geographical influence on the future film star will be explained later, more pressing for the newborn was the spread of measles, a disease that was plaguing the world and killing a sizable population each year. Sometime after her birth, Anna, her sister Lulu, and their mother all contracted the dreaded disease.[12] A virus spread via the respiratory effluvia of infected individuals, measles caused red rashes to appear all over the body, often bringing fever, diarrhea, and pneumonia at the same time. It is especially deadly to young children under five and anyone who was malnourished. In one of the worst recorded epidemics in history, measles wiped out 20 percent of Hawaii's population in the 1850s. Not long afterward, it killed more than forty thousand Fijians in 1875. Thus, it was a true crisis when three people in one household fell victim to the disease. One can easily imagine Sam Sing's anxiety or paranoia, as he sought help from Chinese herbal doctors and advice from his clansmen, wondering whether he had made the wrong decision to venture beyond the boundaries of Chinatown.

Miraculously, Anna, Lulu, and their mother recovered. Within a few weeks, the rashes disappeared, the fevers subsided, and one by one they regained their health. After that scare, Sam Sing decided, with the Chinese New Year approaching, to shell out a hard-earned dollar bill for a full-length family portrait. For the formal occasion, he disdained the stereotyped soft cotton and woolen garment and donned his finest robe, a neat skull cap with a black silk band, and a new pair of padded shoes. In his left hand was a folding fan, probably a studio prop, thus allowing him to affect the leisurely air of a contented man. At the other edge of the portrait, sitting slightly at an angle, was his wife, her smooth black hair finely combed and arranged in a chignon at the back of her head. Draped in a traditional gown that went all the way down to her crossed ankles, she wore embroidered shoes that conspicuously revealed her unbound feet. Having been born in America, Gon Toy did not have to endure the torture of having her feet bound when she was a girl, unlike most women in her ancestral land. But she did follow Chinese custom by sitting to the right of her man in the portrait.

Between the parents, and perched on chairs about three feet high, were the two daughters—Anna next to their mother and Lulu by their father. Both girls were dolled up like princesses, with headgear, tiny shoes, and miniature robes over patterned pantaloons. While the older girl, Lulu, sat straight up like her parents with both hands resting on her lap, Anna gripped the armrest with her right hand, seemingly afraid of falling off the chair. Students of period portraiture can tell you that, in this picture, Anna was not the only one remarkable for her unusual posture. As the shutter box clicked, Sam Sing smiled, a facial expression that defied the era's artistic and cultural norms. In those days, Chinese people did not smile in formal photos, probably afraid to reveal their inner souls, which might then be captured or stolen by the camera, the spirit machine. But superstition be damned, Sam Sing could barely contain his happiness, knowing that his family had dodged a potentially fatal bullet. The coming year would be the Year of the Horse, a creature of hard work and perseverance. Sam Sing was ready.

He had no inkling, of course, and neither did his wife, that their second daughter—a timid, clear-eyed girl of two, sitting aslant on the high stool—would one day rise to become the icon of Chinese femininity, enrapturing millions through the magic lens of the camera. The same machine would be, one might argue, far more effective at capturing her soul.

Lee Gon Toy, Anna, Lulu, and Wong Sam Sing, circa 1907 *(Courtesy of China Film Archives, Beijing, China)*

4

FUN IN A CHINESE LAUNDRY

I T IS MORE THAN a little peculiar that Josef von Sternberg, the charismatic filmmaker who played a notable part in Anna May Wong's career, would one day title his memoir *Fun in a Chinese Laundry*. Creatively inserting a "von" in his own name to make it sound aristocratic, the self-ennobling Jewish Austrian had started out in life as a so-called pants-presser in Brooklyn, a work experience that provided some intimacy with fabric and lace. Yet we can safely assume that he never set foot inside a Chinese laundry, unless it was a film set. Except for the title, Sternberg's unconventional, engrossing autobiography makes no reference to that symbol of Chinese life in America. In fact, according to his most sympathetic biographer, hardship in his early youth had endowed him with "a contempt for working-class Americans."[1] It begs the question, then: Why did Herr von Sternberg choose such an odd title for the personal account of a savant? The answer may lie in—astonishingly—the umbilical cord that ties the birth of Hollywood to the Chinese laundry.

Even before the arrival of the motion picture, the "pigtailed Chinaman"—usually going by the generic name of "Charlie" and sweating over steam and starch while muttering "no tickee, no washee"—had long been a familiar racist trope in America. In songs, vaudeville skits, melodramas, comic strips, and pulp fiction, a Chinese laundryman's eight-pound livelihood (referring to the primitive eight-pound iron he used) was a staple of such racist caricature. Unlike the anonymous horde packed inside Chinatown, launderers such as Sam Sing were the first Chinese to venture outside the ethnic ghetto, hoping for better opportunities. When Jacob Riis asserted that each Chinese person in America is "a homeless stranger among us," he was at best only partially right. A Chinese launderer might be a stranger, but he had a home— his workplace. In San Francisco, Chinese, like European Jews in the shtetls, were forbidden to live outside Chinatown unless they were in their own laundries. Though less draconian in restrictions but nonetheless vehemently Sinophobic, Los Angeles did not see too many Chinese willing to move out of the community safe zone, except for launderers and storeowners catering to non-Asian clienteles. Thus, as one historian notes, laundries were an early target of the anti-Chinese alarmists, for washhouses were highly visible operations: "Laundrymen would locate either a vacant building suitable to their needs or a lot on which they could construct an appropriate building to set up shop. . . . Many residents found such intrusions into their neighborhoods objectionable."[2] Especially at times of economic crisis and labor agitation, the conspicuousness of Chinese laundries and their inhabitants in urban streetscapes made them easy targets for attack and ridicule in political rhetoric, popular art, and everyday life.

Putting aside the patently false but wildly popular notion that cheap Chinese labor stole white men's jobs—a trope conveniently applied to Mexicans in the toxic vapors of the twenty-first century—there were a few things about a Chinese laundry that particularly irked the racists, and some of these features would, somewhat perversely, grab the imagination of the earliest dabblers in the art of the motion picture. Ironically, when it comes to the Chinese laundry, racial bias and cinematic imagination seemed to walk hand in hand.

First, the store sign. We do not know exactly how Wah Lee's sign looked to San Francisco's citizens when it first appeared in 1851, but we can be pretty certain that it was red, since, to Chinese, red symbolizes good luck and prosperity. In a milieu where the prevailing wisdom was "not a Chinaman's chance," people like Wah Lee would need oodles of good fortune just to survive, let alone thrive. For decades, those Chinese laundry signs painted on red backgrounds with white or black lettering, occasionally sporting Chinese ideograms to add exotic appeal, dotted the nation's landscape like red pins on a map. Virtually a poetic collage or even an epigrammatic haiku, a sign can exert a powerful influence on the viewer's mind. We may point to at least two instances where the lasting effects of Chinese laundry signs can be detected. First, the large sign of Grauman's Chinese Theatre, that shrine of Hollywood's chinoiserie, adopts the cartoonish chopstick font, almost a mocking replica of those laundry signs once ubiquitous in America. Second, even into the twenty-first century,

Abercrombie & Fitch would try to sell T-shirts that read, WONG BROTHERS LAUNDRY SERVICE. TWO WONGS CAN MAKE IT WHITE.

As one enters the interior of a Chinese laundry, mystery deepens for the curiosity-seeker. A wooden counter of typical height is built around the front room, with a swinging door attached to the counter as the only passage to the inner chamber. The traplike door is locked from within, its hook hidden somewhere under a loose panel. Experts have explained the peculiar design of the counter: "As the Chinese laundry was founded under conditions of extreme conflict of racial and labor agitation against it, it could be the aftermath of the feeling of insecurity—some protection would be better than none."[3] In other words, the counter facilitates both business transactions and self-defense against intruders.

Following the same rationale, there is a secret cash drawer where the laundryman keeps small change—just enough for the day. It is an old-fashioned wooden box, "usually installed either underneath the counter or under one of the laundry shelves. A little bell is attached to it and every time it is opened it produces a tinkling sound." Someone unfamiliar with the mechanism would have difficulty opening the cash drawer, and the bell would not tinkle unless the box was opened. The adoption of the hidden drawer, further deepening the Oriental mystique, was certainly a marked improvement from the early years when traditional Chinese, much to the chagrin of white customers, would simply stick nickels and dimes in their ears for convenience. One year, the Board of Supervisors in San Francisco actually considered banning the use of one's ears as purses.[4]

Behind the counter, against the walls of the front section, are laundry shelves and "ironing beds." Called *hong-choong* in Cantonese, the latter is so named, rather than the popular term "ironing board," because these rigs had indeed started out as sleeping beds for early Chinese launderers. Once again, Paul Siu, the sociologist son of a Chinese laundryman, knows best the secrets of his father's trade: "As the whole structure looks so much like the wooden bed commonly used for sleeping by the Chinese peasants in China, we might speculate that the pioneer laundryman could have converted his own sleeping bed into the ironing board. Imagine how he might do a laundry job when it was first offered to him in the mining town! . . . Under such a condition he might have tried to iron shirts on his own bed and found it practical."[5]

And then there is the abacus, perhaps the most unique cultural exhibit in the shop that would fascinate or befuddle a non-Chinese visitor. In Chinese, an abacus is called *suanpan*, literally meaning "a calculating plate." Usually made of hardwood, it looks like a long, narrow tray. Siu gives us the most accurate description of this essential tool of the trade: "In the tray a dozen or so metal sticks are installed vertically, parallel with one another, and each goes through seven beads. The tray is divided by another piece of wood horizontally across the upper side of the tray, making two sections. On each column two beads appear in the upper section, and five beads appear in the lower section. Each bead in the upper section represents five points, and each bead in the lower section represents one point. The bead on the left is always ten times the bead on the right."[6]

The next item that appears quaint to Main Street USA is the laundry ticket, almost as inscrutable as a Charlie Chan aphorism. In the earlier times, some laundrymen were illiterate and did not know how to write numbers. So they came up with an ingenious method of issuing a laundry ticket, as recalled by an old-timer: "When a bundle of laundry was done, he had to put down the amount charged for the work. . . . He would draw a circle as big as a half dollar coin to represent a half dollar, and a circle as big as a dime for a dime, and so on. When the customers came in to call for their laundry, they would catch on to the meaning of the circles and pay accordingly."[7] But soon the impromptu method graduated to printed tickets, which nonetheless contain equally cryptic ciphers—Chinese characters. Usually, the customers could understand only the amount charged, written in Arabic numerals, making the ticket another piece of the Chinese puzzle surrounding the laundry. Most important, though, the ticket also serves as the claim receipt. If, as often happens, a customer loses the receipt but still tries to claim the laundry, a problem will arise for the laundryman. The ensuing friction—or even confrontation—thus gave birth to the racist refrain that renders a stereotypical Chinese man the butt of the joke: "No tickee, no washee"—or, more familiar, "No tickee, no shirtee."

The Chinese laundryman's method of sprinkling the clothes for ironing was another major source of his misfortune. In those early years, he would use a brass mouth-blower shaped like an insect sprayer, except a tube was built in it instead of an air pump. To spray water, he would need to blow at the opening of the tube, making it look as if he was spitting. Consequently, rumors circulated about Chinamen spreading virulent diseases through the community via contaminated clothing. "Leprosy, plague, tuberculosis and the like were thought to be directly passed on by the laundrymen's method of spraying clothes with their mouths," though not the aforementioned measles.[8] In later decades, even though the sprayer in the Chinese laundry had progressed from a mouth-blower to a gas atomizer, the urban legend died hard. As late as 1974, in the Roman Polanski film *Chinatown*, the private eye Jake Gittes, played by Jack Nicholson, wisecracked that one could "put Chinamen in jail for spitting on laundry." Not everyone found it funny, and in hyping the slur about the Chinese laundryman's alleged maleficence, it was one of the most racially nasty lines coming out of post–Golden Age Hollywood.

Yet Jake Gittes's Chinese joke—he delivered a few more of that sort in the movie—stood him in very good stead, for Hollywood was hooked on the Chinese laundry and the double-entendres that surrounded it. The earliest filmmakers were eager to draw upon the exotic settings and robotic movements as sudsy material for the nascent art of the motion picture. As Robert Sklar puts it in *Movie-Made America*, films "rose to the surface of cultural consciousness from the bottom up, receiving their principal support from the lowest and most invisible classes in American society." It is important to note that not only were those storefront cinemas, penny arcades, and nickelodeons mostly located in urban slums, appealing to the desires of the working class and the "huddled masses," but also the material for these early movies drew on the lives of "the other half." In the decades of "nickel madness," before filmmakers such as Adolph Zukor figured out the more successful formula of "Famous Players in Famous Plays," typical film contents included vaudeville acts, sporting contests, curiosities and grotesqueries, and, most popular of all, comic scenes of everyday life, such as fun in a blacksmith shop, a dentist's office, a barbershop, and a Chinese laundry.[9]

In 1895, Thomas Edison had made a short reel titled *Chinese Laundry Scene*, followed in 1898 by a technically more experimental work, *Dancing Chinamen—Marionettes*. The latter consists of just one scene in which two marionettes on strings dance together. For the duration of the brief film, the marionettes are "pulled up by the strings above ground, then quickly let down until they sit on the ground doing splits, pulled up, let down, pulled up, let down, and so on." Manipulated by an invisible hand, the dancing figures present an image of strangely multijointed bodies that seem to be able to perform physically impossible feats.[10]

As a trailblazer, the American wizard of early cinema was certainly not alone in having fun in a Chinese laundry. Edison's competitor at American Mutoscope and Biograph made *Chinese Rubbernecks* in 1903, a film that shows one laundryman grabbing the head of his coworker and pulling it until the neck stretches across the screen and then springs back. Such a feat, created with dummies, reflects white fantasies about the supposedly robotic Chinese physique as well as violence toward the Chinese body. In fact, when Senator John F. Miller of California introduced the infamous Chinese Exclusion Act in Congress in 1882, he had not simply denigrated the Chinese as a "degraded and inferior race"—comparable to "rats," "beasts," and "swine"—but he also claimed that Chinese laborers posed a serious threat to white workers with their "machine-like" ways and their "muscles of iron." The cartoonish portrayal in *Chinese Rubbernecks* surely echoed Miller's techno-Orientalist paranoia that the Chinese were "automatic engines of flesh and blood."[11]

Such imagery continued to proliferate. Another Biograph film, *The Heathen Chinese and the Sunday School Teachers* (1904), depicts a different kind of "Yellow Peril"—the Chinese threat to the chastity of white women. The protagonists are once again Chinese laundrymen, who are invited by three good-natured, God-fearing white women to attend Sunday school. Somehow the licentious Chinese manage to seduce the church ladies, and soon they are seen cavorting together in an opium den. Fortunately, the police arrive just in time to rescue the white damsels in distress.[12]

Besides blatant Sinophobia, such an obsession with the Chinese washhouse can also be attributed to Hollywood's fetish for the exotic, and it provided a recipe for commercial success with an audience looking for low-cost peep shows. It fulfilled the wish, as Stanley Cavell puts it, "for the magical reproduction of the world by enabling us to view it unseen."[13] As we will see later, watching Chinese laundry scenes was a cheaper alternative, at least cinematically, to those Chinatown "slumming" tours, which would attract the more affluent consumers.

But in those years when film technology was still in its infancy, the fascination with the Chinese laundry became commingled with the very nature of cinema. As film historians have written, commerce in the earliest phase of cinema was driven by the economics of hardware: "The first film companies were the patent holders and manufacturers of camera and projection equipment. These manufacturers regarded the technological display of moving images in itself to be the prime appeal to audiences. The films themselves were of secondary concern." As a result, early filmmakers between, say, 1895 and 1906, developed what historian Tom Gunning calls "a cinema of attractions," which explored the range of uses for film to simply show something or even transform reality. For example, the Lumière brothers' film *Démolition d'un Mur* (*Falling Wall*,

1895) recorded the reduction of a wall to a pile of rubble and then used reverse printing to create the illusion of the wall returning to its former state.[14]

In this early stage of cinema before the advent of stars, filmmakers were preoccupied with recording the activities of human subjects, using a static camera to capture people in everyday rituals. Besides the two Chinese laundry scenes, the numerous short films coming out of Edison's studio all carried descriptive titles matching their realist contents, such as *Blacksmith Scene* (1893), *Record of a Sneeze* (1894), *Amateur Gymnast* (1894), and *The Barbershop* (1894). In the words of film historian Kevin Brownlow, "During the primitive years, the emphasis was on movement for movement's sake."[15] Besides this addiction to human action, as Siegfried Kracauer points out, film "gravitates toward unstaged reality." Understanding film as a redemption of physical reality, Kracauer reminds us that the most unforgettable figures in D. W. Griffith's early films are those who occasionally walk into them "almost directly from the street."[16]

All these characteristics of film made the Chinese laundry seem like an ideal choice of subject. In addition to the unscripted exotic setting and the foreign appearance of Chinese to most Americans, the laundry was also the locale of noisy operations and repetitive actions. The sounds of washing and the din of the workers' chatter could not make it into those silent films, but the whirring images grabbed the imaginations of the camera and viewers just as they were attracted to the robotic actions of an assembly-line worker in, say, Charlie Chaplin's *Modern Times*, a silent film made as late as 1936, when talkies were already predominant. In fact, films based on Chinese washhouses became so ubiquitous that there were two productions in 1901 bearing the same title *Fun in a Chinese Laundry*, one by Edison and the other by Siegmund ("Pop") Lubin, a pioneer from the 1890s. It seems that those early filmmakers could never get enough fun from a Chinese washhouse.

Here we finally understand not only where Josef von Sternberg had gotten the bizarre title for his autobiography, but also why the phrase has such a strong pull on his career. According to his biographer, "Sternberg dated his own discovery of the cinema to around 1910 and his days of 'sleeping rough,' when a nickel or dime would buy a few hours off the streets in a warm if smelly and noisy nickelodeon."[17] But both versions of *Fun in a Chinese Laundry* were made in 1901, suggesting an earlier connection. Anyway, by borrowing the title, Sternberg obviously compared the backbreaking work in the film industry to the menial labor inside a washhouse on the one hand, and unwittingly acknowledged the umbilical cord that ties the birth of film to that symbol of Chinese adaptation to America on the other.

Thus, it is only fitting—some might say serendipitous—that the first Chinese American star in Hollywood, indeed in global cinema, arose literally from a Chinese laundry.

5

ANNA

Growing up in a Chinese laundry on the fringes of Chinatown certainly gave young Anna a rather unique girlhood in early twentieth-century America. As soon as she reached school age, Anna was sent, along with her elder sister Lulu, to the California Street School. Founded in 1872 and first known as Central Street School and then Sand Street School, the public institution had just been renamed California Street School in 1903, two years prior to Anna's birth. Located in downtown Los Angeles, it attracted mostly white and some Hispanic students.[1] For the handful of Chinese children like Anna and Lulu, their opportunity to attend a predominantly white school was bittersweet fruit that emerged from the toxic soil of American racial politics.

Shortly after California joined the Union in 1850, the state's earliest law establishing public education in the state made no mention of racial restrictions, but subsequent legislative acts were quick to impose school segregation. The 1866 Act, in particular, restricted enrollment in public schools to white children only and required that "children of African or Mongolian descent, and Indian children not living under the care of white persons" be educated in segregated schools. In 1884, when Mamie Tape, the eight-year-old daughter of a successful Chinese businessman and his artist wife, was denied admission to the Spring Valley School, her parents sued the San Francisco Board of Education. On January 9, 1885, Superior Court Judge James Maguire ruled in favor of the plaintiff in *Tape v. Hurley*, which declared that the race-based denial of school admission was unlawful. On appeal, the California Supreme Court upheld the decision of the lower court. But justice was short lived. In response to the state's Supreme Court ruling, the state legislature swiftly passed Assembly Bill 268, which allowed the establishment of "separate schools for children of Mongolian or Chinese descent." The bill added that, "when such separate schools are established, Chinese or Mongolian children must not be admitted into any other schools."[2] What is especially remarkable is that the law passed a full eleven years before *Plessy v. Ferguson*, the United States Supreme Court decree that ushered in nearly a half-century of "separate but equal" legislation.

Elsewhere in the country, such as in the Jim Crow South, the plight of Chinese children was equally parlous. The so-called Mississippi Chinese—hundreds of laborers recruited to the Delta area during Reconstruction—had planted their roots in the South over time. Due to their skin color, however, they fell into a racial vacuum in a bifurcated Black-and-white society. The Chinese children were excluded from white schools, and their parents were unwilling to send them to Black schools because most thought of themselves as non-Black. In 1924, when the eight-year-old daughter of Gong Lum, a Chinese merchant with considerable standing in the white community in Rosedale, Mississippi, was rejected from a white school, he went to court. After his lawyers argued that Martha "is not a member of the colored race nor is she of mixed blood, but that she is pure Chinese . . . [and that] there is no school maintained in the District for the education of children of Chinese descent," the Circuit Court decided in Lum's favor. But the state Supreme Court reversed the decision, citing the 1890 Mississippi Constitution, in which "separate schools shall be maintained for children of the white and colored races," and asserting that Chinese are not white and must fall under the category of "colored races." The case—*Lum v. Rice*—then went to the nation's highest court, which upheld the decision of the Mississippi Supreme Court—an outcome all too predictable in the wake of *Plessy v. Ferguson*. Writing the majority opinion, former president and now Chief Justice William Howard Taft maintained that "It has been at all times the policy of the lawmakers of Mississippi to preserve the white schools for members of the Caucasian race alone. . . . A child of Chinese blood, born in, and a citizen of, the United States, is not denied the equal protection of the laws by being classed by the State among the colored races who are assigned to public schools separate from those provided for the whites, when equal facilities for education are afforded to both classes."[3]

In the years before *Brown v. Board of Education* finally outlawed school segregation in 1954, Chinese children in America walked a fine line, their education subject to the vagaries of local laws and national trends. For Anna and her sister to be able to attend a predominantly white public school in Los Angeles, their parents must have felt fortunate and proud. But as much as the girls took pride in attending the school outside Chinatown and looked forward to making friends, bullying would put a stop to any such dreams. Later in life, Anna would tell an interviewer, "My first school was in the old building on California Street. I was very miserable. The American boys used to chase me around at recess, called me a Chink and pulled my little pigtail." In an autobiographical piece written in the 1920s, she described those horrors in greater detail: The schoolboys surrounded her and her sister and "pulled our hair, which we wore in long braids down our backs. They shoved us off the sidewalk, pushing us this way and that, and all the time keeping up their chant: 'Chink, Chink, Chinaman. Chink, Chink, Chinaman!'" Tormenting the Chinese girls became sport for the other schoolchildren. The Wong girls felt that they were "suddenly thrust into a new terrifying world."[4]

What young Anna failed to realize was that her personal pain was merely part of a collective experience, a rite of passage for Chinese Americans that commenced in the mid-nineteenth century. Bullying or mob violence against the Chinese had already become a staple of American street life. Some linguists believe that the word *hoodlum* derives from the anti-Chinese cry of "huddle 'em," a signal for mobs to surround and harass the long-braided "Celestials."[5] Shrewd readers would know that *Lord of the Flies* is much less a tale about children left to their own devices in a natural state than an allegory of the adult world as a wild jungle. Or, as the Confucian adage puts it, "Human nature is good at first. The same nature, varies on nurture." Perhaps inspired by those nickelodeon reels portraying robotic Chinese bodies that could be stretched or elasticized at will, a boy sitting behind Anna at school stuck pins into her to see if the China doll felt pain differently. The next day, when she wore a thick overcoat for protection, the boy used a longer pin. Soon, as Anna recalled, she had to wear six coats as a barricade against him and got sick from overdressing.[6]

No stranger to these anti-Chinese shenanigans, Sam Sing told his daughters, "We must be proud always of our people and our race."[7] But, concerned for their children's safety, the parents transferred the girls to the Presbyterian Chinese Mission School inside Chinatown. One of the first Christian institutions to enter the Chinese community, the Presbyterian Church was founded in 1876 under the leadership of Ira M. Condit, a veteran missionary who had served in Canton for five years in the 1860s. The school had first begun in a mission house near the old Spanish Plaza, where both English and Cantonese were taught. Then, around 1894, the Chinese Children's School was founded at 766 Juan Street. Twenty years later, public school enrollment figures listed twenty-one children in the primary grades and twenty-three in the middle grades. One early account portrays the Chinese Children's School quite favorably:

> The most interesting and unique place in Chinatown is the kindergarten for Chinese children, maintained by the Presbyterian church. It is situated in a quiet nook, away from the bustling portion of Chinatown. It is tastefully furnished and arranged, and in every respect it is the most pleasant and healthy place. Here gather a dozen or more healthy and active urchins in their quaint dresses, daily.[8]

But other descriptions paint a more unflattering picture:

> Classes in the mission vary. Grades disappear. Regulations are elastic as attendance in this factory of private coaching is not unlike a country school. . . . One boy wrestles with fractions, another scratches his head over complicated verbs of the English language which stick out their tongues at rules. The smaller girls learn to sew and sing psalms interchangeably in Chinese and American until they can do handsprings.[9]

In addition to the Presbyterian School, other church schools were also available. In its heyday, Chinatown boasted eight Christian missions, including Methodist, Nazarene, Congregational, and others, all competing to save Chinese souls, young and old. For many of these children, including the Wong sisters, the mission schools served as a transition to the regular public schools. Forced back to Chinatown for their schooling, Anna and Lulu would later return to public schools as they got older, but they continued to juggle the various school systems, and the long hours became punishing: Regular school went from nine to three, followed by Chinese school from four to seven thirty or eight, with only a half hour for supper. On Saturdays, Chinese school went from ten to four, and then half a day on Sunday.

Nora Sterry, a principal of the Macy Street School in Chinatown, pointed out that the great handicap of Chinese children like Anna was that "they do not know how to play." This observer of Chinatown life went on to say, "The routine of their daily life outside the public school does not allow for play and they must actually be taught what seems instinctive in other children."[10] Though not as condescending as Jacob Riis's comments, this statement does not hold water when we measure it against the life of young Anna. In fact, she recalled fondly the happy times at the Presbyterian School. "Here though our teachers were American, all our schoolmates were Chinese. We were among our own people. We were not tormented any longer." Those were the years when Anna, a tomboyish creature with a grimy face, tousled hair flying, played baseball and marbles, all the while having a good time with her "gang."[11]

6

CURIOUS CHINESE CHILD

IN 1915, AS EUROPE became mired in a protracted war with devastating international reverberations, Hollywood experienced a sea change.

By the second decade of the twentieth century, the movie industry had gained respectability as a form of mass entertainment. Rising from its cradle in largely eastern cities, the industry had already begun to move westward to Los Angeles in the previous decade. Mythmakers of Hollywood claim that the formerly obscure suburb of Los Angeles became the site of the motion-picture colony because the first filmmakers who arrived were fugitives—independent producers evading legal hassles and the monopolizing Patent Trust in the East. They wanted to be, so the story goes, "as far from New York and as close to the Mexican border as possible."[1] Debunkers of this myth are quick to point out that the first movies produced in Southern California were made by the Patent Trust, and that Mexico was a long, five-hour drive from Los Angeles in those days. The more plausible explanation lies in the physical environment of the region. Offering year-round sunshine and warm weather for outdoor shooting, Southern California also boasts a geographical ensemble comprising mountain, forest, desert, city, and sea, making any conceivable backdrop within easy reach of downtown Los Angeles. Economically, land was available and affordable in Hollywood, allowing producers to purchase large tracts to build studios. And, as an added incentive, Los Angeles was an open-shop, non-union city with a constant stream of new residents, providing a steady supply of cheap labor for a rapidly expanding industry. The combination of all these factors led to a geographical shift between 1907 and 1913 as film companies moved toward the West Coast.[2]

Using Hollywood as its headquarters, filmmakers began an industrial-scale model of mass production, in the process grabbing the lion's share of the American public's imagination, not to mention its money. The most successful production opened in 1915: D. W. Griffith's epic, *The Birth of a Nation*, touted as one of the greatest visual experiences in the history of filmmaking. Running for an unprecedented dozen reels, or two and a half hours in screen time, the then-longest film ever made was based on Thomas W. Dixon's novel *The Clansman*, which glorified the rise of the hooded Ku Klux Klan in the postbellum South and ridiculed Black aspirations for political rights. The son of a wounded, impoverished Confederate officer in Kentucky, Griffith was ideologically sympathetic to the theme of *The Clansman*. In the motion picture, Griffith found a powerful medium for propagating the message of white supremacy and the fear of miscegenation at a time when such racist sentiments were on a steady rise. The Nativist Era of the 1910s and 1920s, one of the most xenophobic periods in American history, had just begun.

Besides this explosive message, what made *The Birth of a Nation* such a blockbuster was Griffith's style of narrative and his creative use of the camera. Failing in his earlier ambition as a writer, Griffith had done some acting with little success, but he found his calling in filmmaking. While early films typically were made by anchoring the camera in a fixed position, Griffith, the literary aficionado, drew inspiration from nineteenth-century novels and moved the camera freely through space and time. A skeptic once asked, "How can you tell a story jumping about like that? The people won't know what it's about." In response, Griffith invoked the authority of a master narrator in a different medium: "Well, doesn't Dickens write that way?" In some sense, Griffith, dubbed "The Shakespeare of the Screen," realized his literary ambition not with the quill but with the camera. Like a Jamesian portrait of a lady, Griffith moved the camera "so close to the actors that human figures filled the frame. In some shots they were actually larger than the frame and were shown only from the knee up. For the first time viewers could see facial expressions throughout the film." And like an epic Tennyson poem, Griffith told parallel stories, cutting back and forth between scenes and settings, between long and short shots, creating a dynamic montage of filmlike length. Added to these technical innovations were the spectacles of costumes, architectural form, and crowd movement. With no cost spared, the lavish display was so powerful and appealing to the audiences that they spontaneously applauded at scenes of Klan members rescuing whites from evil mulattoes and lustful Blacks. In the words of Vachel Lindsay, those climactic scenes and the emotions aroused were "as powerful as Niagara pours over the cliff."[3]

While this potent combination of racist propaganda and technical innovation made *The Birth of a Nation* a huge success at the box office, the film also spurred key changes in the industry. The increasingly popular use of close-up shots, in particular, would contribute to the creation of the star system in Hollywood. Early cinema often presented anonymous bodies on screen without credits, whereas close-up shots enabled an emphasis and focus on the actor's face as a fount of

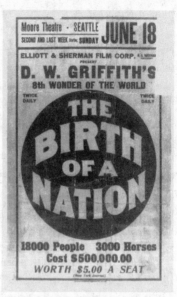

Film poster for D. W. Griffith's "8th Wonder of the World," *The Birth of a Nation*, 1915 *(Courtesy of Library of Congress, Prints and Photographs Division, Reproduction Number LC-DIG-ppmsc-03661)*

meaning. In other words, viewers could finally see facial expressions of characters, with "picture personality" a desired effect. Echoing Adolph Zukor's slogan "Famous Players in Famous Plays," Hollywood finally figured out that stars sold pictures. Name recognition and branding, then, became the magic formula for success. In tandem with these technical changes, the trade press began to publish articles about film actors, circulating information that identified and promoted the images of individual performers. Public interest in all aspects of their lives further increased the value of these actors. Mary Pickford, a child actor in the theater who successfully switched to a career in film under the tutelage of Griffith, was one of the glossiest stars of the silent era. By 1915, she could demand $4,000 a week, with her salary going up to $10,000 a week the next year—this in addition to half the profits of the films and a guaranteed salary of at least one million dollars over two years. At the time, even beginning players with the right charisma, style, and talent could earn $2,000 to $5,000 a year for their film roles.[4] These numbers, astronomical in the eyes of the public, played a big role in Hollywood's rise in cultural sway. The term *movie mogul* came into use around 1915, aptly describing those foreign-born producers, mostly Eastern European Jews, who became "part splendid emperors, part barbarian invaders," seizing cultural authority via the new popular medium.[5] By this point, Hollywood had become—to borrow a cliché—a place, a people, and a state of mind.

It was in this period that Anna came of age, becoming obsessed with the movies and the glamour of being an actor. "At a very young age, I went movie-crazy," she recalled. In fact, she first went to the cinema at the age of ten, using the tip money she had saved from laundry deliveries to buy a ticket. Historians of early American cinema have emphasized the particular appeal of those grubby nickelodeons to poor immigrants, the recently urbanized working class, and women. In *Babel and Babylon*, Miriam Hansen suggests that the nickelodeons, filling a market gap with their low admission fees and flexible schedules, offered the spectators—most of whom had little disposable income or time— "an escape from overcrowded tenements and sweatshop labor, a reprieve from the time discipline of urban-industrial life." Naturally, catering to an audience of such social composition, these movie theaters, particularly the ones that young Anna frequented on Main Street in Los Angeles, not far from Chinatown, were not the most stylish places—they were a far cry from the "picture palaces" with art deco flamboyance or rococo motifs that were proliferating in major cities during Hollywood's golden years. No thought was given, for instance, to ventilation or comfortable seats. In many of the films, the titles were run in Spanish, because the audiences were largely Mexican. However, crouching in the smelly darkness, not minding the Spanish titles, Anna enthralled by the flickering images on the screen. Thereafter, she often played hooky from school and used her lunch money to subsidize her new addiction. When her father caught her, he would beat her with a bamboo stick. "With Chinese logic," Anna said, "my father used to protest that if I had to be a bad girl and play hooky, why didn't I play hooky from the American school, which cost him nothing, instead of the Chinese school where he had to pay tuition."[6] What Sam Sing did not realize was that his second daughter's truancy went beyond those trips to shabby nickelodeons; she had something grander in mind.

At Christmas time, while Lulu asked for a big doll with flaxen curls, Anna wanted a whole lot of little dolls, because she had a purpose. Using her bed for a stage, she arranged those tiny dolls as truly silent actors and made up all sorts of imaginary dramas. When her younger brother James was old enough, she pressed him into service, and the two acted out plays that she had made up. Uninterested in generic kids' games with dolls and teacups, Anna took her performances to a different level. Coming home from the movies, she would retreat to her room and practice for hours in front of the mirror the scenes that most appealed to her. As if anticipating the countless tragic roles she eventually would undertake, she often rehearsed those screen moments of agony: crying in anguish, with tears streaming down her face. She would even clutch a handkerchief to her bosom and then tear it in a paroxysm of sorrow.[7] Her melodramatic reenactments would be a perfect match for the overly wrought style of the era.

Anna's celluloid fantasies did not stop with playacting. She daydreamed of becoming a star. In her reveries, she visualized herself in a scene where, under golden light, she wandered on a path near a white palace and scented gardens. The director, invariably a man with short sleeves and a big horn in front of his mouth, shouted, "Anna May Wong, now you can come down the stairs— We'll do a close-up of that!" And then the photographer moved nearer with a three-legged camera, closing in on her glowing, joyful face. At the end of the scene, the director would say, "You did a great job, Anna May Wong—You are a film star!"[8]

Anna was not alone in her fantasies, at least not if you embrace fiction. Faye Greener, the tragic protagonist in Nathanael West's dystopian portrayal of Hollywood, *The Day of the Locust* (1939), was more methodical in her reverie. "She often spent the whole day making up stories," as the narrative goes. "She would get some music on the radio, then lie down on her bed and shut her eyes. She had a large assortment of stories to choose from. After getting herself in the right mood, she would go over them in her mind, as though they were a pack of cards, discarding one after another until she found the one that suited."[9]

They were called "movie-struck girls." Generations of young American women came to be lured by the glittering promises of a career in Hollywood, swept up by that mirage colloquially known as "The Dream Factory." At a time when the names and faces of Mary Pickford, Alma Rubens, Ruth Roland, and Pearl White were ubiquitous on marquees, posters, and lobby cards, magazines and newspapers all hyped stories of their glamorous lifestyles and sky-high salaries. Any girl with a spark of imagination and a smidgen of ambition might ask, "Why not me?" Whether they hailed from Kalamazoo, Michigan, or Cottage Grove, Wisconsin, they all bought one-way tickets to Los Angeles.[10] When they stepped off the train at Central Station (and later Union Station), or when they joined the long lines of determined young women standing outside Hollywood casting offices, or, if they were lucky enough, when they got as far as the notorious "casting couch," what awaited them would spawn, among other forms, a new genre of American writing in the 1930s and 1940s called *noir*. With cold-eyed realism and hard-boiled language, authors such as Nathanael West, John Fonte, Raymond Chandler, and James Cain would portray the brutal reality facing these Faye Greeners, who had to sell their bodies and souls just to get a part as an extra in a two-reel farce in which they spoke only one line or nothing at all. The Dream Factory would, in the words of West, turn into a "Dream Dump."

But we are getting ahead of the story, so let us get back to the girl dreaming in her father's Chinese laundry.

Fortunately for Anna, she had no need to hop a train to Hollywood; instead, Hollywood came to her. As we saw earlier, the seemingly exotic atmosphere of Chinatown, with its curio shops, restaurants, crooked alleys, and teeming denizens clad in unfamiliar costumes, had always been a favorite backdrop for American movies. In fact, just as the Chinese laundry played a role in the development of film technology, Chinatown's emergence into America's national consciousness coincided with the early growth of the film industry. In the waning days of the nineteenth century, "slumming" trips to Chinatown became a fad. Aided by magazines that began to feature essays on the ethnic enclave, describing exotic menus in restaurants, offerings in curio shops, and the heathen ways of life there, Chinatown became a destination for burgeoning tourism. As one historian writes, "By 1909, so-called rubberneck automobiles, accompanied by a 'megaphone man,' who provided a commentary on the urban landscape, would take the curious spectator on a tour through Chinatown, which included visits to a joss house [shrine], a theater, and a restaurant." Indeed, the touring automobile, with its ascending rows of seats, looked a bit like a mobile theater.[11] Costing one to two dollars per person, these trips attracted mostly the more affluent who had money to spare, while the masses would have to satisfy their curiosity and cravings simply by going to the movies.

A passing glance at the titles and dates of the era's films reveals how eagerly the producers exploited popular fantasies of turn-of-the-century Chinatown. Such films included *Chinese Procession* (1898), *Parade of Chinese* (1898), *Chinese Shaving Scene* (1902), *San Francisco Chinese Funeral* (1903), *Scene in a Chinese Restaurant* (1903), *Scene in Chinatown* (1903), *Chinese Rubbernecks* (1903), *The Heathen Chinese and the Sunday School Teachers* (1904), and *Rube in an Opium*

Joint (1905), among others. Many of them captured real scenes in Chinatown, letting reality, to paraphrase Siegfried Kracauer, walk into the camera, while others, though staged, used the enclave as a readymade set. Like those slumming parties, film crews frequently trekked across town to shoot scenes in the Chinese quarter. With each scripted picture, Chinatown residents were regularly cast as extras or just stood around the shoots, rubbernecking, returning the favor of spectatorship. The more entrepreneurial members not only acted in films but also opened shops that lent props to the filmmakers. The wealth of the illustrious See family, for instance, came partly from rentals of costumes, furniture, utensils, and other bric-a-brac as film props. Neighborhood restaurants also catered to the Hollywood crowd, inventing menus with faux-Chinese dishes like "Chinaburger"—just a good old American hamburger stuffed with a cluster of beansprouts. As a longtime resident recalled, "You couldn't be in Chinatown at that time and avoid being involved in the film industry."[12]

Naturally, Anna, having been movie-struck at an early age, was also eager to be involved. She hung around the shoots, watching the goings-on, always hoping for a bit part. "We were always thrilled when a motion picture company came down into Chinatown to film scenes," she remembered. She would play hooky from school to watch the crew at work—even though she was at risk of being caught and getting a whipping from her teacher or her father. "I would worm my way through the crowd and get as close to the camera as I dared," she said. "I'd stare and stare at these glamorous individuals, directors, cameramen, assistants, and actors in grease-paint, who had come down into our section of town to make movies."[13]

In fact, her presence was so regular and conspicuous that one film crew dubbed her "C.C.C." (Curious Chinese child). Given her tender age, however, the magic wand of Hollywood would not yet reach her. Anna had to find other ways to wiggle her way into this new film world. She began modeling coats for a furrier and then for a department store. Obviously, the innate beauty of an adolescent Anna became quite noticeable—reflected in her luminous eyes, fresh face, and stature tall for a Chinese girl (her adult height would be five feet seven inches). A restaurant on Broadway hired her just to sit around, like a mannequin in a shop window or a Native American statue guarding a cigar store. "I was atmosphere," as she told a journalist years later.[14]

When the door of Hollywood finally opened a crack, she was needed, unsurprisingly, for nothing else but atmosphere, a proverbial face in the crowd. For Anna, however, it became the first step on a journey of a thousand miles.

PART TWO

BECOMING
ANNA MAY

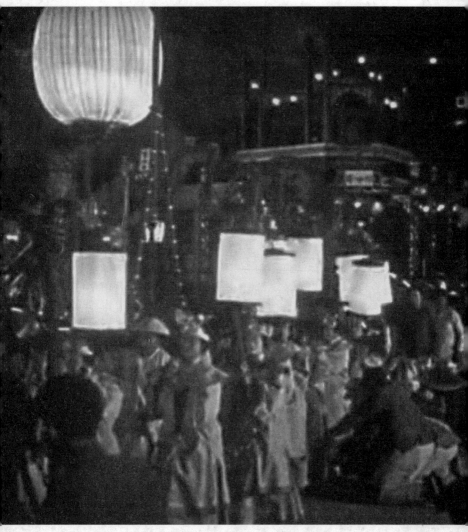

Film debut of Anna May Wong as an unidentified lantern-carrier in *The Red Lantern*, 1919 *(Film still)*

7

THE RED LANTERN

A S THE GREAT WAR was coming to an end and the Spanish Influenza was causing millions of deaths, Hollywood had two major productions in the popular genre of "yellow films" in that epic year of 1918. Ever since Jack London coined the term in 1904, "Yellow Peril" became a popular, if not titillating, motif for Hollywood producers, who in response cranked out a spate of Chinese-themed pictures, including *The Chinese Lily* (1914), *The Yellow Traffic* (1914), *The War of the Tongs* (1917), *Mystic Faces* (1918), and *City of Dim Faces* (1918). All flicks that portrayed Chinese people as opium addicts, white slavers, lawbreakers, thugs, and debauchers, they were awash in the pernicious stereotypes of the era.[1] Each production needed extras from Chinatown, as would two other new ones, *Broken Blossoms* and *The Red Lantern*, both in production in 1918 and released in 1919.

Based on a short story by Thomas Burke, the British master of Limehouse slum fiction, *Broken Blossoms* was directed by none other than D. W. Griffith, whose taste leaned toward the exotic. In addition to *The Birth of a Nation*, the flamboyant auteur had made films about Native Americans, Mexicans, Japanese, and South African Zulus. All were played by white actors and actresses who were made up—crudely for the most part, though expertly on occasion—for the roles.[2]

In *Broken Blossoms*, subtitled "The Yellow Man and the Girl"—a subtler variation of Burke's original title, "The Chink and the Child"—the fledgling silent-screen actor Richard Barthelmess played Cheng Huan in yellowface. The story is set, of course, in London's notorious Limehouse district, where the Chinese congregated. The storekeeper Cheng Huan has come to England from China with the idealistic hope of bringing the Buddhist message of tolerance and passivity to the warring nations, but he falls on hard times and becomes addicted to opium. Lucy (Lillian Gish), a white girl who suffers daily abuse from her father, Burrows, comes to visit his store, and Cheng becomes infatuated with her. One day when Lucy escapes from yet another beating and collapses in front of the store, Cheng takes her in and nurses her back to health. Barely able to control his desire for her virginal body, he treats her like a goddess and goes only so far as kissing the hem of her sleeve. As the title card states, "His love remains a pure and holy thing." Yet, when Burrows learns of this, he gathers a lynch mob, attacks the store, takes Lucy back to his slum quarters, and beats her to death. Devastated, Cheng—The Yellow Man—exacts revenge by shooting Burrows and then, in Wagnerian overdrive, commits suicide next to Lucy's body.

Ingeniously using the soft-focus Sartov lens and diffuse lighting to render Cheng's features less angular and more androgynous in contrast to Burrows's brutish masculinity and Lucy's angelic femininity, Griffith turned Thomas Burke's purple prose and atmospheric sketch of slum life into a melodrama of forbidden love and illicit desire, an admonitory tale against interracial romance. "Drama is exploration; melodrama is exploitation," writes Kevin Brownlow. Like most "yellow films" of the time, *Broken Blossoms* successfully exploited the themes of Chinese exoticism and inscrutability. To help him play the Chinese character, Griffith took Barthelmess slumming in Los Angeles's Chinatown, where they visited restaurants, shops, opium dens, gambling parlors, and temples. In the film, Barthelmess's eyes are demonstrably narrow, an effect achieved by wearing a tight rubber band underneath his Chinese skullcap, thus becoming a pioneer of what renowned cinematographer James Wong Howe would dub "adhesive tape actors"—whites who played Chinese roles with the assistance of a painted, adhesive bandage.[3]

Even though Anna played no part in *Broken Blossoms*, one person who would be instrumental in lining up her first screen role, Reverend James Wang, was in the film. A Christian minister who had arrived from China in the 1880s, Wang found his true calling in the business of motion pictures. Moonlighting at first and then relinquishing his Baptist collar, Wang became an actor, casting agent, and technical adviser. He was effectively the honcho who connected Hollywood to Chinatown.[4] Ironically, in *Broken Blossoms*, Reverend Wang played a Buddhist monk, who fingers his prayer beads while giving Cheng Huan the blessing for his ill-fated journey to the West.

One would think it challenging to compete with the melodrama of star-studded *Broken Blossoms*, but *The Red Lantern*, directed by Albert Capellani and starring Alla Nazimova, proved to be an even bigger production. Unlike the Ohio-born Lillian Gish, Nazimova was a renowned international personage with a storied past and a colorful presence in Hollywood. Originally named Adelaida Yakovlevna Leventon, Nazimova possessed an exotic background as a child of a dysfunctional Jewish family in Yalta, Crimea. Leaving behind a wretched childhood that saw her shuttling among boarding schools, foster care, and charitable relatives, she went to Tsarist Moscow at seventeen and apprenticed herself to Konstantin Stanislavsky at the Moscow Art Theatre. Rising to stardom on stage and touring widely in Europe, she arrived in New York in 1905 and debuted to critical acclaim on Broadway. Her talent and beauty attracted the attention of a fellow Ukrainian and former jewelry dealer from Kiev, Lewis J. Selznick (father of future Hollywood legend David O. Selznick), who in 1915 made her a handsome offer of $30,000 to act in a film. By the time *The Red Lantern* was in production in 1918, Nazimova had become so rich and successful that she was able to buy a sprawling Spanish-style home on three and a half acres at 8080 Sunset Boulevard, where she remodeled the interior and built a pool in the shape of the Black Sea that was surrounded by lush, semitropical landscaping. Dubbed the "Garden of Alla," her stylish residence was a classic movie star's showplace: an immense tiled hallway with a Mexican chandelier, a vast living room with another tiled floor, beamed ceilings, and lavish furnishings upholstered in purple velvet. As if this was not enough, the mansion had a gilded wall sconce, a baronial fireplace, a grand piano, and a broad stairway leading to the upper floor. The garage housed a new Rolls-Royce, while the staff consisted of a chauffeur, a gardener, a cook, a housemaid, and a butler. The place became a popular spot for Hollywood soirees, attracting a largely lesbian following. In fact, Richard Barthelmess, the yellowface actor in *Broken Blossoms*, owed his film career to the encouragement and tutelage of Nazimova, who had studied English with his mother. Young Anna, as we shall see, would also fall under the spell of the prima donna credited with the coinage of the term *sewing circle*, a discreet code for a gathering of lesbian and bisexual thespians.[5]

Mixing history with fantasy, *The Red Lantern* was set in the ancient capital city of Peking during the Boxer Rebellion (1899–1901). Nazimova played the double roles of the Eurasian Mahlee and her white half-sister, Blanche. Mahlee is the illegitimate child of a British man, Sir Philip Sackville, and a Chinese woman who died in childbirth. Abandoning the newborn, Sir Philip threw some money at the Chinese grandmother with the instruction: "You shall never bind her feet." As a result, Mahlee grows up with natural, unbound feet, drawing endless scorns and jeers from neighbors and everyone else. "Big feet—bad luck—everyone knows. Calamity hangs from the tips of the toes," says a cobbler in the film via a Chinese title displayed erroneously. (Occasionally, Chinese words, merely decorative for most viewers, are upside down or flipped in the titles.) After the death of her grandmother, Mahlee goes to live with an American missionary couple and is converted to Christianity. She soon falls in love with the couple's son, who cannot reciprocate her feelings because of her mixed-blood heritage. Instead, he loves Mahlee's white half-sister, Blanche Sackville. Brokenhearted and resentful, Mahlee is lured by an evil Eurasian, Sam Wang (Noah Beery), to join the Boxer Movement. Wang disguises Mahlee as the Goddess of the Red Lantern and incites an uprising against white foreigners. When the allied forces of the Western nations crush the Boxers, Mahlee commits suicide on her peacock throne, muttering her final words: "East is East and West is West."

Billed as "the greatest production of [Nazimova's] amazing career on screen and stage," *The Red Lantern* was produced in the midst of a raging global pandemic. Like COVID-19 almost exactly a hundred years later, the Spanish Influenza brought the world to a standstill. Factories closed, schools went on recess, theaters shuttered, and people were afraid to go out. At the competitor's studio, the leading lady, Lillian Gish, caught the bug. When she recovered and returned to work, germophobic Griffith insisted that Gish wear a face mask whenever possible. As Gish described the horror on the streets, "they were dying so fast in California that they couldn't build caskets, and they were burying the victims in one grave."[6]

Fortunately, no one got sick on the set of *The Red Lantern*, but the need for six hundred Chinese extras was a tall casting order under any circumstances. This nearly impossible task fell to the film's technical adviser, Reverend Wang, who had to knock on doors in Chinatown to scare up live bodies. And that was how luck turned for young Anna. "I ran around to an old Chinese who helped out the movies by getting Chinese actors for them." She remembered her encounter with Wang: "He looked me over critically. 'Well,' he said, 'you are a big girl and you have big eyes; you will do.' I felt flattered until I learned that he had just had an order for 600 Chinese actors in a hurry and hadn't been able to find but fifty."[7]

When Anna broke the news to her parents that she was going to be an extra, they, as the Chinese would put it, flew off the roof. They had always assumed that her playacting in front of the mirror and skipping school to go to the movies was a passing phase. They did not realize how serious she was about becoming an actor. Besides the long Chinese tradition that looked down upon women employed in the entertainment industry, there remained the superstition that every time you have your picture taken, you lose a bit of your soul: The camera was a soul-snatching machine. But for Anna, Chinese beliefs be damned; they were now in the New World, and many of their Chinese friends, as Anna reminded her parents, were engaged in the movie business, even the honorable Reverend Wang. "Just then a squadron of buses stopped at our house to pick me up," she recalled. "There were about 150 Chinese on the way to the studios to play extra parts and my father and mother knew most of them. They stayed so long gossiping in front of the house that the picture was kept waiting; but meanwhile I had slipped without further objection into the bus."[8]

Anna's long-anticipated moment, like most beginnings, was anticlimactic. "That first day I simply walked around with a mob of Chinese," she recalled. But the second day promised to be more exciting, as the director told her to come back and play a part as one of the three girls carrying lanterns. With a bit of adolescent self-aggrandization, she felt "the responsibility of the whole movie industry on my shoulders." Having seen how actresses were made up on the sets, Anna decided to produce a "grand scenic version" of herself: "I borrowed my mother's rice powder rag and fairly kalsomined my face. With the most painstaking effort, I managed to curl my straight Chinese hair. As a finished touch, I took one of our Chinese red papers, wet it and rubbed off the color onto my lips and cheeks."

As she showed up on the set, the director looked at her and gasped: "Good God!" He immediately ordered the costumers to grab hold of her, rub the red off her cheeks, and wash down her hair until they got the curl out of it.

When the film finally was released, she treated five girlfriends to the movie with the lunch money she had saved for more than a week. They went up to the top gallery of the old California Theatre on Main Street to witness her triumph. But they were utterly disappointed: "All we saw were three dim Chinese girls walking by with lanterns. 'Which is you?' my girl friends asked. 'I . . . I don't know,' I faltered. 'I think I must be the outside one.'"[9]

Even though Anna was uncredited and failed to pick herself out of the crowd, it was the opening she had long dreamed of. Unlike the other Chinese extras who gleefully walked away with $7.50 per day (fifty percent more than the usual five dollars, due to the difficulty of finding actors during the pandemic), Anna craved more.[10] And the person who would introduce her to Hollywood was none other than Alla Nazimova, whose scandals in her art and lifestyle continued to defy social norms.

An extant photo shows fourteen-year-old Anna sitting by the pool in the Garden of Alla. Wearing a two-toned swimsuit and a pair of flat-heeled shoes with buckles, she smiles sweetly at the camera. Her naked legs look strong, arms slender, and, under a white bandanna, her signature bangs brush against her new-moon eyebrows. In another photo, she stands on the roof of the bathhouse by the pool, tall like a statue, as if playing a game of truth or dare. Even though she was one of the six hundred Chinese extras on the set of *The Red Lantern*, Anna's youthful charm must have caught the eye of Nazimova, who invited the adolescent to the Garden of Alla, also known as the 8080 Club. At the movie colony's first salon, the guests would drink, gossip, and listen to Nazimova rattling off in her linguistic trifecta of English, Russian, and French about memories of Yalta and Moscow, and her coach Stanislavsky. Maintaining the façade of marriage to a man while romantically involved with various men and women, Nazimova was openly bisexual. "Most of my friends are

Anna May Wong by the pool at the Garden of Alla, 1919, photo by John Springer *(Courtesy of Corbis Historical Collection / Getty Images)*

young girls," she once told journalists, adding, "My friends call me Peter and sometimes Mimi." In addition to splashy gatherings at night, Nazimova hosted poolside parties on Sunday afternoons for young girls only. She also owned Mary's, a dyke bar on the Sunset Strip.[11]

It would be foolish, or perhaps distasteful, to speculate on the nature of young Anna's relationship to Nazimova as anything other than that of a protégé to a mentor. As Gavin Lambert writes in his masterful biography, "Nazimova was the first to cultivate an image of the 'foreign' sexual sophisticate, and supplied the original theme on which Pola Negri, Garbo, and Dietrich created variations." One day, as we shall see, Anna would enter the intimate circle of Marlene Dietrich, perhaps in the same ingenue way she entered the 8080 Club. Regardless, it would not be so hard to imagine how those poolside soirees could affect and transform a fourteen-year-old Chinese girl. The Garden of Alla, as Axel Madsen describes it in *The Sewing Circle* (1995), was a notorious spot for celebrity trysts: It was where Nazimova induced two of her young lovers, Jean Acker and Natacha Rambova, to marry, in succession, Rudolph Valentino.[12]

If nothing else, socializing with the First Lady of the Silent Screen would open doors, as it did for Mildred Davis, Virginia Fox, and Lois Wilson— all young hopeful actresses who frequented Nazimova's parties and later achieved a measure of fame. The list also includes Nazimova's goddaughter, Nancy Davis, later known as Nancy Reagan. Anna was no exception. Soon she became acquainted with many of the important people in Hollywood and was given roles ranging from bit parts to minor characters, and later lead roles. The daughter of a Chinese laundryman was ready to emerge from her cocoon.

8

ANNA MAY

"CALL ME ISHMAEL"—so begins *Moby-Dick*, that pelagic American epic by Herman Melville.[1] As literary scholars have pointed out, the narrator's biblical self-naming—Ishmael being the son of Abraham with his slave woman, whereas Isaac was the rightful heir—is a deliberate act of defiance, affirming his own subversive genealogy. America—a republic born of a war of independence, severing itself from the mother country— also belongs in a subversive genealogy. Consequently, self-naming becomes a quintessential American art. Such a rebirth applies not only to celebrities ranging from Alla Nazimova to Mary Pickford, Warner Oland, Marilyn Monroe, Bob Dylan, and Jon Stewart, but also to almost all Americans who hail from another place, another world. Whether your name in your homeland and original language used to be Yacoob, Ölund, or 黄运特 (Huáng Yùn Tè), anglicization, dropping the umlaut, or reversing the word order would be part of your Americanization, after which you become Jacob, Oland, or even Yunte Huang.

Likewise, one of the first things Anna did when she entered the Hollywood scene was to choose a new nomenclature. At birth, she was given the English name "Anna" by the doctor. In fact, three of the Wong girls had American names with four letters: Lulu, Anna, and Mary; Margaretta, the youngest who died in infancy, was the only exception. "Anna Wong didn't sound well" on screen credits, thought Anna, already dreaming of her own name in lights appearing on marquees. And she also wanted to vary the four-letter format. She ended up choosing "May" because she liked "the suggestion of springtime," when willows turn green.[2] Thus, en route to her rendezvous with American history, Wong Liu Tsong became Anna May Wong.

In her 1919 to 1921 period of apprenticeship, Anna May hobnobbed with Hollywood elites at the 8080 Club and elsewhere, at the same time picking up minor roles in several films. The first one was *Outside the Law* (1920), directed by Todd Browning and starring Priscilla Dean, the popular silent star, and Lon Chaney, who would soon garner the moniker of "The Man of a Thousand Faces." Against the grain of "yellow films" that featured the stereotypically dark side of the Orient, this film presented a romanticized view of Chinese wisdom, anticipating aphorism-spouting Charlie Chan by a few years. The opening scene reveals a volume of *The Sayings of Confucius* on a table covered in Chinese tapestry, followed by a title card: "Confucius said: If a country had none but good rulers for a hundred years, crime might be stamped out and the death penalty abolished."

In this eight-reel silent film, Chaney played the double role of the Chinese servant Ah Wing and the gangster Black Mike. Having seen Alla Nazimova pull the same trick in *The Red Lantern*—simultaneously playing a Chinese role with taped eyes and a white character with more "natural" makeup—Anna

Anna May Wong in *Outside the Law*, 1920 *(Film still)*

May began to get a taste of Hollywood's delicate art of yellowface. As an extra, she sat with a clutch of young girls her age and listened to an old Chinese man doling out nuggets of Confucian wisdom. She remained uncredited in the film, since the camera focused for only a few fleeting seconds on her curled bangs, a knee-length Chinese gown, and a pair of embroidered pantaloons.

In her next film, Anna May received, in her own words, "a real part."[3] It was *Dinty* (1920), directed by Marshall Neilan, in which Anna May played Half Moon, a young maid/mistress of a Chinatown gangster and vice lord, King Dorkh (Noah Beery). She had previously crossed paths with Beery—albeit tangentially—in *The Red Lantern*, but this time she *has* more interaction with him, as King Dorkh tries to seduce Half Moon with money and jewelry. A key turn of the plot involves the abduction of the daughter of a prominent judge, who has been a thorn in Dorkh's side. The method of kidnapping taps into the stereotypical American imagination, an element that would seem almost ironically endearing to Anna May: The thugs hide the victim in, yes, a laundry basket and whisk her away on a horse-drawn carriage marked with the words OONG WONG LAUNDRY.

Perhaps inspired by the scene, Timothy G. Turner, a *Los Angeles Times* journalist, arrived at the Wong Laundry on North Figueroa Street and interviewed Anna May after the release of *Dinty*. In the published feature story, "Maid of Orient Unspoiled by Success Dips Her Ivory Hands in Suds," Turner appeared impressed by the fact that even though Anna May was making $150 a week as an actress, she still toiled in her father's washhouse. "Anna May Wong has a little room in the barn of a building," Turner described. Save for a little Chinese garden, the building was surrounded by vacant lots on all sides, its walls almost paintless and its roof a gallery of floating linen. The journalist, struck by the natural beauty of the young actress, depicted her in an ersatz-Orientalist style: "She is slender, has hands of ivory, carved as delicately as an idol's, and her face is not made of cheeks, ears, eyes and lips, but of petals. Such, after the fashion of the Chinese poet, is Anna May Wong." Applauding her beauty and her work ethic, Turner called her "the Chinese exception to the American rule. The films have not spoiled her." Perhaps he was not clued in, but Turner failed to mention a key development in Anna May's life.[4]

As proverbial as it sounds, art does imitate life. As it turned out, the budding fifteen-year-old actress, while playing a mistress in *Dinty*, had become romantically involved with the predatory director, a married man more than twice her age. Rising from chauffeur to film director, Marshall Neilan, known as "Mickey," was a dandy who liked to splash his high salaries ($125,000 per film) on "wild parties and presents for his many girlfriends." Neilan's affair with teenage Anna May apparently was an open secret in Hollywood, and the two even planned a quick trip south of the border to get a Mexican marriage license in order to circumvent California's antimiscegenation laws.[5]

By 1920, Neilan had become so successful as a director that he was able to establish his own production company, giving him more creative leeway to do his heart's bidding. Captivated by Anna May, Neilan wrote a part specifically for her in his next production, *Bits of Life* (1921). Inspired by a title card in *Broken Blossoms* that read, "Broken bits of his life in his new home," Neilan's new film was an artistic mélange of four short stories. Anna May appeared in the third episode, "Hop" or "Chinese Story." Born in China, the character of Chin Chow (Lon Chaney) had been taught that girl babies were undesirable. Moving to America, he runs opium dens and rises to overlord of the San Francisco underworld. When his wife Toy Sing (Anna May) produces a girl, he beats her and vows to kill the baby. A friend gives Toy Sing a crucifix, which she hammers into the wall, unaware that her husband is lying in an opium stupor on a bunk on the other side. As if only in the movies, the nail penetrates the skull of Chin Chow and kills him.[6]

The film received excellent reviews and was selected by *Photoplay* magazine as one of the eight best pictures of the year, along with *Tol'able David* and *A Man of Stone*, among others. But too many scenes seemed so exotic for middle-class Americans that some states did not even show the film. As one exhibitor put it, "I tell you that Chink stuff of that kind won't do if we expect to stay in the game."[7] While a daring artistic effort, the film was a financial flop.

However, *Bits of Life* set in motion something larger than the film itself. For Chaney, a rising makeup artist, it launched his remarkable career of playing Chinese characters, a legacy that would prove as controversial as Warner Oland's Charlie Chan a decade later. Besides assuming the roles of myriad tortured, often grotesque characters in horror films, such as *The Hunchback of Notre Dame* (1923) and *The Phantom of the Opera* (1925), Chaney would play Yen Sin, a grubby, opium-smoking Chinese laundryman, in *Shadows* (1922); and, later, two Chinese men simultaneously in *Mr. Wu* (1927). Together, the two films would establish a benchmark for Hollywood's representation of Asians. Anna May, who would often appear opposite Chaney's yellowface characters, learned at least one important lesson from *Bits of Life*: As a Chinese woman in Hollywood, she would have rough going in her professional and personal lives.

After the initiation to torture in *Bits of Life*, her various future characters would suffer countless torments and die a thousand deaths. In real life, the rapacious Neilan soon lost interest in his young Chinese paramour and moved on to his next quarry.[8]

Earlier during the shooting of *Dinty*, Anna May's mother had said to her, "I wish you would not have so many pictures taken. Eventually you may lose your soul." Not a believer in her mother's Old World superstitions, Anna May replied that her life could not be lived within the same parameters as her mother's. "It might not be a happier life," she said, "but that was for time to tell."[9]

The up-and-coming actress had chosen May as her new name because it is a hopeful month of spring, but "may" is also part of "maybe." As Charlie Chan says, "Every maybe has a wife called Maybe-Not."

9

MADAME BUTTERFLY
IN TECHNICOLOR

Film poster for *The Toll of the Sea*, 1922 *(Courtesy of Everett Collection)*

IN THE LONG HISTORY of America's Oriental imagination, few tropes have commanded more potency than the character of Madame Butterfly. Originally published in 1898 as a short story written by John Luther Long, a Philadelphia lawyer and writer, the tale of "Madame Butterfly" was inspired by the French writer Pierre Loti's novel, *Madame Chrysanthème* (1887). In 1900, David Belasco adapted Long's story into a one-act play. After a successful run in New York, the play traveled to London, where the already legendary Italian composer Giacomo Puccini attended a performance. Puccini was hooked. Less than three years later, his opera *Madama Butterfly* premiered at Milan's La Scala in 1904 and opened in New York in 1906. Throughout the twentieth century, the doomed love story of a US Navy officer and an exploited Japanese geisha would undergo various incarnations and spawn countless imitations, but Puccini proved prescient in depicting the personal impact of American imperialism a half-century before "the Ugly American" even became a phrase.

In the immediate wake of Puccini's opera, Paramount released the film *Madame Butterfly* in 1915, starring Mary Pickford, who had been a child actor working for David Belasco's theater company. It was followed by a Metro film, *The Toll of the Sea* (1922), featuring the star of our story, Anna May Wong. In midcentury, James Michener's Pulitzer Prize–winning book, *Tales of the South Pacific* (1947), was turned into a Broadway musical by Rodgers and Hammerstein, which included an episode of romance between a US Marine Corps lieutenant and a young Tonkinese woman. Portraying Lieutenant Joseph Cable's fears over the social consequences of interracial marriage, the 1949 musical *South Pacific* featured show tunes like "You've Got to Be Carefully Taught":

> *You've got to be taught to be afraid*
> *Of people whose eyes are oddly made . . .*

It is worth noting that a number like this from the popular "Bali-ha'i" segment of the show was considered too controversial or simply inappropriate for the musical stage at the time. Perturbed by the interracial theme, lawmakers in Georgia passed a bill banning entertainment like *South Pacific*, with one legislator intoning that "a song justifying interracial marriage is implicitly a threat to the American way of life."[1]

Unfazed by the backlash, Michener continued to explore the theme in his next novel, *Sayonara* (1954), in which an American fighter pilot fell in love with a Japanese dancer during the Korean War. The book was adapted to an eponymous film in 1957, starring Marlon Brando and Miyoshi Umeki, and the film won four Academy Awards. The same year saw the publication of Richard Mason's *The World of Suzie Wong*, a novel about a British man romancing a Chinese prostitute in Hong Kong. The bestselling book was subsequently adapted for the stage and the screen, with phenomenal success. And, in the twilight years of the twentieth century, David Henry Hwang's award-winning play, *M. Butterfly* (1988), stood the familiar tale on its head, producing a faux spy-thriller about a French diplomat and his longtime Chinese lover, who turns out to be a secret agent and a man, not to mention Claude-Michel Schönberg's musical *Miss Saigon* (1989), which changed the setting to Vietnam with a similar narrative.

In its infinite variations—perhaps with the exception of Hwang's ingenious retooling—the storyline of Madame Butterfly remains the same: A white man woos an Asian woman and then abandons her to a tragic fate. Pairing Navy officers, Air Force pilots, and US Marines—all heterosexual, hypermasculine symbols—with Asian geishas, dancers, and sex workers, the story creates a stark contrast between dominating white masculinity and submissive Asian femininity, with war and colonialism as a cinematic obbligato. The many lives of Madame Butterfly track, almost step by step, the global footprints of the American empire—from Commodore Matthew Perry's naval fleet opening the bolted door of Tokugawa Japan to the later wars in China, Korea, Vietnam, and beyond. As in the original story, the narrative affords a white man an extended "quickie" in an exotic, faraway locale before he finds or returns to a "real wife" at home, while the Asian woman suffers the consequences of abandonment and childbearing, invariably ending in suicide. It has all the ingredients of an appetizing potpourri ready for consumption by kitsch-thirsty America: romance, war, sex, gunboats, fighter jets, cherry blossoms, geishas, kabuki, lotus flowers, hara-kiri, and more. Like those slumming trips to Chinatown, the Madame Butterfly saga provides Americans with a package tour through the cherry-tree lane of Oriental exotica and erotica.

It is almost serendipitous, then, that Anna May Wong, a rising star who came to symbolize the forbidden East, would assume the prototypical Madame Butterfly persona the first time she secured a lead role—as Lotus Flower in *The Toll of the Sea*. Directed by Chester M. Franklin, the 1922 film was, as the noted screenwriter Frances Marion admitted, "practically the stepdaughter of Madame Butterfly."[2] The story takes place in Hong Kong, where Lotus Flower finds a Caucasian man washed up on the beach. After the rescue, she nurses Allen Carver (Kenneth Harlan) back to health and in the process falls in love. He entices her with the prospect of going to America with him, even as local gossips warn her that white men will only marry her "Chinese fashion" and then forget her when they leave. As one of them puts it, somewhat sarcastically, "It is true! I have already been forgotten by four faithful American husbands." But Lotus Flower refuses to listen. One day, Carver receives a cable urging him to return to America immediately. After his abrupt departure, Lotus Flower gives birth to a son. Despite the passing of many moons, she still pines for his return. To quiet the local gossips, she even forges a letter to herself, pretending it's from her "honorable husband." When he finally comes back, he brings his "real" wife, a Caucasian woman. Brokenhearted, Lotus Flower asks the white woman to take the boy and raise him as her own. And then, à la Madame Butterfly, Lotus Flower throws herself into the sea.

Because she played a tragic part, Anna May had to sob often in the film, as she would do in many more pictures to come. "I cried so that I could not stop crying," as she recalled the ordeal during the production. "Finally the cynical assistant director called out, 'Somebody throw Anna May Wong a raft.'"[3] The film also required her to "speak" pidgin English, with lines such as "Christian lady at mission tell me America fine place. Women free—can spend all husband's money," and "If you no come back to me, you make my heart go dead." Since it was a silent film, she did not actually say these lines, but she had to mime them in a manner befitting the words on the titles. Basically a soprano with no voice, Anna May played these scenes with perfection, in the process garnering glowing reviews. *Variety* noted her "extraordinary fine playing," calling her "an exquisite crier without glycerin." *Film Daily* raved, "The theme is really a very sympathetic one made doubly interesting and sincere by the splendid work of Anna May Wong. She is a clever little actress and displays fine emotional ability." The *New York Times* also gave her a big thumbs-up: "Miss Wong stirs in the spectator all the sympathy her part calls for and she never repels one by an excess of theatrical 'feeling.' She has a difficult role, a role that is botched nine times out of ten, but hers is the tenth performance. Completely unconscious of the camera, with a fine sense of proportion and remarkable pantomimic accuracy, she makes the deserted little Lotus Flower a genuinely appealing, understandable figure."[4]

Unlike *Bits of Life*, which failed miserably at the box office, *The Toll of the Sea* grossed more than $250,000. To make the occasion even more momentous, it was the first film successfully made in Technicolor. Although *The Gulf Between*, a short feature shot in 1917, was actually the first color film, it was largely deemed a failure, abandoned after just one embarrassing screening in Buffalo. In the interim years, scientists and engineers worked to improve the technology so that it could become a practical option for commercial film production. The result was Technicolor No. II, which contained a new subtractive camera and a printing method that could print two color records onto one single filmstrip, requiring no special projector for screening. Bankrolled by Herbert Kalmus of the Technicolor company, *The Toll of the Sea* was therefore a joint venture between Oriental imagination and new technology.

Notably, while applauding Anna May's acting, the reviewers also spilled much ink on the new chromatic medium, especially the relation of color to racial and cultural differences. The *New York Times* opined: "Here are settings just waiting for reproduction in colors, and in them are Chinese people whose costumes of elaborate and finely embroidered silks and severely plain cotton permit richness and the effective variety of contrasts." The reviewer for *Variety*, however, seemed displeased with the effect of the newfangled machine: "Nothing in a moving picture can rise superior to the story. Coloring never will, never has, and doesn't here. The coloring runs without streaks, the camera catching the natural colors apparently, although what seemed something of a freak in this process is that the pallid color given to the complexion of the Chinese people extended to the faces of Americans as well." Apparently, this reviewer was disturbed by Technicolor's inability to differentiate the skin color of Chinese actors from that of Caucasians, calling the tint spillover "a noticeable defect" and "a freak."[5]

Many historians of color cinematography have argued that color in American films was often used to represent racial differences. From the very beginning, Hollywood was concerned with the inability of black-and-white films to showcase, pardon the oxymoron, the beauty of white. "All pretty girls in black and white are pale and consumptive," an author proclaimed in an industry journal in 1927—even the gorgeous white goddess Clara Bow would lose the allure of her famous auburn locks in front of the black-and-white camera.[6] In the years of exploration and prior to the adoption of color cinematography as the industry standard, the subjects chosen to experiment, demonstrate, and market color-film technologies were mostly people of color. As film scholar Kirsty Sinclair Dootson remarks, "Even the briefest survey of landmark films made by American market-leader Technicolor evidences that although whiteness was the structuring principle of color cinema, people of color were routinely exploited as part of the system's chromatic appeals." The examples given by Dootson include the Mexican musical short *La Cucaracha* (1934), which launched Technicolor's three-strip process; the blockbuster *Gone with the Wind* (1939), which secured the firm's market dominance; and the 1922 Orientalist fantasy that debuted the two-color system, *The Toll of the Sea*.[7]

It makes sense, then, that the director would buck the tradition of yellowface and cast Anna May as the lead in *The Toll of the Sea*, an otherwise daring, unprecedented arrangement for a Hollywood film in 1922. In addition, two supporting roles were also played by actresses of Chinese descent, Etta Lee and Ming Young. In fact, Frances Marion had written the script with Anna May in mind—not just because the veteran screenwriter had been impressed by Anna May's appearances in earlier films, but also because there was a need to test Technicolor No. II with real Chinese actors.

Interestingly, as the *Variety* reviewer lamented, the two-color scheme failed to accentuate the differences in skin tones between Chinese and white actors—a technical difficulty to be overcome later with the advent of the tri-color method. But *The Toll of the Sea* successfully exploited the so-called color consciousness of Hollywood by other means. As some scholars have pointed out, the film deliberately contrasts the riot of colors in China with the near-monochromatic palette of the Caucasian world. Besides the display of gay gardens and elaborately embroidered costumes for the Chinese characters, Lotus Flower often appears against a background of flowers and foliage, her dresses and ornaments blending in with the colors of her environment. In contrast, most of the Caucasian characters wear beige or gray suits, making them stand out against the verdant background, as free agents coming and going. Thus, the chromatic harmony between the Chinese heroine and her environment effectively marks her as racially different from the Caucasian characters.[8]

Comments made by a reviewer for *Motion Picture News* prove how successfully the film exploited the interplay between the new technology and Orientalist fantasy: "What land is richer in colors than China? Here we have a Chinese background for a story of an ancient legend. Here are the flowers, the sea, the soft skies in a harmonious arrangement of exquisite shades. Here is the land of the love boat and romance."[9] Although the film was made in California, with the lush landscape of Santa Monica palmed off as faraway China, reviewers raved about the "uncanny excellency" of the colorful reproduction of "actual persons and places," as if "a little bit of life [was] lifted out of the Orient, framed and sent here to delight the eye and sadden the heart."[10]

Just as the blockbuster *The Birth of a Nation* had used cinematic technology to exploit racial differences, *The Toll of the Sea* helped stoke America's Oriental imagination via the new chromatic medium. Presenting a Madame Butterfly–type character for the first time in Technicolor also marked a milestone for Anna May, her first lead role in a feature film. She was even applauded by the *New York Times*, which urged, "She should be seen again and often on the screen."[11]

10

HOLLYWOOD BABYLON

AGAINST A BACKDROP of oil boom, real estate frenzy, and population explosion in Southern California, Hollywood emerged in the mid-1920s to become the nation's fifth largest industry. The big studios—Paramount, Fox, Universal, United Artists, Metro Pictures, Goldwyn Pictures, Warner Bros., imperially run by movie moguls and linked vertically to national distribution systems and theater chains—grossed $1.5 billion a year and accounted for 90 percent of all the films made in the world.[1] Awash in cash, this new class of men and women, "the movie people," were living in such an aura of lavishness and glamour that it would give rise to the epithet "Hollywood Babylon."

To a nation ostensibly founded on the bedrock of Puritanism, the movie people, dedicated to the body and senses, to passions and dreams, were wallowing in a moral cesspool of biblical proportions. Even in its infancy, Hollywood was inundated with scandals of all sorts, Babylonian or otherwise. Infidelity and divorce made constant headlines, destroying or enhancing—depending on public sentiment as fickle as spring weather—the reputations and careers of those involved; tragic suicides revealed the dark side of living in the fast lane; and brutal murders were more shocking in reality than the horror movies they inspired. On September 10, 1920, Olive Thomas, the sister-in-law of Mary Pickford, committed suicide in a Paris hotel, a tragedy induced by drug addiction and despondency over her husband's philandering. A year later to the day, Virginia Rappe, a twenty-five-year-old actress, died during a three-day orgy hosted by Roscoe "Fatty" Arbuckle at a hotel in San Francisco. At the time, Arbuckle, an ex-plumber from Kansas, was Paramount's top-earning actor, whose popularity as a comedian was second only to that of Charlie Chaplin. Arbuckle was arrested and charged with murder on suspicion that he had violently raped Rappe with a champagne or Coca-Cola bottle or a piece of ice. Even though he was acquitted, exoneration by the court of law did not save him in the court of public opinion. Paramount canceled Arbuckle's $3 million contract and shelved his unreleased films. Even though he attempted a comeback by changing his name to Will B. Good, subsequently refining it to William Goodrich, Arbuckle died broke and broken at the age of forty-six, making him the embodiment of the classic American story of rags-to-riches to ruin.[2]

And then there was the shocking murder of the actor and director William Desmond Taylor on February 1, 1922—a never-solved killing that brought to light bizarre details that would shake the foundation of Hollywood: Taylor, the ex-president of the Motion Picture Directors Association, was actually William Cunningham Deane-Tanner, an Irish-born homosexual who had mysteriously disappeared from New York a decade earlier. Since so many movie people were fugitives from their own pasts, the truth about Taylor erected a funhouse mirror for almost everyone. It created an existential crisis in Hollywood, lending credence to the Shakespearean line, "All that glitters is not gold."[3]

The succession of scandals would prompt a period of soul-searching and the appointment of William Hays as the czar of censorship in 1922, followed by the issuing of the infamous Production Code. It imposed restrictions on such subject matter as sex, violence, religion, and race, and it banned portrayals of miscegenation and interracial romance—Madame Butterfly would be out. As we shall see, these puritanical and overtly racist guidelines became a virtual form of foot-binding for Anna May, shackling her career ambitions for the rest of her life.

The Hollywood party, however, must go on. The Roaring Twenties continued to roar. In this age of jazz, flappers, cars, billboards, radios, washing machines, sewing machines, refrigerators, toasters, vacuum cleaners, as well as the Ku Klux Klan parades and cross burnings, America—at least the America portrayed in fan magazines—was a sprawling party that would seem to go on forever. The Dream Factory in Hollywood used the medium of film to supply America's need for dreams: social mobility, a better life, romance, a bigger home, travel, leisure, and excitement of all sorts. And as the headquarters of self-actualizing myth, Hollywood certainly led the way in this epic of conspicuous consumption—of what F. Scott Fitzgerald, as the decade's most recognizable spokesperson and victim, called "the greatest, gaudiest spree in history."[4]

If Anna May thought what she had seen at the Garden of Alla was impressive and overwhelming, she had not seen anything. In fact, after a decade of living in high style, Nazimova had fallen on hard times by the mid-1920s. Her stylish Spanish mansion was converted to a hotel, and she ended up as a tenant renting a room in her former palace. But many more showplaces of the movie people would rise in Hollywood, as would new parvenus, among them Thomas H. Ince, who built a mansion and inaugurated the Aquarian lifestyle of outdoor sports, big cars, and weekend parties. Others followed suit with bigger and costlier homes in the hills above Hollywood and in Bel Air. John Barrymore's Beverly Hills estate consisted of sixteen buildings on seven acres, featuring such amenities as a swimming pool, a skeet-shooting range, a zoo, and an aviary of rare birds. Harold Lloyd's Greenacres, a twenty-two-acre estate, encompassed "a forty-room Italian Renaissance villa worthy of Lorenzo de Medici himself."[5]

The crown jewel, however, was Pickfair, the hilltop residence of Mary Pickford and Douglas Fairbanks, representing the very essence of glamour and respectability in Hollywood style. At their height, "Mary and Doug" were the First Couple of the United States, Pickfair the Buckingham Palace of Hollywood. Both hailing from origins of obscurity and poverty, the couple purposefully lived private lives as public performances, artfully releasing to the press such details as "who came to dinner, who walked the dogs, what Doug gave Mary for her birthday." Shunning such time-honored symbols as rugs, paintings, and antiques, Mary furnished their home with department-store merchandise—or things that George Babbitt, the title character of Sinclair Lewis's 1922 novel, might have used to adorn his middle-class house in the Midwest. In this way, the couple established a deeply personal connection with millions of fans all over the world. The golden ringlets of the Queen of Silent Cinema became the talk of the town in every town, and the former dapper light comedian would make suntan an American preoccupation.[6]

Coming of age in this period of glamour and extravagance, Anna May was certainly inspired by these highly publicized personalities. Who wouldn't want to be "The Most Famous Girl in the World," as Mary was dubbed? However, according to the journalist who, on his days off from his beat outside Pickfair, visited the dingy Chinese laundry on North Figueroa, "Anna May Wong is the Chinese exception to the American rule." To quote Timothy Turner again, "The films have not spoiled her. It is well known what screen success does for the maid of beauty and youth. It is apt to wean her from home in a twinkling, and some of the studio directors say it makes her 'all swelled in the head,' which is the cinema manner of saying 'up stage,' and that is the stage way of saying conceited, opinionated, stubborn, vainglorious and smug."[7] But Anna May remained content with her small room behind the laundry along with her large family of siblings, and when she had time, she would help out at the laundry, manning the counter and doing bookkeeping with an abacus. When a phone call came from one of those directors needing her to play a Chinese maid, she would hop on the Big Red Cars the next morning. After getting off the trolley, she would have to walk for a mile or two to the studio. On the long and lonely trek from the bus stop to the studio lot, according to the city's crime logs, many aspiring young women had encountered unpleasantries of all sorts or simply disappeared, prompting *Photoplay* to publish a series of stories bearing the overall title "The Port of Missing Girls." In a somewhat stereotypical manner, Turner ascribed Anna May's bravery, humility, and diligence to Chinese culture, "For with the Chinese the ties of family and the ideal of work are stronger than any surface things." There might have been a kernel of truth in it. For Anna May, a home was a home, whether it was a chalet in Hollywood or a laundry on North Figueroa.[8]

By this time, around 1922, Anna May had enrolled in Los Angeles High School on Olympic Boulevard, majoring in art. She excelled in tennis, the very sport that Mary and Doug, via their publicized life at Pickfair, were turning into an upper-middle-class obsession. She won singles and doubles matches in school tournaments.[9] Later she would recall her two years at Los Angeles High as the happiest period she had known. Soon, though, an opportunity came—an offer, as they say, impossible to decline—and she would need to quit school in order to pursue, like Icarus, the blinding light of fame.

11

THE THIEF OF BAGDAD

In this torn sea of arabesques,
Looms there no isle of peace?
—SADAKICHI HARTMANN[1]

Julanne Johnston, Anna May Wong, and Douglas Fairbanks in *The Thief of Bagdad*, 1924
(Courtesy of Everett Collection)

SOMETIME IN 1923, impressed by her appearance in *The Toll of the Sea*, Douglas Fairbanks offered Anna May a supporting role in his most ambitious film, *The Thief of Bagdad*. Like Mary—his new better half—Fairbanks had started out as a theatrical actor and made a successful transition from stage to screen. In the early 1920s, he had made a series of escapist costume spectacles, casting himself as a swashbuckling adventurer. In this trilogy of blockbusters—*The Mark of Zorro* (1920), *The Three Musketeers* (1921), and *Robin Hood* (1922)—Fairbanks displayed his exuberant athleticism in sword fights, leaps, somersaults, rope swings, and equestrian stunts.[2] His new vehicle, budgeted at an eye-popping $2 million and produced by United Artists (a company founded by Pickford, Fairbanks, and Chaplin), was expected to top his erstwhile successes.

There is no other way to say it other than that it was a big deal for Anna May to appear in such a major production. It was as close to superstardom as one could possibly get, the equivalent of playing a supporting role in a *Star Wars* sequel today. She would be cast as the duplicitous Mongol slave, serving the Arabic princess in name but spying for her Mongol khan in secret. It was in stark contrast to all of her previous roles, either as a timid Chinese maid or the lovestruck, self-sacrificing Madame Butterfly. Also different was her attire: While in her prior appearances she was little more than a live mannequin showcasing traditional Chinese costumes, in this new production she was going to be clad in a revealing two-piece outfit, showing ample amounts of bare skin. Erotically provocative, she would be paired with Fairbanks's character—a muscular, bare-chested thief, an adult Aladdin dazzling with manly charisma. In a crucial scene, he holds a dagger against the small of her bare back, while she looks back in fear, her seminude body trembling with "a mixture of terror and sensuality."[3]

To get eighteen-year-old Anna May to wear such a revealing outfit and act in such provocative scenes, Fairbanks had to write a letter to her parents to obtain their permission and to promise that there would be no impropriety during the production. Her parents must have heard about her earlier relationship with Mickey Neilan, and there was a rumor that Todd Browning had been romantically involved with her during the making of *Drifting* (1923). In that film, directed by Browning, she made a brief appearance as Rose Li, a Chinese ringleader's daughter who falls for a white man—another instance of the reel and real colliding in Anna May's life. Her parents must have lost not a small amount of sleep worrying about older white men preying on their young daughter.

Fortunately, both Fairbanks and Anna May were consummate professionals. In an interview about the film, he described her as "a very hard worker and usually a modest little person." Ironically, the modest "little" person stood at five feet seven inches, taller than the star himself. More important, she would "give back no chin," as a journalist put it. Fairbanks recalled an incident during the production: "She chanced to say one day that her name meant 'Two Yellow Willows' and a publicity man who had only half heard what she said sent out a yarn saying that Anna May Wong meant 'Two Yellow Widows.' It took some time to tell her that it was an error."[4]

Inspired by *The Arabian Nights*, the film was yet another Oriental fantasy extravaganza, a feast for the eye. The story involves a lowly thief in Bagdad who lives by the motto, "What I like—I take." One day, using a magic rope he stole from a street magician, the thief scales the palace walls and enters the boudoir of the princess. At the sight of the sleeping beauty, he is smitten, and he takes her silk slipper as a souvenir. In order to win her hand and defeat the other suitors, he embarks upon a dangerous and mystical journey to bring back the most desirable treasure ever imaginable. An escapist epic on the surface, the film was actually an allegory for the epoch of the 1920s with its insatiable desire for prosperity, for newer gadgets and products. While the other suitors bring a flying carpet, a crystal ball, and a magic apple that can resurrect the dead (think of the newfangled products of the decade like airplanes, radios, and new medicines), the thief secures the ultimate prize: a powder that can turn into anything he wishes for. That was the kind of magic desired by the likes of the Great Gatsby, as Fitzgerald told us in the novel that defined that decade. It's the beckoning green light, "the orgiastic future that year by year recedes before us," the novelist wrote. "It eluded us then, but that's no matter—tomorrow we will run faster, stretch out our arms farther. . . ."[5]

The Thief of Bagdad certainly went further than any other film, even Griffith's epic, in creating a magic tale for the historical era that begot it. The *New York Times* hailed it as "a feat of motion picture art which has never been equaled."[6] The elaborate sets, designed by William Cameron Menzies, brought out the full splendor of a Disneyesque wonderland: "Palace and city completed with shiny cupolas and towers, surreal bridges and staircases. The floors were glazed and the buildings were reflected on them. Walls were painted silver to make the city seem to float like a balloon, literally to drift off the ground among the clouds."[7]

An Orientalist fantasy that cemented Fairbanks's status as a matinee idol and immeasurably boosted Anna May's reputation, *The Thief of Bagdad* also cast several other Asian actors to spice up the arabesque flavors, particularly Kamiyama Sojin and Sadakichi Hartmann. Playing the avaricious Mongol prince with a Fu Manchu look, Sojin had been the foremost Shakespearean actor in Japan before arriving in Hollywood. In a few years, he and Anna May would work together in *The Chinese Parrot* (1927), a Charlie Chan film based on Earl Derr Biggers's popular novel. Sojin would impersonate the inscrutable, wisecracking Chinese detective from Honolulu, and Anna May would play a Nautch dancer.

The other Asian actor in *The Thief of Bagdad* was, strictly speaking, Eurasian. Born in Dejima, an artificial island in the Bay of Nagasaki—the site of the original Madame Butterfly story, Sadakichi Hartmann was the child of a German businessman and a Japanese woman, possibly a geisha, who died soon after his birth. Virtually abandoned by his father and raised in Germany, Hartmann became, in the words of his biographer, "a soul adrift." Self-taught and tenacious, he arrived in the United States in 1882 and dabbled in theater, art criticism, and poetry. A devotee of Walt Whitman, he published several poetry volumes that showed the influence of the French Symbolists and Japanese haiku, including *Drifting Flowers of the Sea and Other Poems* (1904), *My Rubaiyat* (1913), and *Japanese Rhythms* (1915). Living a precarious existence in the libertine circles of New York, Hartmann was crowned "The King of Bohemia" in Greenwich Village.[8] And, inspired by the Japanese tradition of "listening to the incense," he once did a stage performance in New York, a synesthetic attempt in which he released squirts of perfume timed to the musical notes in a symphony. Such a quixotic act not only intrigued the Anglo-American modernists such as William B. Yeats and Ezra Pound, but it also made Hartmann the perfect impersonator of the court magician in *The Thief of Bagdad*. Sporting a bejeweled turban and a buoyant Houdini cape, the trickster helps the Mongol prince locate the magic apple. Hartmann's skits, whether on-screen, on stage, or in real life, were so entertaining that one day Pound, jailed in Pisa and awaiting extradition to the United States to face trial for treason, would recall fondly his Japanese friend's "vagaries." Sitting in an outdoor steel cage like an animal, Pound wrote that a few more characters like Sadakichi "would have enriched the life of Manhattan."[9] To be thus remembered by the poetic maestro in his darkest hours certainly speaks to Hartmann's charisma as a talented raconteur.

Led by a superstar, supported by Anna May and other Asian actors, *The Thief of Bagdad* premiered at New York's Liberty Theatre, on West 42nd Street, on Saint Patrick's Day of 1924. Fairbanks deliberately turned the opening event into a theatrical extravaganza by providing a memorable "Arabian" atmosphere for the audience. He hired the famous theater producer Morris Gest as the impresario for the screening. At the sold-out theater, hordes of moviegoers pushed their way into the lobby. Police were hired to clear the jam and assist people to their seats, where they were sensorially assaulted by the beating of drums, droning voices singing dirges, and the odor of incense emanating from unknown corners of the theater. During the intermission, as the *New York Times* reported, "ushers in Arabian attire made a brave effort to bear cups of Turkish coffee to the women in the audience."[10] After the premiere, Gest was paid a salary of $3,000 per week to travel far and wide to present the film. The theatricalized screenings went as far as London, Paris, and Moscow. The biggest hit was in Germany, two years later. In fact, *The Thief of Bagdad* became the longest-running American film in Berlin, with an exclusive one-month engagement at the Capitol am Zoo, followed by showings in forty-five theaters across Germany.[11]

Incidentally, the film's popularity in Germany would, as we will see, be vital in shaping Anna May's career. When the *New York Times* ran a story titled "Fairbanks Wins Berlin" on January 23, 1926, they should have, if they had known any better, rephrased the headline as "Anna May Wong Wins Berlin."[12] While German moviegoers were bedazzled by Fairbanks's acrobatics and the extravagant sets, some important directors in the audience, working for the burgeoning German film industry, took notice of the exotic beauty and superb talent of the young Chinese actress. For them, the Mongol handmaid had upstaged the Bagdad thief. Unlike their Hollywood colleagues blindsided by America's racial politics—notwithstanding that Weimar Germany had its own share of race problems (more on which later)—they recognized the ascension of a shining global star.

12

HER OWN COMPANY

I N THE SPRING OF 1924, when *The Thief of Bagdad* was playing to great fanfare, captivating audiences with its splendid arabesque displays and fantasies about a distant land, America was shutting its doors to foreigners. A landmark anti-immigration bill, the Johnson-Reed Act was passed by Congress with overwhelming support and swiftly signed into law by President Calvin Coolidge that May. While the 1882 Chinese Exclusion Act had already halted Chinese immigration, this new law would bar *all* Asians and drastically reduce the number of immigrants from other parts of the world, particularly those from Southern and Eastern Europe. The passage of this exclusionary act resulted from several factors, but particularly from the rise of nativism and the changing structure of global geopolitics in the wake of the Great War. Rejecting the melting-pot concept of the previous decades and envisioning America as a nation that embodied a hierarchy of races and nationalities, the law encapsulated the xenophobic frenzy of the 1920s and deeply impacted the cultural life of America for the next four decades. In the words of John Higham, the Johnson-Reed Act meant that "the old belief in America as a promised land for all who yearn for freedom had lost its operative significance."[1]

Toxic social milieu notwithstanding, Anna May began the year of 1924 with hope and excitement. In January, she used her income from *The Thief of Bagdad* to buy a bungalow in the 1400 block of North Tamarind. Even though she had been bluntly reminded of her ethnic status during her house hunt by the fact that certain areas of Los Angeles were off-limits to Chinese, she was eager to leave her family's crowded residence and find a place of her own. According to a journalist who visited her, Anna May decorated her new house with a distinctly Oriental touch—sandalwood, ivory, and burning incense. She also appeared, in the words of the journalist, to be "re-Chinafying herself" with traditional Chinese attire and makeup, including long fingernails, an old lacquered vanity case, orange-blossom perfume, and golden hair ornaments.[2]

What this journalist saw, however, was only one side of Anna May, or one side of a Chinese American identity that was always caught up in a tug-of-war between two traditions, two almost-irreconcilable ways of life. In fact, to her Hollywood friends, Anna May was known for her flapper style, often sporting "a tip-tilted hat, pure Parisian heels, sheer silk stockings, and a Persian lamb wrap." To attain the ultimate symbol of the American Dream in a city that was fast becoming the capital of automobiles, she bought a Willys-Knight six-cylinder car, a relatively low-priced but high-quality model made in Toledo, Ohio.[3]

Trouble, goes the old adage, is a dog nibbling at the heels of fame. As her reputation rose, Anna May soon attracted some Tinseltown hucksters looking for a quick buck. In March 1924, Anna May signed an agreement with a Hollywood self-promoter, Forrest B. Creighton, to start a company called "The Anna May Wong Productions." At nineteen, Anna May was actually no greenhorn in business. At her father's laundry, from making delivery runs to assisting with management and bookkeeping, she had acquired some business acumen. According to Creighton's pitch, her production company would make a series of films about ancient Chinese legends, and he would raise $400,000 to bankroll the productions.[4] It sounded like a great idea for Anna May to make films about China in ways not dictated by the big studios. And she was not alone in thinking this way.

From the very beginning, dismayed by racially dehumanizing on-screen stereotypes, Chinese in America had tried to make their own films to counter the preponderance of those popular "yellow flicks." In 1916, twenty-one-year-old Marion Wong formed the Mandarin Film Company in Oakland, California. Born in San Francisco to a wealthy family, Wong showed an early interest in theatrical arts and had appeared on stage as a singer, earning the epithet "Chinese Song Bird." "I have never seen any Chinese movies," Wong said, "so I decided to introduce them to the world." She wrote the script for a love story and added scenes depicting people and manners in China. Working on a shoestring budget provided by relatives, she drafted her sister-in-law and her mother as cast members, built a makeshift studio in the back of their home, and borrowed furnishings from neighbors and local shops as props. Her heroic efforts resulted in *The Curse of Quon Gwon* (1917), the earliest known film written, produced, and directed by a Chinese American. But the film failed to find a distributor, and the company folded. Wong moved on to establish a successful restaurant career.[5]

The baton of Chinese filmmaking was then handed, symbolically, to James B. Leong, newly arrived from China. Born in Shanghai, Leong came to the United States in 1913 and attended college in Muncie, Indiana. After graduation, he went to try his luck in Hollywood around the time "yellow flicks" were becoming a fad. He found work at a number of studios and performed various tasks, including working as a technical adviser and interpreter for D. W. Griffith's *Broken Blossoms*. In the early 1920s, after a period of apprenticeship, Leong formed a Los Angeles–based film company financed by the local Chinese community: James B. Leong Productions. According to the *Los Angeles Times*, his goal was to create films that were "made by Chinese for Chinese, but employing American methods and American players until such time as Chinese actors and technicians may be developed to take their places." The first film Leong produced was *Lotus Blossom* (1921), its title an apparent throwback to Griffith's film. Like *Broken Blossoms*, Leong's film, which he codirected and cowrote, was a tragic tale (weren't they all?) adapted from a Chinese legend about a young girl trying to salvage her father's reputation as an artisan. She gives her life so that the sacred bell he is making can be sweet-toned when it calls the people to prayer. Casting the vaudeville singer Lady Tsen Mei as the lead, the roster also included James Wang (the ex-minister who got Anna May her first part) and Noah Beery and Tully Marshall in yellowface![6]

After its premiere at the Alhambra Theatre in Los Angeles on November 26, 1921, *Lotus Blossom* received positive reviews in trade papers. Writing for *Picture-Play Magazine*, Emma-Lindsay Squier applauded Leong's worthy attempt "to produce motion pictures that will show us China as it is," a radical departure from typical Hollywood films that "show us opium dens, singsong girls, slant-eyed Mandarins with queues and long finger nails, mysterious temples where strange gods hold sway." Squier entitled her piece "The Dragon Awakens," presaging a new era of young Chinese such as Leong rising in the film industry.[7] Unfortunately, like Marion Wong's trailblazing venture, Leong's was also a short-lived experiment. *Lotus Blossom* was the only film he made.[8] The dragon awoke but then dozed off again. Leong went on to become an actor, appearing in several Hollywood classics, including *Shanghai Express*

(1932), in which Anna May would play a significant part; *The Hatchet Man* (1932), starring Edward G. Robinson; and *The Good Earth* (1937).

Besides the Chinese, ambitious filmmakers of other ethnicities also tried to loosen Hollywood's stranglehold on racial representations by making their own independent pictures, including Sidney Goldin (Yiddish), Guillermo Calles (Mexican), Oscar Micheaux (African American), and Sessue Hayakawa (Japanese). Hayakawa, who crossed paths with Anna May on screen, was a particularly good model for her to follow in the enterprise of filmmaking. Arguably the first matinee idol, the Japan-born Hayakawa became the symbol of exotic charm and forbidden love with his starring role in Cecil B. DeMille's *The Cheat* (1915). As he became increasingly unhappy with the parts he had played, in 1918 Hayakawa established his own production company, Haworth Pictures Corporation, which made twenty-three films in three years. However, as racial animosity toward Japanese heightened in America, Hayakawa left the country in 1922 to pursue his career in Japan and Europe.[9]

The travails of these predecessors were both inspirations and deterrents for Anna May as she pondered the future of The Anna May Wong Productions. But she did not need to ponder for long. It was soon revealed that Creighton's business proposal was no more than a ploy to use Anna May's name for his own benefit. In fact, Creighton had reworded his copy of the agreement signed by Anna May, binding her to a three-year service term as well as her liability for certain debts he might incur. Recognizing the Barnum-like scheme, Anna May had to go to court, where a judge issued a temporary injunction, prohibiting Creighton from continuing with the fraudulent operation. It effectively ended her dream of having her own company.[10]

Smarting from the fallout of the deception and legal wrangling, Anna May played bit parts in three Paramount films in 1924: as a jealous queen in an Egyptian tale, *The Fortieth Door*; as an Eskimo girl in *The Alaskan*; and then as another Native American character, Tiger Lily, in *Peter Pan*. Despite her phenomenal performances in *The Toll of the Sea* and *The Thief of Bagdad*, as well as her growing international fame, Anna May suddenly was no longer able to find a real part in other American films, the new censorship decrees revealing their long reach. Even though the infamous Production Code would not come until a decade later, the industry had always been mindful of those "Don'ts" and "Be Carefuls" long before their official codification. One taboo, in particular, became a roadblock for Anna May's career: miscegenation, which includes romance or kissing between an interracial couple on screen. Such prohibitions caused filmmakers to pass her over, condemning her almost permanently to secondary roles in romance films, whether comedy or tragedy.

Still, she soldiered on. Her impersonation of an Eskimo in *The Alas-kan* received a nod from *Variety*: "Anna May Wong as an Indian girl scored nicely."[11] And during the making of *Peter Pan*, she deepened her friendship with cinematographer James Wong Howe, whose reputation was on a steady rise. Hailing from Anna May's ancestral home of Canton, Howe came to America in 1904 when his father, a former laborer for the Northern Pacific Railroad, had saved enough money to send for him. Growing up in Pasco, Washington, where his father ran a general store, Howe was the only Chinese boy in town. Wearing a pigtail, he naturally became the butt of jokes and a target for bul-lying by white children. He could play only with Native American kids, who often asked about his queue or what tribe he belonged to. Small in stature but feisty in spirit, Howe became a bantamweight boxer in the Pacific Northwest after quitting high school.

Lured by reports of opportunities in California, seventeen-year-old Howe arrived in Los Angeles in 1916. He picked up odd jobs—one stint as a delivery boy in a photography studio and another as a bellhop at a hotel in Pasadena. He was fired from the latter position after a fistfight with a Korean employee. Drifting, he spent much time in Chinatown, an area that continued to attract Hollywood filmmakers. A chance encounter with a former boxing opponent, who had become a cameraman doing location shooting in Chinatown, helped Howe land a job as a janitor at the Lasky Studio. Cleaning out the camera room and sweeping the sets every day, Howe was always the last person to leave the studio at night. When he missed his bus, he would simply sleep on the set in a bed where Gloria Swanson played her bedroom scenes.

Inhaling the aura of the star actress might have worked wonders. During the making of the Cecil B. DeMille film *Male and Female* (1919), starring Swanson, there was a need for an extra man to carry the fourth camera. That was how the former bantamweight boxer emerged from his janitorial closet and became a clapper loader for the cameraman. When DeMille saw Howe, he was tickled by the sight of a puckish Asian, who wore a gaudy floral shirt and held the slate, while gritting a large cigar between his teeth. "I like his face," said DeMille to his underlings, and he kept Howe on as a camera assistant.

Eventually becoming an award-winning cinematographer—ten Oscar nominations and two Oscars in his long career—Howe in the 1920s was the most sought-after photographer for publicity stills. The secret of his success was his ingenious use of shadows to make actors look their best. It remains Hollywood lore that Mary Minter—an enormously popular actress before a murder scandal sank her career—was so pleased to see Howe make her pale blue eyes "go dark" in photos that she insisted on him as her cameraman for her next films. Having no need for any special effects, Anna May had also ordered some head shots from her illustrious kinsman. By this time, Howe had become so rich and famous that he could afford a $37,000 Duesenberg, and when he gunned it down West Hollywood's Sunset Strip, onlookers would stare in disbelief, wondering what family would let their Chinese houseboy drive around in such an expensive car.[12]

As the cinematographer for *Peter Pan*, a fairy tale about a boy looking for his lost shadow, Howe worked his magic again and adopted the technique of deep focus to bring out both the foreground and distant planes. In addition, he used the diffusion of light to create "an ethereal quality that helps establish the unreality of the fantasy land." Gifted with Howe's elfish sparkle, *Peter Pan* landed on that year's *New York Times* Ten Best Films list.[13]

Besides *The Alaskan* and *Peter Pan*, Anna May was also thrilled to be chosen by Columbia Pictures for its *Screen Snapshots* series, which, as the program notes stated, was intended to "offer a glimpse into the heart of the movie world revealing intimate and unusual views of your favorite stars 'on location' and in the privacy of their homes." The luminaries included D. W. Griffith, Douglas Fairbanks, Sid Grauman, and gossip columnist Hedda Hopper. Anna May's segment was titled *East Is West* and ran about one minute. It showed her changing from a Chinese outfit to a Western dress and then doing a spirited Charleston, before sitting down on a swing lounge. As she wipes her brow in a medium-close shot, the title card reads: "Whew! That's work but I like it."[14]

While Anna enjoyed her work and never tired of fighting against all odds, her personal life as a nineteen-year-old suffered. By Chinese custom, she was old enough to be a bride, and her parents had been nagging her about it. But she was caught in a dilemma, a plight experienced by many Chinese American women navigating a bicultural universe. As Anna May confessed, "Where am I to meet the men who might wish to marry me, from whom I could choose a mate with assurance of happiness? I am tall, and I have large eyes. Both are considered defects in the beauty standards of my race. I am independent, and Chinese men do not like that. Many possible suitors seem afraid of me because I seem too modern. Because of my position, I must be careful with whom I go about."[15] These factors made it difficult for her to date Chinese men.

As for men of other races, the antimiscegenation laws made such marriages unwise, to say the least. Her friend James Howe had been going out with white women. When he eventually married his beloved Sanora Babb in France, the union was not recognized in the United States, and the couple had to keep it secret for years. Anna May had attracted droves of white men and would continue to do so in the future. In addition to her earlier affairs with Mickey Neilan and Todd Browning, there were rumors of her going out with the actor Brent Romney, and later with the English songwriter Eric Maschwitz. But Anna May was determined not to lose her head. "With American men," she told an interviewer, "who seem to like me and whose ideals I like and whose friendship I value—well, what's the use to let one's heart go when nothing can come of it?"[16]

Neither Chinese nor American men, therefore, were feasible options for Anna. And even if she had bisexual desires or experience, she would not let on in a world where she had yet to find her footing or in a profession laden with booby traps. "I have very little social life—am very lonely," she sighed.[17] In short, Anna May had to keep her own company.

13

VAUDEVILLE

Anna May Wong cigarette
card, late 1920s *(Courtesy of
New York Public Library)*

THE CINEMA, said the French symbolist poet Paul
Valéry, diverts the spectator from the core of his
being. What justifies such a striking insight, as the great
German Jewish émigré Siegfried Kracauer explains
in *Theory of Film*, is that "film clings to the surface of
things." Rather than being introspective with spiritual
concerns, a film tempts us with "kaleidoscopic sights
of ephemeral outward appearances." This is why, Kracauer asserts, "Many people with strong cultural learn-
ings scorn the cinema."[1]

Such observations would resonate with Anna May in
1925, as she, turning twenty, felt a personal crisis brewing. "It is hard to get into the pictures, but it is harder to
keep in them," she stated. "Of course, it is nice enough
if one gets a five-year contract as some of the actors do, but freelancing which
I do, is not easy. You see there are not many Chinese parts."[2] The biggest Chinese part that year was the beguiling character of Charlie Chan, newly born in
the Earl Derr Biggers novel *The House Without a Key* and immediately becoming a sensation. But, as we know, the role of a bumbling Chinese sleuth would
eventually go to white actors, following Hollywood's enduring tradition of
yellowface.[3] Unable to secure a female lead role since *The Toll of the Sea*, Anna
May felt that she had had enough of teaching white actresses how to use chopsticks. She wanted to strike out on a new path in acting: live theater.

"I have always wanted to act in serious plays," she said. "In the studio one can act only before the other workers, and can't get the effect."[4] Indeed, in film acting, one does it for the mechanical eye of the camera, which breaks down the human wholeness into fragments, for scenes are shot separately without following any narrative sequence and then put together afterward. "The film actor," opines V. I. Pudovkin, "is deprived of a consciousness of the uninterrupted development of the action in his work. . . . The whole image of the actor is only to be conceived as a future appearance on the screen, subsequent to the editing of the director."[5] Anna May would agree with such a view. "I think I like the stage better," she said.[6]

On January 21, 1925, Anna May debuted as a "speaking actress" at the Orpheum Theatre in San Francisco. In front of a full house, she sang a Chinese lullaby and a popular ditty called "Sally." Her first vaudeville act, exclaimed the *San Francisco Chronicle*, was "pure delight." After all her pantomime and soundless gesticulations in silent pictures, she felt enlivened by having a voice in front of a responsive crowd that cheered or jeered. Before that night was over, she had already thought about adding more routines: "If I go on with the act, and I think now that I shall, I will put in a Nautch dance after the lullaby, and perhaps do a short dramatic recitation. I love dramatic things, and I have picked out several little poems that I should like to do."[7] Always a quick study, Anna May worked hard to expand her repertoire. According to Moon Kwan, a Chinese poet moonlighting in Hollywood, Anna May asked him to teach her how to play the *yueqin*, the Chinese banjo. She explained that it was no novelty to play the piano or violin in a vaudeville act, but the Chinese banjo might do. And she also learned from Kwan how to recite classical Chinese poems. Later, on stage and screen, Anna May would be seen plucking an outlandish moon-shaped instrument, humming lines from Li Po in Cantonese.[8]

After her successful debut, Anna May went on tour with a vaudeville troupe in the spring of 1925. The group she joined, the Los Angeles–based Cosmic Production Company, consisted mostly of veteran actors who alternated between stage and screen, including the company's president, Harry Tighe. As we know, many of the film actors in the silent era had roots in theater, including Alla Nazimova, Douglas Fairbanks, and Mary Pickford. Before becoming the world's most famous on-screen tramp, Charlie Chaplin was an obscure English vaudeville actor, and his coach, Roscoe ("Fatty") Arbuckle, also began as a comedian known for rollicking skits and gags. Among Anna May's colleagues at the Cosmic, leading man Bryant Washburn was a variety comedy star who had begun his career with the Essanay Studio in 1911 and was known for his "Skinner" character. Ruth Stonehouse, starting out at eight as a dancer in variety shows, had appeared in no fewer than fifty shorts and feature films. And Helen Holmes, hailing from Indiana, had been a photographer's model before plodding the well-trodden path from Broadway to Hollywood.[9]

On February 14, 1925, bidding farewell to the snowcapped Sierra Nevada, the motley crew of the Cosmic, dubbed "Bryant Washburn and His Hollywooders," left California for the Midwest. First stop: Kansas City, Kansas. Their advance man had tried to drum up interest by billing the show as "an extravaganza the likes of which the municipality of Kansas City had never seen." The chosen venue was the city's august convention hall, a fireproof stone citadel that had recently hosted a series of rousing Ku Klux Klan rallies. On opening day, a marching band and a police squad escorted the performers to the hall, but that great pre-show fanfare failed miserably—or perhaps the place was cursed by the hooded Klansmen. When the troupe arrived at the convention hall, they were shocked to see that, except for a few eager journalists, the eighteen-thousand-seat theater was empty. But the proverbial show must go on; Li Po would wait for no one. The troupe performed for free to entertain the members of the marching band and the local constabulary, who were unfortunately keener on sniffing out the trails of bandits like Charles ("Pretty Boy") Floyd than on listening to an ancient Chinese poet insinuating in his singsong tongue.[10]

The next two stops—Atchison, Kansas, and Omaha, Nebraska—yielded moderate ticket sales, but then the troupe got a free ride to jail. Thanks to a major screwup by the company manager, the troupe left Omaha without paying the hotel bill. When they crossed the state line and arrived in Des Moines, Iowa, the local police were waiting. Rather than being escorted by the uniformed officers with the festive accompaniment of a marching band, Anna May and her associates were marched off in shame to the jail. Eventually the hotel bill was paid off, and the troupe members were released from jail. When the humiliated performers contemplated suing the hotel for defamation and false arrest, Harry Tighe issued an apology instead, taking full responsibility for the mishap. Obviously, the company was on its last legs. Still, the group soldiered on, traveling to Illinois and then Michigan. Their fifty-minute program at an auditorium in Berwyn, Illinois, received a positive review in *Variety*, with a special mention of the Chinese greenhorn: "Anna May Wong scored the individual hit of the turn with two pop numbers, utilizing the Oriental garb. She possesses a good delivery and would survive in the varieties." Nonetheless, after their last show in Detroit in April, the group disbanded.[11]

Besides the good coverage in the trade paper, Anna May could take consolation in the fact that she had picked up vaudeville as a step toward real theatrical work. It was meant to be a transition to something more serious, a higher art. Such a dream eventually would come true—not in America, but abroad. Even then, though, vaudeville would remain a signature repertoire of Anna May's career as a performer. In subsequent years, she would continue to pick up these gigs to tide herself over during fallow seasons of film acting. And when she finally did appear again on screen, the persona of a vaudeville girl, doing a Nautch dance or plucking a *yueqin*, would come to the aid of her various characterizations in the pivotal year of 1927.

14

1927

*I ain't seen it advertised at Grauman's Chinese,
so how should I know?*
—JAMES ELLROY, *The Big Nowhere*[1]

Grauman's Chinese Theatre, Hollywood *(Photograph by Yunte Huang)*

WHILE THE EARLIEST nickelodeon reels had tapped Chinatown for material and inspiration, and the "yellow flicks" had continued the exploitation of popular stereotypes, Hollywood's Chinese imagination reached an apex in 1927 with the construction of a baroque landmark. Anna May would lend a helping hand, literally and symbolically, to the erection of this shrine to chinoiserie.

After the 1926 failure of the Cosmic troupe, and with the encouragement of her father, Anna May moved back to the family residence on North Figueroa. Proud of his daughter's accomplishments but concerned with her struggles, Sam Sing built her a separate apartment behind the laundry, so she could live with the family while still having a room of her own. Back in the family's folds, Anna May felt safe and grateful: "I believe close quarters promote sympathy and understanding. Lives are interwoven. What affects one affects all and much opportunity is to be had for learning the Chinese virtue, compassion. . . . I am lucky that I am Chinese."[2]

Her luck for being Chinese, though, was both a break and a barrier. On January 5, 1926, two days after her twenty-first birthday, Anna May was invited to a Hollywood ceremony. Following the success of his dazzling Egyptian Theatre, the showman Sidney Grauman teamed up with Mary Pickford and Douglas Fairbanks to raise $2 million for the building of the Chinese Theatre, a spectacularly ornate Mount Olympus in the land of orange groves and poppy fields. At the groundbreaking ceremony, Anna May joined Norma Talmadge in shoveling the first spadeful of dirt. In her silk robe, she looked like her doppelgänger—Lotus Flower—in *The Toll of the Sea*. Indisputably the most authentic female Chinese icon at the time, she stood on the margin of the lineup, next to Grauman, Charlie Chaplin, Talmadge, and Conrad Nagel. With dozens of Chinese extras hovering in the background, she felt like she, too, was an extra hired for the occasion. In the photo op, she bowed her head, eyes closed, hands held together, as if saying a prayer, a bittersweet benediction on this quixotic tribute to her fatherland.[3]

In the coming months, after the building's scaffolding was removed, artisans would install temple bells, pagodas, stone heavenly dogs, and countless other artifacts imported from China. The punctilious process of "Chinafying" was supervised by Anna May's friend Moon Kwan, who had served as a technical adviser for many films. A young Chinese artist named Keye Luke was hired to paint the murals, a temporary job that would lead to his long and illustrious career as an actor, playing such memorable roles as Charlie Chan's Number One Son and the blind Master Po in David Carradine's television series *Kung Fu*.

On May 18, 1927, Grauman's Chinese Theatre opened its doors. Soaring to ninety feet, it boasted gigantic coral-red columns supporting a jade-green roof, silver dragons spreading across the ceiling of a 2,258-seat auditorium, a pagoda posed as the box office, and ushers dressed in Chinese costumes. Although there was no acknowledgment of the brightest Chinese star of the era at the grand opening, an alluring wax statue of Anna May would later be added to grace the lobby. By all accounts, Grauman's Chinese Theatre was a monument to Hollywood's lasting China fever.[4]

Adding to the frenzy, Hollywood released at least four Chinese-themed films that year: *Mr. Wu* (MGM), *Old San Francisco* (Warner Bros.), *The Chinese Parrot* (Universal), and *Streets of Shanghai* (Tiffany-Stahl). Unsurprisingly, Anna May appeared in all of them, but only in the periphery. At a time when her star power could entice an elite gentlemen's club in Los Angeles to name a section of its landscaping "Anna May Wong Garden," no China flick could do without her, but no director could feature her as the lead.[5] The cultural logic at play is as riddling as a Charlie Chan aphorism.

In *Mr. Wu*, directed by William Nigh, Anna May reunited with Lon Chaney six years after *Bits of Life*, playing a handmaid to the female protagonist. Living up to his reputation as the man of myriad faces, Chaney assumed the double roles of Mr. Wu and his grandfather. A mandarin of immense pedigree and wealth, Wu is about to marry off his daughter Nang Ping (Renée Adorée) to the son of a colleague. A chance encounter, however, leads to a secret romance between Nang and a young Englishman. When Wu discovers his daughter's betrayal, he ritualistically sacrifices her at the ancestral altar to protect his family name (ironically, the Chinese character for "Wu" means militant violence). In this Chinese Romeo-and-Juliet story, there are inevitably love scenes between the Chinese girl and the Englishman, clandestine trysts full of hugging, necking, and kissing. Coincidentally, in June 1927, the Motion Picture Producers and Distributors of America passed a resolution codifying a list of "Don'ts" and "Be Carefuls" for films. Judging by these pre-Code guidelines, the kind of interracial romance and physical intimacy in *Mr. Wu* would have raised a red flag. However, since Nang Ping was impersonated by the French actress Adorée, not an actual Chinese woman like Anna May, the white

Romeo could woo his "Oriental" Juliet freely and gallantly, posing no offense to the industry's rules or America's hypocritical sense of decorum.

In a nation whose mythic origin story involves a bevy of Bostonians dressed up as Mohawks and grunting fake Indian words while dumping tea into the sea, the kind of yellowface performance by Chaney and Adorée was exactly what most viewers had come to expect and enjoy at the cinema. Racial mimicry lies at the heart of the American identity. In his studies of classic American literature, D. H. Lawrence astutely identified two streaks of the American character: "First, Americans had an awkward tendency to define themselves by what they were not"—they were not Indians, Blacks, Mexicans, or Chinese. Second, they had been continually haunted by the fatal dilemma of wanting to have things both ways. They abhorred the Indians, driving them off land and killing them in the process, but they also wanted to "play Indian," savoring the freedom and spirit of those "noble savages." Such a dialectic of simultaneous repulsion and desire showed up again and again in America's racial imagination and constituted the foundation of its art and literature.[6]

Nowhere did such a feature reveal itself more clearly than in blackface. From the very beginning, minstrelsy as a form of racial mimicry—white actors blackening their faces to play, and play down, Black characters—defined the birth of popular American entertainment. The same year as the opening of Grauman's Chinese Theatre and the release of *Mr. Wu* and other yellowface flicks, there appeared the first talkie made in Hollywood, *The Jazz Singer*. Adapted from the biography of Broadway's leading blackface entertainer Al Jolson, who played his fictional self in the film, the plot involves a Jewish boy named Jakie Rabinowitz, who is captivated by jazz singing. When his father, a cantor, forbids his distasteful obsession, Jakie runs away. Reborn as Jack Robin, Jakie makes a splash on Broadway as a blackface jazz singer. The film ends with Jakie, wearing a woolen cap and covered with burnt cork, performing a Negro number, "My Mammy," in front of his proud mother and an admiring theater audience.

Perpetuating the American dialectic of repulsion and desire, blackface also attained a new popularity, as *The Jazz Singer* amply demonstrated, at the height of the Eastern European immigration wave. As Michael Rogin argues in *Blackface, White Noise*, blackface in the early decades of the twentieth century gave whites an opportunity to act out and solidify their whiteness by playing and parodying Blacks. To turn European greenhorns into white Americans, the melting pot used racial masquerade—blackface, yellowface, redface, Jewface, and so on—to promote identity exchange but also to exclude unwanted racial groups.[7] In *Mr. Wu*, we see not only Lon Chaney solidifying his stardom by playing two Chinese, but also the French actress Renée Adorée (a stage name that literally means "reborn adored") gaining recognition in America by playing Nang Ping stereotypically, with mincing steps and feigned shyness. At the same time, Anna May, a real Chinese talent slotted to the secondary role of handmaid, could only look on with envy and resignation.[8]

Racial masquerade became even more complicated in *Old San Francisco*, written by Darryl F. Zanuck, who had also produced *The Jazz Singer*. The connection between these two films, both released in 1927, stems also from the fact that Warner Oland, impersonating a Jewish cantor in one film, played a Caucasian thug who hides his Chinese identity in the other. Whether as an orthodox Jew or an evil Chinese, Oland was a prime example of a newly arrived European acclimating himself to American culture by mastering the art of playing a racial other. Born Johan Verner Ölund in Sweden and arriving in America with his parents at the age of thirteen, Oland attended drama school in Boston. After dropping the umlaut and anglicizing his name, Oland took advantage of his vaguely Asiatic features to pick up Oriental roles in films. As talkies began to dominate the industry in the late 1920s, and many stars of the silent era fell victim to the technological transition to sound, Oland would become Hollywood's top choice to play an on-screen Chinese. His signature roles were the supervillain Dr. Fu Manchu and the affable sleuth Charlie Chan.

In *Old San Francisco*, Oland's character, Chris Buckwell, is a gluttonous villain who bullies, robs, rapes, and kills. Concealing his real Chinese identity, he relegates his Buddhist shrine to his basement, where he prays for forgiveness while keeping his disabled brother locked up in a cage. Like the Mongol spy in *The Thief of Bagdad*, Anna May plays a nameless Chinese girl who serves as a stool pigeon for Buckwell. With her assistance, he kidnaps a white girl and sells her to a white slaver. As he grabs for the blood money, an earthquake hits the city and buries him under fallen debris. Perhaps the film historian Kevin Brownlow is right in calling *Old San Francisco* "one of the most racist films ever made in America." Penned by Zanuck, the film is marred by naked Sinophobia. Derogatory allusions are prevalent, the terms "Chinaman," "Chink," and "Mongolian" are used interchangeably, and white slavery by Jews, portrayed openly, is affirmed. In a crucial, revelatory scene that is, in Brownlow's words, "suffused by the kind of religion best practiced by the Ku Klux Klan," the title card reads: "In the awful light of an outraged, wrathful Christian God, the heathen soul of the Mongol stood revealed."[9]

Truth be told, in those early years Hollywood did try to cast a real Asian actor for a leading Asian role. Earlier, Technicolor was using Anna May for the color experiment in *The Toll of the Sea*, and Sessue Hayakawa, before he was hamstrung by rising Japanophobia, had played leads in numerous films. In *The Chinese Parrot*, the second Charlie Chan flick, in which Anna May was a vaudeville dancer, the Chinese detective was actually played by Kamiyama Sojin, who had appeared in *The Thief of Bagdad*. For all the sins committed by Hollywood for casting white actors as Charlie Chan, at least the first three films of the long-running series featured Asian leads: George Kuwa in *The House Without a Key* (1926), Sojin in *The Chinese Parrot* (1927), and Edward Park in *Behind That Curtain* (1929). Unfortunately, the reels of the first two films have been lost, but, judging from the fact that in the third film, Charlie Chan, one of the most popular icons in the print media at the time, appears on screen for no more than one minute—he literally falls out of the picture!—we can surmise that Americans were not so keen on a real Chinese playing a Chinese character. They would have to go to a freak show for that, as they had done in earlier decades, flocking to see the world-famous Siamese Twins at the circus, or the China Lady at Peale's Museum in Philadelphia. For Americans who cut their teeth on playing Indian or doing blackface, there was just not enough oomph—or too much MSG?—in an Oriental playing an Oriental. It would take someone like Warner Oland, the Swedish-turned-American whiz at yellowface, to salvage the legacy of the honorable Chinese detective.

In such a toxic cultural milieu, Anna May did not feel at home, a sentiment shared by many nonwhite artists in the American entertainment world of the 1920s. "I felt it was a crisis in my life," she recalled.[10] Even though picking up a handful of supporting roles a year would be boast-worthy for many movie-struck girls, the daughter of a Chinese laundryman maintained her higher aspirations, undaunted by the welter of prejudice she faced. It was at this point that her fortune veered. At one of those swanky Hollywood parties, Anna May met Karl Vollmöller, a German author who had just adapted his own novel, *Dirty Money*, for a German film to be directed by Richard Eichberg. Film historians have often credited Vollmöller with introducing Marlene Dietrich to Josef von Sternberg, forgetting that the polymath German—he was a poet, philologist, archaeologist, playwright, screenwriter, and auto-racer—was also instrumental in raising Anna May's profile. Vollmöller convinced Eichberg, who had been quite impressed by her performance in *The Thief of Bagdad* and others, to cast Anna May as the lead in the German film. In fact, to entice her to make the long trek across the pond, Eichberg offered her a generous five-picture contract. Although she did not know a word of German and had never traveled abroad except for a quick 1924 trip to Mexico with her family to validate their citizenship papers, this was an opportunity she could not decline. "The door opened," she said, "and I walked through."[11]

Thus, joining the exodus of other nonwhite performers such as Josephine Baker and Paul Robeson, Anna May sailed for Europe to seek a better future. On the eve of her departure, a columnist for the *Los Angeles Times* lamented, "It seems to us the greatest pity in the world that Hollywood producers are going to let that uniquely talented young oriental actress, Anna May Wong, slip through their fingers."[12] Ironically, just as those European greenhorns came to America to become white in the New World's race crucible, Anna May was going to "old Europe" in order to be recognized as an American.

PART THREE

"ORIENTALLY YOURS"

Anna May Wong and her sister Lulu in Berlin, 1928 *(Courtesy of Everett Collection)*

15

WEIMAR BERLIN

ANNA MAY and her sister Lulu arrived in Germany in the spring of 1928. Arising out of the ashes of World War I, the Weimar Republic, to paraphrase the eminent historian Peter Gay, was dancing on the edge of a volcano. For a short, dizzying span of a decade or so, Germany was an incubator for both liberal dreams and nascent fascism. A precarious exuberance, which abetted and even fulfilled the visions of artists, was soon shattered by the rise of the Nazis. Smarting from the military defeat and the detrimental terms of the 1919 Treaty of Versailles, the parliamentary democracy was from the start riven by economic hardships and political upheavals. Nonetheless, out of this chaos came an explosion of creativity in art, literature, music, and film, a Zeitgeist aptly described as the "Golden Twenties." Especially in Berlin, the erstwhile capital of Prussian militarism, there emerged a mesmerizing cultural scene, an untrammeled drive toward everything modern, open, and cosmopolitan.[1]

At the time of Anna May's arrival, the artistic avant-garde—from Bertolt Brecht's *Threepenny Opera* to Fritz Lang's *Metropolis*, from Bauhaus to Dadaism—was in full swing. In mass culture, Berlin became what Ilya Ehrenburg called "an apostle of Americanism."[2] America was a catchword for whatever was cool and modern—everything from jazz to the foxtrot and the Charleston, to Josephine Baker's *La Revue Nègre* and her banana skirt.[3] Galloping inflation and the corollary devaluation of the Deutsche Mark in 1922 and 1923 also spurred a huge influx of foreign tourists and artists, most lured by the affordable and easy lifestyle in the German capital. Cabarets with seminude all-girl chorus lines, cafés filled with the aroma of Turkish coffee and the comfort of velvet armchairs, glitzy picture palaces, high-class bars catering to patrons of all sexual proclivities. Christopher Isherwood, a British literary sojourner whose first visit to Germany coincided with Anna May's, vividly described bar scenes that gave him a "delicious nausea": "Here screaming boys in drag and monocled, Eton-cropped girls in dinner jackets play-acted the high jinks of Sodom and Gomorrah, horrifying the onlookers and reassuring them that Berlin was still the most decadent city in Europe." To Isherwood, a Cambridge-educated gay man fleeing the stuffy British milieu, "Berlin meant boys."⁴ In his memoir, *The World of Yesterday*, the much more straitlaced Stefan Zweig called Berlin "the worst sink of iniquity in the world." He described a scene that occurred on the very street where Anna May and Lulu would be staying: "Youths in wasp-waisted coats, their faces made up, promenaded along the Kurfürstendamm, not all of them were professional rent boys; every grammar-school student wanted to earn something, and state secretaries and prominent financiers could be seen sitting in darkened bars shamelessly courting the favor of drunken sailors. Even the Rome of Suetonius never knew such orgies as those at the transvestites' balls in Berlin, where hundreds of men in women's clothing and women dressed like men danced under the benevolent gaze of the police."⁵ To cultural conservatives, this kind of American craze and Babylonian mongrelism stood for everything that was wrong with the modern world. In a novel by Stephen Spender—another British visitor to Berlin—a character opined that Berlin was a "city with no virgins. Not even the kittens and puppies [were] virgins."⁶ This remark, hyperbolic as it is, offers a measure of the intense human energy—driven by the artistic avant-garde, explosive youth culture, and other popular desires—that would give Berlin its reputation as "the Hauptstadt of vice."

It would be hard to overstate the sense of exhilaration Anna May felt upon arriving in Germany. After having been long inured to America's puritanism and Hollywood's racism, she finally could let down her guard. Not that the Weimar Republic was a haven of racial equity. Au contraire, barely a few years later, men in jackboots and brown shirts would come out of the shadows with their swastikas and billy clubs. But, as we will see, Anna May was entering a far more cosmopolitan milieu, one where she would be treated differently than she was in Hollywood. Of course, confusion and anxiety were also inevitable for any newcomer. As Anna May would later tell Walter Benjamin, a native Berliner and one of the city's most famous flaneurs, when she and Lulu stepped off the gangplank in Hamburg and managed to get to the cavernous Hauptbahnhof, they felt lost. Under the vaulted gloom of the train terminal appeared a sea of strangers and a cacophony of unfamiliar sounds, as if they had just walked onto a film set where they did not know the plot. Knowing no German, they were desperate to hear the magic word *Berlin*. But, as she had hoped, the city, indeed the country, would open its arms to embrace what Benjamin would dub "a Chinoiserie from the Old West."[7]

As an American woman of Chinese descent, Anna May embodied for Germans two cultures that were not really compatible—America and China. Consequently, the seeming contradiction would cause a certain amount of confusion in German perceptions of her, reflected in Benjamin's odd phrase. As an import from America, she was expected to help German filmmakers compete with Hollywood for the domestic and European market—or, in the words of a German film critic, to try to "be more American than the Americans."[8] In the immediate post–World War I era, film had become a perfect diversion for a nation existentially wounded. While the rich could afford seats at Max Reinhardt's classical theater, or wine and dinner aboard a Rhine steamer, the impoverished and beer-besotted flocked to the movies. In 1919, there were more than a hundred film companies in Berlin's Friedrichstrasse district. By the early 1920s, the center of gravity had shifted to the western suburb of Babelsberg, which was becoming a Hollywood-style city. But the competition from America was daunting. As historian David Clay Large describes in *Berlin: A Modern History*, "By 1923, the number of American films showing in Germany almost equaled that of the homemade product. German commentators complained about the intellectual vacuity of the American imports, but the German public found these films, with their canned sentimentality, images of fabulous wealth, extreme violence, and wild chase scenes, highly compelling."[9] In the language of Benjamin, for instance, we can detect a palpable influence of American movies. Describing Anna May as the "Old West," he evokes not only the *Leatherstocking Tales* of James Fenimore Cooper, or the dime novels about Billy the Kid, Buffalo Bill, and Wyatt Earp, but also the cinematic images of the shoot-'em-up Western frontier, rough-and-tumble cowboys, and Dodge City.

By the late 1920s, Hollywood had penetrated the German market not only with its movies but also with capital investment in German film companies. MGM and Paramount both bought into UFA (Universum Film AG), the biggest film conglomerate in Germany, creating a business relationship that would increase the traffic between Hollywood and Babelsberg. The joint venture propelled a constellation of German directors and actors into global stardom, including Josef von Sternberg, Richard Eichberg, Marlene Dietrich, and Emil Jannings, who won the first Academy Award ever presented to an actor for his role in *The Way of All Flesh* (1927). Eichberg, the architect of Anna May's transatlantic migration, was considered one of the "most American of German directors," who had made his name as a producer and director of Hollywood-style action-packed, fast-paced, spectacularly exotic genre films.[10] In 1928, Eichberg had struck a deal with British International Pictures to coproduce films in Germany, the United Kingdom, and France. Signing up a Hollywood star like Anna May was part of Eichberg's plan to develop the European cinema and to out-American the Americans.

At the same time, Anna May was seen by Germans as an icon of China, embodying all the exoticism and mystique of the Orient, thus distinguishing her from other American imports, such as Louise Brooks, known for her roles in German films that explored modern sexual mores. Although it was a role already typecast for Anna May by Hollywood, being a Chinese icon actually meant something different in Germany. In contrast to the United States, where the Chinese presence had been long and prominent, it had been barely visible in Germany. According to census records, the first two Chinese only arrived in Berlin in 1822. The 1904 opening of the Trans-Siberian Railroad brought more Chinese traders and merchants to Germany via Moscow, and they mostly settled around Berlin's railway station, the Schlesischer Bahnhof (today's Ostbahnhof). In no way comparable in size to Chinatowns in the United States or Great Britain, the small Chinese district that emerged in East Berlin became known as the *Gelbes Quartier* (the Yellow Quarter). It was the poorest neighborhood, consisting of squalid tenements and dismal courtyards, with no gardens or trees lining the streets, no supply of electricity or running water. During the Great War, France recruited about a hundred thousand coolie laborers from China to dig trenches, bury the dead, and perform other menial services. After the war, some of those men, especially ones from the southern districts of Qingtian and Wenzhou (my hometown), who were endowed with strong entrepreneurial spirits, remained in Europe and found their way to Germany. They made a living selling trinkets and tourist paraphernalia—porcelain vases, tea services, soapstone carvings, fans, and cheap jewelry. The first Chinese restaurant opened in Berlin in 1923, the same year as Hitler's Munich Beer Hall Putsch. The 1925 census counted 747 Chinese in the entire Weimar Republic, of whom 312 resided in Berlin. Due to their small cohort, the Chinese community in Germany was not as conspicuous as in the United

States and elsewhere. A 1928 report showed only a handful of Chinese restaurants and curio shops dotting East Berlin's drab landscape with their exotic appearance: "Nondescript like all other closely cramped buildings in the eastern district of the city. Only one part of the façade stands out. Around the shopwindow and the door the wall is painted pink. Chinese characters shine forth from this dull ground."[11]

Geopolitically, Germany lost all of its colonies in the Asia-Pacific region after World War I, while America's influence was steadily rising there. Pursuant to the Treaty of Versailles, the rights to the German colony in Qingdao (Tsingtao) were transferred to Japan, a swap that infuriated the Chinese populace. Massive protests in 1919 triggered the firestorm of the May Fourth Movement and changed the destiny of modern China. A defeated empire without colonies, Germany had nonetheless kept alive its colonial imagination, tinted by nostalgia and loss. These lingering sentiments found expressions in popular culture such as Hans Grimm's bestselling novel, *Volk ohne Raum* (People without Space, 1926), and would likewise set the tone for the films made by Richard Eichberg, with the aid of his newly acquired Chinese icon.

Upon their arrival, Anna May and Lulu checked into the Hotel Eden on Berlin's famous Kurfürstendamm, a long, broad avenue lined with shops, hotels, and restaurants—a less elegant version of the Champs-Élysées. Catering to the wealthiest patrons, the posh hotel had gained notoriety in 1919 for its connection to the arrest and murder of two Communist radicals, Karl Liebknecht and Rosa Luxemburg. Its rooftop café, equipped with a minigolf course, was a favorite hangout for such celebrity writers and artists as Erich Maria Remarque, Heinrich Mann, and Marlene Dietrich. Young Billy Wilder, then an obscure freelance reporter, was moonlighting as a hired dancing companion, a so-called taxi dancer, at the hotel's roof garden.[12] Nearby stood the Romanisches Café, described as "the primary waterhole for Berlin's cultural arbiters and their hangers-on."[13] At the end of the long boulevard was the enormous Luna Park, and its opening in spring marked the beginning of a season of merriment.[14] In an article for *Neue Berliner Zeitung*, Joseph Roth, also a young reporter trying to make a name for himself, told the story of a man just released after fifty-one years in jail. Roth depicted the old man's astonishment at the sound and fury of a city he could not recognize, wondering in a Teutonic reprise of Rip Van Winkle what century he was in.[15] Anna May's first impression of Berlin was likely not as bewildering as that of Roth's old man, but she must have been somewhat overwhelmed by the bustle at the Potsdamer Platz, the elevated S-Bahn seemingly flying through the air, the Devil's Wheel roller coaster at Luna Park, or the naked bodies at the immensely popular open-air baths.

"To go to Berlin," wrote Peter Gay in his definitive study of Weimar culture, "was the aspiration of the composer, the journalist, the actor; with its superb orchestras, its hundred and twenty newspapers, its forty theatres, Berlin was the place for the ambitious, the energetic, the talented. Wherever they started, it was in Berlin they became, and Berlin that made them, famous."[16] It's certain that Gay did not have Anna May in mind when he wrote those lines, given that his heroes of the era were the likes of Stefan George, Martin Heidegger, and Thomas Mann. Nonetheless, it was indeed in Berlin that the ambitious, energetic, and talented Chinese American actress, at a continent's and an ocean's remove from her father's laundry, would reach global stardom.

16

"Orientally Yours"

Orientally yours
Anna May Wong
霜 柳 黃
士 女 籍 美

Anna May Wong publicity photo, late 1920s *(Courtesy of New York Public Library)*

LIKE HER GRANDFATHER, who had left Canton hoping to strike it rich in America's Old West, or like the Chinese coolies migrating to Berlin, Anna May got busy acclimating herself to life in a foreign land. Though she was already a star, she never failed to remember her humble origins. More important, she had the uncanny ability to turn working-class aesthetics into high-class symbols, as she would do one day with the coolie hat and jacket.

Taking a crash course in German, she practiced eight hours a day the speech and writing of a notoriously hard language. And she made daily trips to the UFA studios in Babelsberg to rehearse and get ready for the new chapter in her career. Always a quick study, she was soon able to speak, read, and write in basic German. As she stated in an article published in the journal *Mein Film*, "I am very happy in Berlin, so happy as I have seldom been in my life. I really enjoy my work in Berlin, and I also work very well with director Eichberg."[1]

Knowing German was an asset that came in handy just as photographers began to line up outside her hotel room seeking photo shoots. Likewise, journalists came for interviews, and Berlin's cognoscenti invited her to prestigious events. She became a regular at the theater and the opera, in addition to making rounds of private parties. When Anna May got tired of being an American flapper, she and Lulu would go to lunch at the Tientsin Restaurant on Kantstrasse. Run by a Mr. Yu and his German Frau—the sort of interracial union that would soon be rendered illegal by the Nuremberg Laws—it was the first Chinese restaurant in town. Diagonally across the street from the train station, the eatery was frequented by Chinese students and diplomats living in the Charlottenburg area, and it often served as a meeting place for Chinese student activists. It was at Tientsin that Anna May had a chance encounter with Gongzhen Ge, a pioneer of Chinese journalism traveling in Europe. Ge recognized the actress, whose face had graced Chinese magazines since the early 1920s. They talked—he in Mandarin, she in Cantonese—and when communication across the dialectical divide became impossible, they sought the aid of an English–Chinese dictionary. She asked him about China, which was being shredded by warlords, torn apart by the infighting between Chiang Kai-shek and the forces of the Chinese Communist Party. Ge reassured her that, despite the unrest, the Chinese film industry was flourishing, and Anna May expressed hopes to visit China one day, perhaps even to make films there. The next day, she granted him a formal interview at her hotel, accompanied by a photographer. In an article published a few months later in the Chinese journal *Life Weekly*, Ge described his two meetings with Anna May, her Eastern charm in a Western dress, her concerns for her war-torn ancestral homeland, and her dream of visiting China. The article also included a headshot of her with a dedication, "Orientally yours, Anna May Wong."[2] Coquettish and witty, this inscription would become her unique signoff, revealing both a quiet acquiescence and a tongue-in-cheek defiance of the public perception of her as an exotic icon. It was with such wry humor that she would assume her roles on-screen and assert her ostensibly Oriental self in the sophisticated cultural sphere of Weimar Berlin.

Her first German film *Song* (1928) was a smash hit. Ninety-four minutes long, Richard Eichberg's colonial fantasy was in the heavily treaded tradition of *Madame Butterfly*. The story was set at "an unspecified Eastern harbor," but, judging by the architectural landmarks, it is Istanbul, where the East literally meets the West. The title character, Song, is introduced by a title card as "a human piece of driftwood," and Anna May was paired with Heinrich George, a seasoned German actor and a Communist Party member who had appeared in Fritz Lang's *Metropolis*.

As the plot of the silent film unfolds, Song falls in love with John Houben, a rough, abusive cabaret artist and professional knife-thrower. When he is temporarily blinded, she cares for him in disguise, wearing the perfume and fur coat of the woman he once loved. When he finds out the truth and comes looking for her, it is too late, for Song has been fatally wounded in a sword-dance performance in a nightclub. Unlike *The Toll of the Sea*, in which Anna May's performance was stymied by Hollywood's protocols, *Song* provides a vehicle for her star qualities, showcasing for the first time her multiple talents as an actress, cabaret dancer, vaudeville artiste, and a pioneer in that tricky art of racial masquerade.

In the style of German Expressionism, which prioritizes inner emotions over replicated realities, artificial props over natural settings, the camera emphasizes Anna May's expressive face in close-ups and repeatedly isolates her on-screen, as if to carve out from the narrative a separate space just for her performance. In the words of a shrewd film critic, such a *mise-en-scène* establishes "her as an outsider not only in the story, but also in visual terms."[3] Different from, say, Lon Chaney in *Shadow*, where he impersonated a Chinese by yellowface, Anna May assumes the title role here by *mise-en-abyme*, a play within a play. Interestingly, the character's name, Song, is also Anna May's Chinese name, Liu Tsong. Thus, the line between Anna May and her character, between reality and art, often gets crossed in this film. There would be additional examples. In *Piccadilly* (1929), the heroine Shosho signs Anna May's Chinese name as if it were her own. To add another twist, there was another famous Song (or Soong) living in Germany at the time: Qingling Soong, widow of the founding father of modern China, Dr. Sun Yat-sen. Threatened by political enemies after her husband's death in 1925, Madame Sun had gone into exile and sought refuge first in the Soviet Union and then in Germany.[4] For German viewers who had read about Madame Sun in the newspapers, her plight resembled that of Anna May's film character, Song, a shipwrecked Asian damsel awaiting rescue by a strong, knife-throwing white man.

The film also uses Anna May's talents to reflect other manifestations of Germany's colonial obsession with romance and fantasy. In one scene, Song performs a Malay dance to the accompaniment of a one-man mariachi band. In another, as the target for a knife-throwing act, she conjures the image of a native Pacific Islander, clad in a grass skirt with her long hair, adorned with beads and flowers, flowing down her bare back. In the final scene, she appears on stage sporting two eagle feathers on her head, looking like an Aztec warrior princess, wielding a sword, and performing a war dance on a turntable of knives pointed upward—before she accidentally falls onto a blade and dies. In its late nineteenth-century heyday, the German Reich had exerted colonial influence all over the world, including Southeast Asia, the South Pacific, Latin America—locales suggested by Anna May's artistic assumption of multiple female identities in this film.

One particular identity, however, proved tricky for her to appropriate: a white woman. In the story, when Houben becomes temporarily blind, Song takes care of him and helps him recover. As he continues to pine for his old flame, Gloria, Song tries to heal his emotional wound by passing as the white woman. As just described, she puts on Gloria's perfume and fur coat and gets him into an intimate embrace. While interracial romance remained taboo—for European and American films alike—blindness and masquerade in this plotline provided an alibi for transgression. In fact, taking a cue from the original novel, *Dirty Money*, the screenwriters were able to create scenes in which the interracial couple kisses. These scenes of intimacy, however, were not filmed, presumably for fear of censorship.[5] Even though the notorious Nuremberg Laws would not be issued until 1935, eugenics had deep roots in Europe, as it did in America.

Considering how prevalent the practice of yellowface was, and how routinely white actresses played Asian characters, it was rather remarkable for Anna May to be able to return the favor, so to speak, and impersonate a white woman. As Shirley Jennifer Lim rightly points out, "Passing for white is unprecedented in Wong's career as well as for other Asian American actors and actresses." Anna May's scene of passing in *Song* is indeed, as Lim avows, "a revolutionary remaking of the racial masquerade."[6]

The boldness and versatility of the Hollywood émigré did not fail to impress the German audiences and critics. Two weeks after its gala debut at Berlin's Alhambra Theatre on August 21, 1928, *Song* played in ninety-four cinemas across Germany. In a lengthy review for the *Film-Kurier*, Ernst Jaeger lauded the silent feature as "a particularly well-done episode of film history," imbuing Madame Butterfly romanticism into a Dostoyevskian tragedy. The leading German film critic was especially impressed by "the girl from the East, who has filmed long enough in the exotic gardens of California to know how she can pull her facial expressions against the conventional film style." Jaeger was struck by Anna May's mimetic power, describing her, in overwrought language, as "the Mongolian woman with the body of an American girl, in whom, only when she is dancing, does the strange rhythm, a rocking that originates in the plum blossom dance of her native country, make her appear magical." Spellbound by her physique and alien rhythm, Jaeger was most taken by her visage. "The look on her face!" he cried, barely able to contain his enthusiasm:

> Eyes like dark coffers. Her eyelashes hang over you like branches. Her lips mimic English—and yet she has a secret of her race which puts her ahead of all her peers: the masklike expression of her face remains fixed and frozen even when her eyes scream, her lips burn. This makes her the perfect choice for the camera, which under [Heinrich] Gärtner's artistic hand is able to bring us as close as possible to the otherness of that alien expression. This is a great feat of filmmaking: to bring such an alien life into our everyday light.

His language, in retrospect, seems to animalize or "jungle-ize" her, for no German woman presumably would be capable of such uncontrolled passion and lust. It is hardly surprising, Jaeger concluded, that the film was, above all, "the drama of Anna May Wong."[7]

Other German reviewers echoed Jaeger's enthusiasm, agreeing that a star had been born in Berlin. The film journal *Lichtbildbühne* breathlessly proclaimed, "This German film will, in its success, announce the glory of Anna May Wong as one of the greatest film artists." The evening newspaper *8-Uhr-Abendblatt* sounded more nationalistic, as if turning the actress into a new colonial satrapy: "Anna May Wong is ours now, and we won't let her go again."[8]

In September, *Song* was released in Great Britain as *Show Life* and in the United States as *Wasted Love*. The British press recognized the film as "Anna May Wong's first starring vehicle" and praised her performance in glowing terms: "Anna May Wong scores a veritable triumph. . . . the star's personality and acting, which from start to finish enchains the attention. . . . Anna May Wong's acting [is] a masterpiece of subtlety." The American press, however, appeared to be no fan of German Expressionism. Perhaps also trying to justify Hollywood's snubbing of a promising talent, the *New York Times* dismissed the film as "a hapless piece of work that is years behind the times." It went on to state sourly, "Anna May Wong is a competent little actress, but it would take far more than good acting, coupled with pleasing photography, to make this production half-way diverting." Likewise, *Variety* also dissed the film: "Miss Wong is the only one with the slightest knowledge of what to do before a camera. Promiscuous use of tears has robbed the theme of any continuity and makes it unravel like a cumbersome trailer. Story is patchwork."[9]

These sour-grape reviews would do little to deter Anna May's rise in Europe. As she recalled, "The first picture in which I appeared made a hit. Crowds waited in the lobby for me to come out." Everywhere she went in Berlin, she was mobbed by fans. The success of *Song* propelled her to stardom, but more important, it induced in her a psychic shift. "Weaving my way through that pack of admiring fans," she said, "I seemed suddenly to be standing at one side watching myself with complete detachment. It was my Chinese soul coming back to claim me. Up to that time I had been more of an American flapper than Chinese."[10] While one British reviewer was right in saying that, "paradoxical as it might sound, Anna May Wong has gone to Germany only to be Americanized," it is equally true that she had gone to Germany to recognize her Chinese self—a role she had been forced to play not so freely in America, but now with much more ease in Europe.[11] Looking at herself—and with detachment—through the eyes of the other, she could finally claim with irony and sincerity her identity of "Orientally yours."

17

CONVERSATION WITH AMW

*It is essentially a worship of the imperfect, as
it is a tender attempt to accomplish something
possible in this impossible thing we know as life.*
—KAKUZO OKAKURA,
The Book of Tea (1906)

IN "The Work of Art in the Age of Its Reproducibility," a landmark essay
that remained unpublished in its author's lifetime, the philosopher Walter
Benjamin offers a penetrating analysis of the aesthetics of film and photography. He argues that, compared with traditional artworks of painting, even the
most perfect reproduction made by a camera lacks one thing: "the here and now
of the work of art—its unique existence in a particular place." In other words,
film and photography, by virtue of their reproducibility, lack "the aura." Benjamin continues: "What, then, is the aura? A strange tissue of space and time:
the unique apparition of a distance, however near it may be. To follow with the
eye—while resting on a summer afternoon—a mountain range on the horizon
or a branch that casts its shadow on the beholder is to breathe the aura of those
mountains, of that branch."[1]

On a fine summer afternoon in June 1928, Benjamin, a medium-built man
with thick dark hair, awkward hands, and a pair of gold-rimmed glasses shining like small headlights, was breathing the aura—not of a mountain range or
a shadowy branch but of someone he was meeting for the first time. It was a
rendezvous that would, as reported by the native Berliner in a resulting article,
shed light on the souls of both the mesmerized beholder and the beheld in her
unique aura.

It was a private party, at "a friend's house in Berlin," as Benjamin put it.

Maybe a backyard gathering, in the shadow of a copse of trees, since the article later mentions "garden games." It was a time to celebrate the arrival of summer and to toast Anna May's starring role in her first German flick. "As everyone knows," Benjamin wrote, "May Wong has a leading role in Eichberg's great film now in production." He called her May Wong, as did many of her German fans, who felt "Anna" sounded too Scandinavian. In fact, he seemed to like "May" so much better than "Anna" that when he published the article, he even misspelled "Anna" in the title, "Gespräch mit Anne May Wong" (Conversation with Anne May Wong).[2]

To this aficionado of astrology, tarot cards, graphology, and other mantic symbols, a name is vital. Earlier that year, Benjamin had published *One-Way Street*, an experimental book composed of sixty short prose pieces, a Dadaist collage of aphorisms, slogans, dream sequences, philosophical musings, and political pastiche. He dedicated the book to Asja Lacis, a Latvian Bolshevik actress, with a striking inscription:

> *This street is named*
> *Asja Lacis Street*
> *after her who*
> *as an engineer*
> *cut it through the author.*[3]

Asja, or "Asia," was an elusive, and often unsympathetic, object of desire. In his diary, Benjamin compared her to "an almost impregnable fortress."[4] It was a chaotic period in his life. Just separated from his wife Dora, newly experimenting with hashish, he was struggling as a freelancer for newspapers and journals while trying to maintain his love affair with Asja. His entanglement with the latter was a somewhat sadomasochistic relationship, as suggested by the dedication of *One-Way Street*, which conjures up an image of a dominatrix cutting a path through a man's heart or body, searing it with her own name—as he seemingly wished.

For a few fleeting hours on this summer afternoon, the eccentric writer, not yet the intellectual giant he was to become, turned his attention from his elusive Asja to the enigmatic Asian actress. By no means an ardent Sinophile, Benjamin nonetheless held China in high regard, as this gem from *One-Way Street* proves:

"Chinese Curios": The power of a country road when one is
walking along it is different from the power it has when one
is flying over it by airplane. In the same way, the power of a
text when it is read is different from the power it has when it is
copied out. . . . Only the copied text thus commands the soul
of him who is occupied with it, whereas the mere reader never
discovers the new aspects of his inner self that are opened by
the text, that road cut through the interior jungle forever closing behind it: because the reader follows the movement of his
mind in the free flight of daydreaming, whereas the copier sub-
mits it to command. The Chinese practice of copying books
was thus an incomparable guarantee of literary culture, and
the transcript a key to China's enigmas.[5]

The abrupt appearance of China in his musings over the difference between a
flier and a pedestrian, a reader and a copier, is not only the mark of a Dadaist
disdain for flow or continuity, but also a measure of the Middle Kingdom's cultural prestige in the mind of the German thinker.

Indeed, his infatuation with this specimen of chinoiserie began with her
name: "May Wong—the name resonates with color around the edges, sharp
and light like the tiny specks that open into scentless blossoms like full moons
in a bowl of tea. My questions were a tepid bath in which the destinies concealed in this name could divulge a little something of themselves."[6] Rather
than a flier-cum-reader, Benjamin chose the role of a pedestrian-cum-copier,
who lets nature reveal mysteries of its own accord, like watching tiny tea leaves
unfolding in water, then blossoming into full moons. Comparing the poetics of
her name to the hidden secrets of tea, Benjamin, a devotee of Jewish mysticism,
would understand what Kakuzo Okakura avows in *The Book of Tea*, "Teaism
is Taoism in disguise."[7] At that garden party in Berlin, the writer continued,
"we formed a little community around the low table to observe the process
of unfolding."[8]

At the beginning of their meeting, Anna May introduced Benjamin to the
people sitting around her: a novelist, then an artist on her left, a female American journalist on her right, and her sister Lulu. Clad in a dark-blue suit and a
light-blue blouse fronted by a yellow tie, Anna May surprised Benjamin with
her chic attire, leaving him to struggle for words: "Her outfit might be most

fitting for such garden games, [and yet] one would need a Chinese verse to describe this." Trying to reconcile his expectation of a "chinoiserie specimen" with the reality of an American flapper, he added, "She has always dressed like this, having been born not in China but in Los Angeles's Chinatown." He was amused when she told him, perhaps as a tease, that her favorite dress was cut from her father's wedding jacket, and she would wear it on occasion. The writer was indeed tickled, waxing poetically: "The fabric donned was divine/ But the face more than fine."

He had not yet seen her acting, so they did not talk too much about the film that was being made, but she did tell him that the role was perfect for her. Looking back on her arduous ten years in Hollywood, she said, "It is a role that belongs to me like no other before."

As the conversation went on, the two moved to another room, away from the chatter of the party. An inveterate aphorist, Benjamin quoted a Chinese proverb from *Yu-Kia-Li*, a German translation of an old Chinese text: "Idle prattle about people's affairs prevents important discussion." Not to be out-done, Anna May ad-libbed one of her own sayings rather than tap the wisdom of dead ancients: "Bitter truth is only heard from enemies." And she was quick to add, "I want to hear bitter truth from my friends as well."

Reclining on a couch, she loosened her long hair and arranged it in the manner he poetically compared to "a dragon romping in water." She pushed her dragon's mane back over her forehead, and it came down a bit lower, cutting into her oval face and making it look like a heart. Spellbound, he observed, "Everything that is heart appears reflected in her eyes." Perhaps he was recalling a passage in *One-Way Street*, where he depicts the piercing eyes of the woman he loves: "Had she touched me with the match of her eyes, I would have gone up like a powder keg."[9] If earlier he was struggling to find a Chinese verse to describe Anna May, he found it now, in another quote from *Yu-Kia-Li*: "An ample face like a spring breeze/Formally round, spiritually in peace."

Their tête-à-tête continued. She spoke of her desire to play a mother: "The best are mothers. I played one at fifteen." It was her first big break, as Lotus Flower in *The Toll of the Sea*, the young mother of a biracial child. "Why not?" she went on. "There are so many young mothers." He agreed, thinking of Dora and their son Stefan, who had just turned ten, and of Asja, who was reluctant to have children with him.

Like a movie camera, he recorded the scene with the keen eye of an inspired writer. If he had begun the interview by likening it to tea brewing—

his questions became a "tepid bath" in which the tea leaves would unfold their secrets—she had changed the game somewhere along the way. "May Wong turns question and answer into a kind of swinging," he wrote. "She leans back and rises up, sinks down and rises up, and I imagine that now and then I give her a push. She laughs, that is all."[10]

Save for this essay Benjamin would publish in the July 6, 1928, issue of *Die Literarische Welt*, there is no other record from this intimate encounter between one of Weimar Berlin's leading critics and the rising Chinese American actress.[11] About a year after their rendezvous, the stock market crash on Wall Street and the subsequent worldwide economic depression would precipitate, inter alia, the rise of Adolf Hitler to power. Jews such as Benjamin would be expelled from Germany or rounded up and sent to concentration camps. Though spared genocide, the Chinese who chose to stay in Nazi Germany rather than return to China were sent to labor camps. By the mid-1930s, Anna May would not have been able to make films in Germany. Benjamin would flee to France. In 1940, he perished during a desperate attempt to cross the border into Spain, with the ultimate goal of coming to America. His death was recorded by the French police as a suicide.

In retrospect, the meeting of Walter Benjamin and Anna May took place in the twilight of the almost ephemeral glory of the Weimar Republic. To quote the Japanese savant Okakura again, "Meanwhile, let us have a sip of tea. The afternoon glow is brightening the bamboos, the fountains are bubbling with delight, the sounding of the pines is heard in our kettle. Let us dream of evanescence, and linger in the beautiful foolishness of things."[12]

Anna May Wong in *Pavement Butterfly*, 1929 *(Courtesy of Mondadori Portfolio / Archivio GBB / Everett Collection)*

18

THE VAMP

SOON AFTER her meeting with Walter Benjamin in Berlin, Anna May went to France in June 1928 to make her second film with Richard Eichberg. It was a trip that took her from the Parisian streets and the Louvre to the roulette tables of Monte Carlo on the French Riviera—all locations for this new movie. When Benjamin associated Anna May with America's fabled frontiers by calling her "a Chinoiserie from the Old West," he might have had a point. This cultural amalgamation of femme fatale and violence became a proven formula for success as a film subject. The cinematic allure of gun molls is as enduring as happy endings of riding into the sunset. Even before her crowning as the vampirish "Daughter of the Dragon," Anna May's characters had always brushed against danger. In *Song*, her title character dies in a precarious sword dance. Now in *Großstadtschmetterling* (aka *Pavement Butterfly*), her new incarnation would again be ensnared in a plot of death by blade.

Set alternately in Paris and Nice, the film featured Anna May as a Chinese variety dancer. Performing under the stage name of Princess Butterfly, Mah does fan dances at a street fair to accompany a Chinese circus artist, who pulls a stunt of "The Flying Harikari"—jumping through a wooden frame lined with sharp knives. Koko, a spurned and vindictive suitor of Mah, murders her partner and blames it on her. Running through the Parisian streets, Mah takes refuge in the studio of a young artist named Kusmin. She models for him and in the process falls in love with him. Kusmin's portrait of Mah is sold to a rich patron, but on her way to the bank, she encounters Koko, who robs her of the money. Mistakenly accusing her of theft, Kusmin throws her out. Back on the street again, she is rescued this time by the baron who has bought her portrait. He takes her down to Monte Carlo, where she manages to retrieve the money stolen by Koko—only to see that Kusmin has a new love interest. Walking through the layered shadows of a portico fronting a casino, she exits from the life of the man she loves.

Befitting the film's working title *Die Fremde* (*The Foreigner*), *Pavement Butterfly* portrays the story of a "racial other" living on the margins of a Western society. A beautiful and highly desirable woman, she is nonetheless an outsider who does not fit in. Easily misunderstood, she is lovable but untouchable. Writing again for the *Film-Kurier*, Ernst Jaeger noted the poor treatment of the "Chinese girl in saccharine": "The Eichberg team did not dare to let a happy white man share the same bed as the undressed body of a Mongolian woman." He ascribed the film's "erotic hypocrisy" to the British influence (the film was coproduced by British International Pictures), calling it "the Anglo-American icing on the cinematic cake."[1] Another reviewer for a Socialist newspaper was more direct in criticizing the film's sexism and racism, attributing it also to foreign influences: "Following the American scheme, the Chinese woman has to rescue a young white man, a painter, and at the end—because the white race is so sky-high superior to the yellow one—she gets the usual boot."[2]

Despite their harsh critiques of the film, the reviewers praised Anna May as the lead actress, noting her "personality and exotic charm," while recognizing the film as an interesting "vehicle for the varied talent of the charming star."[3] More important, *Pavement Butterfly*, as suggested by the title phrase, introduced a new character type, a role that indeed uniquely belonged to Anna May. While the word *butterfly* implies the familiar Madame Butterfly, and the sorrowful ending confirms the film's place in the Orientalist pedagogy, *pavement* points not only to a new setting for this old character type but also to the advent of a new figure. In his biography of Anna May, Graham Hodges maintains that, "had Walter Benjamin been less overwhelmed by Anna May Wong's beauty, he might have enlarged his creative interpretation of Baudelaire's concept of the *flaneur*, or urban observer."[4] Indeed, Parisian streets, where Anna May's character roams, poignantly evoke the Baudelairean figure of an incognito stroller. As an ethnic outsider, Princess Butterfly may share some characteristics with Charles Baudelaire's Parisian prowler, an alienated yet compassionate male aesthete who "muses on the bizarre in the commonplace, the sublime in the mundane," a witness to a teeming metropolis on the eve of great change.[5] But, as a woman, she is perhaps thematically much closer to another type of character emerging in Weimar Germany as well as European cinema at the time: the vamp.

Even though during those interwar years the proportion of women in employment in Weimar Germany remained constant—rising only slightly from 31.2 percent in 1907 to 35.6 percent in 1925—the expansion of the areas in which women were now working, particularly in modern sectors of industry, commerce, and public employment, represented a shift in women's public presence. With increased access to higher education and better jobs, women also became more involved in politics. In the Weimar Republic, for example, 111 women were elected to the Reichstag. A feminist manifesto, "This Is the New Woman," published in 1929, declared:

> The new woman has set herself the goal of proving in her work and deeds that the representatives of the female sex are not second-class persons existing only in dependence and obedience but are fully capable of satisfying the demands of their positions in life. The proof of her personal value and the proof of the value of her sex are therefore the maxims ruling the life of every single woman in our times.[6]

Reflecting these social trends, a new figure appeared on the silver screen as a male-generated fantasy of a modern woman: the glamorous girl who is "a bit too independent to be true, armed with bobbed hair and made-up face, fashionable clothes and cigarette, working by day in a typing pool or behind the sales counter in some dreamland of consumerism, frittering away the night dancing the Charleston or watching UFA and Hollywood films." As Detlev Peukert states in his study of the Weimar Republic, such a caricature bore little resemblance to the young female white-collar workers whose lives had inspired it. But this did not prevent the mythology of the "new woman" from being promoted by the media and taking on a life of its own. Peukert writes: "The worlds conjured up by the illustrated magazines, serials and hospital romances, by romantic films and musical comedies and by advertising and the new consumerism made their mark on the attitudes and daydreams of many young women."[7] The 1930 film *The Blue Angel*, directed by Josef von Sternberg and starring Marlene Dietrich, did much to further popularize the image of the vamp. Playing a seductress named Lola, Dietrich trotted out her legs on stage and crooned in her husky voice,

love is just a game
to me men are drawn
like moths to the flame.

Anna May's character in *Pavement Butterfly* was no temptress like Dietrich's Lola, but Mah is equally attractive to the men around her, with some even willing, in a noir way, to kill for her. Like Lola, Mah orbits among the demimonde of artists and gamblers, bedecked in the latest Parisian fashions, loving passionately, and yet having the courage to walk away when she realizes the futility of the affection. Her parting words, in particular, reveal her streak of independence as a new woman: *"Ich gehöre nicht zu euch"* (I don't belong to you). Anticipating her signature "Dragon Lady" role in the talkie era, Anna May added a dimension of the "exotic other" to the image of the vamp. In other words, she is simultaneously Madame Butterfly and the vamp.

Speaking of female iconography, Anna May attended the 1928 Berlin Press Ball where she met two figures who defined new womanhood in Germany: Marlene Dietrich and Leni Riefenstahl. In a photograph taken for the occasion by Alfred Eisenstaedt, these three icons of twentieth-century cinema huddle together: A young, pre-Hollywood Dietrich flirtatiously grits a cigarette holder between her teeth; Anna May stands tallest in the middle, smiling into the camera, straight bangs outlining her face, a long string of pearls dangling in front of her sheath dress; and Riefenstahl, the most reserved and matronly of the three, has her arm around Anna May's waist, as if jealously protecting the young woman from her assertive competitor.[8]

When this photo was taken, Dietrich had not yet made her first breakaway film, *The Blue Angel*, but she had been a successful stage actor, demonstrating her talents in musicals, revues, and a few silent features. Riefenstahl was her friend and rival. As Karin Wieland shows in her remarkable duo-biography, both Dietrich and Riefenstahl came of age at the beginning of the Weimar Republic, and both sought fame in Germany's nascent film industry. While Dietrich's depiction of Lola in *The Blue Angel* would soon catapult her to global stardom, Riefenstahl, who missed out on the part, would insinuate herself into Hitler's inner circle and become the Führer's camerawoman. The dissonance of these two women, born less than a year apart and following diametrically opposite paths of life and career, encapsulates the undulations of twentieth-century history.[9] But we should not forget the third woman in this photo, Anna

May, who stood in the center but was continuously pushed to the margins by forces beyond her control.

On this evening at the press ball—an occasion representing the pinnacle of Berlin nightlife in the Golden Twenties— friendship, love, and jealousy were all in the air. Other snapshots taken by Eisenstaedt, already a rising star as a cameraman, show Anna May pouring liquor into Dietrich's mouth, with Riefenstahl standing by, looking naughty.[10] By all accounts, Anna May was a bigger star than the pre-Lola

Marlene Dietrich, Anna May Wong, and Leni Riefenstahl at Berlin Press Ball, 1928 *(Courtesy of Harvard Art Museums / Busch-Reisinger Museum, Gift of Lufthansa German Airlines)*

Dietrich and the pre-Hitler Riefenstahl on this bacchic night. A Hollywooder hired to energize Germany's Babelsberg, she was literally the toast of the town. For an Asian actress like her, however, stardom did not mean acceptance, and fascination could not be mistaken for equity—a cultural lesson she would learn at the next stop of her globe-trotting journey.

19

PICCADILLY

WHEN ANNA MAY, having left her mark in Germany and France, arrived in London in the fall of 1928, the British Empire was near the zenith of its grandeur. Possessing colonies on every continent—more than a quarter of the planet—the empire had never been larger. The stock market's Black Thursday was still a year in the future, and even though there were hints of a crisis—increasing social unrest at home and incipient independence movements in the colonies—the Union Jack remained the symbol of the most powerful nation on Earth. As if sensing that the best days would soon be over, the British Empire mounted a stunning exhibition at Wembley Park in 1924–25, perhaps a last-ditch attempt to project the fading imperial nimbus. Although the spectacular exposition that made Wembley a household name was long over by 1928, no one could forget some of the exotic scenes on display. Visitors to the Hong Kong booth, for instance, would remember dining in its restaurant on bird's nest soup, shark fin, and other delicacies served by Chinese "boys" to the accompaniment of a traditional Chinese band. Stepping into the "street" outside, they would perhaps find themselves bewildered by the bright signs in Chinese characters, announcing the names of the pigtailed, smiling proprietors and the wares for sale.[1]

Yet, British curiosity about China was hardly new to the twentieth century. In 1829, a hundred years prior to Anna May's arrival, the world-famous Siamese Twins, Chang and Eng Bunker, both of Chinese descent, had been displayed as monstrous freaks in Piccadilly—an iconic name that would become the title of Anna May's first British film and one of her most memorable pic-

Anna May Wong in *Piccadilly*, 1929 *(Courtesy of Mary Evans / Ronald Grant / Everett Collection)*

tures. Furthermore, the two Opium Wars (1839–1842, 1856–1860) raised the British stake in the Middle Kingdom and sparked new interest in all things Chinese. In the years leading up to the Boxer Rebellion of 1899–1901, as Britain further expanded its influence in China and dispatched more soldiers, missionaries, businessmen, and diplomats, a small Chinatown grew up along London's dockside streets. Boardinghouses, grocery stores, restaurants, association halls, and laundries catered mostly to Chinese laborers and seamen. Unsurprisingly, such an ethnic enclave in the heart of the metropolis inspired opportunistic writers to exploit its dramatic potential. The long-running series of Dr. Fu Manchu stories, for instance, was born out of novelist Sax Rohmer's obsession with Chinatown as an imaginary locus of drugs, gambling, sex, and other iniquities. The yellow-journalism Limehouse fiction by Thomas Burke also scandalized readers with tales of forbidden romance between Yellow Man and White Girl, provoking Darwinian panic and fears of miscegenation.[2]

Interestingly, Anna May had read all of Burke's books and loved the nightmarish atmosphere of the Limehouse stories. Her new film, *Piccadilly*, set

alternately in Limehouse in East London and in the West End, had a similarly noirish quality that permeated its 105-minute run. And in just a few years,
she would personify the progeny of the insidious Dr. Fu Manchu in *Daughter
of the Dragon*. Besides the popularity of Limehouse fiction and the imaginary
evil doctor, there were other elements in multiple echelons of British society
that contributed to the phenomenal success of a Chinese American actress in
Great Britain.

Among the upper class and cultural elites, China held a particular allure
that could not be undone by the negative images associated with Limehouse.
As Ezra Pound, the American poet then living in London, said in 1914, "China
is interesting, VERY."[3] Pound and his cohort of Anglo-American poets turned
to China for artistic inspirations, a search that gave birth to Imagism. Likewise, Virginia Woolf tried to pinpoint the genesis of literary modernism with
her famous claim, "On and about December 1910 human character changed."
That year was marked not only by King Edward VII's death and the stunning Post-Impressionist exhibition at Grafton Galleries, but also by the June
opening of the British Museum's exhibition of Chinese and Japanese painting,
curated by Pound's friend Laurence Binyon. In *To the Lighthouse* (1927), Woolf
described Lily Briscoe, a painter and a New Woman, as having "little Chinese
eyes" and a "puckered-up face."[4]

In the broader sectors of British society, the aesthetics of chinoiserie,
embodied by embroideries, furniture, utensils, and other objects, had historically defined taste and class standing. In the wake of the Boxer Rebellion,
British forces and their Western allies looted the Summer Palace in Peking
and then burned it to the ground. The spoils from the royal palace were later
exhibited and auctioned off, spurring a spike in demand for Chinese *objets
d'art*. In the same period, Chinese objects and embroidery found their way into
middle-class homes and wardrobes. As a corollary to the Wembley Exhibition,
a marked proclivity for Oriental styles in homes was noted in 1924 and 1925. At
the beginning of 1925, the *China Express and Telegraph* boldly predicted that it
would be "A Great Year of Chinese Fashions": "There are Chinese tea jackets,
rest coatees [jackets or coats], and loose wraps made of vivid colors, embroidered with large white lotus flowers with red fish and orange birds. Chinese
dance frocks made in marocain [crepe fabric] worked in many colored skeins
of silk will be seen in dance halls, and with these will be worn Chinese silk
slippers."[5] Throughout the year, the influential newspaper continued to run
articles about wallpaper portraying Chinese motifs, curtains depicting Chi-

nese dragons or dragon-shaped clouds, eiderdowns having much black in them, lampshades adorned with dragons in gold tinsel, and chinaware glazed in bright colors that imitated the porcelain of the Kang-hsi period. When the Hong Kong section at the Wembley Exhibition closed in October 1925, eager buyers lined up for the auction of lacquerware furniture, ivory, embroideries, mahjong sets, tea, and ginger. As in the United States, mahjong nights across Britain became huge hits, replacing bridge parties.[6]

Such Chinese vogues certainly helped to boost Anna May's popularity in the United Kingdom, but chinoiserie did little to reduce Sinophobia. Just think: It was at the height of American xenophobia in the mid-1920s that Charlie Chan, an iconic Chinese fellow, burst onto the scene and took the nation by storm. Like racial masquerade, cultural appropriation of objects and images helps alleviate racial anxieties by satisfying consumer desires for the exotic and new. It does not necessarily, however, translate into affection for the people. Even when the so-called *coiffure chinoise*—in which the hair is pulled back from the face and fixed in a chignon with an ornamental pin—popularized by the Parisian actress Andree Spinelly, was catching on among British women, a Chinese student in London could not find a barber willing to cut his hair or a room to rent outside cramped Chinatown.[7] This was the kind of cultural reality facing Anna May when she arrived. She needed to bridge the gulf between the China vogue in Bloomsbury and the sordid reality of Limehouse, between the fetish for all things Chinese and a nithering racial condescension no different from what she had been subject to in America.

Piccadilly, her first British film and last silent feature, was another Anglo-German collaborative project. Like its German counterpart, the British film industry was trying to compete with Hollywood and counterbalance the increasing cultural domination by the United States. After Parliament passed the Cinematograph Films Act in 1927, requiring British theaters to show a certain number of domestic films per screen, British studios greatly increased their production pace to meet the spike in demand.[8] Getting Anna May to shoot a film in England, then, would satisfy several prerequisites: Though directed by a German, *Piccadilly* counted as a British film; though American, Anna May was Chinese and could appeal to British viewers with a hunger for chinoiserie. In fact, while in England, Anna May received the honorary title of Cultural Ambassador of China, even though she was an American citizen and had never set foot on Chinese soil.

Written by the bestselling author Arnold Bennett and directed by E. A.

Dupont, *Piccadilly* was a feast for the eye. The story involves Shosho (Anna May), a scullery maid who snatches a job as the dancing star at the fashionable Piccadilly Club from Mabel Greenfield (Gilda Gray), a blonde whose Charleston routines begin to get stale. Using her exotic and youthful charm, Shosho also steals Mabel's place in the heart of the club owner, Valentine Wilmot. In the end, Shosho is shot dead by Jim, her jealous Chinese lover.

Piccadilly is a singular film for a whole variety of reasons. Critics and film historians often consider it a cinematic masterpiece, not in the least because it features Anna May in a starring role. Whereas other films in which she acts play on racist tropes and negative stereotypes, *Piccadilly*, while realistically depicting the rank bigotry that confronted the Asian-English community, seems to pander less to inflammatory stereotypes and "dragon lady" dog whistles that populate many of her other films. It is then significant that the film was made in England, not in Hollywood. What also makes *Piccadilly* historic is the fact that it was filmed in 1928, just as silent movies were yielding to talkies. It is a throwback, yet it distinguishes itself as a masterpiece of the silent era, its cinematography and acting of the highest quality, with Shosho's balletic movements closer, say, to Buster Keaton than to mere slapstick.

Also striking about *Piccadilly* is its larger historical symbolism—its depiction of a hedonistic nightclub society that flourished between the wars, whether in Germany or, so it seems, in a post-Edwardian England. The café society of Berlin, so brilliantly animated by one of its finest chroniclers, Joseph Roth, comes to life here, but this is louche London, not Weimar. It is a world that refuses to recognize that an entire generation, only ten years earlier, was decimated, their bodies fallen in Somme and Verdun, or in Flanders Fields, as John McCrae's eponymous, most poignant war poem describes:

> *We are the Dead. Short days ago*
> *We lived, felt dawn, saw sunset glow,*
> *Loved and were loved, and now we lie*
> *In Flanders fields.*[9]

The opening of the film gives not the slightest impression of the imminent crisis—1929 marks the beginning of a global Depression, the most severe of the twentieth century. Piccadilly is all aglitter, the double-decker buses arriving at the Piccadilly Club, the crowds milling outside, with Gilda Gray, soon to be Anna May's rival, featured on the marquee. The ballroom with its hints of early art deco is especially grand, the twin staircase shaped like a double helix leading to the dance floor, the couples foxtrotting as though they had not a single care but to be narcotized by the rhythmic swaying of the music, the bar inundated by tuxedoed gentlemen angling to catch the bartender's eye.

Here are the spoils—the wealth and the arrogance—of the overseas colonies on full display: the porcine gentleman diner, plucked from a Georg Grosz painting, remonstrating the waiters for a "dirty plate"; the Lucullan display of food; the mink-swathed women in the ladies' room applying lipstick, reaching for a cigarette, and gossiping that Vic and Mabel are "the talk of the town"; the dancers in frenzied motion (women backward, please); and the film itself a dazzling montage of motion and energy that suggests life as an endless party.

It is into this world that Anna May/Shosho is thrust. A spectacular display of the glitter and dazzle in London's upscale West End in contrast to Limehouse's squalor, *Piccadilly* cast Anna May in her most provocatively erotic and seductive role. When Shosho first appears in the scullery scene, the camera tracks Wilmot's coveting gaze and finds her dancing on a worktable, surrounded by a gaggle of dishwashers cheering her on. Then the camera pans over, as if caressing her, slowly tilting down from her fresh face to her braless upper body, her nipples protruding through her sweater. It then lingers for a few seconds on a ragged apron wrapped around her undulating hips, then zeroes in on the runs in her sheer black stockings, finally ending with a close-up of her plain Mary Jane shoes with buckles. As if depicting Anna May as a fashion model, the film shows her in various costumes that match her changing status, at the same time reflecting her shifting psyche. As Shosho emerges as a star performer, her daily attire changes to a keyhole sweater with horizontal stripes of a Parisian apache dancer, then a tight silky black dress with enticing buttons. On a night out as the new paramour of her boss, she dons an elegant coat with fur on the collar and hem. Her most striking attire was the dance costume, an exotic piece she demands that Wilmot purchase for her from a Chinese curio shop in Limehouse for an exorbitant amount. "I dance in that or not at all," she declares. It is a Southeast Asia–inspired piece consisting of a gold headdress with a phallic horn and armorlike shoulder pads and breastplates. In her shimmering armor, Shosho looks like an androgynous goddess triumphant in the game of love and death.[10]

In the final seduction scene, she takes Wilmot back to her flat. Full of kitschy, derivative bric-a-brac like goldfish, pagoda lanterns, a Buddha portrait, and looming shadows of a dragon, the exotic decor suggests a den of an

Oriental seductress ready to ensnare her unsuspecting prey. Appearing behind a diaphanous screen, Shosho has slipped into a braless sequined dress dangling on two thin straps, plus a matching embroidered veil. Not surprisingly, she lures Wilmot into her web.

Compared with any of her previous films, *Piccadilly* becomes a star vehicle in which, as American literary scholar Anne Anlin Cheng points out, "Wong most actively aligns herself with her character."[11] The plot of *Piccadilly* in many ways matches Anna May's own story, as if both the real life and the cinematic one were constructed on a rags-to-riches fantasy, in that the poor Chinese girl is miraculously rescued from her benighted circumstances and suddenly thrust into a starring role, as if she's been crowned "queen for a day." The first time we see Shosho, she dances on a table in the scullery under a set of coolie-hat lampshades and against a background of rising steam. Both the coolie-hat imagery and the vapor from the dishwashing sink seem to complement Anna May's humble origin in a Chinese laundry. Another diegetic moment occurs when Shosho sends Mabel a bouquet of flowers, accompanied by a sarcastic message: "To Miss Mabel: A thought from one who was in the kitchen. Shosho." After her English autograph, we see Anna May's real Chinese name, 黄柳霜. The same thing happens when Shosho signs the contract offered by Wilmot. She again writes Anna May's real name. Thus, the film becomes as much a biopic of Anna May Wong as a Cinderella story of Shosho. That the lives of both Anna May and the scullery-maid-turned-nightclub-dancing sensation would end tragically is not uncoincidental, although it would be more than a quarter century before Anna May's decline led to her death back in Los Angeles.

The alignment of fact and fiction gives *Piccadilly* the feel of a documentary, creating a *mise-en-abyme* that sheds light on what lies beyond the studio lot. At the very beginning of the film, the credits are ingeniously printed on the side of a double-decker bus rumbling through the street, promising a flick full of tourist delights. King Ho Chang, who played Jim, was actually a restaurant owner in Limehouse, which partly accounts for the two realistic restaurant scenes in the film. In the first one, Chinese diners are seen devouring fried chicken and mashed potatoes with knives and forks; in the second scene, the footage depicts Chinese customers brandishing their obligatory chopsticks. In a reprise of those "slumming trips" that took place in turn-of-the-century American cities, the travel agency Thomas Cook began to promote charabanc [open-topped vehicle] trips to the Limehouse district during the same period. As Anne Witchard describes the scene in her study of 1920s London, "At a carefully stage-managed time, doors would burst open and Chinese, complete with pigtails, would chase each other down the street wielding cleavers."[12] It also became trendy for West End clubbers, after a couple of cocktails, to go carousing down Chinatown way, which is exactly what Shosho and Wilmot do on the fateful night when she is killed. In the rough Limehouse saloon, packed with working-class drinkers and women kicking up their legs or slipping pound notes into their nylons, Shosho tells Wilmot, "You see, this is *our* Piccadilly," not his pretentious high-end club. Soon an inebriated white woman dancing with a black man is kicked out of the saloon by the owner, who scolds her, "Are yer blind, or wot?" Realizing the crowd's animosity toward interracial mixing, Shosho and Wilmot beat a quick retreat.

The fear of miscegenation was actually replicated by what lay beyond the camera. Given the preponderance of eroticism in this film, it was especially difficult for the editor to cut the on-screen kissing scene between Shosho and Wil-

Jameson Thomas and Anna May Wong in *Piccadilly*, 1929 *(Courtesy of Everett Collection)*

mot. As the Wilmot actor Jameson Thomas admitted, even though England was less prejudiced about interracial romance than America, they had to be "careful to handle such scenes tactfully."[13] In his influential study of film stars, Edgar Morin theorizes the magic of a kiss: "The kiss is not only the key technique of love-making, nor the cinematic substitute for intercourse forbidden by censorship: it is the triumphant symbol of the role of the face and the soul in twentieth-century love."[14] Without the magic of a kiss, Anna May became a star shorn of stardust.

Despite the absence of such scenes, *Piccadilly* received glowing reviews in the British press and abroad. *The Bioscope* noted, "This is the most striking film issued recently from a British studio and reflects every possible credit on all concerned in its making. Anna May Wong is perfectly fitted as the little scullery maid whose head is easily turned by sudden success." *Close Up* called it "the perfect British film," and *Variety* also opined that "this is one British-made that can go around the world." *The Picturegoer* gave Anna May a backhanded compliment: "By her immobility, her reposeful body movements that are certainly her Oriental heritage, she gave a touch of dignity to the siren she portrayed."[15] Almost all reviewers agreed that just as Shosho steals Mabel's paramour, Anna May outshone the blonde Gilda Gray and was the real star of the two. This newfound glory would open doors to Anna May's enduring dream: to appear on London's live stage.

THE CIRCLE OF CHALK

Cover of London theater program for *The Circle of Chalk*, 1929 *(Courtesy of Masheter Archive / Alamy Stock Photo)*

I T IS A CHINESE TALE as old as the Bible: A beautiful girl named Hai-tang is sold to a brothel by her destitute family. Ma, a childless, married rich man, takes her home as his concubine. After she bears him a son, the first wife becomes jealous. She accuses Hai-tang of adultery and then poisons Ma. She blames Hai-tang for the murder and claims the baby as her own so that she can usurp all the wealth. Hai-tang is arrested and tortured into making a false confession. On the eve of her execution, she is rescued by a wise magistrate who sets up an ingenious ruse. He places the baby inside a circle of chalk and asks the two women to pull the child as hard as they can, in a winner-take-all match. Afraid to hurt her own baby, Hai-tang willingly gives up, and the shrewd magistrate instantly recognizes her as the true mother.[1]

Similar to the biblical story about King Solomon's wise judgment, this Chinese tale was immortalized as 灰阑记 (*Story of the Chalk Circle*), by the playwright Li Qianfu of the Yuan dynasty, before Shakespeare's time. The poetic drama was first introduced to the West through a French translation in 1832 and then liberally rendered into German by the flamboyant poet Klabund (Alfred Henschke) in 1924. In the German version, while Hai-tang works as a teahouse girl—euphemism for a prostitute—a prince falls in love with her, but she is bought by the evil man Ma, who is the root cause of her plight because he bankrupted her father and drove him to his death. After her ordeal, the former prince, now the emperor, saves Hai-tang by the scheme of the chalk circle and marries her at the end. In 1929, James Laver translated the German version into English as *The Circle of Chalk*, which caught the eye of Basil Dean, a former actor turned stage director and an influential impresario in Britain's film and theater world. Deciding to put Laver's rendition on stage, Dean cast about, as he later recalled, "for an actress, almond-eyed, if possible," to play the part of Hai-tang.[2] The original meaning of Hai-tang is "begonia," a delicate flower of bright colors, or a social butterfly. In 1929 London, no one would fit Dean's preference better than the Chinese American flapper who had just stepped into the limelight with *Pavement Butterfly* and *Piccadilly*. Thus, with no professional stage training, and having done only a handful of vaudeville gigs, Anna May was chosen as the principal lady in a major production in Shakespeare's milieu.

Critics were right in calling the 1929 staging of *The Circle of Chalk* a "study of chinoiserie." To ensure that the play was as authentically "Chinese" as

Limehouse fiction, Dean was meticulous about all aspects of the production. He gave exacting directives to the set designer:

> Begin by enclosing the stage space in a box as wide as the proscenium arch itself; swing doors right and left at the back for entrances and exits; ceiling, walls, floors, all in black lacquer; in the center of the stage an oblong turntable on which various scenes—the tea house, the magistrate's court, etc.—can be built back to back. The final scene, the throne room of the Imperial Palace, will occupy the whole platform; all this inner scenery to be painted and decorated in Chinese red lacquer and gold.

In other words, Dean wanted a proverbial Chinese box.[3]

For music, Dean hired composer Ernest Irving, whose taste notoriously bordered on eccentricity. In fact, Irving's orchestra included many strange instruments: gongs, drums of various kinds, a cello adapted for the Chinese fiddle, a marimba, and a woodwind rarity called a heckelphone.[4] It was reminiscent of the ragtag Chinese orchestra that accompanied Shosho's dance at the Piccadilly Club.

For the libretto, Dean sprinkled the dialogue with ersatz Oriental dainties, at times as formalized as a Confucian saying, and at others flowery like a Charlie Chan aphorism: "I am your most unworthy servant," "May a thousand mosquitoes buzz in his brain, and a thousand wasps sting his eyes and blind him!" and "I swear by the bones of my ancestors." Hai-tang's lines were also highly stylized, mixing Ben Jonson's *Volpone* or William Wycherley's *Country Wife* with an Oriental pitch and rhythm: "I fear your Majesty's anger. You glower upon me like a wolf or tiger, ready to devour me if I do not obey you. But I cannot do it. I bore this child under my heart for nine months. Nine months have I lived with him, nine months longer than other people. I have known all sweetness with him, and all bitterness without him."[5]

To prepare for her London stage debut, Anna May binged on British literature, trying to familiarize herself with the dramatic tradition that had produced the likes of Shakespeare, Jonson, and Dryden. She even read up on Bertrand Russell in order to get a better handle on the British attitude toward the Chinese. After his yearlong tour and lecturing in China in 1920, the Cambridge philosopher had written extensively about the millennia-old civilization, culminating in a book of essays titled *The Problem of China* (1922). Writing at a time when China was viewed as weak and backward, or even dubbed "the sick man of East Asia," Russell rose above the racial bias and provided a shrewd assessment of Chinese problems. Contrasting China with the West, Russell praised the Chinese love of "knowledge, art, instinctive happiness, and relations of friendship or affection." He wrote, "China is better than we are. Our prosperity, and most of what we endeavor to secure for ourselves, can only be obtained by widespread oppression and exploitation of weaker nations, while the Chinese are not strong enough to injure other countries, and secure whatever they enjoy by means of their own merits and exertions alone." China may seem weak now, he felt, but it is patient: "It thinks of centuries as other nations think of decades. It is essentially indestructible, and can afford to wait." Russell characterized the Chinese patience as a "pacific temper," which he argued would bode well for the future of China.[6] These assessments by a world-class philosopher had a profound impact on Anna May, who had been looking to reconnect with her Chinese roots, a spiritual journey that would one day take her to China.

On March 14, 1929, *The Circle of Chalk* opened at the New Theatre in London's West End. Though the mob scene was not as raucous as that for Lord Byron or Rudolph Valentino, fans thronged the theater to catch a glimpse of the movie star. They waited on the street, young men in their best clothes, "combing their hair and knotting and reknotting their ties," and young women with their locks sheared in the style of their idol.[7] While various styles of bangs, or "fringes," had been worn by both men and women since ancient Greece, they became controversial periodically when conservative clergy regarded women who cut and curled their hair into bangs as representing "a slide into mortal sin." In the Victorian era, after Alexandra, Princess of Wales (later Queen of England as wife of King Edward VII), started wearing her hair in short, frizzy fringes, the style caught on with young British women.[8] Now Anna May had introduced a new version: The Wong look was not curly or wavy, but blunt in the front and straight in the back. Among her British fans, some women even painted their faces ivory with powder, in imitation of "the Wong complexion."[9]

Despite the frenzy, the show was, shall we say, a mixed bag. As a stage novice, Anna May held her ground pretty well. Her performance of a lotus dance almost brought down the house. One reviewer stated: "She is enchanting. Her bowings, her swayings, her slitherings, her bendings, her stops and her starts excited to ecstasy. As a dancer, she is the soul of eloquence."[10] In contrast, Laurence Olivier, still a young actor of trifling repute, gave a truly lackluster performance. Donning a gorgeous primrose silk robe, the future theatrical giant played the Chinese prince in yellowface and overdid his makeup and his imitation of Chinese gesticulations and speech. He was roundly roasted by reviewers, with one critic commenting sarcastically, "Here he had become what he had always wanted to be, a leading man in the West End. And he was practically throwing away the opportunity to expand himself. It wasn't that Larry was bad because he had insufficient talent and couldn't help it. It was as if he was being bad deliberately."[11] Some years later, Sir Larry would again be "bad deliberately," doing Othello in blackface.

Most of the criticism, however, was reserved for Anna May's vocal delivery. For those expecting to hear a stereotypical high-pitched, bell-like voice with an Asian accent, she shocked them with her *sotto voce* California twang. Taken aback, one critic denigrated her voice as being "guttural and uncultivated," dreadfully incongruent with the lightness and delicacy of her bodily movements.[12] Another reviewer wrote, "As soon as the great Anna May opened her mouth, her squeaky American voice shattered any attempt at illusion."[13] As the director responsible for casting Anna May, Basil Dean was the one most disappointed: "But oh! That California accent! As thick as the smog that now smothers their cities. Try as she might—and she did try—Anna May couldn't get rid of it. In Berlin they had made no complaint. After all, why should they? She was making a silent film." Dean considered it a miscalculation on his part by underestimating "the strong prejudice, amounting to almost total rejection in some cases of the American accent in English plays at that time, just as the British accent was resented on Broadway." Dean regretted his own folly in engaging a silent-film actress when, as he condescendingly put it, "any attractive English ingenue with good voice and gesture might well have carried the production to success."[14] At the end of the eight-week run, Anna May attended a lunch with newspaper critics. Responding to a question about her voice, she remarked that she wished the reviewers "could make up their mind whether she had a New York or Hollywood accent." She then switched to Cantonese so that none of them could understand her.[15]

Her defiance and playfulness notwithstanding, the question of her voice signaled a major issue emerging in the performance world at the time. As the motion picture industry hurtled from silent films to talkies, many stars of the bygone era fell by the wayside, because the utterance of one syllable was sometimes enough to dispel all the beautiful illusions they had studiously curated in the silent world. The same challenge would soon face Anna May. The debacle of *The Circle of Chalk* sounded an alarm gong for her. While some critics, dismayed by her vocal performance, predicted that "Anna in talkies will not be the same as Anna of silent screen,"[16] it remained to be seen whether she could, or would, successfully enter the world of sound.

21

THE FIRST WORD

From Moscow down to Astrakhan
You'll hear love tales from every man
Some girls can't kiss, but some girls can
　　　　—Theme song of the film *Hai-Tang* (1930)

IT IS SOMEWHAT IRONIC that the first word Anna May uttered in a talkie was *"Mitleid,"* German for "pity." It was a plea to authority for leniency.

Prodded by the harsh reviews of her voice in *The Circle of Chalk*, Anna May took singing lessons and hired an elocution teacher from Oxford University to study voice.[1] Paying two hundred guineas per session to eliminate her California accent may seem exorbitant, but with the arrival of sound in the film industry, she was facing an existential threat, the same one experienced by many other silent-film stars. The momentous success of *The Jazz Singer*, the first talkie using the Vitaphone sound system, signaled that the days of the silent film were numbered. Overnight, the small Warner Bros. company leaped to the front ranks of the industry, forcing other studios to catch up. Big investments were made to build recording studios to accommodate talkies. In fact, sound gave the Europeans a tremendous psychological lift in their battle against American domination. The British in particular, always assuming the superiority of the British accent—which Henry James extolled as the "tone standard"—were convinced that their time had arrived.[2]

The impact of the talkie revolution on actors and the cinema was incalculable. As Charlie Chaplin said, "Just when we got it right, it was over."[3] The maestro of pantomime, who would resist the talkies and continue to make silent films until *The Great Dictator* in 1940, was no exception. In *Fun in a Chinese Laundry*, Josef von Sternberg recalled, "With the arrival of sound in films, Mr.

Chaplin lost his cunning. The voice that issued from the mouth of the clown he had invented bore no relation to the mask."[4] At the dawn of talkies, as famously dramatized in *Singin' in the Rain* (1952), many silent stars with squeaky voices quickly fell out of favor, while others remained apprehensive about the new technology. "The problem of speech was a real one," Robert Sklar writes. "Elocution coaches made a killing; actors with clipped British accents hastened to Hollywood; observers predicted that the foreign players who had become so significant in Hollywood silents would be packed off back to Sweden, Germany or Czechoslovakia."[5] Even the great Emil Jannings was worried about his own voice and feared for the loss of his expressive power.[6] Greta Garbo, then a Swedish ingenue, suffered a setback. Having played sophisticated socialites in all of her American silent films, Garbo made her talkie debut in MGM's *Anna Christie* (1930). Speaking to a waiter in a waterfront dive, her long-awaited first movie words were, to be kind, flavorful: "Gimme a visky. Ginger ale on the side. And don' be stingy, ba-bee." The screaming tagline of "Garbo talks!" put out by MGM's marketers as enticement, ironically captured the shock of the audience.[7]

Mindful of the transition, Anna May astutely took steps to ready herself. In addition to the voice lessons, she also started learning French while boning up on German. With the technique of dubbing still a few years away, her first talkie would be made separately in three different language versions: German, English, and French. She was working again with Richard Eichberg, who had arranged with British International Pictures (BIP) and the French company Etablissements Jacques Haik to shoot big-budget, multilingual sound features at Elstree Studios. This new film—titled *Hai-Tang* in German, *The Road to Honor* in English (*The Flame of Love* in the United States), and *L'Amour Maître des Choses* in French—borrowed the heroine's name from *The Circle of Chalk*, even though its plotline had nothing to do with the stage drama. Playing the title character, Anna May was a dancer touring with a troupe in Tsarist Russia. Suffering from unrequited love for a dashing Russian officer, she has to sleep with a villainous archduke in order to save her brother from execution. Feeling ashamed, she, yet again, commits suicide in the end.

In *Hai-Tang*, Anna May spoke her first word in a sound feature. She recalled the vexing moment in an article she wrote for *Mein Film* in 1930: "As the word escaped my lips and was swallowed up by the lurking ear of the microphone, I was gripped by a horrible fear that it had not sounded right." It was another one of those *mise-en-abyme* scenes where the story in the film corresponded to the happening outside the film. On-screen, Hai-Tang utters the word *Mitleid* (pity), begging the archduke, who has just violated her sexually, for leniency: "Pity! Pity! Your Imperial Highness—Oh, have pity on my brother. . . ." Off-screen, the actress was asking for sympathy from those making the film and those listening to her voice recorded in the studio. "It was the most exciting moment of my entire film career," she said. "Of course, even during the close-ups in silent film shoots, I trembled with worry and wondered if the shoots came out flattering. But the film camera usually faithfully transmits play and expression. What one entrusts to it in terms of performing output and emotional input is almost always found unchanged in the projection." Such a certainty was lost with sound. As she explained further, "No matter how hard you work on it and struggle for perfect pronunciation and the right tone vibration, you never know how it will sound in the end when the film is being shown. This uncertainty makes the heart pound and the voice tremble." Fortunately, after the first syllables, with every word that followed, the fear dissipated. "My voice gradually regained its firmness, and I felt proud and happy like a student of swimming who is left off the leash for the first time and I feel he is asserting himself against the element with his own strength."[8]

Besides the anxiety over sound, she was also forced to carry an extra load of work. To make these multilingual films, completely different casts were usually employed for each language version. In the case of *Hai-Tang*, however, the filmmaker, taking advantage of her remarkable linguistic agility and impeccable work ethic, cast Anna May as the lead in all three versions, opposite different partners in each: In the German version, she paired up with Franz Lederer; in English, with John Longden; and in French, with Robert Ancelin. They were essentially working her like a coolie in a Chinese laundry. When all the filming was done, she was so exhausted that she had to check herself into a sanitorium to rest. Even that was interrupted by the urgent demand for her to make an appearance at the film's premiere.[9]

The three versions of *Hai-Tang*, released within months of each other, received mixed reviews. German critics lauded Anna May's fluency in German—some thought she must have used a double—but were not impressed by her first venture into sound. One reviewer wrote, "Anna May Wong's incredibly subtle and expressive art, enhanced by her exotic appeal, was one of the greatest treasures of the silent film. With deepest regret one cannot help noticing that a lot of this appeal has been lost with the introduction of dialogue." Ernst Jaeger, who had written glowing reviews of her earlier German films, reached a similar conclusion: "Anna May Wong was a silent miracle. Her intellectual diction merely adds curious novelty." Jaeger went on to criticize the production, which was heavily influenced by British prudery: "It is interesting to see how well the producer Eichberg has understood the English mentality: eroticism without sex-appeal, exoticism without miscegenation."[10]

The Anglo-American press was equally lukewarm. *The Bioscope* dissed the film but recognized, with a caveat, the star power of the female lead: "This story can hardly be said to rouse emotions, as all the characters belong to the stage rather than to real life. Anna May Wong gives a very effective performance, in which her grace and skill as a dancer are supplemented by her skill as a vocalist. Her speaking voice has hardly the same appeal." Likewise, the reviewer for the *New York Times* had mixed feelings about the English film: "The stilted dialogue of this version makes the entire production seem unreal and obscures the haunting Oriental beauty of the star, Anna May Wong. Miss Wong is one of the few cinema luminaries able to convey poignant emotion with restraint." And *Variety* noted that "Miss Wong talks flat American."[11]

The French press was more receptive, partly due to the fact that the premiere of *L'Amour Maître des Choses* coincided with the opening of the first luxurious cinema on the Champs-Elysées. Reviewers were impressed with Anna May's "impeccable diction" in a language she hardly knew—a feat that would be accomplished again one day by the Japanese actor Eiji Okada in Alain Resnais's *Hiroshima, Mon Amour* (1959). *Cinémonde* praised the "amazing performance from this beautiful and voluptuous woman, this strangely sincere and fascinating interpreter." Even the *New York Times* spilled ink on the French version of the film, calling it "a production with some interesting interludes" but faulting its vocal recording: "Here and there one hears poorly synchronized songs from Miss Wong and M. Ancelin."[12]

Though a financial flop, the tri-lingual films gave Anna May extensive global coverage. More important, they helped to alleviate her apprehension over the technology of sound. While many actors could not survive the transition, she was able to pull it off in no fewer than three different languages.

Change, however, did not happen just in the film industry. As Anna May flourished in Europe, the world seemed to stand on the verge of a cataclysm. The 1929 stock market crash on Wall Street sent the world economy into a tailspin, causing human misery and social unrest that would unleash some of the darkest forces in modern history. In September 1930, the Nazis became the second largest political party in Germany, overtaking the Communists. The Weimar Republic was on life support. Marlene Dietrich would leave for America, while Leni Riefenstahl would emerge as Hitler's propaganda filmmaker. Given the rise of nativism and fascism, Europe was fast turning into an unfriendly place for the Chinese American star.

Perhaps symbolically, Anna May's last cinematic act during her European sojourn was a rowdy revue. Directed by Adrian Brunel and shot in London, *Elstree Calling* (1930) was a spoof of *The Taming of the Shrew*, put out by the Fairbanks–Pickford team. Clad in a risqué two-piece silver outfit and rattling off cries in Cantonese, Anna May threw car tires, furniture pieces, and shoes down a staircase, also hurling custard pies at her Petruchio. Even when the Bard himself showed up, he received a pie in the face. It was the kind of Shakespearean burlesque that could bring some bittersweet laughter to anxious moviegoers. Adding to the symbolism, the assistant director of the on-screen variety show was none other than Alfred Hitchcock, the future explorer of the human psyche's darkest crevices. According to Graham Hodges, one scene cut from the film showed Hitchcock "plastering Anna May with a pie."[13]

Feeling homesick in London after two and a half years abroad, Anna May did not wait to hear what critics had to say about *Elstree Calling*. In a strange dream one night, she and a female friend stood beneath a willow tree, weeping silently. The image reminded her of a scene in Charlotte Brontë's *Jane Eyre*, a novel she cherished. During the time Jane runs away from Mr. Rochester and is about to make a life-changing decision, she feels a premonition, as if hearing Rochester calling her name in the air, an almost-supernatural occurrence. Jane hurries back to Thornfield, only to find that the estate has burned to the ground and her beloved has been maimed and blinded in the inferno. Since "Willow" was Anna May's Chinese name, she interpreted the dream as a bad omen.[14] Perhaps clairvoyant like Brontë's heroine, or like the soothsayer she would play a few years later in *When Were You Born?*, Anna May quickly opted to sail back home to America.

PART FOUR

Daughter
of the
Dragon

22

ON THE SPOT

WHEN THE FOUR-FUNNELED Cunarder RMS *Aquitania* hove into New York's harbor in late October of 1930, Anna May was astonished to see from the deck that long queues of men were waiting on the street for food and jobs. The bubble of prosperity that had inured the previous decade had now burst; America was in the early throes of the Great Depression. After the 1929 stock market crash and the subsequent failure of 3,600 banks nationwide, millions of people had lost their jobs, in the process sending the unemployment rate up as high as 25 percent. To quote a Chinese saying that would have been familiar to Anna May, "Misery does not travel alone." That summer, a historically severe drought had hit the Southern Plains, killing people, livestock, and crops across the region and leading to a prolonged Dust Bowl era. Unprecedented economic woes had dug deep into the pockets and the conscience of the nation.

Responding in the only way they knew, politicians panicked and turned to protectionism in order to stave off further losses of American jobs. In June, Congress passed the Smoot-Hawley Act, increasing tariffs on foreign imports. Reluctantly signing the bill into law, President Herbert Hoover also proposed a $150 million public works program to create jobs. In September, ground was broken for the Hoover Dam, outside of Las Vegas, a few months before Nevada legalized casino gambling. A former oasis in the desert along the Old Spanish Trail would soon rise as the world's capital of sin and entertainment.

Other headlines of the year 1930 included the discovery in February of the planet Pluto by the American astronomer Clyde Tombaugh. Even though Pluto turned out decades later to be a dwarf planet, the discovery inspired Walt Disney to introduce a new animated character, Pluto, as Mickey Mouse's canine companion. In March, the inventor Clarence Birdseye marketed the first frozen foods, while Babe Ruth signed a two-year contract with the New York Yankees. In May, the Supreme Court ruled against Prohibition, effectively opening the spigot to boost the American spirit, or more functionally to soothe the nerves. In June, a *Chicago Tribune* reporter was gunned down by the henchmen of Al Capone, a killing that once again reminded the public of the ruthless brutality of the gangster boss, who had orchestrated the infamous Saint Valentine's Day Massacre the previous year. Earlier in the month of Anna May's return to America, the Philadelphia Athletics had won their second straight World Series after beating the St. Louis Cardinals 7–1 in Game 6. In the movie world, Jean Harlow just had her first major role in Howard Hughes's *Hell's Angels*. After the film's release in November, the icon of "Blonde Bombshell" was born, charming millions with her platinum hair and irresistible sensuality.

By no means less attractive or less talented, the Chinese American actress who arrived in New York on this October day of 1930 had become a force to be reckoned with. Having left America as a flapper in chic clothing, Anna May returned as a sophisticated woman attired in elegant European fashions and affecting an upper-class British accent and highborn manners. One journalist claimed that Anna could speak Chinese, French, German, and English fluently and could switch easily from one language to the other. She was also particularly fond of American slang. "When the use of Americanisms seems proper in a situation, she discloses an amazing knowledge of the patois," the journalist wrote. "She will use a French or German word if it describes a thing better than another language."[1]

While still crossing the Atlantic, Anna May had received a telegram sent from New York by stage director Lee Ephraim, offering her a lead role in Edgar Wallace's play *On the Spot*. Though little known today, except as the original screenwriter for the classic film *King Kong* (1933), Wallace was the most popular British writer during the interwar years. A master of the thriller and crime genres, Wallace wrote more than 170 books, a thousand short stories, and twenty-three plays. He sold two hundred million copies of his works worldwide in thirty languages. Such a stunning output, sustained by copious amounts of caffeine and cigarettes and frenzied work schedules, was not matched by literary quality, and he was considered something of a hack. George Orwell called Wallace a manufacturer of fairy gold. In 1930, though, he was still at the height of his career, with one out of every four books sold in the United Kingdom bearing his name in the title.[2] In the previous year, after the Saint Valentine's Day Massacre, in which seven of Capone's rivals were brazenly killed in broad daylight, Wallace visited Chicago to scout for material for his new work. He was shown the Hotel Lexington, Capone's headquarters; the flower shop where the crime boss's archrival was "put on the spot"; and the restaurants where warring gangs had settled their scores with machine guns. He was also driven around the old red-light district and the flourishing new bawdy houses in the suburb of Cicero.[3]

Upon his return to England, Wallace wrote the play *On the Spot* in four days, crafting a saga of sex and crime involving a "Scarface"-type character, Tony Perelli, and his Chinese mistress, Minn Lee. Starring Charles Laughton as the gangster boss and Gillian Lind in yellowface as Minn Lee, the British play lasted for 342 performances on its initial run in the West End and became Wallace's greatest theatrical success. Anna May had watched the show in London and even went out to lunch with the portly English playwright. As she recalled the rendezvous, "The exceedingly busy Mr. Wallace, like the eternal beaver he is, could grant me only an hour for lunch. During that time he invented three new plots, two for books and one for a play. He insisted on beginning to work on them at once, knowing that it is always well to follow one path to the end. I'm sure the Son of Heaven had three men in mind when he created Mr. Wallace."[4]

After its successful run in England, the play traveled to America with a new cast. Engaging Anna May, who had made a splash in Europe and commanded a virtual monopoly on lead Oriental roles, would certainly be a boost for the theatrical production. To Anna May, this would be her first appearance in front of the footlights on the legitimate stage in America. Mindful of fame's fickleness and uncertain about Hollywood's reception, despite her overseas successes, Anna May knew the importance of Broadway. Therefore, when Lee Ephraim rushed to the docks to meet her, carrying a script in one hand and a contract in the other, Anna May signed the agreement even before she had cleared customs.[5] And when Ephraim got a bit overzealous as he explained to her the high stakes of the production, Anna May retorted, "Quite true. But one actor does not make a play."[6] At twenty-five, she showed a kind of imperturbability that was equal parts innate personality and affected public persona, a quality quite befitting the character she was going to portray.

A creation of Wallace's pen, Minn Lee is a small and lovely woman "with slanting brown eyes and a rosebud of mouth. Skin—like satin. When you saw it, you felt it. Her hair, not the blue-black of the Oriental but a sheeny black."[7] Born of a white father and a Chinese mother, the half-caste Minn was a Barnard College graduate who carried herself in Chicago's crime underworld like a pristine lotus flower rising out of mud.[8] If the playwright's imagination was obviously tinged with clichés, a *New York Times* critic was no better in calling Anna May "an inscrutably loyal jade."[9] Likewise, during the rehearsal, Ephraim insisted that the Minn character walk "short, hesitant steps," in the manner of a geisha with bound feet, but Anna May reminded the director that the dainty gaits of the geisha were to be found only in Japan. Always bold to speak her mind in the face of ignorance, she was also well versed in the art of colloquy, doling out wisdom in nuggets of flowery diction like a female Charlie Chan. On the opening night of *On the Spot*, when the usual jitteriness was palpable among the crew, Anna May told them, "If the play fails, our work merely goes to the four winds." When the premiere was successful, she said to them, "The gods have indeed been kind to us."[10]

The gods might have been kind to Anna May, but they also had a cruel way of evening out the score. Just as Anna May was receiving a standing ovation at a curtain call in New York on the night of November 11, a tragedy befell her family back on the West Coast. Her mother, Lee Gon Toy, was hit by a car in front of their family laundry on North Figueroa and died from her injuries at the hospital. In those early decades of the twentieth century, most American urban roadways were still designed for foot traffic, not automobiles, leading to a high rate of traffic accidents involving pedestrians. Researchers have reported that between 1930 and 1932 there were sixteen thousand pedestrians killed by cars per year nationwide, accounting for almost 40 percent of all traffic-related deaths (compared to about 14 percent today). According to witnesses, the forty-three-year-old Lee had stepped in front of a passing car driven by a man named Joe Rondini, who was unable to avoid striking her. Anna May's *Jane Eyre* nightmare in London had come to fruition.[11]

In the millennia-old Chinese tradition, it remains every parent's wish that as they lie dying, their children will sit at their deathbed and hold their hand one last time, just as that parent had once held the children's hands when they learned to walk. Anna May was traumatized that she could not be at her mother's bedside. Compounding the situation was the fact that *On the Spot* had just had a phenomenal run. Leaving the show and returning to Los Angeles for the funeral would be disastrous. Painful as it was, the dutiful daughter could not attend the last rites. She had to mourn her mother from afar, just as her dream had foretold—with the girl weeping under the willows, only able to shed silent tears.

23

DAUGHTER OF THE DRAGON

STILL IN MOURNING for her mother while taking daily curtain calls on Broadway, Anna May was tapped by a major Hollywood studio to play the daughter of the most diabolic figure in cinema. In 1931, Paramount had paid a princely $20,000 for the rights to Sax Rohmer's new installment of his popular Fu Manchu series, *The Daughter of Fu Manchu*, and planned to lavish another quarter-million dollars on the film adaptation.[1] This would be Anna May's first American talkie, and, by all accounts, the definitive Anna May Wong picture.

As if pitted in a protracted sumo match, for almost half a century, two Chinese icons sparred for the spotlight in the West's popular imagination. Ostensibly, these two Chinese gentlemen could not be more different: Charlie Chan, a funny, courteous, aphorism-spouting detective, works tirelessly to maintain law and order for mainstream (as in white) America. Inspired by a real-life, bullwhip-wielding Cantonese cop in Honolulu, the fictional Charlie Chan was created by Earl Derr Biggers, a young Ohioan educated at Harvard. Chan is rather like a multilayered Chinese box: He may have slanted eyes and a chubby and inscrutable face, but he prefers Western suits to his traditional garments, drinks sarsaparilla rather than tea, and beguiles friends and foes alike with fortune-cookie Confucianism—his trademark singsong Chinatown blues. One may love him or hate him, but the fact remains that he is a crime fighter, albeit with outlandish manners.

In contrast, Dr. Fu Manchu is an archvillain who epitomizes the East's threat to the West. In the words of his progenitor, the British writer Sax Rohmer, Fu Manchu is a superman with a satanic heart: "Imagine a person, tall, lean and feline, high-shouldered, with a brow like Shakespeare and a face like Satan, a close-shaven skull, and long, magnetic eyes of the true cat-green. Invest him with all the cruel cunning of an entire Eastern race, accumulated in one giant intellect, with all the resources of science past and present, with all the resources, if you will, of a wealthy government."[2] Born in the heyday of the "Yellow Peril" frenzy during the 1910s, Fu Manchu is an agent of the Chinese government who moves about, wraithlike, within the opium dens, subterranean passages, and feral dungeons of the modern metropolis. His feline claws can penetrate the rosy bosom of the pristine English countryside or that cradle of Western democracy, the White House. A scientific wizard with almost unbelievable expertise in chemistry, medicine, engineering, botany, and zoology, he is also an omniscient hypnotist who can control someone's mind for hours or days on end, as well as a skilled linguist who speaks English impecca-

Sessue Hayakawa and Anna May Wong in *Daughter of the Dragon*, 1931 *(Courtesy of Album / Alamy Stock Photo)*

bly but with an odd choice of words. In a nutshell, Dr. Fu Manchu is a menace to what Charlie Chan tries to protect.

Despite their apparent differences, the honorable detective and the evil doctor are two sides of the same coin. They were both figments of the West's unrestrained racial imagination. Rohmer once famously admitted: "I made my name on Fu Manchu because I know nothing about the Chinese. I know something about Chinatown. But that is a different matter."[3] The Chinese supervillain was indeed born out of the cradle of Limehouse fiction and the "Yellow Peril" discourse around the turn of the twentieth century, a will-o'-the-wisp made palpable by racial fantasy and fear. Likewise, Charlie Chan, as I have argued in my earlier book, is an American stereotype of the "Chinaman." Even though the inspiration of a real Chinese detective and his own deep dive into Chinese American history helped Biggers mint a character whose strength and virtue extend well beyond a mere chimera of the Chinaman in Western fantasy, Charlie Chan bears the stamp of his time, a birthmark that encapsulates the racial tensions of the nativist, xenophobic America of the 1920s.[4]

Conjoined, then, in one sense like the Siamese Twins, Fu Manchu and Charlie Chan became almost inseparable in the Anglo-American celluloid realm—each jousting to be the foremost Chinaman. Thus, not so strangely, they were even played by the same actor at times. The evil doctor first appeared on the silver screen in a British silent series, *The Mystery of Dr. Fu Manchu* (1923), starring Harry Agar Lyons. His American debut was a Paramount talkie, *The Mysterious Dr. Fu Manchu* (1929), featuring Warner Oland. Having played Oriental villains in half a dozen silent films, as well as the Jewish cantor in *The Jazz Singer*, Oland delivered a rather convincing performance of the evil Chinese doctor. After repeating the baddy role in *The Return of Dr. Fu Manchu* in 1930, Oland was hired by Fox to play Charlie Chan, the good guy. In the previous year, the adaptation of Biggers's third Charlie Chan novel, *Behind That Curtain*, had been a flop. In that hour-long talkie, Chan, played by a balding, San Francisco–born Edward Park, appears for no more than a minute. Despite the debacle, the producers at Fox perceived the enormous promise held by the charming, exotic Chinese character. Having secured the rights to Biggers's new novel, they decided to try Oland, the man who had been the face of Fu Manchu. Premiering in February of 1931, *Charlie Chan Carries On* showcased a Chinese hero with suave manners, a singsong voice, and a bellyful of witticisms that are both enlightening and befuddling. Due to his vaguely Asiatic features, Oland needed no elaborate makeup, and his habit of sneaking a few behind-the-scene nips put a perennial grin on his face and slurred his speech almost to a perfect pitch for a character who speaks broken English. The film was a smashing success. The audience could not get enough of Oland/Chan's pearls of wisdom sprinkled throughout the film, "Only a very brave mouse will make its nest in a cat's ear," "He who feeds the chicken deserves the egg," and "Only a very sly man can shoot off a cannon quietly."

Riding on his success as the wisecracking Chinese sleuth, Oland was about to sail for Hawaii to make a new, on-location Chan flick, *The Black Camel*, when Paramount offered him $12,000 for cameoing in the third Fu Manchu installment. He would team up with Anna May, his costar in *Old San Francisco*, and Sessue Hayakawa, the Japanese Rip van Winkle who had disappeared from Hollywood for twelve years. As its title indicates, *Daughter of the Dragon* was less about the sinister doctor than his female progeny, who has inherited his diabolical power but is far more dangerous with her bewitching beauty and serpentine cunning.

In Rohmer's potent racial imagination, the daughter of Fu Manchu possesses "the uncanny power which Homer gave to Circe, of stealing men's souls." Fah Lo Suee is her name, meaning "sweet perfume," for she wears a faint perfume, which is more an aura than a physical fact. Here is how Sax Rohmer—a pseudonym that suggests an errant Saxon knight on a quixotic quest—describes the witchlike woman from the East: "A delicately slender hand it was, nurtured in indolence—an unforgettable hand, delicious yet repellant, with pointed, varnished nails; a cultured hand possessing the long, square-jointed thumb of domination; a hand cruel for all its softness as the velvet paw of a tigress." Walking stealthily like a cat in a pair of soft, loose slippers, she has a silvery voice and a slender body that retains its "ivory" illusion. Exceeding her father's power as a hypnotist, she can cast spells on a man or a woman with her jade-green eyes and listen to the other's thinking, sort of wiretapping inside the head. She can also leave detailed post-hypnotic instructions to be carried out by the person under her influence. To complete her profile, she smokes cigarettes from a long, enameled holder, which she wields like a dragon lady's scepter.[5]

None of her past roles had sufficiently prepared Anna May for such a character. The Mongol slave in *The Thief of Bagdad* might have been duplicitous, but she was less a villainess than a victim, abused by her mistress and subservient to her Mongol prince. The same was true of her role as a gangster's daughter in *Old San Francisco*. In *Piccadilly*, Shosho was a simple, unabashed hedonist, a seductress with no malice, only ambition for career success. Under

Rohmer's pen, however, Fah Lo Suee is more cyborg than human. She is devoid of the kind of humanity saturating Anna May's previous roles. To bring such a character to life on screen, then, would be quite a challenge, an acting job requiring unusual skills that perhaps only the fabled Daughter of the Dragon might possess.

Taking much liberty with Rohmer's original novel, *Daughter of the Dragon* begins at a revue theater in London, where the exotic dancer Ling Moy (Wong) has just wrapped up her closing act for the season. She is excited to learn that her father has arrived in the city, but she does not know his real identity, this being Dr. Fu Manchu (Oland). Presumably already dead for twenty years after he terrorized London, Fu now returns to finish up his revenge killing of the Petrie family—to "clean the slate," so to speak. After he drugs the elder Petrie and controls his mind, he speaks to his victim in a florid diction that could easily have rolled off the tongue of Oland's Charlie Chan: "In the twenty years I have fought to live, the thought of killing you and your son has been my dearest nurse." He kills the father and is mortally wounded in his follow-up attempt on the son, Ronald. On his deathbed, Fu reveals his identity to Ling Moy and regrets that he has no son who can carry on and settle the debt with the Petries, "Gods of my ancestors—if only thou had granted me another son!"

And here comes the metamorphosis, a radical transformation that turns Madame Butterfly into Dragon Lady, a character type Anna May would forever be known for. Realizing her true identity, Ling Moy immediately offers to inherit the family mantle: "The blood is mine. The hate is mine. The vengeance shall be mine." She also undergoes a gender transition, at least in spirit, as she vows, "Father! Father! I will be your son! I will be your son!" In response, the father no longer addresses her as "my flower daughter," but instead as "man-daughter." He implores her, "Swear, man-daughter, to deliver the soul of Ronald Petrie to me, to our ancestors!" Afterward, he simply calls her "my son." The variations of address may seem like something called for by the plot, justified by a patriarch's dying wish and his progeny's eagerness to please, but the impromptu role-play triggers a more profound change in Anna May's character—or, more precisely, her characterization.

To keep her promise of vengeance, she needs to seduce not one but two men: the blond Ronald, whom she promises to kill, and Ah Kee (Hayakawa), a Chinese detective tasked to protect Ronald. In the first cat-and-mouse game, Ling Moy affects some Madame Butterfly wiles to ensnare the white man. When Ronald begs her to "chuck everything and stay," she replies, "If I stayed, would my hair ever become golden curls, and my skin ivory, like Ronald's?" It may sound like an expression by someone who feels racially inferior—and there is a kernel of truth to it, because she repeatedly hesitates to execute her plot to kill him, partly due to her lingering feelings for the white man with golden curls and ivory skin. But these words are mostly uttered to fuel his fire and thereby give her psychological advantage over this British toff, who responds eagerly, "Strange, I prefer yours. I shall never forget your hair and eyes." Stoking his ardor, she secretly plots his demise. As she confides to an ally, "I am giving him a beautiful illusion. Which I shall crush." Her cruelty is revealed after she and her aides—called Dacoits in Rohmer's original, essentially a pack of sub-human cutthroats—are ready to torture and kill Ronald and his fiancée, Joan. Demonstrating the corrosiveness of the acid she plans to use on Joan's face, she tells Roland gleefully, "My vengeance is inspired tonight. You will first have the torture of seeing her beauty eaten slowly away by this hungry acid." When he begs for mercy, she hisses, "Very well, Ling Moy is merciful." She hands him a knife and barks, "Kill her!"[6]

In her manipulation of Ah Kee, Ling Moy shows the same kind of duplicity but deploys different tactics. Exploiting his infatuation, Ling Moy lures Ah Kee away from Ronald and keeps him occupied while her accomplices abduct Ronald and Joan. She has Ah Kee put on a Chinese robe, and she entertains him like a courtesan, plucking a traditional Chinese pipa (lute) and singing in Cantonese dialect. Totally besotted, Ah Kee kneels in front of her and worships her like a goddess. He begs her to go to China with him, totally unaware either of her real identity or her evil intentions.

With one man at her feet and another at her fingertips, Ling Moy appears as a monstrous female figure who, like Lady Macbeth, cloaks an almost masculine pride in her ability to double-cross and to execute a murderous plot. These gender-bending qualities have led some scholars to argue that Anna May was "cross-dressing" in the film as a man. As Graham Hodges suggests, "Ling Moy's roles switch between male and female characteristics and blur binary differences between the sexes. Even Anna May's female outfits were powerfully cut and mannish and provide coded meaning to homosexual viewers."[7] Or, to borrow the term from Lady Macbeth, they "unsex" her (*Macbeth* 1.5).

The initial reactions to Anna May's newly minted dragon-lady persona were somewhat muted. After the release in August 1931, the *New York Times* gave the top-billing actress a lukewarm compliment, "Miss Wong does quite well in some of her scenes." The reviewer was more impressed by the lavish sets with dragons on the walls, secret panels, and other ersatz-Oriental decor befitting a Fu Manchu lair. *Variety* found faults with the performance, calling the dialogue "mostly amateurish and inept."[8] Many critics were troubled by Hayakawa's heavy Japanese accent. A master of theatrical miming during the silent era, he sounded in a talkie like someone in a losing wrestling match with spoken English. Worse yet, his lines were often more suitable for the stage than the screen, such as: "It is the triumph of irony that the only woman I have ever deeply loved should be born of the blood that I loathe," suggesting that critics were wrongly blaming the actor rather than the clumsy screenwriter. In the last line of the film, as he gently caresses the long hair of Fu Manchu's dead daughter, he says, "Flower Ling Moy, a flower need not love, but only be loved. As Ah Kee loved you." It is as if a technician had suddenly turned on the soundtrack of *Broken Blossoms*, bringing the once-muted soundscape to hyper-melodramatic life in a Hollywood Oriental fantasy.

All these highly stylized dialogues, sets, and actions combined to accentu-ate the image of the dragon lady. A quote from the crowd-sourced *Urban Dic-tionary* would suffice to show how Anna May's Ling Moy provides a definitive profile in the popular imagination: "A 'dragon lady' was a woman of Asian heritage who was thought of as being sexually powerful and generally of a cunning, underhanded, conniving nature, who would use her beauty and sex-uality to get what she wanted. Often accompanied in fiction with an opium pipe, jade jewelry, and wearing a Chinese dress, usually with dragons on it. They were usually depicted as snide, assertive, aggressive, sneaky, and explo-sive in temperament."[9] Undoubtedly, it was the film *Daughter of the Dragon* that introduced *dragon lady* into the English lexicon. In March 1938, *Look* magazine crowned Anna May as "The World's Most Beautiful Chinese Girl." The fea-ture article described her glamour and fashion sense, while the cover image showed her with a sinister gaze as she holds a blood-stained dagger. In its 1961 obituary of Anna May, *Time* magazine eschewed the loaded term of *dragon lady* but apparently implied it when the journal labeled Wong "the screen's foremost Oriental villainess," another throwback to the infamous *Daughter of the Dragon*.

Anna May's apotheosis as a dragon lady would draw the ire of some racially sensitive viewers and historians. They vilified her for helping to create stereo-typical Asian women by performing roles that "call for stylized and patterned displays, requiring less in the way of acting than a series of directed Oriental affectations."[10] This kind of criticism would later be leveled at Nancy Kwan in *China Doll*, Michelle Yeoh in *Tomorrow Never Dies*, or Lucy Liu in *Charlie's Angels* and *Kill Bill*, for their ostensible perpetuation of the dragon lady stereotype. In her self-defense, Anna May confessed to a Hollywood reporter, "When a person is trying to get established in a profession, he can't choose parts. He has to take what is offered."[11] Such a reality check never succeeded in dispelling the disparaging views. More than eighty years later, Lucy Liu, facing the same critique, would supply the same answer—that she did not have much choice. Not surprisingly, it did not quiet her detractors, either.[12] To better understand the iconography of the dragon lady as fashioned by Anna May, we need to open a different line of inquiry.

By condemning the stereotypical performance, most critics, as Cynthia Liu has rightly pointed out, seem to assume that the primary task of film is mimesis, to reproduce the world as is. But film, either as an art or as a technology, never records reality as it is found. In his *Film as Art*, Rudolf Arnheim reminds us that "people who contemptuously refer to the camera as an automatic recording machine must be made to realize that even in the simplest photographic reproduction of a perfectly simple object, a feeling for its nature is required which is quite beyond any mechanical operation."[13] Siegfried Kracauer, perhaps the most ardent apologist for this medium's photographic nature and realist aesthetics, also stresses the indexical rather than the iconic dimension of film. From closeup shots of the silent era to bullet time in the digital age, traditional models of representation have given way to what film historian Miriam Hansen calls "the reign of simulation."[14] Likewise, Anna May's impersonation of Ling Moy should be understood as a performative, not simply mimetic, act. In her essay "The Art of Screen Passing," Chinese American scholar Yiman Wang situates Anna May's career in the context of art deco in America, a popular trend that surfaced in the first few decades of the twentieth century that affected all aspects of design. Wang considers the practice of yellowface to be a component of the art deco aesthetic, because it "provides a vehicle within which whites can play out a fantasy of otherness." The audience was drawn to a simulation of reality rather than a realistic representation, for the escape from realism and history was consistent with the art deco aesthetic, "which decontextualizes icons and objects and repackages them for decorative purposes."[15] It is symptomatic, then, that the *New York Times* reviewer was more enthused by the film sets than the performance in *Daughter of the Dragon*.

Within such an elaborately Oriental setting, Anna May, as Wang argues, performed "screen passing," by which she means Wong's "ability to act and overact in a wide range of racialized roles, by which she brings to the fore the stereotypical and Orientalist underpinnings of these roles."[16] In other words, Anna May drew attention to or even exploded the stereotype by overacting these roles. A comparison with another controversial actor of the 1930s would help shed light on this thorny issue. Once the best-known and most successful Black actor in Hollywood, Stepin Fetchit played characters who exploited all the clichés about a so-called nitwit negro. In *Charlie Chan in Egypt* (1935), for instance, Fetchit portrays Snowshoes, a fez-wearing, hookah-puffing, and superstitious Black servant who harbors a native sentiment toward life on postbellum Southern plantations. His characterization is so overblown, flashy, and exaggerated that, as film critic Ken Hanke put it, "the very stereotypical images they ostensibly represent become mocked by the format in which they are confined. . . . One might go so far as to make the case that Stepin Fetchit was subversively antistereotypical."[17] As the film scholar Donald Bogle suggests in his classic study of Black film history, the essence of blackface or yellowface is not found in the racial stereotype itself but rather in "what certain talented actors have done with the stereotype," or what they have accomplished with even stereotyped roles.[18] In the same vein, what Anna May achieved with the dragonlady persona and other roles was sharing with her audiences the thrill of being part of what might be deeply shameful, an almost illicit pleasure. The goal of such a performance is to expose the stereotypes as human construction rather than simple mimesis.[19]

Such a delicate dance between stereotype and imagination, convention and subversion, has made Anna May both revered and reviled in Asian American history. Between Madame Butterfly and the Dragon Lady, there lies the alluring art through which Anna May Wong continues to haunt us all.

24

SHANGHAI EXPRESS

WHILE THE SPECTERS of the insidious Dr. Fu Manchu and his diabolical daughter continued to resonate in the West, the "Yellow Peril" would soon find a more menacing manifestation in the real world.

On September 18, 1931, just days after the release of *Daughter of the Dragon*, Japanese troops, using the pretext of an explosion along the Southern Manchurian Railway, attacked the Chinese city of Mukden (Shenyang). With Fu Manchurian cunning, a cabal of renegade officers from the Imperial Japanese Army had concocted a plot to destroy the rail track and blame it on Chinese brigands, in much the same way that the Germans would invade Poland on a *casus belli* in 1939. Mukden fell in just one day, with the loss of five hundred Chinese lives. By January 1932, Japan's military takeover of China's three northeastern provinces was complete. In March, Japan established its puppet state of Manchukuo and installed Puyi, the former emperor of China, as the figurehead of state. Long before the official start of World War II, the Mukden Incident would provide the initial salvo for a protracted, fourteen-year world war in Asia.

The Japanese aggression sparked worldwide condemnation. After the League of Nations released the Lytton Report and exposed the Japanese deception, Japan found itself diplomatically isolated and withdrew from the league. The invasion of Manchuria was so barbaric that it prompted Anna May, not a political activist by any means, to pen an opinion piece entitled "Manchuria" for Rob Wagner's *Beverly Hills Script*. In the article, echoing Bertrand Russell's

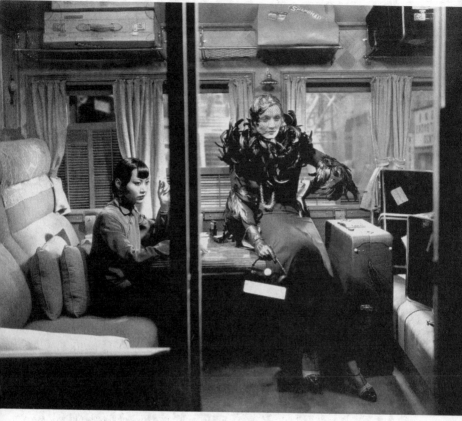

Anna May Wong and Marlene Dietrich in *Shanghai Express*, 1932 *(Courtesy of Everett Collection)*

analysis, she drew a stark contrast between China's ancient, patient wisdom and the modern, aggressive, and bellicose culture of Japan:

> Never has the world so felt the need of spiritual rejuvenation to relieve it of the weariness of the whirl and clock of machines and the nerve-strain of speed and crushing size. Thus we are witnessing the greatest renaissance in history, which will culminate in a new interest and happiness in the philosophy of life. Just as fate destined the exquisite lotus to bloom above polluted torrents, thus, despite the iron heel of Japan, will the

endangered bud of Chinese culture bloom forth in its consummate moral purity and spiritual elegance above the mire of blood and destruction.[1]

Expressing a wish that China could rise above this plane of blood and destruction, these words in some ways served as a philosophical manifesto for Anna May, who would now appear in a major film about war-torn China. Produced by Adolph Zukor and directed by Josef von Sternberg, *Shanghai Express* has a storyline full of brigands, train robbers, torture, rape, murder, and garden varieties of moral decay.

As a so-called China flick, *Shanghai Express* becomes part of the enduring Hollywood tradition of casting a white actress, yellowface or not, in the exotic setting of faraway China. Earlier we had Alla Nazimova in *The Red Lantern*, and the 1930s brought Myrna Loy in *The Mask of Fu Manchu* (1932), Barbara Stanwyck in *The Bitter Tea of General Yen* (1933), and Luise Rainer in *The Good Earth* (1937), to name just a few. Likewise, Sternberg's new film was a star vehicle—not for Anna May but for his own "discovery" and new German import, Marlene Dietrich.

Dietrich's breakaway film, *The Blue Angel* (1930), made in Berlin and directed by Sternberg, had become in only a few years a rousing success and a cultural classic in its own time. But the rise of nationalism changed the social dynamics of Germany and Europe at large. In his memoir, Sternberg, a Vienna-born Jew, recalls the censorship of *The Blue Angel* in the Nazi era: "The Germans did not then consider the film to be German in essence. When he became Lord High Executioner, Adolf Hitler ordered the negative and all but one copy to be destroyed." Curiously enough, Hitler would repeatedly screen the remaining copy and secretly considered it to be his favorite film.[2] This anecdote speaks not only to the lure of the film or the perversion of the Führer, but also to the irresistible charisma of the lead actress whose legs, as Peter Gay puts it, embody the Weimar Zeitgeist as palpably as the Bauhaus buildings, Kandinsky's abstractions, and Rilke's *Duino Elegies*.[3]

Fleeing Germany, Dietrich arrived in Los Angeles in 1931, beginning there her permanent exile in America. In the ensuing years, she would reject repeated overtures from the Führer, who tried to lure her back to make films for him, as her rival, Leni Riefenstahl, did. Dietrich would eventually renounce her German citizenship and become a naturalized citizen of the United States, while

Riefenstahl ascended to infamy as "Hitler's camerawoman." Thus, two of the three women in that memorable Eisenstaedt portrait from the 1928 Berlin Press Ball were reunited in Hollywood. Renewing their friendship, they would make a major film for Sternberg, the quirky, imperious savant.

Like Walt Disney's Magic Kingdom, the exotic China of Sternberg's *Shanghai Express* was created out of cardboard and fantasy. Borrowing some footage taken by James Howe during his trip to China in 1928, the film was mostly shot on a railway set built in California's San Bernardino Valley. Haunted by the Mojave Desert just beyond the mountains and devastated by the hot dry Santa Ana winds, the valley was always, as Joan Didion termed it, "an alien place."[4] Recalling this supposedly halcyon era, Sternberg describes how the production team conjured up a Middle Kingdom in a harsh landscape: "A China was built of papier-mâché and into it we placed slant-eyed men, women, and children, who seemed to relish being part of it. We borrowed a train from the Santa Fe, painted it white, and added an armored car to carry Chinese soldiers with fixed bayonets." Every detail was carefully thought out. They even raised a cow and had it give birth to a calf. When the camera was ready to roll, Sternberg had the cow nourish its calf near noisy railroad tracks, "so that it would be undisturbed by clanging bells and hooting whistles when my train came along through the crowded streets to be stopped by an animal suckling its young."[5]

Dietrich's daughter, Maria Riva, only seven at the time, was allowed to accompany her mother to the film sets. In a biography about her diva mother—her "Mutti"—Riva gives us a close-up of how the famous opening scenes of *Shanghai Express* were manufactured in the San Bernardino Valley: "A dreary railroad yard, deserted except for a few lonely Pullman wagons and . . . suddenly, CHINA! Bustling, frantic, hot, dusty, crowded, milling, scurrying, overpopulated China. Chickens, goats, paper lanterns, straw-hatted coolies, ragged urchins, scrawny dogs, bags, trunks, crates, and boxes, roped parcels in all shapes and sizes. Above, a sea of banners, long, narrow white cloth panels painted with Chinese letters." In the midst of this dramatic chaos, Maria saw a real train with its huge black locomotive belching steam, and high atop it appeared Sternberg, a little man who was busy painting white shadows onto the train. It seemed that Mother Nature had dealt Sternberg a personal affront by refusing to supply clouds that day, but, "undaunted, he was painting his own."[6]

As usual, the several hundred Chinese extras were recruited from Los

Angeles's Chinatown; some of them were Anna May's old friends or neighbors, including James Leong, who had continued acting to subsidize his dream of producing more Chinese films. Tom Gubbins, dubbed the "Mayor of Chinatown," worked as the film's interpreter to translate the director's instructions for the Chinese extras and help Warner Oland, playing a half-caste character, to ad-lib a few singsong lines as the occasion demanded. After plenty of practice as Charlie Chan and Fu Manchu, Oland could now pass so easily that an old Chinese man who had never worked in a film thought Oland was genuinely Chinese. Through the interpreter, the old man asked Oland whether he was from Canton, because he looked like a boy he had known there many years earlier.[7] Such a friendly rapport between total strangers was thematically perfect for a film that featured an eclectic group of globetrotting travelers boarding a train in Peking on what would be a harrowing and unforgettable journey to Shanghai.

Among these passengers is Shanghai Lily (Dietrich), a notorious "coaster" who lives by her wits along the China coast. Symbolizing the modern, decadent West, she arrives at the swarming train station in an automobile, sporting a vampish black gown, a veil, and a feather boa. In contrast, Hui Fei (Wong), a reformed Chinese prostitute on her way to Shanghai to live a respectable life, arrives at the scene in a palanquin, clad in a loose cheongsam. Their first glances at each other set up a dynamic between the two women that will enliven, like electrical currents, the film. As one reviewer wrote, "They look at each other, neither intently nor curiously, but in that look, the attitude each takes to life finds its perfect and complete expression."[8]

The unusual chemistry between the two stars extended beyond the screen. Once again, through the innocent eyes of Dietrich's seven-year-old daughter, we can sense their cozy intimacy—if not, as some have suggested, sapphic love. As Riva recalls, "Anna May Wong and my mother became chummy. Between takes, they talked, not rehearsing their scenes, just soft conversation, smoked, sipped cool coffee through their straws. My mother fussed over Miss Wong's square bangs and had Travis redesign one of her kimonos so it would be more flattering. She liked Miss Wong much better than her leading man."[9] Sometimes the two would simply relax together in Dietrich's grand dressing room, listening to Richard Tauber's records on a gramophone—Dietrich had a sizable collection of work by Tauber, her favorite crooner—just as Shanghai Lily and Hui Fei would do in their shared compartment on the Shanghai Express.[10] Such intimacy fed persistent speculations about Anna May's sexual orientation, especially since the Blonde Venus was openly bisexual. As Donald Spoto describes it in his biography, "Dietrich openly discussed her casual amours, which included men from film studios with whom she spent an occasional night, actors from the theater who she thought required a little attention, and those like Anna May Wong and Tilly Losch, who were clever, amusing and exotic companions."[11] In fact, Dietrich was not alone in counting Anna May as her lesbian lover. Dolores del Rio, the Hispanic actress who would one day be immortalized next to Anna May in a public-square shrine on Hollywood Boulevard, was also said to number Wong, besides Henry Fonda and Orson Welles, among her paramours.[12]

In *Shanghai Express*, Shanghai Lily's love interest is Captain Donald Harvey (Clive Brook), a British medical officer, with whom she had a fling five years ago and who still burns a torch for her. In the midst of all the intrigues of civil war, espionage, kidnapping, and killing, the rapprochement of Shanghai Lily and her Doc constitutes a major thread of the plot. Off-screen, though, as Riva reveals, Dietrich was not fond of her leading man, who turned out to be a predictably wooden type: "a photogenic jaw, British, and little else."[13]

Thrown into the mix was Warner Oland as Henry Chang, a Chinese warlord traveling incognito, a degenerate who covets both Shanghai Lily and Hui Fei. A half-caste, Chang was born of a white father and a Chinese mother. Later in the film, someone queries his ethnicity: "I can't make head or tail out of you, Mr. Chang—are you Chinese or white or what are you?" Unlike Chris Buckwell, Oland's other half-caste character in *Old San Francisco*, who hides his Chinese identity and passes for white, Chang admits, "I'm not proud of my white blood." His racial self-hatred plays out in his hostility toward all of the white characters aboard the train: Sam Salt, an American peddler of knockoff jewelry; a Frenchman dishonorably discharged from the army but still wearing a uniform to disguise his disgraceful past; a German opium smuggler posing as a coal baron; a missionary with a hypocritical sense of morality; and Mrs. Haggerty, a querulous boardinghouse owner desperate to keep up her façade of respectability. It seems that everyone has a secret, giving credence to what David Selznick once said about Sternberg's films: They all dealt with completely fake people in wholly fake situations. Only Shanghai Lily and Hui Fei, two women of apparent ill repute, live carefree by their charm, wits, and grit. The former speaks one line that encapsulates the disposition of a femme fatale: "It took more than one man to change my name to Shanghai Lily." The latter, by giving the pompous, Cockney-accented Mrs. Haggerty a sardonic putdown, reveals a soul comfortable in her own skin: "I must confess I don't quite know the standard of respectability that you demand in your boardinghouse, Mrs. Haggerty."

Carrying such a motley cast of passengers, Sternberg's hand-painted Shanghai Express chugs precariously through the maelstrom of wartime China. Using a Chinese-character clock as a timekeeper, the story unfolds like a murder mystery that has to be solved by a supersleuth before the train reaches its destination. Every time the train stops, the drama turns, comically at times and violently at others. Barely clearing Peking, the express is halted by a cow tethered to the tracks with a suckling calf, attended by a peasant vociferously bickering with the engineers while gently coaxing the animals out of the way. At the next stop, government troops order everyone off the train for inspection and they arrest a Chinese fellow, later identified as Chang's right-hand man. In the midst of the commotion, Chang sends a telegram to his rebel forces, informing them of the arrest and ordering the hijack of the train. At midnight, rebels ambush the train at a remote station, killing all the government soldiers onboard. Chang now reveals his true identity and changes into a military outfit. After interrogating each of the foreign passengers, Chang decides to hold Captain Harvey hostage to exchange for his own lieutenant. He then makes advances to Shanghai Lily but is rebuffed. Frustrated, Chang satisfies his bestial craving by violating Hui Fei. In revenge, Hui Fei kills Chang with a dagger. With the rebel leader dead, the train rumbles on, arriving in Shanghai without further ado.

The railroad journey might have set a good tempo for the plot, but Sternberg was never known to be a zippy storyteller. He was far more interested in making love to his star with the camera. Every time Dietrich's character appears on-screen, she is almost always shot full frame, as if every gesture, look, or word was loaded with significance. Under special lighting, Dietrich's face glowed in the dark like a silver moon, and her "limp, wispy hair took on thickness, life, and incredible sheen."[14] It might have just been a rumor, but it was said that real gold dust, instead of Sternberg's butterfly lights, was sprinkled in Dietrich's hair to create those starry sparkles. But it was certainly true that Paramount had insured Dietrich's legs with Lloyd's of London for a million dollars.[15] Such an obsession with megastars drew the ire of the critics. A reviewer for *Vanity Fair* wrote that Sternberg "traded his open style for fancy play, chiefly upon the legs in silk, and buttocks in lace, of Dietrich, of whom he has made a Paramount slut. By his own token, Sternberg is a man of meditation as well as a man of action; but instead of contemplating the navel of Buddha his umbilical perseverance is fixed on the navel of Venus."[16] Not everyone, however, was offended by Sternberg's penchant for visual luxury and highly stylized performances. Ayn Rand, the patron saint of libertarianism, once told Sternberg that rarely had any film so impressed her as *Shanghai Express*. When pressed for a reason, Rand spoke of a scene that was unforgettable to her: "The way the wind blows through the fur-piece around Marlene's shoulder when she sits on the back platform of the train!"[17]

Next to the aura of the Blonde Venus, Anna May held her ground quite well, as her character commands a force field of her own in the film. While Shanghai Lily prances around like a dressage mare in heat, Hui Fei plays solitaire and smokes cigarettes alone, minding her own business. Shanghai Lily may speak some clever lines, but it is Hui Fei who delivers the most hardboiled quips in the film. In fact, on the occasions of their *bon mots*, their respective roles as lead and support are often reversed, with Shanghai Lily setting things up for Hui Fei to deliver the punch. In one scene, when Captain Harvey is held hostage by Chang and Shanghai Lily despairs over his plight, Hui Fei asks, "When are we leaving?" Shanghai Lily has a proverbial blonde moment, as she replies, "I wish I knew. I suppose as soon as Captain Harvey comes down."

"If he's up there," Hui Fei deadpans, "he may never come down."

After Hui Fei kills Chang and saves everyone, Shanghai Lily says, "I don't know if I ought to be grateful to you or not." Hui Fei replies in a sultry voice, with the steely firmness of Fu Manchu's daughter (or a gun moll in a classic noir film), "It's of no consequence. I didn't do it for you. Death canceled his debt to me."

It is worth emphasizing that, in this saga, with all its guns, armies, and imperial powers, no one has the power or will to change the course of history, except for the lowly prostitute who has the courage to take down a supervillain to settle a personal account. In other words, Hui Fei is the real engine driving the Shanghai Express.

Released on February 17, 1932, the film received mixed reviews but did well at the box office, grossing more than $1.5 million worldwide. It was nominated for Academy Awards in three categories—Best Picture, Best Director, and Best Cinematography; Lee Garmes took home the Oscar in the last category. Most film historians agree that if there had been a category at that time for Best Supporting Actress, Anna May would have been the strongest contender that year.[18] While Hui Fei collects the $20,000 bounty for Chang's head, Anna May earned only $6,000 for the film, merely a fraction of Dietrich's salary of

$78,166. Paramount did not only lowball Anna May—for her top-billing role in *Daughter of the Dragon* a year earlier, her salary was also $6,000, whereas her costars Oland earned $12,000 and Hayakawa $10,000. More frustratingly, the studio also refused to give her a contract after her sparkling performance in *Shanghai Express*.

As Hollywood plunged into the Golden Age of the 1930s, Anna May's Tinseltown fortune was merely chugging along, like a train without a destination.

25

To Be Kissed, or Not

Curiously, the stock market crash of 1929 and the Great Depression of the 1930s turned out to be good fortune for American filmmakers. Long rebuked and vilified as hell-bent subverters of middle-class values, Hollywood Babylonians saw the heavenly gates swing open under the sheer forces of social and economic devastation. A depression-wracked nation yearned for distraction and entertainment, and filmmakers were ready to provide a cinematic salve. Having successfully transitioned to sound, the industry was maturing, with new genres forming, new stars being born, and studios achieving extraordinary power. The movies would continue to rise in popularity and influence until 1946, when theater attendance reached its all-time peak before the arrival of television.[1]

Laws of nature, however, dictate that, to reach the top, one has to hit bottom first. Even la-la land was not depression-proof. Trouble in paradise began when nearly a third of theaters nationwide were shuttered and admission prices fell by a third in 1933. Half of the eight major studios were in financial disarray that year: Paramount, the famous house that Adolph Zukor built (and Anna May's lifeboat), sank into bankruptcy; RKO and Universal were in receivership; Fox underwent a major overhaul and would be taken over by a much smaller company, Twentieth Century. It was no surprise, then, that Paramount, already a broken ship at the time of *Shanghai Express*'s release, was unable to offer the biggest Chinese star a new contract.

Without stable employment, Anna May became footloose again. Between

1932 and 1935, she crossed the Atlantic Ocean many times, acted in half a dozen films, and appeared in revues all over Europe and North America.

When she was still finishing up *Shanghai Express*, Anna May signed a contract with World Wide Pictures, a small Hollywood studio, to play the female lead in a Sherlock Holmes adaptation. World Wide Pictures, the American distributor of her breakaway British film *Piccadilly*, also would soon fall victim to the hard times hitting the industry, and *A Study in Scarlet*, made in 1933, was its final production. Inspired by Arthur Conan Doyle's eponymous novella about the supremely deductive and eccentric resident at London's 221B Baker Street, the film has virtually nothing to do with the original plot except for a sentence spoken by the supersleuth: "There's the scarlet thread of murder running through the colorless skein of life, and our duty is to unravel it, and expose every inch of it."[2] Adopting that line as the epigraph, the film shows a series of murders involving a secret society, the Scarlet Ring, which holds meetings in a deserted building in Limehouse. Reginald Owen played Sherlock Holmes, a role coveted by many aspiring actors due to the immense popularity of the character. In fact, Clive Brook, the male lead in *Shanghai Express*, had impersonated the detective in the first Sherlock Holmes "talkie" in 1929, and he was reprising the role in a new adaptation produced by Paramount in late 1932, apparently in competition with *A Study in Scarlet*. It seems that global audiences could not get enough of the hijinks of the cocaine-addicted, violin-playing detective.

Cast in a smaller production by an impoverished studio, Anna May cameoed as Mrs. Pyke, an elegantly dressed widow who puts on a façade of respectability and sophistication but is actually in cahoots with the mastermind of the murderous ring. When playing second fiddle in *Shanghai Express*, Anna May was costumed more plainly in order to supply a contrast for the domineering Dietrich. Now cast as the female lead, each of her appearances was choreographed like a walk down the runway at a Milan fashion show, even though her entire screen time is no more than eight minutes. Speaking with an upper-class British accent, Anna May's character constantly switches wardrobes that range from a double-breasted tweed coat accompanied by a soft slouching hat to an evening pantsuit evoking a Shanghai motif, to a satin gown with wide sleeves that she wears while holding a cigarette à la Bogart. As Anthony Chan aptly puts it in *Perpetually Cool*, it seemed that *A Study in Scarlet* "was merely a showcase for Anna May Wong's modeling talents."[3]

Anna May Wong in her coolie hat, displaying golden, gem-studded nail guards, 1934 *(Courtesy of Everett Collection)*

This focus on Anna May's wardrobe signaled an interesting turn in her career and would contribute to her enduring legacy as a fashion icon. Ever since her first starring role in *The Toll of the Sea*, the camera had always loved the Chinese actress who could wear any costume like her second skin, and *Piccadilly* extended the romance. After a decade of acting and a long sojourn in European metropoles, Anna May had developed a keen sense of fashion, intuiting astutely that the essence of celebrity is as much skein as skin. As she once said to a German reporter, "You can forgive a woman for a face that is not beautiful more easily than for a dress that isn't."[4] When good parts were hard to get, she found other ways to make herself visible and continued to project her star power via fashion, both on and off the screen.

In late 1931, after Anna May returned from Europe, she delivered the equivalent of a present-day TED Talk on makeup before an adoring audience of three hundred women in San Francisco. Sponsored by the *San Francisco Chronicle*, the program announced that the film star would lecture on "her theory of what actually constituted Oriental beauty," "the fine points of Celestial comeliness," and "the feminine preparations for the stage and the street."[5] In her talk, Anna May spoke of her own starstruck childhood and her first encounter with makeup, which involved Chinese red paper, white rice powder, and "a board of burned matches." She then gave advice on daily work and street cosmetics, and her counsel simply boiled down to three rules: "Use powder the exact shade of the skin, blend color with powder with the utmost care, and use makeup so that it will be as inconspicuous as possible."[6] Turning herself into a fashion icon with expertise on makeup eventually paid off. In 1934, the Mayfair Mannequin Society of New York named Wong "The World's Best Dressed Woman." It was an honor that surely brought her much consolation, if not income, when major studios continued to snub her.

In 1934, after *A Study in Scarlet*, Anna May went to England and starred in three films. The first, *Tiger Bay*, is a noirish tale with a touch of the Western. Originally set in London's notorious Limehouse, it was relocated to an unspecified South American port due to British censorship. In the native quarters of Tiger Bay, a slum full of the riffraff of the seven seas, Lui Chang (Wong) runs a popular nightclub with tastefully exotic Chinese decor. A local gang, led by Olaf, targets the club for its protection racket. When rejected, Olaf and his men begin to make trouble for the seemingly delicate Chinese hostess. What the gangsters do not know is that Lui Chang is actually the daughter of a Manchu nobleman, and that she had to flee China after a bloody war had killed everyone in her family. A gutsy survivor, she is not intimidated by a few local ruffians. With the cunning of a dragon's daughter and the courage of Gary Cooper's Marshal Kane in *High Noon*, she faces off with the gang, killing Olaf and then jabbing her wrist with a poisoned ring. Dying, she whispers an ancient Chinese poem.

The film gave Anna May ample space and time to show off her wardrobe, dance skills, and exotic charm. Her first appearance is shot in the style of Dietrich's Shanghai Lily: full frame of her upper body, her face glowing against the glitter and sheen of her jewelry and costume. Some of her lines were well written, reminiscent of her badinage in *Shanghai Express*, such as "I have my business to think of. Police and business don't go together in Tiger Bay." But overall, it was a run-of-the-mill B-movie with stilted dialogues and droll scenes. One segment in which Chang recalls the battle in the Chinese capital is particularly egregious: It shows an immaculately dressed Chinese man sitting in a flying rickshaw and aimlessly shooting a gun as if setting off fireworks. It seems as if he had forgotten how to act or simply given up trying. Or, more likely, the director of an uninspiring film did not care enough about such details.

Anna May's next film, *Chu Chin Chow* (1934), was a far more ambitious production. Ever since its introduction to Europe in the seventeenth century, *The Arabian Nights* had been popular in stirring the Western imagination about the Arab world. Characters such as Scheherazade, Aladdin, Sinbad, and Ali Baba were household names as familiar as Snow White and Cinderella. In the twentieth century, after Oscar Asche adapted the tale of "Ali Baba and the Forty Thieves" into the comic operetta *Chu Chin Chow*, the Arabian tale with a Chinese meringue was staged at His Majesty's Theatre and ran for 2,238 consecutive performances—from August 31, 1916, to July 22, 1921. A welcome distraction in the dark days of the Great War, the musical was also produced in New York, playing at the Metropolitan Opera House for 105 performances between 1917 and 1918.

Counting on its sustaining appeal, British producers decided to bring *Chu Chin Chow* onto the screen with a sizable budget of half a million dollars. Directed by Walter Forde, the cinematic adaptation had a star-studded cast, including the top-billing George Robey, a legendary musical hall comic, also known as the "Prime Minister of Mirth"; Fritz Kortner, one of Austria's foremost stage performers; John Garrick, a noted British actor/singer; and Pearl Argyle, Britain's leading ballerina. In addition, Erno Metzner designed lavish sets for the musical extravaganza, and Mutz Greenbaum worked the camera. Kortner, Metzner, and Greenbaum were all top artists from the German Expressionist era who, as Jews, had escaped the tightening net that constricted the lives of German Jews in the years before Kristallnacht in 1938 transformed the country into a killing field.

Joining the impressive cast, though billed third, was Anna May, who was featured most prominently on publicity posters. In one still, the publicists went so far as to make her wear an Egyptian cap, channeling the ancient Queen Nefertiti, even though Anna May was playing Zahrat, a slave girl. Serving in the house of Ali Baba's wealthy brother Kasim Baba, Zahrat is actually a spy, sort of an aide-de-camp, for the robber chief Abu Hassan. It was a role similar to the Mongol mole Anna May had played in *The Thief of Bagdad*. There was, in fact, much similarity between these two films. Both were spectacular Orientalist fantasies that feature flashy—if not fleshy—costumes, kitschy sets, and Caucasians dressed up as Arabs, Chinese, or Blacks. While Douglas Fairbanks capered around like an adult Aladdin in *The Thief of Bagdad*, the Austrian-born Kortner played *Chu Chin Chow*'s Abu Hassan alternately in brownface, yellowface, and blackface. The difference here for Anna May, however, is that her conniving character this time gets a chance for redemption. Zahrat is initially responsible for sending intelligence via carrier pigeon to the robber chief and setting in motion all the havoc Hassan and his band will wreak. Later she repents and inhabits the role of the clever Morgiana in the original story from *The Arabian Nights* by identifying the forty thieves hiding inside oil jars and spoiling Hassan's plot. In the end, it is Zahrat who spots Hassan in disguise and kills him with a knife. Once again, like Hui Fei in *Shanghai Express* and Lui Chang in *Tiger Bay*, Anna May's character rises to the occasion and takes the matter into her own hands.

Released in Britain in July 1934, and two months later in the United States, the film received glowing reviews. The *New York Times* called it "a tasteful, spectacular and robust adaptation." *The Film Daily* singled out Anna May for being "very alluring as Zahrat." *Motion Picture Exhibitor* commented on the film's international appeal, adding: "There are a few names familiar to American audiences, but the vastness of the picture and its scope are dominant." London's *Times* observed that *Chu Chin Chow* is "easily the biggest thing in its class that has ever come from England [and] marks a definite challenge by Great Britain to American producers."[7] Not minding the transatlantic challenge, President Franklin D. Roosevelt took his mother to a private screening in New York to celebrate her eightieth birthday that September. Less than two years into his tenure, the thirty-second president could only wish that digging the nation out of the Great Depression was as easy as saying "Open sesame."[8]

In contrast to the great fanfare generated by *Chu Chin Chow*, Anna May's third film made in England that year was, to quote her most sympathetic biographer, "a dud."[9] Produced by Basil Dean—the theatrical director who had given Anna May her first part on the British stage—*Java Head* is a diluted version of *Madame Butterfly* that takes place not in the Far East but in a bucolic English seaport. Gerrit Ammidon (John Loder), a British trader in China, marries a Manchu princess named Taou Yen (Wong) and brings her home to England. Like a freak show, the arrival of a "heathen Chinese" with long fingernails and outlandish manners causes a stir in the English hamlet. In addition to wearing exotic Manchu costumes, Taou Yen kneels down on all fours when greeting an elder; she never shakes hands but prefers to kowtow; she prays at a Buddhist altar rather than to the Christian God. Feeling the heat of public and familial outrage, Gerrit begins to question his own choice while rekindling his flame for Nettie (Elizabeth Allan), an English girl. Noticing her husband's affection for the other woman, the Manchu princess metamorphoses into an archetypal Cho Cho San or Lotus Flower by sacrificing herself so that the two white lovers can live happily ever after.

By and large a flop, *Java Head* is nonetheless noteworthy for being the first and only film in which Anna May's character is kissed by a Caucasian man. Under the pretext of a married couple, Gerrit is seen kissing Taou Yen in one scene. Taking place demurely in their bedroom, it is less a kiss than a light peck on the chin, with the camera angle purposefully blocking the view of the lips. It is in no way comparable to another scene where Gerrit and Nettie are engaged in a passionate kiss to consummate their declaration of love.

The "kissing taboo" might have been broken, but the curse remained. Anna May Wong, the fashion icon who had won the honorary title of "The World's Best Dressed Woman," was still a beauty no one was allowed to kiss.

26

Not So Good Earth

Portrait of Anna May Wong by Carl Van Vechten, 1935 *(Courtesy of Library of Congress, Prints and Photographs Division, Carl Van Vechten Collection, Reproduction Number LC-USZ62-135273)*

A N ACTOR, as Josef von Sternberg put it bluntly, is a puppet subject to the manipulations of a director and the camera.¹ Just for that reason, Anna May always preferred the live stage, allowing her to bask in the applause of a live audience. In her peripatetic years of 1932 to 1935, she traveled all over the world to do live shows.

In early 1932, she worked the vaudeville circuit that took her to Canada and the Northeast. In a musical revue at the Mastbaum Theatre in Philadelphia, she sang a highly suggestive song, "Boys Will Be Girls and Girls Will Be Boys," and took a curtain call by thanking the audience in Cantonese, French, German, English, and Yiddish. In July 1932, she entertained a packed auditorium at New York's grandiose Capitol Theatre, dancing, singing, acting, and reciting a Chinese poem. After returning to England in 1933, she did cabaret at the Embassy Club in London for two weeks. It was the first time that the uptight British club had allowed a cabaret performance, which greatly improved their business. In October, she was in Dublin as the star of a variety show called *Tuneful Songs and Intriguing Costumes*. Switching between Chinese costumes and European dresses, she "offered an aural tour of global melodies, accompanied by a small orchestra."² Her performance of the Chinese folk song "The Jasmine Flower," with its simple melody and hauntingly sweet lyrics, brought down the house:

> *What a pretty jasmine flower!*
> *Buds and blooms everywhere,*
> *Pure and fragrant we all declare.*
> *Let me pluck one with tender care,*
> *And give it to someone dear.*

Eighty years later, at her highly anticipated appearance on China's CCTV New Year Gala in 2013, the Canadian star Celine Dion would sing the same song in Chinese in front of a billion viewers, bringing full circle the global exchange of pop culture.

In January 1934, the same week that *A Study in Scarlet* was playing in Liverpool, Anna May made an appearance at the city's Shakespeare Theatre as part of a revue called *1001 Marvels*. An article in the *Liverpool Evening Echo* called her "that American-Oriental film and stage star." As the top-billed thespian, she performed "a song and piano act" and entertained "the eye with novel frocks and intriguing 'creations.'"[3]

After the British Isles, Anna May continued to continental Europe, taking her vaudeville talents to France, Italy, Switzerland, Spain, and Scandinavia. Her Italian tour in the winter of 1935 was the most extensive, including Rome, Milan, Florence, Venice, Naples, Turin, Palermo, Catania, Messina, Trieste, and Genoa. She took a cram course in Italian and made it known that one-third of her act would be delivered in that language. Also touring widely in Europe at the time was that other American cabaret icon, Josephine Baker, whose career is often compared with Anna May's. Known for her comic, banana-skirted persona, Baker flaunted her loose-limbed athleticism and artful clumsiness, while lyricizing the primitive-to-Parisienne narrative in a falsetto voice. By contrast, Anna May, clad alternately in elaborate Chinese costumes and chic European clothes, while speaking multiple tongues with affected fluency, projected an Asian mystique in a cosmopolitan world. Yet, for most of the European audiences, both Baker's primitivism and Wong's mystique appeared as deadly seductions, representing in essence forbidden love.[4]

To extend the parallel a bit further, Baker, despite her stardom in Europe, never attained popularity in her home country, a land where "separate but equal" still remained on the books. In 1936, her revival of the *Ziegfeld Follies* on Broadway was a flop, with *Time* magazine referring to her as a "Negro wench . . . whose dancing and singing might be topped anywhere outside Paris," while other critics considered her voice "too thin" and "dwarf-like" to fill a theater.[5] Heartbroken, Baker returned to Europe and renounced her US citizenship a year later. Similarly, after an extensive European tour, Anna May returned to America in 1935, hoping to land her dream part in what would become a landmark Chinese-themed film, *The Good Earth*. After lavishing $100,000 on the rights to Pearl S. Buck's novel published in 1931, MGM had taken its time to develop the potentially blockbuster film. The studio heads predicted that an epic story about the rise of a Chinese peasant from rags to riches would resonate well with Depression-weary Americans. Who can't see, they reasoned, the connection between the devastation of famine, drought, and locust swarms in faraway China and the ravages of the Dust Bowl here? They extravagantly budgeted more than $2.8 million for the movie and hired a veritable army of coolie workers for nearly four years to carve a California hillside into a replica of rural China, turning dry desert into rice paddies. They also obtained the services of General Ting-Hsu Tu from China as a technical adviser, rather than rely on Chinatown honchos as usual.[6] When it came to casting, however, Hollywood's imagination was stuck in its old ruts, much to Anna May's dismay.

When MGM first acquired the film rights in 1932, Buck, who was born in China to missionary parents and considered herself bicultural, wrote to a studio executive, hoping for "an entirely satisfactory Chinese cast."[7] When the author met with another MGM executive for lunch in 1935, she again expressed her wish for the casting of Chinese actors in the leading parts. But she was told that this would be impossible because of the Hollywood star system. At the time of testing for parts, there were two obvious stars: Luise Rainer and Paul Muni. Rainer, an Austrian-born actress who had just arrived in Hollywood, was touted as the next Greta Garbo. Her limited appearance in a supporting role in *The Great Ziegfeld* (1936) was so impressive that it garnered her the Academy Award for Best Actress. Dubbed the "Viennese teardrop" for her dramatically emotional performance, she convinced producers that she could play any part, even a poor, plain-as-shoe wife of a Chinese peasant, the part coveted by Anna May. Similarly, Muni was an Austro-Hungarian actor who had cut his teeth in Yiddish theater in Chicago. After his breakaway role in *Scarface* (1932), Warner Bros. gave him the rare privilege of choosing his part in any film. In the same year Rainer won an Oscar, Muni won his for Best Actor in *The Story of Louis Pasteur* (1936), a biopic about the famous French chemist. Now the impersonator of the crazy scientist who revolutionized agriculture would walk in the tattered shoes of a Chinese peasant.

As soon as Muni was cast as Wang Lung, the male protagonist in *The Good Earth*, Anna May knew that it would be virtually impossible for her to get the female lead part as O-lan, because Hollywood was always queasy about casting an interracial pair as a couple. If the male lead would be a yellowface actor, then the female had better follow suit to avoid offending delicate American sensibilities. As Anna May told a friend, for her to continue to seek the O-lan role would be like bucking up against a stone wall. What she did not realize, however, was that this particular stone wall had been fortified not only by Hollywood's deep-trenched racism, but also by a China factor.

Since her screen debut, Anna May had received mixed reviews in China. While the Chinese print media had closely followed her career—a beautiful compatriot's travails in foreign movielands always made good copy—Anna May's stereotypical roles in some films had raised the hackles of Chinese critics. Censorious scrutiny became intense as Hollywood, entering its Golden

Age, enjoyed greater popularity in China than in any other country. The Chinese government began to fight battles over Chinese images in American films. Domestically, the government established a review board that maintained an iron grip on the importation of foreign films, banning those perceived to have tarnished the image of China, including *The Thief of Bagdad* and *Shanghai Express*. Overseas, through shrewd diplomacy, the Chinese also scored occasional victories by pressuring studios to change a script or even shelve a project. In 1932, when MGM tried to make a Fu Manchu sequel after the successes of *Daughter of the Dragon* and *The Mask of Fu Manchu*, the Chinese Embassy vehemently protested. The United States Government, eager to recruit China as an ally against the Japanese expansion in the Far East, pressured MGM to pull the plug on the production. Even so, in the 1930s, China's influence in Hollywood was still a far cry from the tremendous clout it carries today. As Erich Schwartzel wrote in *Red Carpet: Hollywood, China, and the Battle for Cultural Supremacy*, China had by 2020 become a market "too big to ignore and too lucrative to anger," giving it the ability to green-light film projects and change scripts like an invisible studio chief.[8] But the Great Wall was not built in one day, and neither was China's soft-power astrosphere. What is generally not well known is that, as early as the 1930s, China had already made its presence felt in Hollywood.

As the technical adviser for *The Good Earth*, General Tu exerted considerable influence on the film's production. A member of China's Central Film Censorship Committee, which had banned several of Anna May's flicks, Tu made it known to MGM producers that, given her alleged "tainted reputation," casting her would be detrimental to the film's fate in China. "Whenever she appears in a film," he told them, "the newspapers print her picture with the caption 'Anna May again loses face for China.'"[9] If the producers had already preferred to cast Rainer in yellowface, Tu's cautionary message became the last straw.

Even so, pressured by a spontaneous campaign launched by Los Angeles newspapers, and sensing the absurdity of not casting the indisputably biggest Chinese star in a big China flick, MGM executives decided to audition Anna May for the part of Lotus, a youthful concubine of Wang Lung. After her first test for the small role on December 10, 1935, associate producer Albert Lewin wrote a casting memo about Anna May: "A little disappointing as to looks. Does not seem beautiful enough to make Wang's infatuation convincing; however, deserves consideration." Four days later, after yet another audition,

Lewin wrote again: "Deserves serious consideration as possibility for Lotus— Not as beautiful as she might be."[10] Having been snubbed for the leading part, Anna May felt torn over accepting a secondary role even if she got the offer. As she confided in a letter, many of her friends were advising her to take the part if there was enough money in it.[11] But when MGM, after testing hundreds of Asian actors for the various minor roles, found most of them not fitting the producer's conception of "what Chinese people looked like," Anna May was so incensed that she decided to have nothing to do with the production. As she told a journalist soon afterward, "I do not see why I, at this stage of my career, should take a step backward and accept a minor role in a Chinese play that will surround me entirely by a Caucasian cast."[12]

In the absence of the biggest Chinese star, and with a predominantly Caucasian cast, *The Good Earth* became a yellowface extravaganza. Asian extras were hired only for subordinate roles and "for atmosphere." After Muni and Rainer, the third-billing Uncle part went to the American actor Walter Connolly, while the fourth-billing Lotus part went to another Austrian starlet, Tilly Losch, effectively producing what one critic called "MGM Chinese."[13] But even with its partial Viennese cast, the Chinese-themed film still did well at the box office. It would garner five Academy Award nominations, winning two of them, including Rainer as Best Actress.

To Anna May and her fellow Chinese Americans, the success of the film added salt to their wounds. As the Chinese American film historian Stephen Gong reflected on the legacy of *The Good Earth*, "It's big and prestigious. You were going to have a big cast, and there was a lot of interest in China at that time with political troubles and strife in Asia. It would have been, could have been, and should have been our *Gone with the Wind*. If you're Chinese American and you're interested in film, it seems like this great graveyard for all our dreams and aspirations."[14] Incidentally, Anna May's younger sister, Mary, did get a tiny part as the Little Bride in *The Good Earth*. Three years later, depressed by her dim prospects in Hollywood, Mary hanged herself in the family garage. Tragically, Gong's graveyard metaphor struck home.

Forced to endure this shameful slight, Anna May became increasingly disgusted by Hollywood's racism. She thought about leaving the country again, as she had done in 1928 when she escaped to Germany. But this time, Europe was standing on the verge of an inferno, and no longer an option. By now, most of her family members had left for China. Their family laundry had been destroyed, along with Chinatown, to make room for the new Union Station.

After a prolonged legal battle, California's Supreme Court approved the construction of the iconic, Mission-style train terminal. As the old American saying goes, "They bring the hammer down to Chinatown"—the demolition of old Chinatown commenced on December 22, 1933, with sledgehammers and axes. The children's school on Apablasa Street was the first building to go, followed by the once-bustling vegetable market, and then all the other structures. Arriving to witness the destruction, a reporter for the *Los Angeles Times* observed that two senior Chinese residents, "whose wrinkles and shuffle bespoke many years spent in the area, hurried to their small garden and began pulling the vegetables from the ground. . . . Others tossed their few belongings into a modern shopping bag and, with their favorite cooking utensils in hand, slowly plodded from the scene of a quickly wrecked home." Just like that, a community that for half a century had survived massacres, arsons, and all forms of racial violence and harassment was shattered, leaving more than 2,500 residents virtually homeless.[15]

With his business gone and dotage beckoning, Sam Sing felt more palpably the pull of his ancestral land. The Chinese notion of *luoye guigen,* "Fallen leaves return to the roots," was no mere fortune-cookie truism. On August 5, 1934, accompanied by four of his brood, the old man who had toiled all his life in an LA-based Chinese laundry sailed for Canton. There, his first wife, last seen as a young bride many moons earlier, was still living and waiting, along with their now-adult son. It would be a bittersweet reunion after a four-decade hiatus across the ocean, an occurrence that was nonetheless a textbook saga of Chinese immigrants in America.

Her family's presence back in China gave Anna May a great impetus to make a visit there, to get her mind and body away from Hollywood's—both literal and figurative—noisome air. All these years she had been pegged as a Chinese actress, even though she was born in California and, by all accounts, as proverbially American as apple pie. Maybe it was time for her to visit the real "good earth," not the one fabricated by the movies, or heard in the stories.

Always conscious of her public image, she told the press that she was going to China to study the Chinese theater. "I'll be a neophyte there, for all my stage experience," she stated. "I want to work with the old Chinese plays and, eventually, I want to select two or three of them, find good translations, and take a group of English-speaking Chinese on a world tour."[16] Deep down, however, she was going to China to find out, as she put it, "whether I am really Anna May Wong or Wong Liu Tsong."[17]

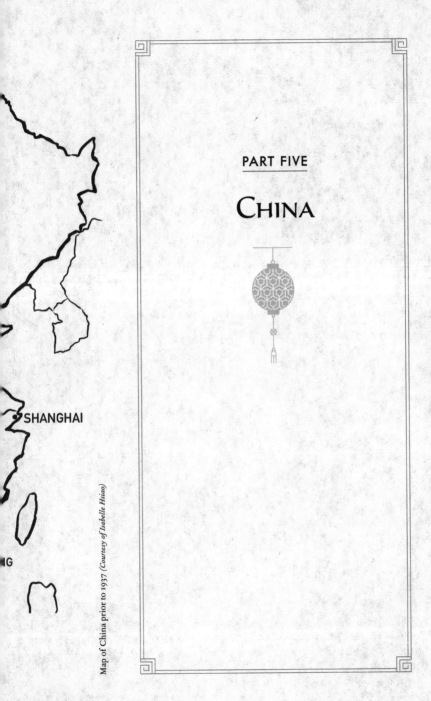

PART FIVE

CHINA

Map of China prior to 1937 *(Courtesy of Isabelle Hsiao)*

SHANGHAI

27

TRANSPACIFIC INTERLUDE

WAVING GOOD-BYE to friends on the dock, Anna May sailed out of San Francisco Bay on January 24, 1936. It happened to be Chinese New Year, a day when, as her father had told her, everyone in China would don their best clothes and make social calls, while the air would be heavy with the smoke of firecrackers. "Every Chinese tries to pay off his debts before the New Year," she wrote in her stateroom aboard the SS *President Hoover*, owned and operated by the Dollar Steamship Lines. "He who is unlucky enough to fail must carry a lighted lantern when he goes on the street, to indicate that for him New Year's Day has not yet dawned."[1]

As the luxury liner passed the still-unfinished Golden Gate Bridge, she could see through the porthole the skyline of the city that boasted the nation's first Chinatown, where her parents had tied the knot. In the sprawling bay, there was the citadel of the federal prison on Alcatraz—the Rock, where Al Capone was serving time for tax evasion, while neurosyphilis ate away his brain. Anna May recalled with a shudder her role as the mobster boss's Chinese mistress in the play *On the Spot*. Right next to Alcatraz was the hulk of Angel Island, where Chinese immigrants were detained inside wooden barracks, waiting to be examined, interrogated, and processed like cattle going through a stockyard chute.

Imagining the plight of her Chinese compatriots in detention, Anna May began to understand why her father had been so determined to go back to

LEFT: Anna May Wong, circa 1936 *(Courtesy of Mondadori Portfolio / Archivio GBB / Everett Collection)*

China. As she wrote in her first serial article for the *New York Herald Tribune*, "My father and his friends passionately loved their native country, and I was brought up on stories of tree-shaded villages set on the edge of old canals; of Buddhas seated on gold-leafed lotus flowers; of the kitchen-god who is burned with much ceremony every year after his mouth had been rubbed with sugar, so that when he ascends in smoke, he will report only good things to the heavenly authorities." Growing up on stories like these, she felt, on the one hand, that "I am going to a strange country, and yet, in a way, I am going home."[2] On the other hand, as she confessed to a San Francisco journalist right before her departure, "Perhaps upon my arrival, I shall feel like an outsider. Perhaps, instead, I shall find my past life assuming a dreamlike quality of unreality."[3]

To alleviate her anxieties, while boning up on her knowledge of a country that so far had been more of an idea than a place, she devoured Lin Yutang's *My Country and My People*. Assisted by Pearl Buck and published by her husband's John Day Company in 1935, Lin's book about the Chinese way of life caused a great flutter in the English-speaking world. It was reprinted forty times and propelled Lin to global fame. Mrs. Eugene O'Neill, one of Anna May's confidantes, had claimed that she was going to throw away all her other books on China and stick to Lin's sensational volume.

The trip offered Anna May time for reading and writing, but it also allowed her to catch up on her rest, sleeping around the clock twice before the ship even reached Honolulu. As the shipboard life became a pleasant monotony, punctuated only by the soft-toned gongs announcing meals, she walked around on the deck and chatted with fellow passengers, among whom there was Clarence E. Gauss, a career diplomat recently appointed American consul general in Shanghai.[4] We do not know what the Hollywood actress and the future US ambassador to China talked about, but we do know that Anna May enjoyed even more her conversations with two other gentlemen who remained anonymous in her account. "Today I talked to a leading Chinese businessman of Shanghai, who came to the United States to study the American reaction to the depression," she wrote. As an economic slump was ravaging China, the patriotic man was anxious to help his country by introducing American optimism. The other gentleman spoke to her about feminine beauty, a topic dear to her heart. According to this man, the classical Chinese ideal of beauty implied a complexion of jade, eyebrows like a moth's antennae, and a walk resembling a swaying willow. "It was also important that the lady's neck should not be rigid; her head should swing as if set on her shoulders by a thin copper wire," the man added. "Girls were taught not to show their teeth when smiling." However, Anna May was relieved to hear that "in the larger cities this old ideal has undergone a change. Eyebrows like a moth's antennae are still appreciated, but the creamy jade complexions are often hidden by Western cosmetics, and girls who learned basketball in middle school disdain to walk like swaying willows." As a global icon of Chinese feminine beauty, Anna May was very much intrigued by these remarks.[5]

When she became weary of upper-deck socialization, Anna May began to explore the lower decks and ventured down one afternoon to the third class. There in the bow of the ship she found mostly working-class Chinese, like her father, returning to their native country, "some to die there and leave their bones among the ancestral grave mounds; some to visit their children they had not seen for twenty years; some to help out parents whose homes had been destroyed during the internal wars." These homebound passengers all seemed to be enjoying themselves, despite the congestion of the deck. One man showed her a talented canary he was taking home as a present for his brother; he told her in Cantonese about the Chinese hobby of taking a stroll in the park while carrying a bird chirping inside a cage. It was the kind of leisurely lifestyle Lin Yutang passionately espoused in *My Country and My People*.[6]

After visiting the third-class deck, Anna May went out to the end of the ship's bow, looking at the glorious sunset over the Pacific, what Herman Melville once called "the tide-beating heart of earth."[7] As the prow sliced into foaming swells, schools of flying fish leaped into the rainbow-colored air. "I found it most exciting to face that broad ocean," she wrote, "and to realize that far to the westward lay China, the country I have known only in shadowy dreams."[8]

On January 28, the *President Hoover* sailed into the harbor of Honolulu, the first outpost of the East and the stomping ground of the legendary Chinese detective Charlie Chan. Naturally, Anna May's first glimpse of Honolulu was the hulky mass of Diamond Head looming above the bay and majestic palms lining the curving shore. As she wrote in her second installment for the *Herald Tribune*, neat houses lay "half hidden behind banana and banyan trees and smothered in flowering vines; the avenues, shaded by giant tree ferns, [led] to the windswept Pali." Finding the city to be the loveliest place she had ever seen, she was even more interested in the people and their colorful clothes, including "Japanese children in bright kimonos that made them look like walking flower gardens, and Chinese youngsters dressed in gay native costumes, some of them with little bewhiskered tigers on their shoes, to frighten away evil spirits." She also saw native Hawaiian women dressed in *holoku*, "a Mother

Hubbard originally cut out, it is said, from the nightgown patterns of the first lady missionaries."[9]

As soon as the ship docked, Chinese Consul General K. C. Mui came onboard to greet Anna May, carrying an armful of flowers so massive that it concealed his face and made him look like a walking bouquet. "He brought blossoms of every color," she wrote, "so as to be sure that some of them would match my costume." News had traveled fast, and the Chinese government obviously did not make light of the visit by a Chinese celebrity from Hollywood. Accompanied by a local teacher, her host took Anna May for a long drive over the island, followed by a lunch at a palatial Chinese restaurant. No Chinese feast would be complete without that quaint delicacy called bird's nest soup, made of the saliva of South Seas birds. Keeping her American readers in mind, Anna May wrote that the soup was "a little too subtle in flavor to be appreciated by most Western palates." But she also assured her curious readers that the authentic Oriental meal did not include their favorite chop suey, which was in fact "a Western adaptation of the Chinese cuisine." To bring the gastronomical tour to a comical end, she added, "I heard today of a restaurant in Shanghai which displays the sign, 'Real American Chop-Suey Served Here.'"[10] Apparently, her host did not bring her anywhere near Wot Fat Chop Suey, a historic joint in the heart of Honolulu's Chinatown, a favorite of tourists and locals alike, and even frequented by Detective Charlie Chan (both the real and the fictional).

Following lunch, they continued the drive to downtown, through streets hedged by hibiscus, shaded by flowering limes and giant monkeypods. They made a stop at Honolulu's famous aquarium. Reflecting her keen interest in fashion, Anna May observed that some of the fish they saw might have been designed by a Paris couturier, "especially the butterfly fish, with its enchanting tints; the convict fish, striped in black and white; and the octopus, glaring at us with evil, lidless eyes."[11]

The day ended with an obligatory dip at Waikiki Beach and a bonus ride in an outrigger canoe. Paddling through the opalescent surf, she noted that it was a most exciting sport, comparable to skiing in Switzerland. When her twelve-hour whistle stop concluded and the Dollar liner finally steamed away to the melancholic music of Aloha, she waved good-byes to the hula dancers and her new acquaintances, tossing leis one by one into the harbor. "With each," she said, "I sent a wish that I might someday return."[12]

Two days later, when the ship reached Yokohama, Anna May finally set foot in Asia for the first time. Through a veil of drifting snow, she saw a picturesque scene of "women in thin kimonos, looking like half-frozen hummingbirds; stevedores in straw raincoats that made them resemble shredded-wheat biscuits; and jinrikisha lanterns bobbing in the snowy dusk." Her absorption with her first glimpse of Asia was shattered by a trampling cavalcade of Japanese reporters, who galloped up the gangplank like a band of sword-wielding samurais. Taken aback, she soon recovered her composure and became rather amused by the peculiar manner in which the mass interview commenced: "Each reporter came forward, presented me with his card, bowed low and drew in his breath in that audible way considered the acme of Nipponese politeness. 'Please'—deep bow and prolonged hiss—'you got sweetheart?' 'Please'—ditto—'you think Oriental ladies should have permanent wave?' 'Please, you like Japan?'" Responding to the machine-gun fire of queries, Anna May answered by speaking metaphorically that she was wedded to her art, and then she repeated for the umpteenth time the gist of her life story. Satisfied, the squad of reporters smiled in unison, launched into a reverie of even more deep bows, and retreated down the gangplank as rapidly as they had come.[13]

Having a few hours to look around, she went ashore and explored the seaport's waterfront district. In the thickening twilight, she could distinguish little of the city, but the snow falling softly on the lovely papier-mâché houses made her feel as if she had just walked into a movie set built for a new production of *Madame Butterfly*. With no film crew around, the star actress recalled her breakaway role in *The Toll of the Sea*. Even though it had been only fourteen years since that film, it felt like a lifetime ago.[14]

The twilight excursion brought her to a dancing place called the Sunshine Bar. The place was empty of clients, and there were no customary geishas. The latter had been replaced by taxi dancers—a cultural import from Weimar Berlin—dressed in Western clothes and high heels, huddling around a charcoal brazier like small sparrows in the deserted ballroom. Lamenting the sad sight, the actress reflected on the trade that was often compared to her own: "A geisha's training was long and arduous; during the course of it she had to expose herself to bad weather so that her voice would be broken by repeated colds and thus acquire a much-admired huskiness. Her difficult training made her an expensive luxury as an entertainer. [Taxi dancers] are cheaper, but Japanese night life is losing its elegance and ceremony."[15]

When she finally got back to the ship, she found an evening edition of a local paper. There was an article about her arrival, in which it was also stated that she was engaged to a wealthy Cantonese man named Art. Such, she sighed, were "the hazards of interviews in the East," where miscommunication was frequent and malapropisms were legion. At least, it was not as quixotic as the sign on a Yokohama curio shop she had heard about: FOREIGNERS WELCOME, AND WILL BE PROMPTLY EXECUTED.[16]

After spending an almost-sleepless night on the ship, she was excited the next day to continue her exploration of Japan. As soon as dawn light streaked the sky, she went down to the Yokohama station and took the first electric train to Tokyo. Upon her arrival in an icy rain, the largest city in Asia appeared as a wet pandemonium: the incessant braying of car horns, the clanging of trolleys, the shriek of the elevated rails, and the clack-clacks of thousands of wooden *getas* (sandals) worn by people trudging along the watery streets. "There seemed to be millions of automobiles," she observed, "nearly all of which were driven with a degree of recklessness great enough to astonish a New York policeman." By portraying the recklessness on the street, she appeared to be making a not-so-subtle allusion to the rising militarism in Japan, which by 1936 had cemented its occupation of Manchuria and revealed its larger ambitions in the Pacific region. Traveling in Japan in the 1930s, a Chinese person would naturally have mixed feelings. Addressing her American readers, most of whom probably could not tell the difference between Chinese and Japanese, Anna May asserted, "The Chinese are closer to Americans in mental make-up than any people of the East."[17] In retrospect, such a grandiose statement should be construed not as an ethnographic fact but an attempt to rally support for her own people in face of increasing Japanese aggression.

Perturbed by the growing military specter in Japan, Anna May nonetheless delighted in watching fashion on the street: "There were women in Japanese dress, the outer kimonos over their stiff obis [sashes] giving them the effect of being strangely round-shouldered. There were pale students in semi-military uniforms, businessmen in ordinary Western suits, youths arrayed in kimonos and cowboy hats, and several workmen dressed in knitted sweaters and long woolen underwear."[18]

From the modern capital, she traveled to the ancient city of Kyoto, making quick stops in Kobe and Osaka. Along the route, an endless series of tiny thatched houses, rural temples with curving eaves, and stunted pines outlined against the sky made her feel as if she was riding through a long scroll of Japanese prints. Osaka, an industrialized city smothered under veils of smog, reminded her of Pittsburgh. Kyoto was overrun by pilgrims and tourists, who carried their lunches and up-to-date Thermos bottles and hurried from shrine to shrine. Only the sound of temple bells, booming in the air and bouncing off cobbled streets, reminded her that the city used to be the sacred site of Japanese learning and the mighty Shoguns.

"Although I have reveled in the beauty of Japan and admired its modern achievements," she concluded, "I have not yet found the serene spiritual tempo I had hoped to discover in the East."[19] With ever-mounting anticipation, she looked forward to reaching China.

28

SHANGHAI

*Nobody belongs in Shanghai. Everyone is either
just going or just arriving.*
—LOUIS L'AMOUR,
"Shanghai, Not Without Gestures"[1]

SHANGHAI, a name as beguiling as Baghdad, Paris, Istanbul, or Timbuktu,
evoked auras of romance, mystery, and adventure. Once only a mudflat at
the mouth of the murky Whangpoo River, Shanghai had by the early 1930s
become the fifth largest city in the world. With a population surpassing three
million, the bustling treaty port was carved like a jigsaw puzzle into the Chinese sections in the north and south, and the foreign enclaves in the middle. At
the heart of the so-called *shili yangchang* (ten-mile-long foreign zone) was the
Bund, a strip of riverfront embankment famous for its majestic profile lined
with edifices of colonial power—the British Consulate, the Palace Hotel, the
Shanghai Club, Sassoon House with its Cathay Hotel, and the Hong Kong and
Shanghai Bank.

Within the International Settlement and the French Concession, foreigners, or Shanghailanders, enjoyed their lives of privilege and luxury beyond
the reach of Chinese law, while the local populace maintained a love–hate
relationship with such imported symbols of modernity as department stores,
movie theaters, racetracks, coffeehouses, dance halls, and public gardens.
Tossed into the mix were boatloads of White Russians and Jews, all refugees
fleeing the Bolshevik Revolution or growing Nazi persecution. These stateless
émigrés were legal nonentities subsisting at the mercy of Chinese hospitality
and rule. In the words of Louis L'Amour, America's most prolific Western
author, who had in his youth drifted ashore on the Bund as an itinerant sailor,

Aerial view of the Bund, Shanghai, circa 1927 *(Courtesy of Adrienne Livesey, Elaine Ryder, Irene Brien, and Special Collections, University of Bristol Library)*

Shanghai was an amalgam of men, women, and children of all nationalities "buying and selling, fighting and gambling, loving and dying . . . eating the food of many countries, speaking in tongues I had never heard of, praying to many gods." Or, as Aldous Huxley saw it, the essence of Shanghai was "life itself, dense, rank, richly clotted. . . . Nothing more intensely living can be imagined."[2]

Around the time of Anna May's arrival, Mao Tse-tung's Red Army had already completed the epic Long March and found a foothold in the northwest hinterland. During that odyssey— comparable to Napoleon's retreat from Moscow—the Red Army trudged six thousand miles in 368 days, evading countless ambushes by the Nationalists and provincial warlords, and enduring hunger, fatigue, and inclement weather. When they finally reached their destination on October 20, 1935, the formerly ninety-thousand-strong army had been reduced to only eight thousand. Using the remote enclave of Shaanbei

as their base, the Red Army consolidated resources and were slowly rebuild-
ing their military strength. Meanwhile, Chiang Kai-shek's Nationalist regime,
facing internal opposition from the Communists and an external threat from
the Japanese, was caught in a quandary. With the nation mired in economic
depression and military conflicts, famine, inflation, and crime defined the daily
lives of many in the population of four hundred million.

In Shanghai, the contrast between the haves and the have-nots was especially staggering. In the shadows of soaring skyscrapers and elegant art-deco
buildings festered another world marked by the pain and suffering of ordinary
Chinese. Desperate, disease-ridden prostitutes and starving beggars swarmed
the streets. J. G. Ballard, born in Shanghai and having seen many gruesome
scenes on the street from his family's chauffeured Buick on his way to school,
had this to say about his birthplace: "If Shanghai's neon lights were the world's
brightest, its pavements were the hardest."[3] The preponderance of fetid back
alleys, gambling dens, and opium parlors had compelled Edgar Snow—a
sojourner in the city before he became the loudest megaphone for Mao's
revolution—to dub Shanghai "a fascinating old Sodom and Gomorrah."[4]
Traveling through wartime China in 1938, W. H. Auden and Christopher Isherwood characterized the city as an "unhealthy mud-bank." Nonetheless, they
declared, "the tired or lustful businessman will find here everything to gratify
his desires. You can buy an electric razor, or a French dinner, or a well-cut
suit. . . . You can attend race-meetings, baseball games, football matches. You
can see the latest American films. If you want girls, or boys, you can have
them, at all prices, in the bathhouses and the brothels. If you want opium you
can smoke it in the best company, served on a tray, like afternoon tea. Good
wine is difficult to obtain in this climate, but there is whiskey and gin to float a
fleet of battleships. . . Finally, if you ever repent, there are churches and cha-
pels of all denominations."[5] Thanks to the city's reputation, *shanghai* entered
the English lexicon as a verb that means, as defined by *Webster's Dictionary*,
"to render insensible, as by drugs, and ship on a vessel wanting hands," or "to
bring about the performance of an action by deception or force."

❦ ❦ ❦

"SHANGHAI AT last," Anna May exclaimed upon arrival, unable to contain
her excitement. At 2 o'clock in the afternoon of February 11, 1936, the *President
Hoover* entered the broad mouth of the muddy Whangpoo. The first craft she

saw was a junk, with ribbed sails and large eyes painted on either side of the prow so that the vessel, as the Chinese imagined, could see its way. Flat fields, dotted with peasant shanties and rural shrines, stretched out to the horizon along the river. Moments later, big factories loomed with their chimneys stuck up like dirty fingers, smudging the sky with smoke. As soon as the giant liner moored at the buoys, swift sampans crowded alongside like a gaggle of hungry children encircling a limousine on the street. "These are the homes of the river people," Anna May observed. "Their cats and children were tethered on the tiny decks, and they stretched up their hands to beg for anything we had to offer—a penny, an old newspaper, a cigarette." It saddened her to see people struggling for survival, and yet, upon closer look, she realized that the river people all seemed happy and their babies looked as fat as little laughing Buddhas. "Perhaps there are worse things in the world," she mused, "than being a nomad on the great Whangpoo."[6]

Soon a ferryboat arrived, carrying a throng of reporters and her brother, James, a graduate of the business school at the University of Southern California, who had been teaching at a Shanghai college. Coming aboard, the newshawks immediately surrounded the Chinese actress, who was dressed in an elegantly cut mink coat and a London-designed black hat that resembled a tiger. Befitting the grand occasion, she wore shoes, gloves, and a handbag—all in chic black. The eager reporters ignored the other dignitaries aboard the same ship, including the US Consul General, and inundated Anna May with questions on the deck, while photographers, like the precursors of the paparazzi, snapped shots of her from all angles. Some of the cameramen, including "Newsreel Wong"—a famous Chinese photographer working for the Hearst Corporation—climbed into the lifeboats in their pursuit of unusual angles. As *The China Press* noted in its front-page lead article published the next morning, "More newshawks and cameramen turned out for the actress than had been seen on the waterfront since the visit of the United States Congressional party first arrived here some months ago. . . . Perhaps never in the history of Shanghai has any person been sought after as Miss Wong was yesterday."[7]

For about an hour, Anna May held court on the deck overlooking the Whangpoo and spoke like a savvy celebrity. "I can see I have a great deal to learn," she told the reporters. "When the Chinese go to America for the first time, they are making a new beginning in life in one sense, and now the process is just reversed with me. Here I am in China!"[8]

She spoke of the film industry and answered the question of why American movies were so popular in China by stating that they had great speed, continuity, and were knitted together better. As for the stereotypes found in these films, she opined, "China has grounds for resentment on the type of picture that has commonly been made in portrayal of Chinese characters. I believe that there is now a field for making a picture that would portray the finer type of Chinese woman as she really is." She then told of an incident while making *Shanghai Express*: She was on location one morning and saw the train had been decked out and painted to be used in the shoot. She approached Josef von Sternberg and asked whether he thought the train was a little too fancy, to which the auteur replied that it was his idea of "how a train ought to be."[9]

Unfortunately, most of the questions were asked either in Mandarin or in the Shanghai dialect, which sounded to the Cantonese-speaking actress as foreign as Gaelic. Thus, she had the strange experience of talking to her own people through an interpreter.

When Anna May finally broke free from the reporters and boarded the tender to the shore, she took a good look at the fabled "Paris of Asia." "My first glimpse of Shanghai," she wrote in her third installment for the *Herald Tribune*, "with its tall, modern buildings rising above the curving Bund, filled me with such a rush of emotion that I didn't know whether to laugh or weep." As soon as the ferry reached the Customs jetty, six uniformed British guards marched up and told her that they had been sent to escort her safely through a mob of admirers assembling outside the dock. At first, she thought someone was pulling a prank, but when she walked toward the gate, she realized that she was in danger of being overwhelmed: "Old ladies teetering precariously on bound feet, scholarly looking gentlemen in long silk robes, school girls in tight jackets and short shirts, and returned students in Western dress were pointing toward us and talking excitedly." Only after the guards led her through a side door was she able to sneak out of Customs and avoid a stampede of her fervent fans.[10]

When she reached the Park Hotel, she was "breathless, somewhat disheveled," and without her luggage. But she felt proud and happy. "This tumultuous greeting from my own people," she said, "touched me more than anything that ever has happened to me in my motion-picture career." However, as the Chinese saying goes, rising tides can lift a boat but can also capsize the vessel. Anna May would soon find out how capricious public opinions were among the people she proudly called her own.

In the evening, she was feted at a posh dinner party at the hotel. Built in

1934 and designed by the Hungarian-Slovakian architect Laszlo Hudec, the art-deco Park Hotel soared 275 feet into the sky and, until 1963, was the tallest building in Asia. The dinner reception on the hotel's Sky Terrace was hosted by Dr. and Madame Wellington Koo and attended by about one hundred guests. The Koos were about to leave for Paris, where the Columbia-educated Dr. Koo would assume his new post as the Chinese Ambassador to France. The guest list read like a breathless piece on the society page. As the *guibin* (VIP) of the night, Anna May was seated, according to Chinese custom, to the left of the host; on her other side was T. V. Soong, the J. P. Morgan of China and brother of the famous Soong sisters. Also in attendance were Lin Yutang and his wife. As a fan of Lin's work, Anna May found him to be a most delightful person, garbed in a scholar's robe and smoking a pipe, spouting gems of Oriental wisdom and humor, almost as if he were the real-life incarnation of Charlie Chan. In the wake of his tremendously popular *My Country and My People*, Lin had been urged by his publisher to relocate to the United States. The prospect of a life-changing move, he told Anna May, had frightened him into a state of inaction. But inaction, he added with a touch of irony, was the Taoist modus operandi of being in the world. Tickled by the attention that the beautiful Hollywood star lavished on him, Lin promised her that he would let her read some of his unpublished manuscripts soon.[11]

A sleepless city, Shanghai was known for its epic nightlife. As Madame Koo recalled in her memoir, "During these hectic boom years Shanghai night life blossomed extravagantly. It was smart to have a good time and even the most staid people made the midnight rounds with surprising frequency. Everyone had money to burn. Dinners of sixty to eighty were not unusual."[12] Rather than the dull ceremonious occasion that Anna May had expected, dancing soon brought the dining room to throbbing life. Except for the killjoy Mr. Soong, all the other guests proved to be enthusiastic dancers, and they kept Anna May busy tripping the entire evening. Just when she thought the party was over, the group adjourned to a Dr. Yen's house to play *pai-gow*, a baccarat-like card game. The party went on until 5 am, when the festivities finally ceased.[13]

After a few hours of sleep in her luxurious suite overlooking the Shanghai Racecourse, she was treated to a Chinese luncheon, or tiffin, as it was called locally, by Madame Koo. A socialite and the heiress of a Chinese tycoon in colonial Indonesia, Madame Koo (née Hui-lan Oei) had previously been married to a British consular officer before becoming the third Mrs. Koo. A free spirit, she commanded much admiration for her impeccable fashion sense, especially her ingenious adaptions of traditional Manchu clothing, which she wore with lace trousers and jade necklaces. In Madame Koo, Anna May had found a kindred spirit and a perfect guide to Shanghai's world of glamour and fashion. Incidentally, although the spellings are different, *Oei* and *Wong* are actually the same Chinese family name, 黄 (Huang), making the two women distant cousins, according to the Chinese belief that two people sharing a last name must be related if you retrace the genealogical lines far enough.

After the tiffin, Madame Koo took Anna May to a silk shop called Laou Kai Fook's on the bustling Nanking Road. It proved to be an enormous place, heaped to the rafters with shimmering bolts of silk, the fabric that had for millennia given China its sterling reputation as the land of abundance and wealth. Dazzled by the richness of colors, Anna May felt that "it seemed as if the aurora borealis had been broken into bits and distributed through the shop." As a privileged client, Madame Koo had access to the VIP room, where rare silks more than a century old were kept. Not to miss an opportunity like that, Anna May ordered several pieces that she could later turn into Chinese gowns.[14]

Back at her hotel, Anna May jotted down her impressions of the first two days for her readers in the United States, focusing on the Chinese clothes that she would soon make trendy there. "Modern Chinese dresses are made very simply. They consist of a high-necked, short-sleeved coat, falling straight to the ankles. . . . Since the gowns are split on both sides to the knee, some ladies wear trousers of lace. Those who belong to the less conservative younger set display silk stockings topped by a few inches of creamy skin—an effect which certainly would have startled the ancient sages."[15] In her memoir, Madame Koo also commented on the Shanghai fad. In fact, the languages these two women used to describe the sartorial changes resembled each other so much that it was clear that Anna May had benefited from her friendship with the Chinese fashion icon. "I was impressed by the chic of Shanghai's modern young women," wrote Madame Koo some years later. "They had inaugurated a successful revolution against China's traditional costume, substituting long, slim gowns, becomingly molded to the figure, for the cumbersome pleated shirt and bulky jackets. . . . I started a Chinese wardrobe and in the process accidentally made several adaptations which, because they were widely copied, set me up as a fashion leader. The new dresses reached to the ankle and were slit only a few inches up each side. Any impatient step tripped me so I ripped the original slits recklessly to the knee, then, abashed by the show of leg, designed lace pantalettes which were decorative yet concealing."[16] Like Madame Koo, Anna May would soon make headlines with her new Chinese wardrobe.

In the evening, Anna May attended a mahjong party, a favorite pastime among Shanghai's leisure class. Having worked all her life, she was no expert at the game and had a hard time keeping up with those seasoned players. She could only watch in awe their skillfulness at the game, tiles flying faster than her eyes could follow. Fortunately, the usual "Shanghai restlessness" set in after a few hours, and the group headed out to the Tower Club, an elite night-club on the ninth floor of the Cathay Hotel on the Bund.

Designed by the Hong Kong–based architects Palmer and Turner and erected in 1929, the Cathay Hotel was the crown jewel of the vast commercial empire of the Sassoons, a family of British Sephardic Jews originally from Baghdad. The scion, Victor Sassoon, was a particularly visible figure in Shanghai's high society. Educated at Harrow and Cambridge, Sir Victor was an aficionado of horse racing, photography, dancing, women, and all the pleasures a supposedly worry-free life provided. The man he hired to run the exclusive Tower Club also had a storied past. Freddy Kaufmann, a gay German Jew, had been a well-known figure in Berlin's cabaret and nightclub scene. A fixture at Berlin's Jockey Club, Kaufmann claimed to have first brought Josef von Sternberg together with Marlene Dietrich, contrary to the popular belief that it was Karl Vollmöller.[17] Escaping from Nazi Germany and arriving in Shanghai in 1935, Kaufmann did a stint at the Rubicon Inn before becoming the emcee of the Tower Club, which offered refined dining, jazz, and dancing for an elite crowd. Regular patrons of the club included Baroness De Steiner, Madame Du Pac, a young von Papen (son of Franz von Papen, Germany's last chancellor before the ascension of Hitler), and, of course, Madame Koo.[18] Also frequenting the scene was Edda Ciano, daughter of Benito Mussolini and wife of the Italian ambassador to China, Count Galeazzo Ciano. Known for her fondness for dry martinis, poker games, and fast cars, Edda carried on affairs with dashing Chinese warlords, such as Zhang Xueliang, while her husband chased women in the city's dance halls and nightclubs.[19]

Entering the swanky club, Anna May was, in her own words, "blinking with astonishment." Kaufmann was a charming man with a rosy complexion, who as a homosexual seemed like a perfect walker for the seductive movie star. He proudly showed Anna May his collection of autographs of Marlene Dietrich and Lillian Harvey. An American orchestra was playing jazz, and the star entertainer that night was a Filipino singer. "So this is China!" Anna May mused. Hastily revising her earlier mental pictures of her ancestral homeland, she tried to reassure herself, "But undoubtedly the hinterland is still true to the ancient ways."[20]

She had no way of knowing that, as Shanghai partied on, Mao's Red Army was biding its time in the hinterland, growing stronger like a young beast in the jungle, determined to revolutionize the ancient—now decadent—ways. Later in 1936, Zhang Xueliang, the young warlord who stole the heart of Countess Ciano, would kidnap Chiang Kai-shek in the hinterland city of Xi'an and try to force the Nationalist leader to make peace with Mao in order to fend off an imminent Japanese invasion.

In retrospect, the frenzied nightlife Anna May witnessed in Shanghai was a replay of what she had seen in Weimar Berlin, a mad dance with eschatological overtures on the edge of an erupting volcano—an endless party before the end of the world as they knew it.

CHINESE ALICE IN SHANGHAILAND

Anna May Wong on the cover of *Liangyou* magazine

"NOTHING SURPRISES ME ANYMORE," observed Anna May on her third day in Shanghai. "So many of my preconceived ideas have been upset that I feel like a Chinese Alice who has wandered through a very strange looking-glass." The sound and fury of the glitzy Chinese city made Hollywood seem like a sleepy backwater. Twenty-four hours a day, she could hear the blare of car horns, the shouts of rickshaw coolies, the rattle of buses, and the high-pitched, blood-curdling squeak of the wheelbarrows that brought farm produce into the city. Hardly a stranger to the demands of an international partygoer, she was amazed by the galloping tempo of social life, with invitations pouring in, the telephone ringing steadily in her hotel suite like a burglar alarm out of control.[1]

That day's tiffin was at Sun Ya's, a restaurant featuring haute Cantonese cuisine. In typical Chinese fashion, a simple lunch turned out to be a fifteen-course meal, including four kinds of soup. Not wanting to insult her host, she had to sample every item. By the end, she seriously considered fasting for a week, a luxury impossible for a visitor suddenly thrown into the fabled world of Chinese hospitality.

After lunch, Anna May visited the Civic Center to witness a mass wedding ceremony officiated by Mayor Wu Tieh-cheng. A diehard follower of Dr. Sun Yat-sen, General Wu had become a close ally of Sun's son, Sun Fo, following the 1925 death of the founding father of modern China. In 1948, when Sun Fo came to power as the premier of China in 1948, Wu would rise to the lofty positions of vice premier and foreign minister. Assuming the mayoralty on the eve of the first Japanese assault on Shanghai in January 1932, Wu was largely responsible for the erection of the Civic Center, an impressive structure built in Peking style with a curving roof and walls adorned with colorful porcelain tiles. Several times a year, the mayor would host gigantic receptions attended by all the elite of Shanghai. One of the most memorable occasions was the lavish banquet given in honor of the US vice president, John Nance Garner, nicknamed "Cactus Jack," who made a stop in Shanghai after the inauguration of Manuel Quezon as the first president of the Philippine Commonwealth in November 1935. As recalled by Madame Koo, who had a front-row seat, the event featured about two thousand of Shanghai's "crème de la crème," a roster that would dwarf even one of Jay Gatsby's guest lists.[2]

Anna May was invited to witness an event that blended East and West. It was one of the series of mass marriages held at the Civic Center since 1934 as a means of encouraging young people who wanted to marry but could not afford the extravagance of a traditional Chinese wedding. "It was an economic move," recalled Madame Koo. "Yet because romance and economy do not jell, the Shanghai officials cleverly sugarcoated the idea with adroit publicity and made the ceremonies exciting as well as novel. Some sixty couples were married simultaneously at a cost of a few American dollars per couple." Anna May was particularly struck by the ingeniously designed bridal gowns. "The brides' costumes were a strange medley of Eastern and Western styles," she observed. "As a rule, white outfits appear only at funerals, but some of the brides compromised by wearing a pink jacket and trousers, combined with a long white veil of mosquito netting."[3]

Still, a few couples who could afford it, or were unwilling to cut corners, stuck to tradition. Earlier, Anna May had seen several old-fashioned bridal sedans being carried through the streets, with the brides concealed behind red lacquer walls, while Chinese bands played loudly. Since some of the brides were graduates of primary or middle schools—a sign that China was catching up and girls were beginning to attend school—their diplomas were displayed proudly at the head of the processions.

After the mass wedding, Anna May was treated to a tour of the Civic Center, including a massive library, a great ballroom, and a sprawling sports stadium. In about a year, the Japanese would bomb the city with ruthless precision and decimate the Civic Center, leaving only a ghostly shell.

At five o'clock, Mayor and Mrs. Wu held a reception for Anna May at their resplendent mansion on Avenue Haig, a street that straddled the International Settlement and the Chinese section of Greater Shanghai. Residents on that street could enjoy the prestige and extraterritorial protection of the foreign zone, which reinforced strict curfew laws and disallowed late-night clubbing. When they wanted to "do the town," the nighthawks conveniently stepped across the avenue and hit a joint such as Del Monte, run by White Russians. In the words of Madame Koo, who also lived on that bifurcated street, White Russians were the backbone of the city's nightlife. "They began to trickle into China after the Russian revolution and arrived in increasing waves until they reached a flood tide after the Japanese occupation of Harbin," Koo recalled. "They were ambitious, industrious and had no false pride about earning a living. The men became bodyguards, policemen, chauffeurs, masseurs, hairdressers, night club impresarios. . . . The White Russian women were more conspicuous, because literally hundreds became dance-hall girls. You found them in every kind of amusement place from the lowly Hong Kew halls, patronized by sailors, to the glittering night clubs where evening dress was obligatory. They were decorative, gay, charming and added a sophisticated touch to Shanghai gaiety."[4]

In "Malady of Spring Nights," one of the most celebrated stories about love and despair in prewar Shanghai, the Chinese writer Yu Dafu captured aptly the ambience of a nocturnal world segregated by streets, with White Russians serenading in the background: "By now the inhabitants of the slum had all gone quietly to sleep. On Dent Road, facing me, there stood the modern blocks of Rixinli, with a few high windows lit up with colored lights. Balalaika music and snatches of melancholic songs, clear and lyrical, drifted into the chilly dead of night—probably it was a White Russian émigré making her living as a singer. Above it all, a layer of ashen clouds, heavy like decaying corpses, draped themselves over the sky."[5] Such a spectacle made Anna May feel nostalgic for Europe, where she or her friends could wander along the cold pavement of an unfamiliar metropolis, suffering the pangs of exile and yearning.

On this winter night, men and women of Shanghai's high society, including many film executives, gathered at the Wu mansion, just a stone's throw from the slums, to toast the Hollywood star. Hobnobbing among these social elites, Anna May was most delighted to see Mei Lan-fang, the "Queen of Peking Opera." She had met him a year earlier in London, an encounter that had in fact inspired her to come to China and study traditional theater with virtuosos like him. Considered among the greatest female impersonators, Mei had never taken a male role in his distinguished career—actresses were taboo in classical Chinese dramas. In person, as Madame Koo put it, he was "extremely masculine," and his natural voice, octaves below the falsetto demanded by the stage, often surprised others.[6] A native of Peking, Mei owned a pleasant house in the Western Hills, as well as a pad in Shanghai, which he frequented now and then. Anna May found him "a quiet, unobtrusive person, with beautiful long hands and a dignified, courteous manner." They chatted about *Lady Precious Stream*, an old Chinese play adapted to English, which was becoming a big hit in London and New York at the time. Mei told Anna May that he knew the original drama so well that he could perform it in his sleep.[7] This second meeting with Mei further deepened her admiration. In a month or so, she would go to Peking and try to apprentice herself to the maestro of Chinese theater.

The ensuing days continued to be a whirl of tiffins, receptions, and dance parties lasting till dawn. Originally, Anna May had planned for sightseeing trips, but seasonal cold rains dampened that hope. She did, however, venture beyond the boundary of the foreign concessions on her own. When the Chinese tailor who was going to come for a fitting failed to show up one morning, Madame Koo sent her amah to escort Anna May to the tailor shop in the Chinese section. "The native city," she wrote, "proved to be a maze of narrow, crooked streets, flanked by buildings in Chinese style and brightened by swinging signs of red and gold."[8] During his trip to America in 1842, Charles Dickens complained about how "distractingly regular" many of the urban thoroughfares were in the New World. After walking around Philadelphia, a city laid out in a rigidly rectangular grid of roads distinguished from one another only by number, the English novelist proclaimed, "I would have given the world for a crooked street."[9] Dickens would easily have had his wish fulfilled in any Chinese city. As Anna May explained, "Streets in Chinese towns are always crooked, because of the old belief that evil spirits can travel only in a straight line. The beautiful stone 'spirit walls' that screen the entrance to Chinese homes are also meant to thwart the straight-flying devils. Some houses add little mirrors to the screen, so that the evil spirits will be frightened by their own horrid faces."[10]

Having dodged a few "honey wagons," which collected the contents of chamber pots every morning along the street, Anna May and the amah finally got to the tailor shop, located in a side alley that curved like a limp noodle. The Chinese proprietor apologized profusely for having been ill and unable to keep the previous appointment. He then proceeded to take the measurements in a way that astonished his American visitor: "He merely hurled a few strings around me, rather as if they were lariats, and then tied a knot in each one to indicate the measurement. How, considering his orders, he manages to remember what each stands for is something only Buddha knows." Inside that dark little shop were heaps of pretty dresses in various stages of creation. A fresh-faced boy apprentice was trying to stitch in a straight line while stealing curious sidelong glances at the radiant actress who could speak neither Mandarin nor Shanghaiese. It reminded Anna May of her years working in her family laundry, folding, bagging, delivering, and at times sewing up tears or sewing on lost buttons. "Here men are the dressmakers," she observed, "and most of the embroidery was done by small boys."[11]

As if specially created for a movie-lot background, Shanghai had become a mecca for refugees, adventurers, smugglers, entrepreneurs, missionaries, spies, and tourists. For comparison, Humphrey Bogart's *Casablanca* might not be far off: Connection was the key for anyone desiring success in life or simply wanting to have a good time. Thanks to Madame Koo, Anna May had gained access to the highest echelons of Chinese society. In the foreign community, however, her adventure as a Chinese Alice proved to be rather more unpredictable. Her guide in that world of expats and mountebanks was Bernardine Szold Fritz. A native of Peoria, Illinois, Fritz had started out as an actress in Chicago before moving to Paris, and she mingled with Gertrude Stein's Lost Generation—Ernest Hemingway, Dorothy Parker, F. Scott Fitzgerald, among others. Having married three times before age thirty, she arrived in Shanghai in 1929 to marry her fourth husband, Chester Fritz, an American silver broker. Comfortably situated in the foreign concessions, she established her own version of Stein's Parisian salon (or Rick's Café Américain), attracting Chinese and foreign writers, artists, musicians, and actors. She also established the International Arts Theatre, promoting ballet and modern dance. Always sporting a head turban in public, she was a fixture at the whirl of parties, balls, club meetings, and other events that made up the social scene in Shanghai's foreign community. In those years, few prominent American visitors did not have a letter of introduction to Fritz or did not seek her out. Anna May had met her in London a few years earlier, and they also shared a mutual friend in Fania Marinoff, a dancer and the wife of Carl Van Vechten. This time, Anna May finally got together with her after several unsuccessful attempts. She found her charming, admired by many for the wonderful things she had done for the theatrical world of Shanghai. They quickly formed a friendship, which would further blossom as Anna May later traveled north to Peking with letters of introduction from Fritz herself.[12]

Through Bernardine, Anna May was warmly received by various clubs where her socialite friend was either the hostess or the soul of the party. The American University Club entertained Anna May as the guest of honor at a club tiffin, as did Fritz's own International Arts Theatre. The Rotary Club invited Anna May for its annual Valentine Dance. Also in the midst of those scenes at the time was Emily Hahn, a talented and vivacious American woman who had made a career—indeed, an art—out of scandalizing 1930s Shanghai.

Originally from St. Louis, Hahn arrived in China with a résumé that read like a dime-store adventure novel. The first woman to receive a degree in mining engineering at the University of Wisconsin–Madison, she traveled, at the age of nineteen, 2,400 miles across the United States in a Ford Model T, disguised as a man. After her brother-in-law forwarded her letters from the road to *The New Yorker*, that jump-started her career as a writer and a lifelong correspondent for the journal, which would publish many of her witty, elegant essays between 1929 and 1996. In 1930, she spent two years living with a pygmy tribe in the jungles of the Belgian Congo, before crossing Central Africa alone on foot. Arriving in Shanghai aboard a cruise ship in 1935, she was seduced by the siren call of the decadent but foreign city and stayed on. As one of her biographers writes, "She threw herself into it wholeheartedly—taking in the races, inspecting Chinese factories, dining with diplomats, entertaining millionaires and opera stars, visiting White Russian artists, attending garden parties, learning Mandarin, teaching English to a Japanese spy, and having a new dress made every day."[13]

Living on the income from her work for the *North China Daily News* and *The New Yorker*, Hahn rented an apartment in Shanghai's red-light district, became involved with Sir Victor Sassoon and, more scandalously, carried on an open affair with a married Chinese poet, Sinmay Zau (Shao Xunmei). The latter introduced her to the art of *dayan*, opium-smoking, to which she became addicted. One of her most provocative essays in *The New Yorker*, titled "The Big Smoke," opens with an unabashed teaser: "Though I had always wanted to be an opium addict, I can't claim that as the reason I went to China."[14] One other notorious item was her pet gibbon, Mr. Mills, dressed in a diaper and a dinner jacket made of trimmings from her fur coat. She went everywhere with Mr. Mills perched on her shoulder, and he would jealously bite any man who dared to look at her the wrong way or tried to touch her. Around the time of Anna May's arrival, Hahn had outraged the foreign community with her vampish acting in an International Arts Theatre production of the ancient feminist Greek play, *Lysistrata*. Some members of the more straitlaced audience stormed out of the theater in protest.[15] As she stated in her memoir, *China to Me: A Partial Autobiography* (1944), of all the cities in the world, Shanghai was her town, where nothing seemed impossible. "Let the aesthetes sigh for Peking and their dream world," she declaimed. "I don't reject Peking. Like Carmel, Santa Fe, Fiesole, it is a reward for the afterlife. Shanghai is for now, for the living me."[16]

Though there was no record of Anna May meeting Emily Hahn, it would have been virtually impossible that they had not brushed shoulders, with Mr. Mills looking on mischievously, especially when they shared a mutual friend in the indefatigable hostess Bernardine Szold Fritz. In fact, it was the flamboyant "China coast correspondent" of *The New Yorker* who, with a keen nose for scandal, recorded in her memoir an otherwise-unreported incident involving Anna May. In *China to Me*, Hahn wrote, "Our own American country club, the Columbia, wouldn't take Chinese as members or guests. Some businessman created a scandal by bringing Anna May Wong, American citizen, to bowl in the Columbia bowling alley. They wouldn't let her do it. 'You have to be careful,' the committee would say vaguely when they were asked what it was all about."[17] Founded in 1918, the Columbia Country Club was a palatial retreat for American expats, most of whom lived at the nearby Columbia Circle. Designed by Shanghai's eminent American architect Elliott Hazzard, the sprawling set of Spanish Revival buildings contained facilities for swimming, tennis, squash, bowling, and baseball.[18] Even though Anna May was an American citizen and a Hollywood star, her Chinese ethnicity was cause enough for her exclusion from the club, along with the millions of Chinese in the city. A similar indignity was experienced at another club by Liza Roos, wife of the business tycoon Silas Hardoon, who at one point was the richest man in Asia. The Race Club admitted Hardoon, born in Baghdad to Jewish parents, as an Englishman, but his Chinese wife could attend only as her husband's guest, even though she was half-French.[19] Perhaps also reflecting on her own experience as a Jewish woman, Hahn stated, "Shanghai wasn't perfect on that score, not by any means."[20] The racism of the Shanghai club scene was as ubiquitous as an infamous sign, NEITHER CHINESE NOR DOGS ALLOWED, hanging over the entrance to a park policed by the British.

Anna May had arrived in a foreign city thousands of miles from Hollywood, but racism nonetheless followed her around like a monkey on her back. Being denied entry in China because she was Chinese sounded as baffling as Alice's jabberwocky. However, the American club was not alone in snubbing her. As Anna May would soon find out, the Chinese themselves were no strangers to ostracism.

30

FRAGRANT HARBOR

Victoria Harbor, Hong Kong, circa 1940s *(Courtesy of Hedda Morrison Collection, Harvard-Yenching Library of Harvard College Library, Harvard University)*

SOME YEARS EARLIER, while basking in the afterglow of her captivating performance in *The Thief of Bagdad*, Anna May would often sing a melancholic ballad that someone had written for her at a Hollywood house party:

> *I'm Anna May Wong*
> *I come from Old Hong Kong*
> *But now I'm a Hollywood star*

I'm very glad
Dream in the nap, Bagdad[1]

And now, after ten days in Shanghai, Anna May sailed for the Chinese city that rhymes with her family name. Originally, Hong Kong was going to be her first destination on this China trip, for she was eager to cross the border to visit her ancestral village outside Canton, where her father and siblings had been living for more than two years. But Shanghai, agog with the thrill of having a movie star in their presence, had planned so many events in her honor that Madame Koo and her brother begged her for a longer layover, to which she acceded.

On February 21, 1936, after a bumpy passage on the SS *President Grant* through the rough and nippy waters of the East China Sea, Anna May arrived in Hong Kong. Literally meaning "Fragrant Harbor" in Chinese, Hong Kong had been no more than a cluster of fishing villages on the fringes of the Qing empire when it first appeared on the global stage in 1842. After its humiliating defeat in the First Opium War (1839–42), China ceded the island to Britain for 150 years, a concession that infuriated Lord Palmerston. Belittling the island as a barren rock that would "never be a mart of trade," the bellicose foreign minister sacked the entire negotiating team. History, however, proved Lord Palmerston's shortsightedness. By 1936, after about a century of British colonial rule, Hong Kong had metamorphosed into an international city with a population close to one million. A vast emporium of commerce with a veneer of lacquered wealth, it stood at the crossroads of East and West, a crown jewel on the British imperial map, even though life on the island was a bit—shall we say—stale, thanks to the rigidity of colonial rule. Compared to fast-paced Shanghai, where competing forces of governance bred vitality as well as chaos, Hong Kong suffered from the parochial and restricting snobbery of the ruling British elites, addicted as they were to precedence and protocol. It made Hong Kong, pleasant as it was, more or less a colonial backwater, an impression confirmed by Anna May upon her arrival.

"Hong Kong is a lovely place for its cleanliness, healthiness, and order," she said. "Shanghai, on the other hand, is a place of activity, or shall I say, hectivity."[2] From the ship's deck, she saw a bustling harbor crammed with sampans, skiffs, and Chinese junks. The lush green Victoria Peak (better known as The Peak), dotted with white mansions where wealthy Europeans luxuriated in the panoramic view and temperate climate to the exclusion of Chinese, loomed in a misty haze. To the north, the blue hills of Kowloon rose like ramparts guarding a city with an invisible army. To the west and south, the ocean's bald rocks evoked bobbing sea turtles. Anna May once again recalled scenes from *The Toll of the Sea*, with its story set in Hong Kong. In the far distance, the dim coast of the Chinese mainland curved like a fading eyebrow of an ancient empress dowager.

Walking down the gangplank a little wet from the drizzle, Anna May wore a crimson coat, a black hat with a veil, and a gray fox-fur stole around her shoulders. Stepping onto the wharf, she was so overjoyed to see her sister Lulu, her old friend Moon Kwan, and the welcoming party they had brought, that she totally forgot to greet the quayside mob of journalists and fans. It was later announced that her apparent aloofness was caused in part by the fact that she had caught a cold crossing the East China Sea and was exhausted from the journey. Public sentiments could be fickle. Among those who felt slighted on the wharf were the representatives from the Association of the Taishan District, where her ancestral village, Chang On, was located. Founded on the bedrock of patriarchal order, filial piety, and inviolable rules for propriety, such an organization would often consider any small deviation or affrontery as serious as disturbing the equilibrium of the universe, the Way of Heaven. As a result, the welcome scene turned vengeful, as some members of the delegation yelled at her, screaming, "Don't let her go ashore!" She then rushed to the Hong Kong Hotel, the city's first luxury hotel, which had opened in 1868 and faced the waterfront on Queen's Road.[3]

The next morning, Anna May was upset by the headlines in the local Chinese papers. They faulted her for having given the press "the cold shoulder" and called her interpretations of Chinese in her films "an insult to Chinese people." To remedy the situation, she invited the journalists to her hotel room for an interview. Fighting off flu symptoms, she held court for hours, patiently answering questions and addressing topics that ranged all the way from the modern Chinese woman and *Lady Precious Stream* to Hollywood's ongoing Shakespearean fad and the state of world cinema. "The modern Chinese woman," she said, "seems to be holding her own with the outside world. She is giving the world a chance to get acquainted with her. The older generation always stayed at home and the Chinese woman was a person of mystery except to her family or immediate friends." Having compared the old and new images of the Chinese woman, she explained her own part in shaping some of the stereotypes, insisting that "she was not responsible for the interpretation of

Chinese roles in American films as these parts were given to her by the directors. She had no say in the matter."[4]

When words failed to change minds, Anna May turned to fashion to soften her image. On the day before her departure from Shanghai, she had done a session with Tsang Tsing-ying, a *China Press* artist, who made sketches of the actress in her various haute-couture dresses from Paris, London, New York, and Hollywood. Now these sketches appeared in the paper, creating quite a stir in Shanghai and Hong Kong—two centers of modern Chinese fashion. The dresses featured in the sketches, accompanied by brief remarks and captions, included a gown specially designed by the famous Hollywood designer Howard Greer, which was made of gold lamé with a train that could be converted into either a cape or a sari; a printed satin tunic blouse over a black satin skirt, and a black mandarin-style coat to match; a black broadtail three-quarter coat, cut straight with slits on both sides and buttoned almost all the way down; and a "calla dress," a tunic of white satin over a pleated skirt with sleeves cut to resemble the calla lily. All of these designer dresses showed a combination of Oriental and Parisian influences.[5] Quite soon, when her back-alley Shanghai tailor finished her orders, she would have even more new clothes with which to show the world her impeccable taste and creative ideas.

Even her improved reputation in the Chinese media, however, could not undo the damage caused by Anna May's unintentional slight of the Taishan welcoming committee, whose members sent a cable to her father, urging him not to allow her to visit Chang On. If she insisted on coming, they warned, "The entire family might be expelled." It seemed that her long-awaited "homecoming" would have to wait a bit longer.[6]

Meanwhile, as in Shanghai, Hong Kong's social elites opened their arms to embrace the Hollywood star. Peter Sin, an influential lawyer who sat on the boards of several charity organizations, hosted a lavish reception at the Peninsula Hotel. The venue, a colonial-style establishment founded in 1928 by the Kadoorie family, was a favorite meeting place for the local elites. Sin had made Anna May's acquaintance four years earlier in London, where he had become the first Chinese barrister permitted to practice in Britain.[7] Also attending the reception were US Consul General Charles Hoover, Moon Kwan and his colleagues from the Grand View Sound Film Company, and other dignitaries and parvenus.

The next day, Sin accompanied Anna May and Lulu to visit Sir Robert Ho-tung Bosman at his private residence on The Peak. Known as "the grand old man of Hong Kong," Bosman was the son of a Chinese woman and Mozes Hartog Bosman, a Dutch Jewish tycoon who had made his fortune in the Chinese coolie trade. Having built an empire in shipping and real estate in the colony, the wealthy Bosmans were the Rockefellers of Hong Kong. Ho-tung's maternal half-brother, Kom-tong, had a harem of twelve wives, countless mistresses, and reportedly more than thirty children. One member of the brood was Grace Ho, born of his British-Chinese mistress in Shanghai. Defying her family by marrying a poor Cantonese opera singer, Grace would sever her connections with the Bosmans and tour America with an opera troupe. On November 27, 1940, between curtain calls in San Francisco, Grace would give birth to a boy she named Bruce Lee. Thus, unknown to most, the man who would become the icon of Asian masculinity and introduce the word *kung fu* to the English language turned out to be a circumcised Jew. Bruce Lee, the great-grandson of Mozes Bosman, was five-eighths Chinese, one-quarter English, and one-eighth Jewish.[8]

Though Eurasian, Ho-tung identified himself as Chinese, a choice clearly reflected in his sartorial preferences. Educated locally at Queen's College, Ho-tung inherited his family's commercial empire and became the richest man in Hong Kong by the age of thirty-five. His private residence on the lush hills of The Peak consisted of several buildings named Ho-tung Gardens. Prior to the opening of the Peak Tram in 1888, the residents of the exclusive Peak area were carried up and down the steep slope on sedan chairs. According to a city ordinance, and in a decree reminiscent of South African apartheid, no Chinese were permitted to live on The Peak, and Chinese servants of white residents were given passes to enter the "holy land." Visiting the area in the spring of 1936, Emily Hahn was struck by the rank discrimination, as she wrote in her China memoir: "Only one Chinese, an old fellow named Sir Robert Ho-tung . . . was permitted past these magic if imaginary portals. Sir Robert was too rich to ignore, so the British allowed him to build his house on his own Peak land, and to live there when he wanted to."[9]

Around five in the afternoon, just as the sun dipped over the edges of the Western Hills, Anna May, clad in a black Western dress under a fur coat, arrived at the Ho-tung Gardens with her entourage. The Grand Old Man lived by himself in a separate house called the Neuk, but he entertained guests at the gardens, where he had received the US vice president a few months earlier. At seventy-three, he was in great health, with a back straight as a rod and a gait like a young man's—he would live until his mid-nineties. Above his Chinese robe was a long, bony face, sculpted like ancient Greek art and fine-lined like a map of Asia. Over the delicacies provided to accompany afternoon tea, Anna May chatted with the host in Cantonese, mixed with English when necessary or convenient—her native Taishanese being slightly different from the Cantonese spoken in Hong Kong. She told him about her trip thus far, her wish to cross the border to see her aging father, and her plan to study Chinese opera in Peking. Ho-tung nodded approvingly, impressed by the chiseled beauty and unusual résumé of the laundryman's daughter.[10]

Later that evening, Cao Shanyun, a prominent esquire, invited Anna May to attend the races in Happy Valley. The racecourse was another popular venue for local elites and ordinary citizens alike; even the Shanghai-based tycoon Sir Victor Sassoon kept some of his prized thoroughbreds in a stable there, and he would often bring his female guests, such as Emily Hahn, down to Hong Kong to watch the races. Anna May did not find Sir Victor and his entourage at the crowded tracks that night, but she was introduced to Hong Kong Governor Sir Andrew Caldecott. With the unique distinction of having the shortest tenure of governorship (1935–1937) in Hong Kong colonial history, Sir Andrew was a stickler for rules that perpetuated class divisions. He became notorious for explaining in excruciating detail whether Britons of various ranks visiting the colony should make their presence known by signing the visitors' log in the embassy or Government House: "Heads of Department *must*, their deputies *should*, other officers of more than ten years seniority *might*. . . . Members of the Legislature *must*, Town Councilors *should*, heads of mercantile houses and persons authorized to sign for them 'per pro,' *might*. . . . All others *might not*."[11] With a prig like that, Anna May could not do much except exchange some polite pleasantries, as if scripted by a bored screenwriter.

Still waiting for the misunderstanding with the Taishan Association to sort itself out so that she could visit her father, she decided to take a break from Hong Kong's unseasonable cold and seek sunshine elsewhere. Coincidentally, arriving in the colony on March 12 with his fiancée, Paulette Goddard, was Charlie Chaplin, who also complained about the coldness of Hong Kong.[12]

On March 2, 1936, Anna May left for Manila on the SS *President Polk*. As she told a friend afterward, she went to Manila for sunshine and rest but got only the sunshine.[13] She tried to enter the Philippines incognito to avoid attention, but word spread fast on the street. It was not long before she was spotted, and a platoon of reporters then trailed her everywhere. In consolation, she not only enjoyed excursions into the beautiful countryside outside Manila but also was treated royally by the social elites in the newly established Commonwealth. Since the Spanish-American War of 1898, the Philippines had been an American territory, which lasted until 1934, when Congress passed the Tydings-McDuffie Act, granting independence to the islands after a ten-year transition period. In 1935, a constitution was written and the Commonwealth of the Philippines was established. Manuel Quezon, son of a Chinese mestizo, was elected president. The inauguration ceremony, held in November 1935 and attended by a US congressional delegation led by Vice President John Nance Garner, drew a crowd of around three hundred thousand.

Now, less than four months into his presidency and still savoring his landslide victory in the election, President and Madame Quezon invited the visiting Hollywood personage to dinner at the Malacañang Palace. Afterward, there was a party for Anna May, attended by Nicasio Osmeña (son of Vice President Sergio Osmeña) and the two Elizalde brothers, Joaquin and Manolo, who virtually owned the entire country through their sprawling business empire. Anna May was having a glorious time, except that, between the Elizalde brothers and young Osmeña, she did not have a spare moment to herself.[14]

After a busy week in the Philippines, she returned to Hong Kong aboard the *President Pierce*, docking on March 9. To her delight, she found a package waiting for her—her photographs taken by Carl Van Vechten back in New York. She was flattered to see the glamorous portraits, many saturated in a voyeuristic intrigue, by an amateur but renowned photographer who would, unknown to her at that moment, become an important part of her legacy in popular culture. Even more exciting was the news that she would finally be allowed to visit her father in China. She and Lulu immediately stepped on the Kowloon-Canton Express, carrying enough candy and red envelopes for the entire village.[15]

As the train rolled through the rural landscape of the Pearl River Delta, Anna May saw vast fields dotted with mist-shrouded hamlets. The tableaux included dim profiles of peasants in bat-wing straw capes driving water buffalo at a pace slower than time, and an endless esplanade of dwarf palms waving their green leaves as if welcoming her home. Standing at the southern edge of the Middle Kingdom, this region had historically borne the brunt of China's disastrous clashes with Western powers. It was here that the first salvo of the Opium War was launched. This was also the birthplace of Dr. Sun Yat-sen, who came of age in Hawaii and returned to China to lead a revolution to overthrow the Manchus. And here was also where the real Charlie Chan, Chang

Apana, the bullwhip-wielding Honolulu cop-turned-movie-icon, had grown up. Even the world-renowned Siamese Twins, Chang and Eng Bunker, could find their roots here, their father having been a Cantonese fisherman who had migrated to Siam.

As the source of the earliest waves of the Chinese diaspora, this area was the spiritual home for overseas Chinese. Old people would come back here to die; failing that, they asked that their bones be sent back here for burial. Anna May recalled the passengers crowding the belly of the *President Hoover* crossing the Pacific, the looks of longing on their faces during their homebound journey. She finally understood why her father, having worked and lived in America all his life, was so eager to return to the land of his ancestors. It was a land under a spell.

Disembarking at her destination, she found Canton to be the most Chinese city she had visited. Shanghai was too international to be called China, and Hong Kong was a British colony in name *and* in appearance. Anna May and Lulu, however, had no time to sightsee in Canton, the first Chinese port open to the world. They got into a car headed for Taishan, the county seat, and from there they trekked the three-mile muddy country road to Chang On, where their father was waiting.

For this China trip, Anna May had made an arrangement not only with Randolph Hearst's *New York Herald Tribune* to write a series of articles, but also with Hearst Metrotone News to make a documentary film to be broadcast later. As a result, Newsreel Wong, Hearst's man in China, was there to film the family reunion in the rustic village.

As she reached the end of the dirt path between rice paddies with her younger brother Richard, Anna May was greeted by her father. She had never seen him so happy. Surrounded now by his offspring from the two worlds that were once a galaxy apart, he displayed a wide grin on his wizened face. While *The Good Earth*, embodying America's cinematic imagination of China, was being shot in the California desert, Newsreel Wong's camera was capturing a slice of Chinese life that was as real as the soil on which they stood. Although the former Los Angeles laundryman's story might not have been as epic as peasant Wang's saga under Pearl Buck's pen, Anna May felt ecstatic walking into the camera's frame in a venue that was, for once, not a fabricated set—and there was no domineering director barking orders at her through a megaphone. In fact, both the father and the daughter, as principal actors in this "homecoming" scene, had in some sense built the set with their own hands. During his long absence from Chang On, Sam Sing had continued to send funds to his first wife, who was raising their son by herself. When Anna May began to make money as an actress, she gave part of her income to her father to help him with the upkeep of his two families. With steady financial support from Sam Sing and Anna May, her half-brother had been able to study in Japan and eventually graduate from the prestigious Waseda University, and the family had also been able to buy quite a bit of land and property in Chang On. The house Anna May was now entering—a two-story, half-timber and half-brick structure typical of southern China—had in fact been built with the money the father–daughter team had earned with sweat and toil over the years.[16]

After sending young Richard off to school, Anna May and her father chatted for a while on the stone steps of the house, and then went back inside. Newsreel Wong's footage showed only a passing glance at the two sitting at a wooden table while enjoying tea together. The film quickly cut to a lengthier scene outdoors, in which Anna May and her father walked around to survey the fishponds and surrounding fields. As she later recalled, perhaps she was overwhelmed by the strange sense of standing on the land walked on by generations of her ancestors, for she felt a deep connection to that corner of the earth that was almost "heavenly."[17]

In the ensuing days, visitors from Chang On and more distant villages came to take a peek at the film star. "Many women could not believe I really existed," she recalled. "They had seen me on the screen but they thought I was simply a picture invented by a machine." For most, she might as well have been a fairy princess descending from the sky. Following tradition, a big banquet was held for the entire village to celebrate her "homecoming." It was a communal feast of forty-three courses, and, in order to be polite, she had to eat "liberally of all of them."[18]

After spending a few days in her ancestral land, Anna May returned to Hong Kong, where another pleasant surprise awaited her. Her old friend Warner Oland, having played Charlie Chan about a dozen times, had come to China for a quick tour of his "homeland" and to promote the new Chan movie that would hit Chinese theaters later that year: *Charlie Chan in Shanghai*. Unlike his character's fictional journey, which is troubled from the start by murderous malfeasance aboard ship, Oland's arrival in Shanghai on March 22 via the *Empress of Asia* was a celebratory event witnessed by hundreds of fans and journalists. They referred to him as Mr. Chan and saluted his "homecoming." As I have described in *Charlie Chan*, Oland, always a good sport, reciprocated the Chinese enthusiasm by staying in character and blurring the line, as usual, between fiction and reality. During a press conference, he responded to questions by maintaining the Charlie Chan persona, riffing a few Swedish-accented Mandarin lines from the movies.[19] After a quick trip to Peking, Oland landed in Hong Kong on the last leg of his China tour.

Delighted that their paths crossed in that corner of the world, Anna May treated her longtime costar to a dim sum lunch. Over a tableful of delicacies, the two compared notes about their China trips. Despite the huge gap in their backgrounds—a Swede and a Chinese girl from Los Angeles—they had one thing in common: Each had made a career out of portraying Chinese, which had brought them both fame and notoriety. The significance—or, rather, the irony—of this rendezvous did not escape the notice of some sharp-eyed Chinese observers. The famous cartoonist Wang Zimei drew a somewhat satirical sketch accompanied by a parodic vignette, titled "Anna May Wong and Charlie Chan (Warner Oland)." Set against a noirish background of a bat flying over a ghostly tree under a full moon on one side and soft willows and a ribbed sail with a boatman's silhouette under a new moon on the other, we see an immaculately dressed Charlie Chan/Warner Oland with a smooth haircut looking quizzically at Anna May Wong, clad in a trendy cheongsam. The imaginary dialogue between Anna May and Oland in his double role is light banter:

> WONG: Your trip to China as the great Detective Charlie Chan seems to be going quite well.
>
> CHAN: Thank you so much! Have you not also received a warm welcome from your compatriots?
>
> WONG: Yes, but they are not so impressed by what I've done. As you know, due to restrictions of Hollywood I had to play some roles not so flattering to Chinese. Even though I haven't been officially criticized, the fact that my home-town folks refused to let me visit really broke my heart.
>
> CHAN: So sorry, Miss Wong grieve over such affair, but it was ineluctably a misunderstanding.

By putting words into the duo's mouths, the anonymous author aptly captured the dynamics at work in this global mishmash of icons and meanings.

While most Chinese conveniently forgot Oland's role as the insidious Dr. Fu Manchu and chose to embrace him as the honorable Detective Chan, they found it hard to forgive a Chinese woman for ostensibly tarnishing the image of China. As Charlie Chan says, "Public mind is fickle like spring weather"—except, Anna May learned, when it came to Chinese women.[20]

Cartoon depiction of Warner Oland and Anna May Wong, *Manhuajie*, 1936

The day after her rendezvous with Oland, Anna May hosted a farewell tea party at the Hong Kong Hotel, an enjoyable event attended by the US Consul General and his wife; Peter Sin, Paramount's rep in Hong Kong; and others. After the party, and under the cover of darkness, she left for the dock and, once again, boarded the SS *President Coolidge*.[21] Bound for Shanghai, she would continue her rocky romance with a land she still hoped to call home.

31

CHINESE GESTURES

Portrait of Anna May Wong in Chinese theatrical costumes, 1937 *(Courtesy of Library of Congress, Prints and Photographs Division, Carl Van Vechten Collection, Reproduction Number LC-USZ62-115194)*

"Anna May Wong Slipped into City" was a front-page headline in Shanghai on the day after her return from Hong Kong. Also in the news was the announcement of a military exercise to be conducted by Japanese naval forces in the Whangpoo, which would include the firing of blank ammunition.[1] "Bloody Saturday"—a full-scale Japanese attack on the city—was still more than a year away, but Shanghai citizens had not forgotten the earlier mayhem in 1932. After the Japanese invasion of Manchuria, protests and boycotts of Japanese goods broke out in China, a nationwide movement particularly fervent in Shanghai. In response, Japan sent a coterie of militant Buddhist monks to the city to stage counterprotests in the streets and openly promote Japan's imperial interests. When one of the ultranationalist monks was killed by an angry Chinese mob, the Japanese used the incident, as they had done in Manchuria, as a pretext for military action. Bombs rained on Chapei, a densely populated Chinese district of Shanghai, and troops landed from warships. While the Chinese 19th Route Army, defying Chiang Kai-shek, put up a stiff and heroic resistance, thousands of civilians were killed and many more wounded. An overflowing river of refugees fled the war zone under the watchful eyes of the foreign powers, who were appalled but did virtually nothing to stop the carnage. Mindful of President Woodrow Wilson's inactivity following the German invasion of Belgium in 1914, US Secretary of State Henry Stimson issued a warning to Japan. But it was a toothless threat immediately rendered ineffective by President Herbert Hoover, who announced that the United States would not impose economic sanctions on Japan.[2]

Although the air raid on Chapei had become a distant echo by the spring of 1936, the Nippon aggression had been increasing day by day, as evidenced by the pending military exercise by the Japanese navy in the harbor. Still, Shanghai citizens tried to go about their lives as usual. While the United States government had no interest—not yet—in getting directly involved in China's fight against the Japanese, new films from America certainly created a sense that nothing was wrong and even might have helped to calm nerves. Playing at the Metropol Theatre was Charlie Chaplin's *Modern Times*, a silent satire on the ills of industrialization, featuring comically the Little Tramp struggling on the assembly line; at the Capitol Theatre was Shirley Temple's *The Littlest Rebel*, in which the child star tap-danced and sang, "Polly Wolly Doodle"; and at the Nanking Theatre was Robert Montgomery and Myrna Loy's *Petticoat Fever*, a romantic comedy that ends with the loving couple riding off in a dogsled. The highly anticipated *Charlie Chan in Shanghai* would only be released later that year. For the musically inspired or those who could afford the one-dollar tickets, Sunday concerts at the Lyceum Theatre featured Mozart's *Overture: The Marriage of Figaro*, Shostakovich's Piano Concerto, and Dvorak's *Symphony No. 5*, conducted by the Italian maestro Mario Paci.[3]

It was still too cold to go north to Peking, so Anna May planned to spend the month of April in Shanghai, boning up on Mandarin, studying Chinese drama, and making occasional trips to nearby scenic spots, such as Suzhou and Hangzhou, two southern cities known for their natural beauty, gardens, and cultural milieus. As she told a journalist, she wanted to "delve deeply into the mysteries of China's theater," and she was especially interested in the traditional gestures, wishing to learn their meanings and significance. Asked whether she thought the elements of Chinese drama might be applicable to the motion picture, she said no. But she quickly added that Mei Lan-fang's performance should be filmed in sound and color, "so that the world could become better acquainted with his great work and the dramatic art for which he stands."[4]

She mentioned Mei in this interview partly because her friend Bernardine Szold Fritz had been trying to sponsor the Chinese master's performance at her International Arts Theatre. When she was still in Hong Kong, Anna May had heard from Fritz about the difficulty in staging Mei due to costs. To Fritz's dismay, her plan to bring Mei to London did not pan out either, because Hsiung Shih-I, whose English rendition of *Lady Precious Stream* was making splashes in London and New York at the time, succeeded in preventing Mei from putting on an authentic Chinese play abroad, perhaps out of professional jealousy. All these hurdles for popularizing Chinese drama in the world further galvanized Anna May. Her vision was to combine several ancient Chinese plays into one modern drama, maybe telescoping three stories into one. Western audiences demand an emotional plot full of action, she explained, "while Chinese audiences are more interested in the intellectual aspects of the drama. A Western drama based on a single Chinese play would not have enough action in it to suit European and American tastes."[5]

Interestingly, her view of the fundamental difference between Chinese and Western dramas was shared by one of the world's most celebrated playwrights, Bertolt Brecht. Mesmerized by a rare performance by Mei in Moscow in 1935, Brecht drafted an essay, titled "Alienation Effects in Chinese Acting," which would exert a profound influence on the Western theater of the twentieth century. Prior to his encounter with Chinese drama, Brecht had already experimented with some non-Aristotelian techniques that intentionally created distance between the audience and the play. Watching cross-dressed Mei impersonating a female character on a Moscow stage, the author of *Threepenny Opera* was struck by the use of what he came to call the "alienation effect" (*Verfremdungseffekt*) in traditional Chinese acting. Like Anna May, Brecht was interested in the symbolisms and gestures used in a Chinese play: "A general will carry little pennants on his shoulder, corresponding to the number of regiments under his command. Poverty is shown by patching the silken costumes with irregular shapes of different colors, likewise silken, to indicate that they have been mended. Characters are distinguished by particular masks, i.e., simply by painting. Certain gestures of the two hands signify the forcible opening of a door." Acknowledging the difficulty of exporting these culturally grounded techniques from China, Brecht nonetheless proclaimed that one might be able to learn from the alienation effect achieved in the Chinese theater. "The Western actor does all he can to bring his spectator into the closest proximity to the events and the character he has to portray," Brecht wrote. "In contrast, the Chinese artist's performance often strikes the Western actor as cold. . . . The coldness comes from the actor's holding himself remote from the character portrayed." Sharing Anna May's view on the intellectualism of traditional Chinese theater, Brecht concluded, "Acting like this is healthier, [for] it demands a considerable knowledge of humanity and worldly wisdom, and a keen eye for what is socially important."[6]

In the essay, Brecht told of an incident during the Chinese performance. When Mei was playing a death scene, a spectator sitting next to Brecht exclaimed with astonishment at one of his gestures. "One or two people sitting in front of us turned round indignantly and sshhh'd," Brecht wrote. "They behaved as if they were present at the real death of a real girl. Possibly their attitude would have been all right for a European production, but for a Chinese it was unspeakably ridiculous."[7] As we know, in later years when Brecht was living in exile, he would ingeniously integrate the aesthetics of the alienation effect into his own avant-garde work, producing China-related dramas such as *The Good Woman of Setzuan* and *The Caucasian Chalk Circle*—an adaptation of the play *The Circle of Chalk*, which Anna May had performed earlier in London.

Undoubtedly, Brecht's fascination with Chinese acting exemplifies China's influence on Western modernism, a trend also seen in art, poetry, and philosophy. Of course, cross-cultural influences often go in both directions. When the lacquered gate of millennia-old China was busted open by foreign powers, the West's impact on Chinese cultural life was seen nowhere more palpably than in film. As soon as the motion picture emerged in the West, the Chinese were quick to adopt the new technology and art, which they called *dianying* (electrical shadows). The first cinema opened in Shanghai as early as 1896, when a French Lumière cameraman brought a film as one of the "numbers" in a variety show at the Hsu Gardens that featured acrobats, a magician, and a juggler with fireworks.[8] The first Chinese film, actually just a recording of the Peking opera *Dingjun Mountain*, was made in 1905. When Hollywood entered its Golden Age in the 1930s, China also saw a surge of its film industry. The first sound film, *Singsong Girl Red Peony*, directed by Zhang Shichuan and starring Butterfly Wu, was made in 1931. Before the Japanese invasion in 1937, Shanghai, as the epicenter of the film industry from the very beginning (and the home of about 141 studios out of the 175 in China), had three major production companies: Unique Company (Tianyi), founded by the Shaw Brothers in 1925, focused on folklore dramas; Star Studio (Mingxing), built by Zheng Zhengqiu and Zhang Shichuan in 1922, began with comic shorts and then transitioned to feature-length family dramas; and United China (Lianhua), founded by Luo Mingyou in 1930, was the first studio that took advantage of vertical integration, streamlining production, distribution, and theater.

In 1935, the year before Anna May's visit, the Chinese film world was rocked by the scandal of the actress Ruan Lingyu, a tragedy as disturbing as the death of Marilyn Monroe. Born into poverty but emerging at sixteen as a film star, Ruan had endured a difficult marriage to an abusive man who had frittered away her income with his gambling addiction. Finally having the courage to leave him, she lived with a tea tycoon who turned out to be no better, and, to add to her woes, her ex-husband filed a lawsuit seeking financial compensation. Hounded by relentless tabloid mobs and exhausted from mental and physical abuse, Ruan overdosed on barbiturates during the night of March 8. Dead at the age of twenty-four, she left a note that read, "Gossip is a fearful thing." Her memorial service extended over three days, while the funeral procession, attended by more than a hundred thousand people, stretched for miles on the streets of Shanghai. Three women committed suicide during the event. In a front-page story, the *New York Times* hyperbolically called it "the most spectacular funeral of the century," the reporter perhaps unaware of Rudolph Valentino's spectacular funeral only nine years earlier.[9]

Having just buried a shining star, Shanghai saw another spectacle later that year, the wedding of Butterfly Wu. Like Ruan, born in Shanghai, Wu rose quickly in China's embryonic film world of the 1920s. In 1926, the Shaw Brothers signed her as a long-term actress for their Unique Company. Two years later, she switched over to the Star Studio and acted in a series of popular films. Her starring role in the first sound feature, *Singsong Girl Red Peony*, followed by *The Flower of Freedom* (1932) and *Twin Sisters* (1934), enabled her to surpass Ruan and gain the title of "China's Movie Queen." However, just like Ruan, Wu had her own share of publicity scandals. One of them was the persistent rumor that on the night of the Mukden Incident, Wu had been dancing with Zhang Xueliang, who was supposed to be defending the city against the Japanese attack. She was publicly condemned for allegedly enjoying herself at the moment of national humiliation. Having learned a painful lesson, Wu became circumspect about her personal life and did not publicize her year-long romance with Pan Yousheng, a young comprador, until they announced their engagement in the fall of 1935. Like Ruan's funeral, Wu's wedding became a major social event in the glamorous world of Shanghai, with famous actors serving as the bridesmaids and groomsmen, child stars as flower girls and page boys.[10] After the marriage, she dialed down her acting work to no more than one film per year. When Anna May first arrived in Shanghai in February 1936, Wu was, as the gossip columns reported, vacationing in the Wuyi Mountains in Fujian, recuperating from tonsillitis surgery. This time, when Anna May returned to Shanghai, the two women, who had met each other briefly in England a year earlier, reconnected and became close friends.

At their previous encounter in London, the two had not spent much time together due to Wu's busy itinerary. As part of the Chinese film delegation, Wu, Mei, and other Chinese stars had made stops in Moscow, Berlin, Paris, London, Geneva, and Rome. It was on that trip that Mei's performance in Moscow had inspired Brecht. At a tea party in London, Anna May met Wu, Mei, and the rest of the Chinese delegation. In her memoir, Wu recalled her first impression: "Miss Wong was a tall woman, clad in a colorful dress with wide sleeves and a burgundy straw hat that resembles the cap of a Manchu soldier." Wu lamented that because Wong's Taishanese and her Cantonese were as different as Spanish and Italian, the two had trouble communicating in depth at that meeting.[11] In Shanghai, however, with Wu's ability to speak Mandarin, English, Cantonese, Shanghaiese, and several other regional dialects, she could serve as Anna May's interpreter to help her navigate the multilingual world of China.

On a chilly spring afternoon, two motorcars rolled across the Maple Bridge in the Xuhui District and turned into a sycamore-shaded lane along the Zhaojia Creek. When the cars stopped in front of a brick building, which was the head-quarters of the Star Studio Company, out came the immaculately dressed Pan Yousheng. He opened the car doors and led the way for his wife, Butterfly Wu, and their guest, Anna May Wong, followed by a small entourage consisting of a cameraman and reps of MGM. Dressed in a gray *qipao* under a black coat, Wu smiled like a happy bride, her newly curled hair rippling with soft waves, a pair of diamond earrings sparkling in the sunlight. Standing a head taller than Wu, Anna May wore a dark-green spring coat over a light-blue *qipao* and a pair of open-toe high heels. She wore her hair with short bangs on the forehead and a chignon in the back. She was holding a black purse with her name embroidered in white on the front, apparently a gift specially designed for her.

Walking in locked arms like sisters, Anna May and Wu went up to the sec-ond floor of the building, where several Chinese gentlemen were busy finaliz-ing a shooting script. They were all members of the company and veterans of the industry, including Zhang Shichuan, director and cofounder of Star Studio; Ouyang Yuqian, a playwright and a top Peking Opera singer, widely regarded as the southern counterpart of Mei Lan-fang; and Hong Shen, a Harvard-educated playwright and author of the first Chinese screenplay, *Shentu Shi* (1925). After a round of formalities, they continued to stand around rather than sit down to chat over tea. Learning of Ouyang's background, Anna May invited him for a meeting at the Park Hotel in a few days so that Bernardine Szold Fritz could join them for a lengthier discussion about Peking opera. Asked about her progress in the study of Mandarin, Anna May tried her best to count from one to ten, but her strong accent induced hearty laughs from everyone present. When she was asked for autographs, Anna May gladly obliged but committed a faux pas by adding 女士 (Lady, or Madame) to her Chinese signature, trig-gering another round of guffaws. The native Chinese were too polite to inform the visitor from America that only others can address you with titles like Sir or Madame.

After the visit to the company's headquarters, the group made a stop at Star Studio 2, where the production of a Chinese film, *Jingang Zuan* (*The Diamond Drill*), was in progress. Having just spent time with Warner Oland in Hong Kong, Anna May was amused to meet the director Xu Xinfu, who would soon start making "homegrown" Charlie Chan flicks. Somewhat bizarrely, in these Chinese knockoffs, a real Chinese actor would follow Oland's incarnation of a

Chinaman in almost all aspects: walk, talk, and dress. We would thus reach the twilight zone of yellowface, where a real Chinaman would imitate a Swede's imitation of a Chinaman while someone like Anna May was considered too Chinese to play a Chinese.

Toward the end of the visit, a journalist took Hong Shen aside and asked quietly what he thought of the Hollywood actress. Hong nodded his head, saying under his breath, "She seemed quite modest and sincere. Not a bad person." Most Chinese knew that a few years earlier, in 1930, at the showing of Harold Lloyd's *Welcome Danger* in Shanghai, Hong had led a protest against the negative portrayal of Chinese. That protest turned violent, with some in the audience throwing chairs at the screen and the projector. Given the Chinese sensitivity and Hong's position in the film world, it was a reassuring comment from him.[12]

Such approvals, however, were not always so easy to come by. Over the years, Chinese tabloids had preyed on the global celebrity in the same way they hounded domestic stars such as Ruan and Wu, printing rumors about Anna May's liaisons, her pet peeves, and other salacious matters. Her smoking habit got much press, for cigarettes were often construed as the symbol of a modern woman. One gossip column in the *Linglong* magazine reported that Anna May not only loved dogs but also liked to kiss them, because "a dog's mouth has a special taste, as Miss Wong explained." Several opinion makers published articles condemning her roles in films. For her perceived offenses in appearing in the likes of *The Thief of Bagdad* and *Daughter of the Dragon*, one critic believed she should be expelled from China, and another even suggested that she should be shot.[13]

China's Nationalist government also had mixed feelings about Anna May. Upon her initial arrival in Shanghai, the Bureau of Foreign Intelligence sent her a letter, offering its services "to assist her studying the cultural and social aspects of China."[14] Knowing well that such services meant surveillance in the name of assistance, Anna May politely declined the offer and tried to avoid any contact with the Chinese government. In May, however, the same bureau issued another missive, inviting her to visit Nanking. She could no longer put off the Chinese version of "a walk to downtown," to face the authority who would determine the fate of her future films in the Chinese market.

On May 9, 1936, Anna May left Shanghai and arrived in Nanking, an ancient city by the Yangtze River and the seat of the Nationalist government since 1927. There she was received like a visiting foreign dignitary by top officials from the Bureau of Foreign Intelligence, Ministry of Foreign Affairs, and Central Film Industry Office. Appearance-wise, it was a friendly reception, and the guest of honor was treated to a lavish banquet. The bureaucrats, however, took the occasion to make condescending speeches to air their long-held grievances. "They made speeches that lasted for four hours," she recalled. "Instead of the usual stereotyped 'welcome to our city' speeches, they all took turns berating me for the roles I played." Feeling indignant, and recognizing the hypocrisy in the way they had treated the Swede, Warner Oland, she navigated the treacherous waters as diplomatically as possible. Still a neophyte at speaking Mandarin, she had to answer in English. "When a person is trying to get established in a profession, she can't choose parts. She has to take what is offered," she explained. Appealing to the goodwill of all present without sounding apologetic, she stated that she had come to China to learn, and that she hoped she would now be able to interpret China in a better light. To her relief, there was the kind of happy ending her films rarely had, for her erstwhile interrogators ended up apologizing to her for the chastisements.[15] A dramatic headline befitting a movie star appeared the next day: "Anna May Wong, the daughter who lost her Chinese soul, is 'resurrected.'"[16]

After two days of speechifying and sightseeing in Nanking, Anna May Wong, now "resurrected," boarded the fabled Shanghai Express for Peking on May 11, under the cover of darkness. In that ancient capital, she would continue to recover her Chinese soul.

32

THE DUST OF THE EARTH

Forbidden City, Peking, 1930s *(Courtesy of Hedda Morrison Collection, Harvard-Yenching Library of Harvard College Library, Harvard University)*

CONTRARY TO ITS NAME, the Shanghai Express was a very slow train. Josef von Sternberg, who arrived in China after Anna May had left the country in late 1936, admitted, "The actual Shanghai Express, which I took out of Peking, was thoroughly unlike the train I had invented." Another American traveler, George N. Kates, who had forsaken his Hollywood career to spend some "fat years" in China, took the same trip in 1931 and described it as running "like a cruising tramp, stopping in mid-country, spending leisurely half hours at local stations." Puffing and chuffing, the iron horse lumbered along, like a sedated water buffalo, "over the broad stretch of this earth's surface extending from the Yangtze River in the South to the great plains of North China." There is, as Sternberg candidly acknowledged, "quite a difference between fact and fancy."[1]

After a protracted journey, Anna May's train arrived in Peking on May 14, 1936. Disembarking at Chienmen (Qianmen) Railway Station, she was greeted by a large crowd of reporters and local cinephiles. Standing under the archway of the lofty Water Gate, she announced that she intended to spend three months in the city, "sightseeing and studying the old Chinese drama with a view to making eventually a picture with a Chinese background." Having done so much traveling, she was in fact also contemplating a film about China in which she would act as a travel guide.[2]

Anna May, once out of the teeming station, was struck immediately by the thick, impenetrable medieval walls enclosing the Tartar City, where the ruling Manchus used to live. Despite the sky being blue, Peking was steeped in a color of gray that gave the ancient city its unique character. As a result of sands blown in from the Gobi Desert combined with the muddy mule-cart ruts lining the broad boulevards, Peking seemed permanently swathed in a gauze of dust. As a local proverb says, "On a windless day there are three inches of dust, and on a rainy day there is mud all over the ground." In *Imperial Peking*, his magisterial study of the city, Lin Yutang writes, "In Peking one revels in the blue of the sky but eats the dust of the earth." This prevalence of dust and the universal gray, accentuated by the tinted roofs and painted walls of imperial palaces, conferred a sense of timelessness, an almost ineffable charm that had permeated the city for centuries. Lin compares Peking to a benevolent grandmother who represents to her children, growing up in her all-embracing protection, "a world vaster than one can explore or exhaust." Compared to money-mad, thoroughly modernized Shanghai, the old Imperial City, bearing the indelible time stamps of the Mongol, Ming, and Manchu dynasties, presented a uniquely Chinese vista to a visitor like Anna May. The perspective delivered by a garrulous character in Harold Acton's novel *Peonies and Ponies* (1941) encapsulated the city's allure: "Peking's such loads of fun. Jugglers, fortune-tellers, acrobats, puppet-shows, temple tiffins, treasure hunts and Paomachang [racetrack] picnics—not to speak of costume jamborees, galas and fancy-dress affairs— always something original! Home-made natural fun, not imported or artificially manufactured as in Shanghai. And there's always a delicious spice of the unexpected."[3]

What was unexpected—indeed, alarming—was the increasing reality that Peking's tattered charm was disappearing as a result of the deep inroads made by Japan in northern China. After usurping the three northeastern Chinese provinces and establishing the Manchukuo regime in 1932, the Japanese army headed south, expanding its area of control all the way to the perimeter of Peking. Exerting all sorts of military, political, and economic pressures, Japan coerced the Nationalist government into an uneasy rapprochement, thus creating an environment advantageous to Japan's immediate goal of detaching northern China as an autonomous state like Manchukuo. Massing troops along the demilitarized zone outside Peking, Japan launched a smuggling campaign designed to paralyze China's economy and sever the country's revenue from customs. As Barbara W. Tuchman describes in her study of wartime China, "Bales and shiploads of cotton goods, rayon, sugar, kerosene, cigarettes and other manufactures were smuggled in by armed truck from Manchuria and the seaports. Local officials were bought or bullied into connivance. An enormous business in heroin and morphine was conducted through the Japanese Concession in Tientsin."[4] A front-page article in *The China Press*, appearing next to news about Anna May's Peking arrival, reported the loss of $30 million in customs revenue from August 1, 1935, to May 10, 1936, as a result of smuggling into Tientsin. After issuing an ultimatum for the separation of northern China, the Japanese intensified the smuggling operation, causing a $1.8 million loss in revenue just six days prior to Anna May's arrival.[5] As US Ambassador Nelson Johnson soberly noted, the Japanese attack on Chinese Customs was "as cold-blooded an act by one country against another as any I have read of and I have no doubt that it will succeed."[6] The anxiety was palpable as northern China began to crumble under Japanese pressure, while Hitler reoccupied the Rhineland unopposed in March and Mussolini, using poison gas, annexed Ethiopia in May. Fascism, like a political virus out of control, brooked no borders in its global contamination.

On that seemingly calm spring day, Anna May rode in a car from the train station to her hotel. Passing the Legation Quarter, where the foreign powers had their embassies or consulates, she could see Japanese infantry and cavalry performing daily drills, accompanied by shrill bugling. In fact, the Japanese presence was not only alarming but also ubiquitous in the city. As Tuchman describes, "Japanese officials in cars bearing the flag of the Rising Sun sped through the streets. Japanese officers rode about on horses invariably too large for them which they could not mount without assistance; in case of need orderlies trotted along behind on foot. Japanese businessmen and other civilians filled the hotels, opened their own cafes and brothels, played on the golf courses. Groups of Japanese schoolchildren on conducted tours of Manchukuo and north China visited the Temple of Heaven and Summer Palace."[7]

The Grand Hôtel de Pékin was Anna May's destination, past the Legation Quarter and down the broad Chang An Chieh, also known as the Avenue of Eternal Peace. A seven-story Beaux-Arts building made of steel and concrete and clad in red bricks, the hotel was one of the grandest in Asia when it first opened in 1915. Since then, it had become the center of activities for the established members of the city's foreign colony. Like a scene in a film set, diplomats, military attachés, and secret agents shook hands in the hotel's cavernous lobby, fretting over world affairs and jousting for positions of power. On the hotel rooftop, guests would drink cocktails with the Forbidden City as a backdrop, watching swallows dart in the twilight while listening to the wind-driven temple bells. Desperate Russian émigrés down to their last ruble, and esurient American tourists with Mexican silver dollars in their pockets, would mingle in the mirrored ballroom, eating, drinking, and dancing to the music performed by the hotel's own orchestra. It was in this hotel that Bessie Wallis Warfield Simpson Spencer, the twice-divorced gold digger from Baltimore, after a brief stint as a nude cabaret dancer in Shanghai, began her ascension to the title of Duchess of Windsor, becoming "that woman" who would force a king to choose between her and his crown. It was here that John P. Marquand, the Boston novelist entrusted by *Saturday Evening Post* to mint a new Oriental icon following the sudden death of Earl Derr Biggers, would find inspiration for Mr. Moto, a suave Japanese agent who inherits the inscrutability of Biggers's Charlie Chan. It was also here that Zhang Jingyao, a traitorous Chinese warlord who assisted Japan in setting up Puyi as a puppet monarch, was assassinated in 1933. The Grand Hotel, in the words of Paul French, was "Grand Central, Times Square and Piccadilly Circus all rolled into one."[8]

Checking into the hotel, Anna May could see why it rivaled, if not exceeded, her favorite New York hotel, the Algonquin. A mile's remove from the train station, the Grand Hotel was centrally located near both the Legation Quarter and the shopping district. As French writes in *Destination Peking*, "In the lobby was a branch of the Thomas Cook Travel Agency, American Helen Burton's famous The Camel's Bell store (which also had a showroom on the third floor), and the bookshop of Frenchman Henri Vetch who bought up the libraries of any members of the Peking colony leaving and sold new libraries to any 'griffins' arriving. The lobby also had a number of smaller shops selling antiques, curios, carpets, embroidery, jewelry and jade." Like most "griffins"—China-coast slang for new arrivals and parvenus—Anna May took the American-made Otis elevator and headed straight to the rooftop. There, in the spacious open-air garden, she found the legendary watering hole, equipped with bamboo tables and chairs, a bandstand, and a dance floor that would soon open for the summer season.[9] But the bird's-eye view was the most breathtaking: majestic palaces of the Forbidden City with golden-yellow roofs; a chessboard of avenues symmetrically laid out along a central axis; ancient city walls with empty bastions; and, in the far distance, on a clear day, one could see the Western Hills and a forest that would glow like a bonfire each autumn.

Unlike Emily Hahn, who preferred fast-paced Shanghai over Peking, Anna May was immediately smitten with the quiet beauty of the Imperial City. "I always had a weakness for Chinese art," she said, "but I thought it was exaggerated." In Peking, however, she found that it was no exaggeration. "The trees look like they do in a Chinese painting. Even the ruins are alive in Peking, not dead like the ruins in Rome. If I could ever leave my work, I'd choose Peking for my home."[10] For the next five months, Peking would be her home.

The first few days were spent sightseeing, and Peking provided an abundance of sights. Outside the Forbidden City's high walls, there were countless temples, altars, and towers with august names, all relics of the imperial past: Temple of Heaven, Temple of Earth, Altar of Sun, Altar of Moon, Bell Tower, Drum Tower, and so on. Artificial lakes and verdant parks dotted the cityscape. Seven miles to the northwest of the city rose the Summer Palace, Empress Dowager Cixi's favorite place for sheltering from the unbearable summer heat. Nearby lay the ruins of the old palace, bearing the same name, destroyed and burned to the ground by the Eight Nations Allied Forces during the Boxer Rebellion at the turn of the century.

The Great Wall was also within easy reach by car, and Anna May managed to get a ride from US Senator Burton Wheeler, who was visiting China. A supporter of Franklin D. Roosevelt, the senator from Montana was nonetheless a critic of the president's pre–World War II foreign policy. The Frank Capra film *Mr. Smith Goes to Washington* (1939), adapted from the unpublished novel "The Gentleman from Montana," was loosely based on Wheeler's experience in the 1920s as a freshman senator fighting corruption in the Warren G. Harding administration.[11] This time, Mr. "Smith" and Anna May went to the Great Wall of China to stand in awe at the feat of ancient civil engineering comparable to the Egyptian pyramids. From there, they traveled by sedan chairs (the alternative being donkey rides) to visit the burial ground of the Ming emperors. Anna May bowed before each of their thirteen mausoleums. Apparently, she was carried away by the stony grandeur of Chinese history, or perhaps the story she had just heard when visiting the Coal Hill the previous day still resonated: On the last day of China's longest dynasty, as rebel forces stormed into the Forbidden City, the Ming Emperor Chongzhen drew a sword and cut off the arm of his fifteen-year-old daughter, crying over her ill fortune to be a princess. He then hanged himself at the pavilion on the Coal Hill behind the palace.[12]

It was exactly the kind of Chinese saga that Anna May hoped to take back to America and put on stage or screen. To achieve that goal, and to get a sense of Peking's daily life, she soon started looking for a place to rent. It was also to cut down on her cost of living: The posh Grand Hotel, equipped with running water, flush toilets, and elevators, was certainly nice, but Anna May needed, as she told Bernardine Szold Fritz, to watch her "shekels" carefully. In fact, she had arrived with letters of introduction from Fritz, who set her up with the British writer Harold Acton.[13] Sir Harold, author of the novel *Peonies and Ponies*, was an Oxford-educated poet and historian who had sojourned in Peking since 1932. He was part of Peking's American and European aesthete circle, a largely gay community that included Desmond Parsons and his lover Robert Byron, the American illustrator Thomas Handforth, and the notorious recluse Sir Edmund Backhouse.

Each of these soigné dilettantes was living a life worthy of an entire book. Parsons was the most revered of the group, independently wealthy and naturally gifted as a linguist. He had arrived in Peking in 1934 and rented an old-style house on Tsui Hua Alley, where he re-created a Taoist courtyard, gardens, and traditional room settings full of Chinese porcelain, fans, scrolls, screens, and ceremonial robes. Byron was an explorer and travel writer who had arrived in China via Greece, India, Russia, Persia, and Afghanistan. Author of one of the most influential travel books of the 1930s, *The Road to Oxiana* (1937), Byron was noted for his unconventional wit. Once asked what he most wanted to be, Byron quipped, "To be an incredibly beautiful male prostitute with a sharp sting in my bottom." Sir Edmund Backhouse, the subject of a mesmerizing biography by H. R. Trevor-Roper, was dubbed "The Hermit of Peking" for his eccentric lifestyle. Arriving on the Chinese scene in the final years of the nineteenth century, when the Qing dynasty was on life support, the young English nobleman was a brilliant sinologist who soon found his way into the imperial archives of the Manchus and, allegedly, the bedchamber of the Empress Dowager. While many of his so-called research items, deposited into a collection at the British Museum, turned out to be forgeries, his colorful and hilarious memoir, *Décadence Mandchoue*, was perhaps rightly called a work of fiction. Nonetheless, as a masterpiece of gay porn, if we can even use the word *masterpiece* for such a louche genre, his shocking account of the sexual deviancy and debauchery practiced by the inner circles of the Manchu dynasty would make William Burroughs's *Naked Lunch* "look like a fairy tale for children."[14]

By the spring of 1936, Parsons had departed for Europe, leaving his extravagant abode on Tsui Hua Alley to the care of Byron. Through Acton, Anna May expressed interest in renting the courtyard house. Either hoping his terminally ill lover would soon return, or out of sheer snobbery, Byron refused to rent it to her.[15] Disappointed, Anna May turned to the friendlier crowd, her American compatriots, among whom she found the young, debonair Frank Dorn. Going by "Pinkie," Dorn was a graduate of West Point and a dabbler in fiction and cartography. After serving in the Philippines for three years, followed by a brief stint as a field artillery instructor at Fort Sill in Oklahoma, he arrived in Peking in 1934 with the intention of studying language. In 1937, when Japan launched an all-out invasion, Dorn would be assigned as an aide to the US military attaché in China, the charismatic General Joseph Stilwell.

When Anna May met Pinkie, he had just settled into a nice courtyard house on Tung Ts'ung Pu Alley. Rent was so cheap in the city that most foreigners could afford at least two servants. On a US army officer's salary, Pinkie hired five and paid only $26 a month for the entire household staff—his Number One Boy, Kao; the cook, Sun, who had worked for several years at the Russian Legation and prepared for Pinkie a daily variety of Russian, French, and Chinese dishes; the gardener, Wang, who would change the garden six times a year to feature various plants in their season; the chauffeur, Chou, who drove his master's newly acquired Studebaker sedan; and a coolie for general work.[16] Within an arrow's range from the Grand Hotel, the alley had a storied past. Due to its proximity to the onetime civic exam hall, it was known in the old days as a neighborhood for the literati. Famous residents along the alley in the 1930s included "the dream couple," Liang Sicheng and Lin Huiyin, famous architects educated at the University of Pennsylvania; Peking University professor and philosopher Jin Yuelin; John King Fairbank, the future "Father of China Studies"; and Sven Hedin, the Swedish explorer who had completed a six-thousand-mile trek across High Asia to China.

With Pinkie's help, Anna May found a place to rent on the same alley. According to a Chinese journalist who visited her, Anna May's new digs had a red lacquered gate, behind which was a small granite pavilion in the garden. From her correspondence with Fritz, we may also speculate that it was most likely a section of a traditional compound, or *dazayuan* (mixed court), an architectural design popular in Peking, which consists of several walled-in houses sharing a courtyard in the middle. In her letter, Anna May urged Fritz to visit her in Peking, but she apologized in advance for her small house, where the two women would have to bunk together.[17]

In the summer months of 1936, a year before the fall of Peking, Pinkie was busy researching the history of the Forbidden City. Earlier that year, he had published his first book, *Forest Twilight*, a novel about the life of the pygmy *Negritos* in the Philippines. And then he completed a map of Peking, published by a German-owned press in Tientsin. Based on extensive research and numerous field trips, it was such a finely drawn map that it is still on sale today in the city. By then, he was "thoroughly bitten by the writing bug," working furiously on his next book, which he would publish years later as *The Forbidden City: The Biography of a Palace* (1970). The ambitious military officer-cum-writer and the fun-loving Hollywood actress seemed to hit it off. As neighbors, they could ride around town in Pinkie's Studebaker, all the way to the Western Hills. They would also frequent the Grand Hotel for hard-boiled eggs, a Pernod, or a nightcap; or the Alcazar, a nightclub; or the Hotel du Nord, owned by two affable, potbellied Bavarian brothers, who served the best München beer in town and the delightful house specialty, steak tartare. The five-hundred-year-old T'uan Che Te, specializing in Peking duck and chicken velvet, was another favorite spot for visitors and locals alike. No question, a sense of joie de vivre was in the air.[18]

Since Pinkie and Anna May were both avid collectors of Chinese *objets d'art*, the curio shops, jewelers, and department stores lining Morrison Street, within walking distance from their alley, as well as the nearby Tung An Shih Chang, provided plenty for their picking. The latter, also known as the Morrison Street Bazaar, was an arcade covered by a roof of steel, glass, and iron. In their classic guidebook, *In Search of Old Peking* (1935), L. C. Arlington and William Lewisohn describe it as a huge rabbit warren, "a kind of covered-in miniature town of its own, crammed with small shops and stalls, where you can buy anything from a cent's worth of melon seeds to the latest in radio sets, and everything at very reasonable prices."[19] Pinkie and Anna May probably also enjoyed forays to the Thieves' Market under the walls of the Altar of Heaven, which was held in the small hours of the morning before it was light enough for either the seller or his goods to be seen too distinctly. According to Arlington and Lewisohn, "It is generally believed that all the articles sold here were stolen goods and can therefore be picked up for a song." But as Pinkie noted in his unpublished memoir, the market was "no more a gathering of thieves than happen in the cloister of a secluded nunnery."[20]

Anna May Wong and Frank "Pinkie" Dorn, Peking, 1936 *(Courtesy of Frank Dorn papers, Box 8, Envelope H, Hoover Institution Library and Archives)*

When they tired of fooling around, Anna May and Pinkie could simply kick back and relax in their courtyards, enjoying the quiet hu-tong (alley) life. An extant photo shows them sitting on a backyard lawn, basking in the sun. She is holding a Chinese folding fan with one hand and fondling his pet dog with the other. He is sitting in a matching wicker chair, wearing a pair of short pants and a polo shirt, hair trimmed like a teapot cozy. Another photo shows her standing at a moon gate, wearing a traditional Chinese robe with split sides. She appears tall as a willow in her high heels, looking sideways at the camera, against a background of slanting tree branches, flower beds, carved rails, and traceried windows. In his memoir, Pinkie describes his garden, where the moon gate was "reflected in the still waters of the pool and the branches of weeping willows swaying with each breeze like a woman's long hair brushing over beds of flowers."[21] It was as if he was recalling the image not of the moon gate but of the willowy figure who once stood at the gate.

Even though summer days were long in the north, Peking, unlike Shanghai, did not have much nightlife to brag about, and people generally went to bed early. John Marquand, who had found his inspiration for Mr. Moto in a city under constant threat by Japan, penned the following lyrical passage in *Thank You, Mr. Moto*, published in 1936:

> There is no place in the world as strange as Peking at night, when the darkness covers the city like a veil, and when incongruous and startling sights and sounds come to one out of the dark. The gilded, carved facades of shops; the swinging candle lanterns; the figures by the tables in the smoky yellow light of tea houses; the sound of song; the twanging of stringed instruments; the warm strange smell of soy bean soil; all come out of nowhere to touch one elusively, and are gone. A life in which one can never be a part rolls past intimately but vainly. At such a time the shadows of old Peking stretch out their hands to touch you.[22]

Such were the quiet days and evenings in the long summer of 1936, before the conflagration that would upend the post–World War I geopolitical order, in the process hurling tens of millions of lives into chaos, ruin, and often death. For now, however, Anna May was getting settled in her temporary home on a dusty Peking alley, looking to enter the penetralia of a culture she had been representing on the world stage. When asked about her favorite cities at the end of her China trip, she would once again reaffirm her fondness for the ancient capital: "Of all the Chinese cities I've visited, Peking is the best. To see a real Chinese society and experience the authentic Chinese way of life, it has to be in Peking. Definitely not Shanghai, and not Nanking either." Peking, she added, is like a hidden treasure: "Outside you may see only gray walls. You enter a gate and before you may be a most beautiful garden."[23]

33

AT THE PALACE
OF THE DRAGON LADY

WHILE ENJOYING the distinctly Chinese way of life in the ancient capital, Anna May did not forget the main purpose of her visit: to study
classical Chinese drama with an eye to presenting the traditional art to the
world. Among all the regional variations of Chinese drama, such as Kunqu,
Cantonese Opera, Yue Opera, and Huangmei Xi, Anna May was particularly
interested in Peking Opera.

A relatively new development in Chinese drama, Peking Opera was generally believed to have been born with the blessing of Emperor Qianlong
on the occasion of his eightieth birthday celebration in 1790. Known for its
elegant music, Mandarin librettos, and acrobatic feats, Peking Opera quickly
became the favorite style of drama for the educated nobility, while the com-
moners continued to enjoy the regional variations performed in their own
dialects. Empress Dowager Cixi, for instance, was a Peking Opera enthu-
siast; she had two open-air stages built in the Summer Palace, as well as
another small one in her private quarters, and she regularly summoned the
best talents to perform for her.

As the birthplace of the opera that bears its name, Peking had many drama
schools that trained actors from very young ages. Also, reputable masters
would routinely take on apprentices on their own and pass the skills down
to the new generations in order to keep the artistic tradition alive. Mei Lan-

fang, for instance, was born into a family of Peking Opera and Kunqu performers, and he started training in acting, singing, and acrobatics at the age
of eight. His theatrical debut, as a weaving girl, took place in 1904, when he
was only eleven. Another universally celebrated maestro, Cheng Yanqiu, born
into poverty, was sold to an opera teacher and started tutelage at the tender age
of six. For Anna May to study such an art, which requires rigorous training
from childhood, seemed virtually fruitless. There was another insurmount-
able obstacle: In addition to singing, acting, and acrobatics, the operatic performance also demands impeccable elocution of Chinese words in Mandarin.
One mispronounced syllable or an incorrect tone would create utter havoc.
As Anna May acknowledged, "To study traditional Chinese drama, one must
have a solid foundation in the Chinese language. Only then can she sing and
speak the lines. I started learning Mandarin only after I came to China. With
such flimsy knowledge, I can't even speak it fluently, let alone learning to sing
the opera."[1] As a result, her study was limited to learning how to appreciate
the art, knowing its history, and figuring out how to facilitate its propagation
in the broader world.

In those pleasant but increasingly fraught months of 1936, Anna May
made frequent trips to drama schools in Peking, visited Mei and Cheng at
their homes, and attended performances at local theaters every time she had
a chance. Despite her reputation as a gadfly and a socialite, she was a serious student with scholarly inclinations. In fact, one of the reasons that she had
wanted to rent the house of Desmond Parsons on Tsui Hua Alley was that it
was close to Mei's residence. Regardless, she became a regular at Mei's, and
the fact that he had recently broken the taboo by accepting female apprentices further increased her admiration for the Chinese maestro. As an outsider
and a seasoned actor, she was able to identify the strengths and weaknesses
of Chinese drama in comparison with Western drama, an issue that also concerned Mei. As we know, he had made a few trailblazing trips to perform in the
United States and Europe, but with mixed results. One of the strong points of
the Chinese theater, Anna May reminded the master, is that it allows audience
members to use their own imaginations. "Chinese plays produce their effects
through suggestion," she said. "They don't hit you between the eyes." But she
also pointed out some elements of Peking Opera that might irritate Western
audiences, such as the protracted cacophony of gongs, drums, and cymbals at
irregular intervals and the lengths of the performances, which could drag on

for four or five hours. From the master, she learned the meaning of the gestures and the stories of some iconic female characters he had famously impersonated, such as Mu Guiying, Mulan, and others.[2]

Meanwhile, she also collected books on Chinese drama, everything from history to criticism, plays, and stories. The pride of her collection, however, was her array of exquisite costumes. Being a fashion star, she was enamored with the ornate wardrobe on the Chinese stage. As Bertolt Brecht noted, these outfits often carry symbolic significance in color and design. "The costumes worn by actors in Chinese plays," Anna May said, "are so beautiful with their vintage appeal." She asked Bernardine Szold Fritz to help her buy the best silk in Shanghai and ship it to her in Peking so that she could have beautiful gowns made. Sparing no "shekels," she planned to take these authentic Chinese dresses back to the United States and bedazzle everyone. "I'd never worn real Chinese dresses before—only costumes," she said. "They may have looked right to Western audiences, but they weren't. I'm busy now having a complete wardrobe made. Any woman will tell you how much fun that is!"[3]

Summer heat in the northern city was notorious. In his Peking-based novel *Rickshaw*, completed in the infernal heat of 1936, Lao She compared the sun to a "poisonous flower" that scorched and split the skin on the bony backs of ragpicking children and rickshaw coolies. The asphalt pavements melted, as did the brass shop signs. "The whole city was like a fired-up brick kiln," the novelist observed. To escape the sweltering haze that hung over the city, ordinary folks would go outside the city wall and take dips in the moat. The more affluent would flee into the woodland shades of the Western Hills, or to Beidaihe, China's version of Cape Cod. Anna May chose the latter and spent a few weeks at the seaside resort, along with some American friends. Before long, her bathing-suit photos appeared in Chinese newspapers.[4]

At one point, Anna May also took a side trip to Tientsin, one of the first treaty ports open to the West in 1860 and the gateway to Peking via the sea route. There she visited the Temple of Heavenly God Mother, also known as the Palace of the Dragon Lady. Built in 1326, it was a rare shrine in the north for the sea goddess Mazu, who was popular mostly in southeastern China and Taiwan. After kowtowing with burning incense sticks, Anna May drew lots to seek divine guidance from the patron saint of seafarers. When her lot was cast, it was a Chinese quatrain that read:

Crossing mountains and seas,
One shakes off the bondage of the dusty world.
Growing horns to the sound of a thunderbolt,
One soars up to the sky over the vast land.

The first two lines seemed to acknowledge her hitherto-long journey in life, while promising the ultimate escape from worldly concerns. The last two lines predicted her metamorphosis into a dragonlike creature with horns, ascending to the higher stratosphere. It sounded like an auspicious augury of her path forward, and Anna May was happy with it, especially because it was from a deity commonly known as the Dragon Lady or Dragon Daughter.[5]

With the summer over, Anna May began preparing for her return to China's south and then back to the United States. She had packed several trunks of trinkets, art, and books harvested during her visit. The theatrical gowns—made with great care and at no little expense by the best costumer in Peking—were stunning. With these outfits—alternately suitable for a nun, a warrior, or a princess—she expected one day to present short scenes from a selection of Chinese plays to Western audiences. In fact, she had already booked an engagement for a play in London, where she planned to spend Christmas. One of the gowns, paired with a headdress, was for a traditional warrior, "for she hopes to present Mulan—China's Joan of Arc," as a newspaper article reported. "Like the Maid of Orleans, Mulan wore masculine garb. Another is that of Yang Kuei Fei, the Imperial concubine whose beauty is still a legend, and for whom an Emperor was willing to lose his Empire."[6]

In October, she repaired to Shanghai, followed by a couple of trips farther south to Hong Kong and Canton to see her family. Butterfly Wu hosted a delightful tiffin party at the Cathay Hotel to bid farewell to Anna May. "China has been wonderful," Anna May told her gracious host and others. "It is very hard for me to leave—even harder than I had thought it would be. I have seen and felt so much that it is a little difficult for me to feel that it is part of me as yet. I would like to go to California and think it over under one of our palm trees."[7]

On the evening of October 23, as the United Kingdom remained shocked by ex-King Edward VIII's abdication scandal, and Hitler ordered the Nazi Condor Legion to Spain to fight for the Nationalists, Anna May boarded the *President Pierce* and departed Shanghai for the United States. Over the horizon, war clouds were looming. As Japan sounded its drumbeats and increased its aggression day by day, "the blood-red blossom of war," as Emily Hahn phrased it, was about to burst into full bloom. The war would change, and unpredictably so, the lives of countless millions, including Anna May. If she had left China wondering whether China had become part of her after her nine-month sojourn, it would not take her too long to find out the truth.

PART SIX

THE BIG
NOWHERE

34

THESE FOOLISH THINGS

DESPITE WORLD WAR II still being three years away, November 1936 proved to be an anxious time in twentieth-century history. The noose of fascism tightened on Spain as planes of the German Luftwaffe, acting in support of Generalissimo Francisco Franco, began striking Madrid. No doubt, China felt more vulnerable, as Japan and an increasingly militaristic Germany signed the Anti-Comintern Pact in the middle of the month, while Franklin D. Roosevelt was reelected president in one of the biggest landslides in American history, signaling the utter despair of a country in the throes of a punishing Depression.

Anna May was not totally unaffected by these developments. After being marooned for two weeks in Honolulu due to a maritime strike, she returned to California on November 28, 1936, determined to do something in support of China. In a Paramount press release, she announced, "Though I am American born of American born parents, I am a full-blooded Chinese and more Chinese than ever."[1] However, such a sentiment of divided belonging would appear suspect in the eyes of highly racialized American law.

Arriving at the Port of San Francisco, Anna May had to pass through Immigration on the dreaded Angel Island. Dubbed the "Ellis Island of the West," Angel Island had been a detention station for Chinese immigrants for decades. After the 1882 Chinese Exclusion Act, which effectively banned immigration of Chinese laborers, the US Immigration and Naturalization Service (INS) had a hard time preventing the arrival of "paper sons," who claimed to be direct descendants of native-born citizens and therefore could enter the country to become citizens, according to the Fourteenth Amendment. Villages in southern China, like Anna May's ancestral home, Chang On, developed a sophisticated paper-son slot system and sent over thousands of people every year to claim nativity. Faced with such wide-scale immigration fraud, one federal judge once commented, "If the story told in the courts were true, every Chinese woman who was in the United States twenty-five years ago must have had at least 500 children."[2] In order to stop the trend, the INS set up the Angel Island detention center to process all Chinese entering the country from the West Coast. The new arrivals would undergo medical examinations and lengthy interrogations, and many were kept in jail-like wooden barracks, often more suited for a tiger or a panda. (And, interestingly, the first panda had just arrived in the United States in 1936, a cub named Su Lin, triggering a still-unabated American obsession with giant pandas.)[3] Even Ai-ling Soong, the eldest of the three sisters of the influential Soong family, was detained for two weeks in 1904 in a cell block that was, in the words of an immigration officer, "not fit for a self-respecting animal." It was an ordeal Ai-ling would not easily forget, and President Theodore Roosevelt heard an earful of her complaint when she visited Washington a year later.[4]

As a native-born American citizen carrying a re-entry certificate, which she had taken the trouble to obtain prior to her trip, Anna May would not have to suffer the same kind of indignities as most other Chinese passengers. However, because an impostor had stolen her brother James's identity, she had to spend hours answering questions about each of her family members, identifying them in photos, and filling out forms.[5] The lengthy grilling brought back the memory of her last run-in with immigration officials. In 1932, when she was going to Canada for a vaudeville tour, Anna May made the mistake of stepping off the train in a border town and was stopped by Canadian Customs. Consequently, her tour group had to continue without her, while she traveled alone for a few hundred miles to enter Canada from a designated port of entry.[6] The cold shoulders she received from the INS officers in 1936 was a sobering reminder of the benighted status of Chinese in North America.

Settling back into her old apartment on Wilshire Boulevard, Anna May unpacked several trunks of gorgeous Chinese clothes and other goods she had brought back from the trip. At the same time, she started to dispose of her European clothes and other tchotchkes. A sartorial change is always a sign of mental shift. Meanwhile, her father asked her to get rid of some property owned by the family. For the first few months, life was fraught with little things. And then came an unpleasant surprise.

On March 23, 1937, Anna May received an extortion letter demanding $20,000 under a threat of disfigurement, for acid had become a not-infrequent tactic used by American mobsters to disfigure a face or other body parts. We should not forget that, in *Daughter of the Dragon*, Ling Moy exacts her vengeance on the young Petrie by threatening to disfigure his fiancée with corrosive acid. And what would be portrayed in *Touch of Evil* (1958), in which Miguel Vargas (Charlton Heston) is attacked with acid but fights off his assailant, touched upon a major theme in movies and a huge concern for actors in those decades. Especially for women, the threat of disfigurement was all too horrifically real. The fact that, as late as 2012, *Saving Face*, a documentary about acid attacks on Pakistani women, would win an Academy Award speaks to the pervasiveness and longevity of this evil tactic.

In addition to disfigurement, the extortionist also threatened to maim Anna May's father and harm those close to her. A similar note was sent to the producer David Selznick, warning him that his two sons would be crippled and blinded if he did not fork over the same amount. Coincidentally, the Golden Age of Hollywood also happened to be a golden time for American mobsters to place chokeholds on the big film studios and manage to extort millions of dollars from Hollywood.[7] But it seemed that organized crime was not behind the scheme this time. Los Angeles Police Department investigators determined that, rather than being a mobster, the perpetrator had to be a "movie maniac," for the letters showed a distorted mind fascinated by Hollywood. The letters outlined a film scenario, a proposed cast of biblical characters, and a pipedream that MGM would produce it. To prove his credibility, the writer also claimed responsibility for the attempted assassination of Burton Fitts, district attorney of Los Angeles County, who was shot in the arm while riding in a car. "I can strike quick like I did to Fitts," the writer bragged. "Had I desired to kill him I could have done so. Look at him; that will be you if you do not comply." To add more twists to the story, the notes stated that a local chiropractor, Dr. E. J. Foote, had been chosen to play Jesus Christ in the imaginary movie and would be the designated person to receive the funds, while the Pentecostal evangelist Aimee Semple McPherson, who had orchestrated her own abduction in 1926, was said to be among the cast as well. When the investigators approached Dr. Foote, it appeared that he too had received a threatening letter, to which the signature "The Gang" was attached.[8]

Two weeks later, Anna May received a second letter that read, "You are not yet safe. What is money compared with your life?" It was simply signed "SHE." Strangely, this note, as if part of an early Hitchcock psychodrama, was written by perforating cheap writing paper with the point of a pen, each hole being punched into legible form. The investigators believed that the second note was sent by a copycat who had learned from news reports about the first letters. The FBI stepped in, and the agents interviewed Anna May and others involved. J. Edgar Hoover, the bureau's director, who had a perversely prurient interest in the lives of Hollywood Babylonians, demanded daily reports on the developments. But the investigation went nowhere, and the case eventually was dropped.[9]

Anna May Wong threatened, 1937 *(Courtesy of Herald Examiner Collection / Los Angeles Public Library)*

Understandably, Anna May was rattled by the extortion threats. Usually cool and calm, she began having trouble sleeping at night. A press photo shows a visibly distraught Anna May holding the wildly scribbled threat letter with one hand and nursing an apparent headache with the other. Looking askance pensively, she wears a worried expression with bags under her Bette Davis–like eyes. Accordingly, she avoided her Wilshire Boulevard apartment and went to stay with friends, preferring to spend each night in a different Hollywood home. The only silver lining was that, as a somewhat tongue-in-cheek newspaper article put it, she acquired a "boyfriend"—a police guard. Lieutenant W. E. Engstrom stood six-feet-four in his stockinged feet. The Caucasian officer said very little, but he carried a gun on his right hip. "Wherever Miss Wong goes, he goes. He always sits so that he can watch the doors and windows." Everyone wanted to give parties to cheer her up, but her new "beau" put a crimp in all social activities, stopping her from going to costume parties or even to Chinatown for dinner.

"Chinatown! Yeah, where there's enough dark alleys to hide an army," he snorted. "You wouldn't like to go down to the waterfront and play bridge on the docks, would you?"

Being a good sport under duress, Anna May hassled a consent out of him to go to dinner with her at a Japanese restaurant, where guests removed their shoes and sat on the floor with tiny tables. "If you've got a hole in your sock," she teased him, "we can get you some slippers."

The scene appears almost comical. Imagine the burly policeman trying to squeeze his huge bulk under the short-legged tables without bumping his knees. Having now tortured her own giant cop for hours, she relented at the end of the dinner, "I guess you've suffered enough to even the score between us."

They both roared with laughter.[10]

While the bodyguard story was fodder for a good laugh, there was real romance blooming in Anna May's life. The lyricist of the popular song "These Foolish Things," Eric Maschwitz was a noted British playwright working for the BBC. A charming, Cambridge-educated man with a rictus, Maschwitz had first met Anna May in the early 1930s. Years later, Maschwitz, in his memoir *No Chip on My Shoulder* (1957), reminisced fondly that his younger self had been smitten by the woman who had a lasting influence upon his life: "I can see her now, as she opened the door of her apartment to us, a slender exquisite person in a white blouse and long black skirt. I could not have known then what her friendship one day was going to mean to me but I was entirely enchanted and so overwhelmed with shyness that, as far as I remember, I hardly spoke a word."[11]

In the spring of 1937, just when the extortion episode was winding down, Maschwitz received a six-figure offer from MGM to adapt *Balalaika*, his musical play—which had been running successfully at His Majesty's Theatre in London—for the screen. MGM invited Maschwitz for a discussion, and he took a four-week leave from the BBC to make the trip to California. After a fourteen-day crossing and an overnight flight from New York to Los Angeles, Maschwitz arrived at the Burbank Airport, where Anna May was waiting for him. In the ensuing days, when he made the rounds of the studios, Maschwitz was fortunate to have Anna May as a duenna of sorts, someone who knew the ins and outs of Hollywood. "In the state of mental confusion into which my various small and sudden success had thrown me," he recalled, "I was glad of her cool commonsense." Besides the fat check for his play, MGM also made a handsome offer for Maschwitz to join the pool of writers kept on the company's regular payroll, a roster that included the then-screenwriter William Faulkner. Tempted, Maschwitz nonetheless hesitated, because it meant he would have to quit not only his job at the BBC but also the London theater milieu. Once again, Anna May helped him get out of his dithering. As Maschwitz wrote, "The Chinese are a remarkable people; everyone should know and love at least one educated Chinese person in their lives. Calmly, kindly, shrewdly, Miss Wong analyzed my situation for me, and as we said goodbye at the airport I knew that my time with the B.B.C. was at an end."[12]

It was not a long good-bye, at least not yet. After Maschwitz's departure for Britain, Anna May did some theater work on the East Coast, showing off her newly acquired Chinese wardrobe and musical skills. She performed for a week at Loew's Capitol Theatre in Washington, and then a week at Loew's State in New York. Afterward, she beelined across the ocean to London, where Maschwitz was wrapping up his business at Savoy Hill, then the BBC's head-quarters. He took her to see his play *Balalaika*, after which they went on a quick trip to Paris on July 1, staying at the elegant Hotel Crillon. Unlike most film stars who exploited their romances or scandals for publicity, Anna May was a very private person and kept her love life out of the prying eyes of the public. In the letters to her most frequent confidantes, she mentioned Maschwitz only once in passing.[13] In fact, Maschwitz at this time was still married to his first wife, Hermione Gingold, although the couple had been apart for some years. It seemed to have been a tragic pattern for Anna May to fall for married men, an eerie reflection of the fate of her lovelorn characters.

After Anna May returned home, Maschwitz soon followed her, arriving in Los Angeles in September. To welcome the newest addition to its New Writers' Block, MGM sent out a flock of reporters and cameramen to greet him at the airport. But he was happiest to see Anna May, who drove him to the Roosevelt Hotel and then to Culver City, where he reported for duty at the studios. In the following days, she helped him find a house, a charming Spanish bungalow in Beverly Hills, near her Wilshire apartment. He also bought a secondhand black Packard, and, through her connections, hired a chauffeur and servant, a Korean man named John, who was also an excellent cook. As Maschwitz put it with a touch of his wry British humor, "I now had everything that a new young writer could aspire to, apart from a swimming pool and a British butler!"[14]

Those were the boom days of the movies, when studios hired writers profligately and seldom had enough, if anything, for them to do. It remains Hollywood lore, even today, that Faulkner, on being told to "go home and take it easy, feller," packed his bag and returned to Mississippi, while MGM was unaware for months that he had gone missing. With exorbitant time on his hands and a not-insubstantial paycheck, Maschwitz was thoroughly enjoying Southern California in the company of Anna May. The two went sunbathing on the beach in Santa Monica, visited the racecourse at Santa Anita, explored the desert oasis of Palm Springs, flew up to San Francisco, and drove south over the Mexican border to gamble at Tijuana. Hollywood, an artificial Paradise with no water of its own, was a surreal place for the Briton inured to a very different clime. With hyperbolic British overstatement, Maschwitz wrote that it was "a pantomime Garden of Eden where the huge vegetables have no flavor, the giant flowers no perfume! Nevertheless for a while it had the appeal of novelty; I had never known a town so neatly beautiful, nor so rich." Creating almost parodic images, he described the endless parties, café-crawling, or just "doing the town" in the evening, hitting the Clover Club, Trocadero, Perino's, Cocoanut Grove, Cock'n Bull, Chasen's, Tropics, and Seven Seas in the neon moonlight of the Sunset Strip. The couple also dined frequently at Chinese restaurants downtown, allowing him to try his luck with chopsticks and "a few halting phrases in Chinese." When Maschwitz's friend and former BBC colleague Val Gielgud (brother of John) came to town for vacation, the trio drove to Santa Barbara for fun, stopping by Charlie Chaplin's Flying A Studio in downtown, visiting the quaint Danish colony in Solvang, or just doing 90 mph on the highway passing Ventura.[15]

All, however, was not well in paradise. Two Pacific storms brought a once-in-a-fifty-year flood to the Los Angeles Basin in early 1938. Maschwitz saw firsthand the devastation caused by floodwaters hurtling down the canyons, ripping houses from their foundations, and sweeping them out to sea. Alarmingly, cracks appeared in the walls of the Hollywood Hills reservoir, and police launches sped through streets to rescue those trapped inside houses. The natural disaster led to the loss of more than a hundred lives and unprecedented damage to the area. Fortunately, Maschwitz's rental house on the hill was safe—rising water merely submerging the sidewalks and lapping at his front door. Anna May's Wilshire apartment building also stood unscathed above the deluge.

We do not know whether the storm had anything to do with it, but the novelty began to wear off, and Maschwitz itched for London. In April 1938, as Los Angeles, still caked in mud, was recovering, Maschwitz left for England. At the train station, as if in a cinematic scene, he bade farewell to friends and to the woman who had meant so much to him. "Most of all I hated leaving Anna May," he confessed in his purplish memoir. "As the reader may have realized, she was somebody very precious to me, a friend, a counselor, a piece of porcelain too delicate for my rough hands to handle with any safety. The bell sounded, the last confused farewells were said, and, all of a sudden, knee-deep in chocolates and novels by Pearl S. Buck, with tears in my eye, I was on my way!"[16]

One of Maschwitz's lyrics memorialized the occasion, for it is widely believed that he had written the song "These Foolish Things" for Anna May, a song rendered timeless by the golden voices of jazz singers from Billie Holiday and Ella Fitzgerald to Nat King Cole:

> *A cigarette that bears a lipstick's traces*
> *An airline ticket to romantic places. . . .*[17]

35

DAUGHTER OF SHANGHAI

Philip Ahn and Anna May Wong in *Daughter of Shanghai*, 1938 *(Courtesy of Everett Collection)*

IT WAS WHILE Anna May was crossing the English Channel from Le Havre to Portsmouth on her way from Paris to London that she heard the disturbing news about China. Under a full moon on July 7, 1937, the Japanese army had exchanged fire with Chinese troops on the Marco Polo Bridge outside Peking, in the process shelling a nearby walled town with mortar and artillery fire. The eight-hundred-year-old stone bridge, an architectural gem with parapets adorned by marble lions that spanned the river on graceful arches, was a monument so named in honor of the first Westerner who crossed it in the thirteenth century. The skirmish and subsequent bombardment proved to be the start of a full-scale Japanese invasion.[1]

Within days, the Japanese army marched into Peking and also began to attack other cities. On August 14, a day that would be known as "Bloody Saturday," ill-trained Chinese pilots badly missed their target, mistakenly dropping bombs on crowded areas and luxury hotels on Shanghai's Bund, instead of on *Idzumo*, a Japanese warship anchored in the Whangpoo.[2] Two weeks later, another round of aerial bombardment, this time by Japanese aircraft, hit Shanghai's South Station, killing hundreds of refugees trying to flee the besieged city by train. Gruesome images of the carnage—comparable to the German Condor Legion's bombing of Guernica in the Spanish Civil War earlier that year—were captured by none other than Newsreel Wong. Less than a year after he had photographed Anna May's visit to China, and likely using the same Leica, Wong alarmed and angered the world with a picture of a crying baby sitting alone in the debris of the bombed-out Shanghai train station. The

Bloody Saturday, Shanghai, 1937 *(Courtesy of National Archives)*

tragedies in Shanghai were just a grim forerunner of the Nanking Massacre in December, when the Japanese army engaged in a barbaric rampage, killing an estimated three hundred thousand civilians and committing mass rape, looting, and arson.

For Anna May, the news from China was personally devastating. Not only had she cultivated an almost patriotic affection for her ancestral land, but also most of her family members were still there. Her eldest brother and younger sister, in particular, were both living in Shanghai: James had been teaching there, and Mary was working as a secretary to the Inspector-General of Customs. Fortunately, James had left for Hong Kong on August 14, two hours before the bombing started; and Mary was convalescing at home from a cold and did not go out that day.[3] But the rapid onset of the war would pose an existential threat to everyone, including her father and other siblings in Hong Kong and Canton, areas that also would fall to the Japanese.

The outbreak of war in China riveted America's attention and piqued Hollywood's interest. Ironically, World War II would prove to be a windfall to Hollywood impresarios, who always knew that with a good script, patriotism and profit could go hand in hand. Many of the classic films exploiting war and postwar themes, such as *The Great Dictator* (1940), *Casablanca* (1942), *To Have and Have Not* (1944), and *The Stranger* (1946), were all made during the period from 1937 through the end of the Korean War in 1953.

With China now in the headlines every day, it was no surprise then that Paramount finally offered Anna May her first American starring role since *Daughter of the Dragon*, marking her return to the screen after a three-year hiatus. Even though the new film, as she confided to a friend, was plain hokum, Anna May took Hollywood hokum seriously.[4] In *Daughter of Shanghai*, she played Lan Ying, the daughter of a San Francisco Chinatown importer. After the murder of her father, Lan Ying becomes a detective on the trail of smugglers, traveling as far as the Caribbean and occasionally having to don men's clothes. Because of the intensity of the action involved, the director, Robert Florey, asked Anna May to trim her long fingernails. For a dozen years, she had diligently cultivated the stiletto tips of her slender fingers and protected them against breakage by wearing gold guards. Like Mary Pickford's golden ringlets or Veronica Lake's peek-a-boo cascade, these gilded cuticle attachments had served to exoticize her presence. Yet, for the sake of making her character more believable in the film, Anna May sacrificed her nails.[5]

Dubbed "The Anna May Wong Story" by the studio insiders, *Daughter of Shanghai* did well upon its release in January of 1938 and received good reviews. The *New York Times* praised the lead actress as an "attractive Oriental" in a tense melodrama. *Motion Picture Exhibitor* also considered the film as being "well made, holding enough punch for action houses." Secretly mourning the loss of her fingernails, Anna May was happy that the film, given the outpouring of sympathy for China, now portrayed the lumbering giant of a country in a more positive light. "I like my part in this picture better than any I've had before," she declared. "This picture gives Chinese a break—we have sympathetic parts for a change."[6]

In addition, this was the first film in which Anna May's character is given a happy, romantic ending, although it was, of course, with an Asian man, and Americans were hardly aware that there were cultural differences between a Korean and a Chinese. In her star vehicle, Anna May paired with the Korean American actor Philip Ahn, who played a federal agent, Kim Lee. The combined factors that Wong and Ahn were chums from high school and that Kim Lee proposes marriage to Lan Ying at the end of the film spurred the Hollywood rumor mill into wild speculations that the two Asian American actors were romantically involved, unaware that Ahn was, quite possibly, gay.[7] Interestingly, both Anna May and Ahn added fuel to the speculative fire themselves. In a joint interview, Anna May teased the journalist by remarking, "Of course, I'm very fond of Philip, we've been good friends for many years, but marriage—," and Ahn chimed in, "But who can tell where love is concerned?" In a separate occasion, on CBS Radio, Ahn responded to the rumored romance by proclaiming, "All I can say is that she is one of the finest young ladies I know, and we have been friends since childhood. Further than that, I think you had better ask her. And that's the truth."[8]

Being ambivalent and elusive might have been a good publicity tactic, for, in typical Hollywood fashion, unfounded gossip always creates buzz, keeping curiosity alive. But it is also possible that these two Asian American actors, living in an era when homoeroticism was taboo, were using each other as a proverbial "beard." Especially in an industry where being "outed" as a homosexual could easily doom one's career, there were countless examples of "lavender marriages" or "tandem couples"—Judy Garland and Vincente Minnelli, Charles Laughton and Elsa Lanchester, Laurence Olivier and Jill Esmond, Barbara Stanwyck and Robert Taylor, to name just a few.[9] While she was making *Daughter of Shanghai*, Anna May resumed her cozy relationship with Marlene Dietrich, who was shooting *Angel* on the same Paramount lot. According to Maria Riva, her Mutti found Melvyn Douglas, the male lead in the romcom, rather boring. "He is a talented light comedian," Dietrich opined, "but for my taste, not a romantic lead. He has no glamor—no sex appeal." Still married to her husband while maintaining an on-and-off triangle relationship with Mercedes de Acosta and Greta Garbo, Dietrich was at the time romantically involved with Douglas Fairbanks Jr. And she enjoyed hanging out with Anna May, androgynous John Barrymore, and others. "Anna May Wong got her green tea piping hot at four," as Riva writes in her recollection of how Dietrich and her friends spent their time together on the studio lot and at Mutti's private bungalow at the Beverly Hills Hotel.[10]

Unfortunately, except for these sketchy allusions that occasionally appear in the biographies of other stars, we know very little about how Anna May navigated the *sub rosa* lesbian world of Hollywood in the 1930s and 1940s. Anna May's rumored liaisons with Marlene Dietrich, Leni Riefenstahl, Dolores del Rio, and others were not the kind of sapphic love affairs openly discussed or graphically described as those in, say, de Acosta's *Here Lies the Heart* (1960)—a controversial memoir that serves as an indispensable chronicle of "the sewing circle." Instead, Anna May's fluid sexuality manifested itself mostly in her myriad images, thus giving credence to contemporary feminist views that gender or sexual identity is socially performative rather than biologically determined. In her screen roles, vaudeville skits, and publicity photos, Anna May used costumes, coiffures, and gestures to curate an image of Oriental femininity, while also projecting a style of what would be called, in today's lingo, "lesbian chic."[11]

In a series of studio portraits of Anna May taken by Carl Van Vechten, Edward Steichen, and others in the 1930s, there is an impressive array of aesthetic styles and erotic appeals. Exploring the liminal space between submissive Madame Butterfly and mannish Dragon Lady, these photographs are full of elements of camp theatrics—some showing her in drag, wearing a blonde wig or a Japanese kimono, some nude or seminude. In one photo by Van Vechten, Anna May is attired in a tuxedo and a top hat, holding a cocktail glass close to her glossy lips, while her stiletto fingernails curve around the alcoholic nectar. In a period when famous Hollywood butches like Garbo and Dietrich flaunted their menswear and constantly looked for so-called trouser roles both on and off the screen, homoeroticism latent in Anna May's cosplay with a tuxedo and a coquettishly slanting top hat became unmistakable. In fact, Van Vechten, a bisexual white author who served as a patron and dealmaker in the Harlem

Renaissance, claimed that Anna May was his "first subject" when he began to dabble in photography in 1932. In the ensuing years, he not only took celebrity shots of notable white and African American cultural elites—including Eugene O'Neill, Zora Neale Hurston, Langston Hughes, Henri Matisse, and Georgia O'Keeffe—but also took numerous images of nonwhite male nudes often posed in highly suggestive scenarios. The latter, along with collected hard- and soft-core homopornography, circulated within a closed circle of Van Vechten's most

trusted male acquaintances, most of whom were gay or bisexual, and remained sealed in the archives until twenty-five years after his death.[12] Finding Anna May's provocative images lying next to this clandestine cache of photos certainly gives us a sense of the racialized cultural space in which she negotiated and performed her evolving sexual identity.

While Anna May continued to orbit in Hollywood's gender-fluid sewing circle, Ahn actually served as a precursor for gay actors, such as Rock Hudson and Tab Hunter, who were constantly linked to starlets to throw audiences off a forbidden trail. Straitlaced studio heads could be willing to look the other way as long as actors were discreet about their sexual orientations—and, if they were not,

Portrait of Anna May Wong by Carl Van Vechten, 1932 *(Courtesy of Library of Congress, Prints and Photographs Division, Carl Van Vechten Collection, Reproduction Number LC-USZ62-42509)*

as long as they remained viable as "cash cows." But the standard "moral turpitude" clause in an actor's contract, which could be cited to end a career, always hung like the sword of Damocles over the heads of those having to lead secret lives. As already marginalized Asian actors, Anna May and Ahn faced double jeopardy and would have to tread even more carefully in a pre-Stonewall world.

As soon as *Daughter of Shanghai* finished shooting, Paramount gave Anna May a three-picture contract, in addition to a salary of $4,166 for the film, while Ahn earned a paltry $1,000. With her film career seemingly back on track, Anna May celebrated her thirty-third birthday on January 3, 1938. To her relief, her younger sister was able to return from shell-torn Shanghai, where Mary's office at the Customs House had been splattered by shrapnel.[13] The horrific stories and the daily headlines—the six-week savagery in Nanking happened during the Christmas season—made Anna May eager to do more for the Chinese cause both on and off the screen. She sent money to Dr. Margaret Chung, who was raising funds in San Francisco to send medical supplies to China. In March, as mentioned earlier, *Look* magazine proclaimed Anna May "The World's Most Beautiful Chinese Girl," with a cover photograph and a feature article describing her sense of fashion. Riding a wave of newfound prestige and glamour, she auctioned off her film costumes to raise money for China war relief.[14]

On June 25, New Chinatown opened to great fanfare, and Anna May was invited to join the impressive lineup of dignitaries, celebrities, and community members who gathered at the Central Plaza to celebrate the first Chinese-owned enclave in the United States. After the demolition of Old Chinatown in 1933, proposals were put forth for a new settlement that would continue to serve as a tourist attraction and also house a displaced population of about 2,500 Chinese. It resulted in two competing projects, setting the stage for a "Battle of the Chinatowns."[15]

One was China City, which opened three weeks earlier than its rival and should more appropriately be called Hollywood Chinatown. Led by the social activist Christine Sterling, it was built from the props that had been used in the film production of *The Good Earth*. Combining Hollywood's Oriental vision with pure fantasy, China City sported a centerpiece that was a replica House of Wang set from the Oscar-winning film, designed and crafted in consultation with Paramount Studios. It also featured rickshaw rides, curio stalls manned by Chinese merchants in proto-Disney costume, and children dressed as hungry peasants roaming the streets of an imaginary Chinese city, as depicted in Pearl Buck's novels.[16]

A few blocks away, bounded by Broadway and Castelar, lay the competing vision of a Chinese enclave, New Chinatown. Spearheaded by prominent Chinese community members, the development was architecturally designed to look like Peking's Forbidden City, with an open-air Central Plaza and two lofty gates facing east and west. Part of the West Gate was made of 150-year-old camphor wood and adorned with an inscription by Chinese Consul General T. K. Chang. As a daughter of Old Chinatown, Anna May understandably preferred to affiliate herself with this community-based project rather than the kitschy Hollywood-made fantasy. At the grand opening of New Chinatown, she had the honor of planting a willow tree named after her. Today, this homage to the star persona, whose name means "Yellow Frosted Willow," still stands in front of a wishing well, inspired by yet another old China landmark, the Seven Star Caverns in Canton.[17]

As the Chinese in Los Angeles were celebrating the reopening of their American stand-in for China, their distant homeland was in shambles. After seizing major cities like Peking, Shanghai, and Nanking, the Japanese army in 1938 was making rapid advances into the Chinese heartland. To stall the enemy's momentum, Chiang Kai-shek ordered the opening of dikes on the Yellow River in June, flooding a large swath of densely populated area across three provinces and destroying thousands of villages and towns. An estimated four hundred thousand people drowned, and an additional ten million became refugees. Chiang's desperate measure failed miserably. By October, the Japanese army had begun the siege on Wuhan, forcing the Nationalist government to retreat to the southwestern city of Chungking.

Under the circumstances, China required enormous aid. On October 8, concerned Chinese Los Angelenos turned their annual Moon Festival into a fundraiser. Choosing what remained of Old Chinatown as the venue for the event in order to maximize media exposure, the organizers erected three elaborate gates through which twenty-five thousand visitors would enter. They cordoned off a section of Los Angeles Street, which was decorated with Chinese lanterns and flags and lined with concession stands. Beneath the light of a full moon, the festival kicked off with rituals at the Altar of Blessings to the Moon Goddess, followed by a lantern-and-dragon-boat parade, in which two hundred young women in colorful Chinese gowns carried lanterns and preceded the dragon boat. Using terminology typical of that bygone era, the *Los Angeles Times* reported: "Pretty Chinese girls rode in a grotesque dragon boat, seeking to appease the wrath of the dragon on the fifteenth day of the eighth moon in the Chinese Calendar."[18] A precursor of scenes from the postwar Broadway musical *Flower Drum Song* (1961), the parade also featured a spectacular, high-spirited performance by the Mei Wah Girls Drum Corps. At the climax of the festival, an elongated dragon held up by dozens of athletic men gyrated down the street, while lion dancers dazzled the crowds with their nimble moves, accompanied by cymbals and gongs.[19]

Amid the festivities, a highlight of the night involved the famed Daughter of the Dragon. Placed next to a concession stand where a Dr. Edward Lee told fortunes and sold horned nuts, the Anna May Wong booth was filled to capacity by her fans. The crowds were eagerly lining up to get autographs and have their pictures taken with the star, who looked as though she had just stepped out of a movie screen. The nominal fees they paid would go to the United China Relief Fund.[20]

The full moon being a symbol of reunion, the Moon Festival was usually celebrated by the Chinese as an occasion for family gatherings and thanksgiving. In 1938, Anna May had much to be thankful for but more to be worried about. With the relentless advance of the Japanese forces, her family in southern China was no longer safe. In just a few weeks, the Japanese would capture Canton, forcing millions of people to flee—an Asian forerunner to the exodus from Paris in 1940, when millions fled the city ahead of the Nazi invasion. Even though her father and siblings would make it back safely to the United States in November, all the places she had visited only two years earlier were now engulfed in a fiery cauldron of war. In Shanghai, the Civic Center, where she had once witnessed a mass wedding, had been decimated by the Japanese with precision bombing, leaving only a spectral façade. Sir Victor Sassoon's posh Cathay Hotel and Palace Hotel were also shattered—albeit accidentally by Chinese bombers—causing the loss of many lives. In Peking, the commander of the Japanese army ordered Mei Lan-fang to perform for them, with a reward of a high-ranking position, but the Chinese maestro refused to sing and chose a life of impoverishment and silence for the duration of the war. In fact, the legendary female impersonator purposefully grew a mustache and feigned toothaches to avoid performing. Similarly coerced and tempted, Cheng Yanqiu, the other opera singer Anna May had befriended, chose a life of disguise and exile, tilling the fields as a peasant in the countryside. Pinkie, her handsome neighbor and accomplice in escapades around the old Imperial City, had become the right-hand man of the Commanding General US Army Forces in the China–Burma–India Theater, Joseph Stilwell. Several years later, Pinkie would march by the side of General "Uncle Joe" in a long, perilous walk out of Burma in 1942.

But now, surrounded by her fans and looking at the sea of humanity down the street that used to be so familiar to her as a child, Anna May recalled images of the past, as she had once described nostalgically in her autobiography: "The narrow streets lined with grimy buildings, the shops where Chinese herbs and drugs were sold, the gambling places where white men and Chinese mingled, the overcrowded tenements where the Chinese lived, sometimes entire families in one room, the gaily painted chop-suey restaurants with their lanterns a soft, many colored blur in the dark."[21]

At this moment, she had a premonition: As a Chinese icon, no matter what incarnation she assumed—whether as Daughter of the Dragon, Daughter of Shanghai, or "The World's Most Beautiful Chinese Girl"—the war was going to consume her waking hours and ideological passions. She felt ready for it.

36

YOUR NAME IN CHINESE

PERMIT ME TO DIGRESS a bit from the story of Anna May Wong. In the fall of 1846, when six decades of booming China trade had helped to turn Boston into a hotbed of American Orientalism—or, if you will, a clearinghouse for all things Chinese—a fifteen-year-old girl named Emily Dickinson rolled into town with her parents. Living in Amherst, Massachusetts, the future "Poet Recluse of America" had been struggling with health problems. In late spring through early summer, her cough had become so severe that she had had to take a leave from her classes at Amherst Academy. After she recovered, her parents thought it would be a good idea to take her to Boston for sightseeing, as well as to visit her Aunt Lavinia. After an impressive train ride, Emily spent a month in Beantown, visiting the glorious "City of the Dead"—Mount Auburn Cemetery, America's first garden cemetery, which had opened in 1831—then climbing Bunker Hill, where she enjoyed a panoramic view of the city, before attending two concerts and a horticultural exhibition.

What really tickled her adolescent mind, however, was the Chinese Museum. Newly opened in the Marlboro Chapel on Washington Street by John R. Peters, who would soon sell it to the humbug P. T. Barnum, the Chinese Museum was "a great curiosity" to the young Emily. As she told her friend Abiah Root in a letter, the collection consisted of twenty-five tableaux, each displaying facets of Chinese life and culture, including objects, paintings, and an "endless variety of Wax figures made to resemble the Chinese & dressed in their costume." To make the exhibition more enticing (and lucrative), two Chinese men were also installed at the museum: One of them was a musician and the other a teacher. Apparently quoting from the exhibition pamphlet, Dickinson confided to her friend, "They were both wealthy & not obliged to labor but they were also Opium Eaters & fearing to continue the practice lest it destroyed their lives yet unable to break the 'rigid chain of habit' in their own land, they left their family's & came to this country. They have now entirely overcome the practice." Confessing to a lack of interest in the musician, she was barely able to stay awake as he played upon two Chinese instruments and accompanied them with singing. But she was intrigued by the Writing Master, who was "constantly occupied in writing the names of visitors who request it upon cards in the Chinese language—for which he charges 12½ cts. apiece." Always obsessed with the slipperiness of signs and their meanings, Emily shelled out twenty-five cents to acquire two cards for her sister Viny and herself. We do not know what Chinese characters the Writing Master used to transliterate "Viny" and "Emily," but the perennial punster was satisfied to see the names appear in a mysteriously pictorial script she could not decipher. As she told Abiah, "I consider them very precious."[1]

Fast forward about a century, during the years of World War II, when Americans were attending charity fundraisers and would experience essentially what Emily Dickinson had once seen at the Chinese Museum in Boston. The only difference was that, rather than a reformed opium addict, they would espy a beautiful Chinese actress, bedecked in a finely cut cheongsam, offering to write their names in Chinese for ten cents. Thus, on top of their regular exposure to the signage of Chinese laundries and restaurants (or Ezra Pound's imagism, if they happened to be students of poetry), Americans found that their fascination with Chinese characters and culture just took on a new, humanitarian meaning.

In September 1939, using a ruse similar to Japan's descent on China, Germany invaded Poland under false pretenses. Next, the Nazis seized France in the summer of 1940, before bombing Britain—all while Europe seemed paralyzed. Even then, millions of Americans held on to their "Never again" mentality, weary of becoming involved in another round of Old World quarrels. Before the Japanese bombed Pearl Harbor, the United States desperately sought to maintain neutrality, relying mostly on financial and material aid to support its allies, particularly Britain and China. When Japan officially joined the Axis powers in September 1940, Congress quickly approved a loan of $25 million to China, followed by another $50 million that November.[2] Among the general public, many China aid societies were established, most of them controlled by white businessmen, former missionaries, and local Chinese American organizations. Well before America's entry into the war, which would induce a huge outpouring of patriotic fervor in Hollywood, Anna May was the industry's most active China supporter, crisscrossing the country on fundraising missions.

Having already auctioned off some of her stylish costumes and donated cash to the United China Relief Fund, she became the most visible face of the China cause in the United States. On January 22, 1940, she sponsored a sale of rare Chinese *objets d'art* at the Beverly-Wilshire Hotel, with proceeds going to the American Bureau for Medical Aid to China. In May, she helped Father Charles Meeus host a charity event at the Wilshire Ebell Theatre. A prominent missionary in China and head of the Chinese Boy Scouts, the Belgian-born Catholic priest was employed by the Chinese Ministry of Information to combat the lingering anti-Chinese sentiment among Americans. At this event, Father Meeus showed a short film he had made of rural western China. He spoke highly of Anna May, calling her the leader in relief work.[3] In October, in the midst of a heat wave and several earthquake tremors in Los Angeles, Anna May attended a China Aid Council benefit held at Pickfair. In November and into December, she made whistle-stops on the East Coast, attending Bowl of Rice parties—highly popular fundraisers popping up in affluent areas nationwide—at the Waldorf-Astoria in New York, as well as in Boston and Ridgefield, Connecticut. In June 1941, she directed an evening program for the United China Relief Fund in Santa Monica, attended by Chinese Consul General T. K. Chang and such Hollywood luminaries as Cary Grant, George Murphy, Una Merkel, and Fanny Brice. Besides a lion dance, a sword dance, and a fashion show, Anna May showed the crowd a homemade film of her China trip: *Where the Wind Rocks the Bamboo.*[4] She had wanted to call the film *My Country and My People*, but Lin Yutang's publisher refused to let her borrow the title of the bestseller.[5]

Nothing, however, revealed her passion for the China cause better than her trip to Australia, where Anna May performed revues on the Tivoli Theatre circuit for two and a half months. As part of a variety program titled "Highlights from Hollywood," she arrived in Sydney aboard the ship *Aorangi* on June 4, 1939. Hailed as "the illustrious daughter of China," she appeared as an ambassador and spokesperson for China more than for the United States. Besides a gaggle of journalists and a crowd of fans, the enthusiastic throng greeting her on the dock included Dr. Chun-Jien Pao, the Chinese Consul General in Australia,

Anna May Wong in Australia, 1939 *(Courtesy of New York Public Library)*

and Doris Chen, a Chinese government representative who had been working in Australia to raise funds for Chinese war refugees. The reporter for *The Sydney Morning Herald* was struck by Anna May's distinctly Chinese outfit and demeanor: "Miss Wong, who has a quiet, serene manner, and a low-pitched speaking voice, was an impressive figure in a slim black frock, ankle-length and slit to the knees, to display long white trousers of embroidered sheer. She added a smooth black turban with a gold ornament, and a silver fox cape. Her finger and toe nails were lacquered with a new colored polish, crushed strawberry, which is a deep red with an opalescent sheen."[6] Subsequent news coverage also played up Anna May's Chinese-ness, obviously reflecting her own self-image.

At the time of her arrival, Australia's attitude toward China had become more tolerant. Just as in the United States, prejudice against Chinese immigrants had marked the birth of modern Australia. In fact, throughout the Anglophone world, "anti-coolieism" was foundational to Western identities of nation and empire; and Australia was no exception. As Mae Ngai shows in her magisterial study, *The Chinese Question*, Chinese communities in those far-flung gold-producing regions of Australia routinely faced marginalization, violence, and exclusion from self-described "white men's countries."[7] The rise of Japan as a rival in the Pacific triggered a strategic shift in Australia's China policy, eliciting slow changes of public sentiment in favor of the Chinese. After the Japanese invasion of China, and with war looming in the Pacific, China was now an ally of Australia and the United States.

On a professional level, Anna May appeared to have reached a turning point in her career. By 1939, she had completed the three films dictated by her contract with Paramount. These films, *Dangerous to Know* (1938), *King of China-town* (1939), and *Island of Lost Men* (1939), in addition to *When Were You Born?* (1938), in which she was on loan to Warner Bros., received mixed reviews, but they earned her a good sum of money—enough to splurge $18,000 on a nice house in Santa Monica, just blocks from the ocean.[8]

The first of these films, *Dangerous to Know*, was an adaptation of *On the Spot*, the Edgar Wallace play in which Anna May had made her American stage debut in 1930. It was dismissed by *Motion Picture Exhibitor* as "repetitious claptrap," and by the *New York Times* as a "second-rate melodrama, hardly worthy of the talents of its generally capable cast."[9] The reception of *King of Chinatown* was better, with *Variety* singling out Anna May for her "nice portrayal" of a Chinese woman, based on the real-life San Francisco doctor Margaret Chung, who led the Red Cross campaign to help war-ravaged China.[10] In the film, Anna May teamed up for the second time with Philip Ahn, as well as the Russian-born, strongly accented Akim Tamiroff. An excellent addition to the cast was Sidney Toler, soon to be chosen by Fox as the new Charlie Chan after the untimely death of Anna May's friend Warner Oland. The making of *When Were You Born?* at the Warner Bros. lot provided a respite from most of her previous roles attached to her Chinese identity. Playing an astrologer who accurately predicts the imminent death of a fellow passenger on a cruise ship, Anna May made her entrance in the film with a pet monkey on her shoulder, like a Chinese Emily Hahn. The fourth film, *Island of Lost Men*, returned her not only to the familiar setup at the Paramount studio, but also to her stereotypical role as a café singer plucking a Chinese banjo and sporting a clichéd moniker, "China Lily." The *New York Times* dismissed the film as a portentous burlesque, while *Variety* lauded Anna May for her "dignified, capable" performance.[11]

With *Island of Lost Men*, Anna May entered into what an astute critic has called "the twilight of her film career."[12] Paramount declined to offer her a new contract, nor would any other major studio enlist her. As she complained to her friends privately, film work had dried up for her as fast as puddles under a scorching sun. Some scholars suggested that the real purpose of Anna May's visit to Australia was to escape Hollywood in order to ponder her future. Even if that was true, she had at least chosen a good cause to go along with her private concerns: the humanitarian pursuit of China aid.

After a week of rehearsal, "Highlights from Hollywood" opened at the Tivoli Theatre in Melbourne on June 12. With Anna May as the lead, the program included actress Betty Burgess, a platinum blonde in a handful of films, and tap dancer Sonny Lamont, who had appeared in Fred Astaire and Ginger Rogers's *The Story of Vernon and Irene Castle* (1939). Accompanied by the musical prodigy Merrill La Fontaine on the piano, Anna May sang her favorite Chinese song, "The Jasmine Flower," and a French chanson, followed by a dramatic monologue from *Shanghai Express*. As *The Argus* reported the next day, "Her presentation is original and 'color' is added by the many beautiful Chinese costumes she wears," and her charming versatility was "met with hearty approval" by the audience.[13]

Two weeks later, Anna May added a dramatic episode called "At the Barricade" to her repertoire. In the skit, which was a response to the war raging in China, she impersonated a brave Chinese woman arrested by Japanese soldiers in occupied Tientsin, while the impressionist Bugs Wilson played a Japanese commander. To simulate gunfire, firecrackers obtained from Melbourne's Chinatown were used in the episode. Such a hybrid of entertainment and propaganda would become an inspiration for future films she would make in wartime.[14]

With the added episodes, "Highlights from Hollywood" concluded its successful run in Melbourne and traveled to Sydney in late July. On top of the busy work schedule—two shows per day, six days per week—Anna May participated in many fundraisers and charity events. On August 8, she hosted an "Anna May Wong Ball," attended by the Chinese consul general and other dignitaries. As the *Sydney Morning Herald* reported, during the event, Anna May "autographed photographs of herself at a small charge, and the money was donated to the relief fund."[15] Playing on the variation of "Your Name in Chinese for 10 Cents," she attempted to rally support for China in any way she could.

After two and a half months in Australia, Anna May left Sydney for Los Angeles on August 18, aboard the SS *Monterey*.[16] Just as the luxury liner sailed into the port of San Pedro on September 3, she learned that France and Britain had declared war on Germany. World War II had officially started.

37

GODDESS OF MERCY

Anna May Wong and Hayward Soo Hoo in *Bombs over Burma*, 1942 *(Courtesy of Everett Collection)*

I T MAY SURPRISE readers to know that, in September 1939, when war had commenced in Europe and China, the US Army was ranked nineteenth among the world's armed forces, a notch behind Portugal and just ahead of Bulgaria. With an active army numbering merely 174,000 men, plus Army Reserves, it ranked forty-fifth in the percentage of population under arms.[1] After World War I, the isolationists in Washington had pushed a clutch of laws through Congress limiting any military buildup, and most Americans had lived with the conviction that the country would never again send boots on the ground to fight a war elsewhere. When Winston Churchill uttered, "We shall fight on the beaches . . . in the streets . . . we shall never surrender," his words sounded surreal to many Americans, as if from a soundtrack heard at a movie theater. Trying to drum up assistance for the US allies, President Roosevelt tried to create a sense of urgency in one of his Fireside Chats: "For us this is an emergency as serious as war itself. We must apply ourselves to our task with the same resolution, the same sense of urgency, the same spirit of patriotism and sacrifice as we would show were we at war." Earnest as these words were, they acknowledged that while the United States was willing to provide economic and moral support to its allies, the nation was not at war, at least not yet.[2]

In paradisiacal Southern California, the 1940 Tournament of Roses Parade took place as usual on New Year's Day in Pasadena. As a river of floral floats flowed down Colorado Boulevard, keen observers noted that not one float made reference to war in Europe or elsewhere. That afternoon in the Rose Bowl, the USC Trojans walloped the University of Tennessee Volunteers, 14 to 0. If the New Year was any indication, the mood in California—indeed, the whole nation—was one of "willfully oblivious, even defiant, well-being."[3]

Despite the ongoing carnage in China, 1940 began with hope for Anna May. After returning from Australia, she maintained her steady pace of charity work while trying to fix up her new home in Santa Monica. Located at 326 San Vicente Boulevard, the L-shaped, green-tiled Spanish-style house sat on two lots on the corner of San Vicente and Fourth Street. After remodeling, she converted the property into four units and promptly named it Moongate Apartments, for the sake of the red moon gates and other Chinese features of its architecture and setting. The garden was lush with exotic tropical plants, including passion fruit and pineapple guavas in season. She also planted her own favorite flowers, the simple ones that she preferred, such as geraniums, stock, ginger, and Chinese forget-me-nots. Next to a bamboo grove, she placed a Chinese wheelbarrow, almost as if she was designing her own film set.[4] Keeping the main section of the complex for herself, she rented out the other units to defray the costs of housekeeping and repairs.

In February, her Shanghai friend Sir Victor Sassoon came to town, as did Hilda Yan, the famous Chinese aviatrix, who in May 1939 had been flying solo across America to speak against Japanese aggression—until her plane crashed near Montgomery, Alabama. (She suffered severe injuries but miraculously survived.)[5] Anna May showed her friends around Hollywood and accompanied Yan to an event in Chinatown. In May, she tried to help Madame Koo—whose husband was stuck in Paris as the Chinese ambassador to Vichy France—to sell a precious jade necklace for $5,000 as a contribution to Chinese war orphans and refugees.[6] In July, she was getting ready to travel east for the opening of the play *On the Spot*, at the Deerlake Theatre in Orwigsburg, Pennsylvania, when tragedy struck the Wong family again.

On July 25, Mary, who had fled war horrors in China less than three years earlier, committed suicide. According to the *New York Times*, Mary was having lunch with her father and Lulu at their family house on North Figueroa. After arising from the table, she walked to the garage in the rear of the home and "hanged herself from a clothes-line suspended from a rafter." Her body was found an hour later.[7] There was no specific reason given for the suicide, but Mary might have suffered from PTSD after witnessing her Shanghai office destroyed by shrapnel. Besides, her dream of a Hollywood career had reached a stalemate. Her best gig had been a bit part in *The Good Earth*. The fact that Anna May's career seemed deadlocked also weighed on Mary, who felt that if Anna May at thirty-five could no longer find work, her own career was hopeless.

Anna May was devastated by Mary's death. She was, to quote the *New York Times*, "prostrated by the news" in her Santa Monica home. She did not want to talk to the media or even her friends about the tragedy. Since the early death of her mother, and especially after her father's retirement, she had been acting as a surrogate parent to her younger siblings. In the US Census of 1940, she was listed at the San Vicente address as the head of household, which included Mary, Roger, and Richard. With Mary gone and Roger, at twenty-four, old enough to make it on his own, Anna May took the youngest one, Richard, under her wing. After weeks of mourning, Anna May and Richard left for the East Coast on August 15 for the postponed premiere of *On the Spot* in Pennsylvania. In the ensuing months, as war clouds gathered over the Pacific horizon, she zigzagged across the country for various engagements.

On December 7, 1941, the surprise Japanese attack on Pearl Harbor not only dragged the United States into the global conflict but also brought the war directly to the coast of California. As the so-called garrison state by virtue of its history and geography, California was on high alert. During the days immediately following the Pearl Harbor debacle, air-raid sirens blared constantly in San Francisco and the East Bay. Blackouts ensued. On December 9, a tabloid-like banner headline in the *San Francisco Chronicle* screamed: JAPANESE PLANES NEAR S.F.—4 RAID ALARMS. Quoting a military commander, the paper reported, "There was an actual attack. . . . It was the real thing." Only it wasn't. On the same night, hysteria also roiled Los Angeles. A series of false alarms about air raids that never happened triggered massive blackouts, resulting in the deaths of several pedestrians run over by vehicles in the darkness.[8]

Rampant fear swelled two months later with the shelling of Santa Barbara, a California coastal town affectionately dubbed "the American Riviera." On the evening of February 23, 1942, a Japanese I-17 submarine surfaced in the Santa Barbara Channel, off the rich oilfields at Ellwood. After surveying the Santa Inez Mountains and the city nestled below through the lens of his binoculars, Commander Kozo Nishino of the Imperial Japanese Navy ordered the firing of twenty-five shells across the scenic highway in the direction of the storage tanks of the Bankline and Barnsdall oil companies. Fired from eight miles offshore, these five-inch shells caused only superficial damage to an oil refinery standing in a field of eucalyptus and live oak. But the first attack on continental soil set off mass panic, not to mention a political storm.[9]

The next day, Santa Barbara's Representative Alfred Elliott rose to speak in the US Congress, calling for the internment of all Californians of Japanese ancestry as enemy aliens. "Don't kid yourself," Elliott intoned as he pounded the podium, "and don't let someone tell you there are good Japs."[10] With anti-Japanese hysteria rising, President Franklin Roosevelt signed Executive Order 9066 three weeks later, on March 18, authorizing the incarceration of *all* Japanese on the Pacific Coast. By June 5, more than 120,000 Japanese Americans, mostly US-born or naturalized citizens, were rounded up and sent to ten internment camps scattered in seven inland states.

In the midst of the hysteria and the ensuing roundups, Chinese Americans, no strangers to racial exclusion and discriminatory laws, tried, often desperately, to distinguish themselves from Japanese Americans. Many of them wore buttons that said, I AM CHINESE or just CHINA. Exploiting the ethnic division, *Life* magazine published "How to Tell Japs from the Chinese," showing contrasting diagrams of a Chinese man and a Japanese one, accompanied by a pseudoscientific analysis of the differences. Using terms recalling the language of phrenology and eugenics, while resorting to crackpot theories, the article claimed that a Chinese face is longer and narrower in shape. It depicted a supposedly Chinese person whose complexion was parchment yellow, with no beard or rosy cheeks; in contrast, the purported Japanese face was broader and shorter, displaying an earthy yellow complexion, sometimes with rosy cheeks, and often a heavy beard.[11]

Increasingly hostile to Japan ever since its invasion of Manchuria, the Chinese American press played no small role in fueling anti-Japanese sentiment. Mostly neglecting to mention the injustice and pain caused by the massive roundup of Japanese—which was strikingly similar to the ongoing detention of Chinese immigrants on Angel Island—Chinese newspapers reinforced the idea that Japanese Americans, if unhindered, could become the so-called "fifth column" to aid Japan. Having long resented the presence and competition of Japanese-owned businesses in the vicinity of Chinatowns in San Francisco and Los Angeles, some Chinese used the internment as an opportunity to take over those vacated properties, thereby benefiting economically from the Japanese plight, as did many white business and property owners. Scholars believe that the fortune cookie—that obligatory lagniappe given at the end of a meal in American Chinese restaurants—was, in fact, a Japanese invention, a so-called *senbei*, a rice cracker invented by a Japanese baker in San Francisco as a tea dessert. After the Japanese internment, however, the Chinese entered that niche market and modified the cookies, turning them into a hallmark of Chinese fast food.[12]

In yet another niche market—Hollywood ethnic extras—Chinese bit players also took over the tiny turf after their Japanese counterparts had been sent away to the camps. Due to the rise of Japanophobia in the 1920s, there had been only a handful of Japanese extras in Hollywood to begin with, including the two Yamaoka siblings (Otto and Iris), as well as Tochia Mori, Daro Haro, Mike Morita, to name a few. Otto Yamaoka, for instance, had appeared in no fewer than thirty films between 1930 and 1940, including *Libeled Lady* (1936) with Jean Harlow, Myrna Loy, William Powell, and Spencer Tracy; and *The Letter* (1940) with Bette Davis and Herbert Marshall. He mostly had demeaning roles, often as a servant. His most notable performance was in *The Black Camel* (1931) with Warner Oland, Bela Lugosi, and Robert Young. Yamaoka played Charlie Chan's bungling Japanese sidekick, Kashimo, who would soon be replaced by Keye Luke as the "Number One Son" in later Chan flicks. After he was sent off to the Heart Mountain Camp in Wyoming, along with his entire family, Yamaoka virtually disappeared from the silver screen, with one exception being a cameo as a Burmese sailor in an episode of the TV police series, *The Naked City* (1962), starring William Shatner, the future Captain Kirk in *Star Trek*.[13]

All was not lost, however. Yuki Shimoda, a young Hollywood aspirant imprisoned at the Tule Lake Camp in California, actually spent his internment time honing his thespian skills. An extant photo shows a scantily dressed Shimoda doing an imitation in drag of Carmen Miranda's "Mama Yo Quero" inside the camp. After World War II, Shimoda's performance career took off, with notable appearances in the film *Auntie Mame* (1958), starring Rosalind Russell, in which he was cast as an overly excitable, squealing houseboy; the NBC television movie *Farewell to Manzanar* (1976), which recounts the Japanese internment ordeal; and Stephen Sondheim's Broadway musical *Pacific Overtures* (1976).[14]

In the absence of Japanese actors between 1942 and 1945, the increasing popularity of Pacific War–themed films created a significant demand for Chinese players. After Pearl Harbor, Hollywood immediately jumped on the patriotic, anti-Japanese bandwagon, producing a slew of Japanese-bashing films, including *Little Tokyo, U.S.A.*; *Wake Island*; *Gung Ho!*; *Danger in the Pacific*; and *Halfway to Shanghai*.[15] Caught up in the period of toxic jingoism, Anna May was equally vocal, her anti-Japanese behavior having already begun a decade earlier with the Japanese seizure of Manchuria. In 1937, after the commencement of the full-scale Japanese invasion of China, including "The Rape of Nanking," a Paramount press release claimed that she had "moved from one residence to another to avoid looking down at a Japanese garden." Later, during her USO tour in Alaska and Canada, she was quoted as saying, "Many of the boys I met had fought the Japs in the Aleutians, and in spite of the fact that they are terribly anxious to get home, they have an outspoken urge to take another shot at the enemy. They think of Japs only in terms of extermination."[16]

Her loudest anti-Japanese pronouncement was conveyed, of course, by her film work. In March 1942, Anna May signed a contract with Producers Releasing Corporation (PRC) to star in four films, although only two would be made. Born in the cradle of the antitrust crackdown and industry-wide restructuring in the late 1930s, PRC emerged in the 1940s as a prolific producer of low-budget B-films. Mostly shot in six days or less, PRC films concentrated on Westerns, comedy, horror, war, jungle settings, and noir. Finding its niche in the lower end of B-movies, PRC was rather creative in snatching up talents who were temporarily out of work, putting them in front of and behind the cameras, and delivering a number of low-budget hits.[17] Even though Anna May's first PRC film, *Bombs over Burma* (1942), was dismissed by film critics at the time as war propaganda, it is remembered today by both Anna May Wong fans and film students as a unique piece made by Joseph H. Lewis, an auteur with a reputation for fostering a sustained and coherent style within budgetary constraints. Born in New York City of Russian Jewish parents, Lewis began his eclectic directorial career in B-Westerns. He acquired the moniker of "Wagon-Wheel Joe" because he liked to use wagon wheels in the foreground for visual effects. In the 1950s and '60s, he would be known for directing the dark romance *Gun Crazy* (1950) and popular Western television series, such as *The Big Valley*, *Gunsmoke*, and the hugely successful *Bonanza*.[18]

Shot in two weeks on a shoestring budget of $25,000, *Bombs over Burma* provided a perfect vehicle for Anna May's two chief interests: acting in a movie and campaigning for China. The film opens in Chungking, the wartime capital of the Nationalist government. Following stock footage of the streets crowded with running rickshaws, pannier carriers in coolie hats, and sauntering pedestrians, the scene cuts to a classroom where the teacher Lin Ying (Wong) sits at her desk and reads in Cantonese-flavored Mandarin to a roomful of small children. The idyllic setting is soon spoiled by the ominous droning of approaching Japanese planes. Mixing stock footage with staged scenes, the film depicts a horrendous air raid with frightened citizens running along the streets and into shelters. Ling, a mischievous child in class, is killed when he, oblivious to danger, sings "Yankee Doodle" and watches the planes flying over him. Cradling Ling's lifeless body in her arms, Lin Ying is determined to seek revenge on the enemy.

After the dramatic prelude, the film turns into a road-trip mystery—a tale of war, espionage, murder, and propaganda. Traveling incognito on a bus to Burma, Lin Ying is on a secret mission to deliver a vital message. In reality, as part of the China–Burma–India Theater of Operations, Burma was a strategic staging ground for the Allied forces fighting the Japanese. Under the command of General Joseph Stilwell, with the assistance of Anna May's old Peking neighbor, Pinkie, the United States military provided matériel support via convoys headed from Burma to Chungking. The plot of *Bombs over Burma* centers on the operation of those convoys, many of which have been destroyed by the Japanese on mountainous roads. As in *Shanghai Express*, the bus that Lin Ying rides is filled with seedy characters, many with divided loyalties—a slick Briton with dubious credentials, an oafish Portuguese, a dagger-toting Hindu, a fresh-faced American couple, and a straight-talking Yankee driver by the name of Slim. When the bus arrives at a remote monastery, the motley group becomes stuck because someone has sabotaged the bus by stealing the distributor. In the end, the treacherous spy among the group is caught, and the next convoy carrying medicines and supplies to Chungking sets out on the road under the protection of American planes. *Bombs over Burma* concludes on an upbeat, patriotic note, with a Chinese monk telling Lin Ying, "There will always be a road into the heart of China."

Ironically, by the time the film was ready for release, Japan had captured Burma, a complete military catastrophe for the United States and its allies. The road to China was cut off. In May 1942, Stilwell and his party of 114 men, including Pinkie, were forced to abandon their vehicles and travel on foot to reach the Indian border. It was a gruesome ten-day journey through the wilderness, in which the group, low on supplies, was chased not only by the Japanese but also by an approaching monsoon.

On July 9, *Bombs over Burma* premiered in Los Angeles along with another PRC release, *Prisoner of Japan*, making it a doubleheader in what was billed as "Slap the Jap Week."[19] In a city from which all the Japanese had been "relocated," no one would be there to mind—let alone protest—the crude racial slur. While Anna May's hometown crowd applauded her new performance, with the *Los Angeles Times* reviewer praising her "very fine work," critics elsewhere were not so generous. They were troubled by its propagandistic impulse, with *Variety* seeing it as a "wartime programming of very minor grade," and the *New York Times* bluntly calling it a "dud."[20]

Anna May's second PRC film, *Lady from Chungking*, was directed by William Nigh, another veteran of B-movies. It carried an even heavier dose of war messaging and less of Joseph Lewis's technical finesse. Nigh had directed several Mr. Wong flicks, a copycat series modeled after Charlie Chan, or what some would call "the poor man's Charlie Chan." Caught by the war fervor, Nigh had just made an anti-German, anti-Japanese comedy, *Escape from Hong Kong*, before taking on *Lady from Chungking*. In the film, Anna May played Madame Kwan Mei, a guerrilla leader fighting against Japanese occupiers. The character's name poetically blends "Kwan Yin," the Goddess of Mercy, with "Anna May." Once again, the plot required her character to work in disguise, this time as a seductress to gather information from a Japanese general about the deployment of his troops so that the Flying Tigers could bomb them. During the Sino-Japanese War, at the invitation of Madame Chiang Kai-shek and under the command of retired Captain Claire L. Chennault, more than three hundred American pilots volunteered in China and achieved a stellar record of combat success against the formidable Japanese aerial power. In the months after Pearl

Harbor, and before its replacement by the officially dispatched squadrons of the US Air Force in July 1942, this American volunteer group allegedly shot down 296 enemy aircraft and lost only fourteen pilots. Like *Bombs over Burma*, Anna May's new film with PRC touched upon an important chapter of the anti-Japanese war by incorporating the Flying Tigers story.

A star vehicle for Anna May, *Lady from Chungking* also featured Harold Huber, who had appeared in several Charlie Chan films, often as a bungling police chief. A Brooklyn Jew, Huber also had a knack for playing Asian characters in yellowface, such as Wang's cousin in *The Good Earth*, bandit General Ho-Fang in *Outlaws of the Orient*, and Ito Takimura in *Little Tokyo, U.S.A.* This time, with no viable Japanese actors to choose from—the biggest Japanese name, and Anna May's one-time costar, Sessue Hayakawa, was living in Vichy France during the war—the producer conveniently cast Huber again in yellowface, as General Kaimura. To be fair, Huber's characterization of the general, aided by his fake accent, was actually quite convincing. Seduced by the beautiful Kwan Mei, Kaimura unwittingly divulges vital military intelligence. When the train carrying Japanese troops is blown up by the Flying Tigers, Kwan Mei reveals to Kaimura her true identity as the rebel leader. Facing the firing squad, Kwan Mei gives a defiant speech, proclaiming that many more in China will rise to replace her. Using superposition, the film shows her spirit rising above her lifeless body, continuing the speech that no gun can silence: "China's destiny is victory. It will live because civilization will not die. Tyrants, dictators, the murderers of peace, all will be betrayed. Not even ten million deaths will cripple the soul of China." In this collage of body and spirit, Anna May not only assumed the role of a martyr who symbolizes the unconquerable China, but she also appeared iconically like Kwan Yin, the Buddhist bodhisattva of compassion and mercy.

Such a strong propagandistic message did not sit too well with the critics. *Harrison's Reports* opined that the film was "slow-paced and void of virile action, but it manages to maintain the interest fairly well, despite the familiarity of the plot." *Variety* put it subtly: "This is just grist for the grinds." But Anna May did not care much about the reviews. In the spirit of compassion and mercy, she donated her salary of $4,500 from these two PRC films to the United China Relief Fund.[21]

By the fall of 1942, the war had entered a new phase. Even though Japan had been successful in Asia by capturing Singapore, Philippines, Malaysia, Dutch East Indies (Indonesia), Burma, and Thailand, as well as threatening Australia, the US Navy in June had won the Battle of Midway, making it the Allies' first major naval victory against the seemingly invincible Japanese, thus turning the tide in the warfare of the Pacific Theater. In China, the war reached a stalemate. Distracted elsewhere, the Japanese forces were not able to make more inroads into China's heartland, while facing stiff resistance from guerrilla bands, as portrayed in *Lady from Chungking*. In the European Theater, the Battle of Stalingrad had commenced in July. One of the bloodiest battles in human history, it would result in an estimated two million casualties on both sides when the siege ended in February 1943 with Germany's defeat. Still, the war was far from over.

Even though no battle had been fought on the American mainland, the war was closer than one might have imagined. In Southern California, there was a lingering suspicion after the shelling of Santa Barbara that Japanese submarines were still prowling the coastline. Therefore, Civil Defense authorities imposed dimout restrictions on the region, ordering residents to turn off all lights that could be seen from the sea at night. They feared that shore lights would silhouette American merchant ships, making them "floating ducks" for enemy fire from a ghostly submarine. Consequently, all houses pulled down their shades, neon signs flickered off, and motorists drove in the dark.[22] Because many of Anna May's social engagements happened at night, she had to ask her brother Richard to drive her around with only the parking lights on, so she plied him with vitamin A and carrots for bettering his night vision. During the day, she heard spasmodic firing up and down the coast and often saw planes flying overhead—all signs of a region where everyone's nerves were raw, strung taut.

On the first anniversary of the Pearl Harbor disaster, Anna May volunteered as an official air-raid warden, outfitted with a steel helmet, gas mask, and an armband. During the swearing-in ceremony at the Civil Defense headquarters in Santa Monica, she told journalists that even though she had been busy with bond sales, China relief, and other war work, she felt strongly that, since there was so much need and so much suffering, "One can't do too much."[23] Like Kwan Yin, the Goddess of Mercy, whose Chinese epithet literally means "the one who perceives the sounds of the world," Anna May witnessed universal miseries, whether far away in China, nearby on the streets of Los Angeles, or even at home—her sister's death in the family garage. She felt constantly that she could always do more.

38

WILL THE REAL LADY FROM CHUNGKING PLEASE STAND UP?

WHEN *Lady from Chungking*, released on December 21, 1942, was showing at movie theaters across the country, the United States welcomed another—one might be tempted to say, real—Lady from Chungking. Invited to the White House, Mayling Soong, more commonly known as Madame Chiang Kai-shek, had come to America for a speaking tour to rally support for her country—but, more important, for her husband's government, which was facing severe economic woes and social ills in its war against Japan. The American interest in her visit was predicated on the need to present a united front in the Pacific Theater and to counter Japanese propaganda that Japan was fighting against the white race on behalf of all the other races, fostering the so-called Greater East Asia Co-Prosperity Sphere. Given America's own treatment of minorities, it was not easy for the State Department's propaganda machine to present a strong rebuttal to the Japanese. Case in point: Even though patriotic Asian Americans were joining the military enthusiastically and fighting heroically in Europe and Asia against the Axis powers, the inherently racist Chinese Exclusion Act had remained the law of the land since 1882, and a sizable number of Japanese Americans were confined to internment camps, unlike citizens of German or Italian descent. Aware of these issues, the Office of War Information had issued directives to Hollywood studios, urging them to dial down excessively racist portrayals of Japanese.[1] At a time when Hollywood was trying to emphasize patriotism, opening its canteens to GIs, and sending out stars for USO tours, it seemed that the American public could also use a little pep talk by foreign celebrities who were eager to celebrate American values.

China's First Lady seemed like a good candidate for such a task. First educated at Wesleyan College in Georgia and then at Wellesley College in Massachusetts, Madame Chiang was fluent in English, suave in manners, and charismatic in public. Born into a Southern Methodist family in Shanghai, she was also a devout Christian. It remained Chinese lore that she had converted Chiang, a polygamous Buddhist, to Christianity as a condition for their marriage. Yet, as Charlie Chan says, "Front seldom tell truth. To know occupants of house, always look in backyard." Behind Madame Chiang's beguiling public image lay a prima donna of enormous guile, a person variously described as "a hard, shallow, and selfish woman, [who] can turn on the charm to melt the heart of the most hardboiled foreigner"; or, a power grabber capable of the "most sophisticated bitchery."[2] Of course, such unflattering depictions were obviously tinted by racism, mixing firsthand testimonials with long-held American stereotypes about Chinese women as despotic temptresses, i.e., Dragon Ladies.

One popular American narrative about Madame Chiang, repeated by most biographers, relates to her relationship with Wendell Willkie, a political maverick who lost his presidential bid to Franklin Roosevelt in 1940 but remained popular and influential. An Indiana lawyer-turned-politician, Willkie was ebullient and handsome, sporting a homespun manner that appealed to both Main Street and Wall Street. It was widely expected that the rambunctious Midwesterner would make another run for the White House in 1944. In the long summer of 1942, the war had reached a nadir; despite the US victory in the Battle of Midway, the Allies suffered multiple setbacks elsewhere. Roosevelt decided to send Willkie on a worldwide goodwill tour to reassure beleaguered nations that Americans were united and determined to win the war.

On October 2, after stopping in Africa, the Middle East, and the Soviet Union, Willkie and his entourage, flying on the US Army bomber the *Gulliver*, arrived in the Chinese wartime capital, Chungking. The Chinese rolled out the red carpet for the American VIP and inundated him with long parades, military reviews, and lavish banquets, even though countless Chinese were dying of hunger or wartime injuries every day. Madame Chiang led the charm diplomacy by striking a personal chord with Willkie, literally. According to Willkie's traveling companion and close associate, Gardner Cowles, Madame Chiang became intimately involved with the man she thought might become

Wendell Willkie and Mayling Soong at the official residence of Generalissimo Chiang Kai-shek, Chungking, October 1942 *(Courtesy of Library of Congress, Prints and Photographs Division, Farm Security Administration / Office of War Information Photograph Collection, Reproduction Number LC-DIG-fsa-8e09297)*

the next president of the United States. Falling under her spell, Willkie, who was married and had also been carrying on a long-running affair with Irita Van Doren—the Sunday book-review editor of the *New York Herald Tribune*—invited Madame Chiang to fly back to Washington with him on the *Gulliver*. After Cowles convinced his friend that such a scandal would, among other things, hurt his chance of making a second run for president, Willkie came to his senses, but he was too sheepish to rescind the invitation himself. When Cowles broke the bad news to Madame Chiang on Willkie's behalf, she became so furious that, in Cowles's words, "she reached up and scratched her long fingernails down both my cheeks so deeply that I had marks for about a week."[3]

Cowles, the publisher and editor of *Look*, seemed to be conjuring up the image of an ill-tempered, vampirish Dragon Lady—personified, as noted earlier, by Anna May in a cover photo of his own magazine in 1938.

Always a go-getter, Madame Chiang refused to let a minor setback stop her. In fact, a month earlier, she had already received a letter from Eleanor Roosevelt, indicating that an official invitation from Washington was pending. When that invitation finally came, Madame Chiang followed Willkie to America in November, traveling aboard a Stratoliner provided by the US Government. Reunited with Willkie in New York, she spent the next three months at the Presbyterian Hospital for an undisclosed illness. The entire twelfth floor of the hospital was cleared for her and her entourage, guarded around the clock by the Secret Service and FBI agents. Living under the code name "Snow White" (assigned by the State Department), she convalesced in her suite like a princess, or as a queen, and was tended to daily by a hairdresser and a beautician.[4]

On February 17, 1943, Madame Chiang arrived in Washington and began her official visit. Staying for two weeks as a guest in the Large Pink Room at the White House, she irked the staff with her impetuous behavior: Claiming an allergy to cotton, she had brought her own silk bedsheets and insisted on having them changed every day; and, rather than use the bell or the telephone in the room, she would clap her hands to summon White House staffers as if she were calling coolies in China.[5] Watching her up close, Eleanor Roosevelt also saw another side of Madame Chiang. "I was much amused by the reactions of the men with whom she talked," Eleanor wrote in her memoir. "They found her charming, intelligent, and fascinating, but they were all a little afraid of her, because she could be a coolheaded statesman . . . the little velvet hand and the low, gentle voice disguised a determination that could be as hard as steel." Eleanor was alarmed to notice "a certain casualness about cruelty" that emerged sometimes in Madame Chiang's conversations with others.[6] Perceptive as these observations were, it seemed that even the First Lady, a well-known champion for racial justice, had played into the racist tropes of the period by referring to Madame Chiang as someone with "a little velvet hand."

Her misgivings notwithstanding, the First Lady accompanied her Chinese counterpart on February 18 to Capitol Hill, where Madame Chiang delivered two speeches, first to the Senate and then to the House of Representatives. Lobbying for China and the Sino–US alliance, her speeches were broadcast live nationwide and presumably touched so many Americans that, four days later, a bill was introduced in Congress to repeal the Chinese Exclusion Act.

Truth be told, the success of her speeches might have had less to do with what she said than how she sounded and looked to her intended audience, appearance being the essence of celebrity. The extraordinary oratorical event was, in fact, a theatrical drama in which, not so different from Anna May's cinematic performances, Madame Chiang played her part almost to perfection by exploiting and exploding America's expectations. Clad in a tight-fitting black cheongsam slit to the knee, Madame Chiang spoke in a slow, clear voice that blended Dixie softness with New England urbanity. Tracing invisible lines in the air with her red-lacquered fingernails, she entranced the audience with her Circean spell and Ciceronian eloquence. The striking incongruence between her "exotic" looks and her almost flawless American diction—she deliberately sprinkled her speeches with arcane words and obscure references like *obtunded*, *Gobineau*, and *ochlocracy*—had a disarming effect on her mostly white male audience in the congressional chamber. "In just a few minutes, Mme. Chiang had Congress in the palm of her hand," wrote one reporter. Having trouble transcribing some of the words in her speeches, most reporters fawned over her appearance. One newspaper dubbed her an "Almond-Eyed Cleopatra," another referred to her as "China's lissome Joan of Arc," and yet another depicted her as "petite as an ivory figurine." Ironically, such an almost prurient obsession with her looks actually worked to her advantage. As one biographer astutely observes, by projecting her image as "a tiny woman, frail yet valiant," Madame Chiang was trying to present "China as the damsel in distress and America the knight in shining armor."[7] It was a calculated move, playing on the lasting American fascination with Asian females, a cultural tradition that had both enabled and handicapped a career like that of Anna May Wong.

After Washington, Madame Chiang traveled across the country, making public appearances and giving speeches on similar themes. She also made a stop in Macon, Georgia, a bustling railroad town with antebellum-style architecture lining its main thoroughfare, Mulberry Street—as if the Old South was unwilling to let go of its plantation days. Macon was where Madame Chiang had spent a couple of adolescent years with her two older sisters and then later attended college. It was indeed a bittersweet "homecoming" for her. When she was a grade school student in Macon, the local Board of Education had denied her admission to a white school because she was considered an "alien." Now she had returned as the First Lady of China, who was about to receive an honorary doctorate from Wesleyan College. Interestingly, someone managed to scare up the only Chinese children in town, those belonging to the laundryman

Ben Jung, and put them in a lineup to greet Madame Chiang, who had been dubbed "My Heathen Chinee" by one of her college professors.[8]

The grand finale of Madame Chiang's speaking tour was at the Hollywood Bowl on April 4, an event that drew thirty thousand people, including Hollywood stars such as Ingrid Bergman, Barbara Stanwyck, Ginger Rogers, and Loretta Young. Her rousing speech was preceded by a spectacular pageant produced by David Selznick, a symphonic narrative accompanied by a parade on stage of Chinese moppets and coolies, whose "peaceful" world was dramatically shattered by the Japanese invasion. Over a simulated bombing attack that scattered the "villagers," there came the voice of Edward G. Robinson as Generalissimo Chiang Kai-shek, encouraging people to "go West" to join the fight and to help build a new China. The narrative conflation of the old American shibboleth, "Go West, young man," with the new reality of China's western region as the bastion of resistance to Japanese invaders was either a stroke of genius or just pure Hollywood hooey. The deployment of Robinson as the voice of the Generalissimo was also a curious choice. In the pre–Hays Code days, Robinson had been paired with Loretta Young—one of the stars seated next to Madame Chiang at the event—and done a not-so-convincing yellow-face performance in *The Hatchet Man* (1932). It was a movie about Chinatown tong wars and a murder committed with a flying hatchet. Now, in "China: A Symphonic Narrative," the former hatchet man was deployed to channel the furious falsetto of China's most powerful man, who had, in fact, terrorized his nation through his own combination of brutality and massacre. As Hollywood's lavish tribute to a thoroughly imagined China ended with Robinson/Chiang's crying encouragement to the nation, Madame Chiang, the Lady from Chungking, stepped up to the podium to deliver her speech.[9]

Yet, in all the hoopla, there was a glaring absence: Anna May, the woman who had been Hollywood's face of China. Perhaps Madame Chiang did not want to be outshone by another beautiful Chinese woman. Or perhaps, since she was born with so-called blue blood, she did not deign to share the stage with the daughter of a Chinese laundryman. Or perhaps those in charge of the event had decided, with the stroke of a pen on a studio executive's notepad, who should be the face of China. Anyway, it was one of the greatest, most hurtful snubs Anna May had suffered, after she had worked so tirelessly and wholeheartedly as the leading spokesperson for the China cause. The tricky dynamics between the real and reel Lady from Chungking did not go unnoticed by columnists, many of whom cried foul on Anna May's behalf. But neither the snub by the snooty Madame Chiang nor the Hollywood rebuff would dampen Anna May's enthusiasm for war work. As Hedda Hopper noted in her column, Anna May went "right back ahead working for China relief."[10]

In August 1943, her kid brother Richard turned twenty-one and became one of the ten million Americans inducted for military service during the war. He was sent to England and assigned to a military intelligence unit near London, where Anna May still had friends and connections. During his leaves from the base, some of his sister's old pals would show him around the city and take him to luncheon at places like the Café Royale, providing Private Wong a luxurious respite from dull meals at the canteen.

Anna May herself, thinking more nationally and internationally, followed the examples of Marlene Dietrich, Bob Hope, Judy Garland, and others by volunteering for USO tours. During the 1943 Christmas holiday, she visited air bases in Nebraska. Unlike the other stars, who sang and danced for the troops, she did not entertain on this tour. Instead, she spent the time having meals with "the boys," visiting patients in hospitals, and giving brief speeches in camp theaters. Some of the bases had large units of Black soldiers, and she was appalled to find that these servicemen had their own racially segregated canteens, theaters, and mess halls.[11]

Anna May applied to the Hollywood Victory Committee for overseas USO tours, hoping to go to England so that she could see Richard. Instead, she was sent to Alaska and Canada. In May 1944, a month before the Normandy invasion, while Marlene Dietrich was playing her musical saw in front of homesick GIs in Europe, and opera diva Lily Pons was singing in the sweltering jungles of Burma and India, Anna May landed in Fairbanks for the first leg of her tour. In the arctic region, she found plenty of sunshine that lasted till 10 pm and an equally warm reception from the servicemen. At the canteen, when she was served a plateful of a strange concoction that looked like genuine American chop suey, the sharp-witted actress whipped out a pair of chopsticks, like a cowboy doing a "quickdraw" in a standoff. The hilarious, almost vaudeville, act caused an uproar in the mess hall.[12]

In fact, her chopstick skit, while vintage Anna May Wong, relates to an interest she had begun cultivating in wartime, a new platform for her to present Chinese culture to America: food. Earlier in 1935, she had contributed a recipe to *Milady's Style Parade and Recipe Book*, an almanac that paired a celebrity with his or her favorite food. The 1935 edition included Shirley Temple's menu for children, Will Rogers's baked ham in cider, and Barbara Stanwyck's chicken mousse. Anna May's page features a photo of the actress in a black-and-red velvet gown that trails on the floor. The accompanying recipe is for tea cakes.[13] During her trip to China the following year, Anna May continued to introduce Chinese food to her American newspaper audience. In her serialized letters in the *New York Herald Tribune*, she often went into great detail about the multicourse meals offered by her hosts, glamorizing haute cuisine in China at a time when some Americans continued to portray Chinese as a subhuman species whose dietary preferences included rats, skunks, or anything with legs except tables or chairs.

Anna May's culinary interest also extended to cookbooks. In 1942, she wrote a preface to *New Chinese Recipes*, a cookbook by chef Fred Yuen Wing and home economist Mabel Stegner. Originally published by the Edelmuth Company in New York in 1941, the book was reissued a year later to raise funds for the United China Relief Fund. Containing nearly two hundred Cantonese recipes, the book focused on home cookery using locally available ingredients. In other words, these were, as Anna May put it in her introductory essay, "recipes made with American ingredients by the Chinese method." This emphasis on the ingredients related to the fact that meat was in short supply during wartime. The material shortage made Chinese recipes, which call for a good balance of meat and vegetables, often at a ratio of 1 to 3, sound particularly appealing.[14]

Eager to bring Chinese food to mainstream America, Anna May, as Graham Hodges astutely points out, invented a fictional character, "an American house-wife"—a prototype of the future Margaret Anderson (*Father Knows Best*) and June Cleaver (*Leave It to Beaver*)—who desired culinary adventures beyond the confines of her white middle-class kitchen.[15] In Anna May's conception, the American homemaker was trying to stretch every dollar to bring appetizing, healthy food to the family dinner table. She wanted to learn to cook Chinese but found the process as puzzling as a Chinese box. "She discovered that Chinese chefs measure by 'feel' and judge the temperature and cooking time by experience," Anna May wrote. "All their movements are so deft and swift, she found herself at a loss to follow them." Here Anna May echoed what she had said earlier to a journalist in Australia about her fledgling culinary hobby: "I have been learning Chinese cooking since I visited China, and it is absorbingly interesting, much more of an art than a science. You do not measure by teaspoons, but have to be able to guess when the proportions are right." But the modern American homemaker needed someone who could help her translate measurements from dabs and pinches into cups and teaspoons. In the cookbook collaboration between Wing and Stegner, the home economics consultant translated the Chinese chef's artistry into precise measurements and scientific terms that any American housewife could follow. Moreover, the authors of *New Chinese Recipes* had judiciously left out items like bird's nests, water chestnuts, and exotic Chinese vegetables available only in large Chinatowns, where an ordinary American housewife was unlikely to venture.[16]

To make Chinese food more tempting, Anna May appealed to the American housewife's concerns about nutrition, taste, and economics. Because Chinese food is usually cooked for a very short time, and in a small amount of liquid, the method, Anna May opined, "saves the minerals and vitamins, and they are bound together with a delicious sauce which enhances the flavor of the other ingredients." Sounding like Lin Yutang singing the praises of Chinese culture, Anna May remarked: "Evidently, centuries ago, the Chinese people knew by instinct what our nutrition authorities are learning through scientific research—that a short cooking period in a small amount of liquid with none of that liquid discarded is the ideal method for cooking vegetables, and that a short cooking period for most meats is equally desirable." Delicious and nutritious, Chinese food also would save money. "Just compare it with the cost of the food usually served on [your] dinner plates," Anna May wrote. She concluded her sales pitch by addressing the American housewife's sensibility as a homemaker: Chinese recipes are "new and exciting to serve to guests, and they appeal to children and husbands who have never enjoyed vegetables."[17]

In fact, Anna May did more than contribute a two-page essay to the cookbook. In September 1943, after starring in *The Willow Tree*, a play at the Cambridge Summer Theater in Harvard Square, she went to New York City and did a cooking demo to promote *New Chinese Recipes*. Speaking to a reporter from the *New York Herald Tribune*, she once again emphasized the advantages of Chinese cooking: "Many of our important Chinese dishes are a combination of vegetables, with the meat or fish reduced to the role of little more than a garnish." The dish she showcased that day was a basic item, string beans with beef. It used a pound of string beans, "Chinese or any kind," cut into one-inch pieces, and a half-pound of flank steak cut into half-inch dice. The ingredients were cooked separately and then combined, creating a one-dish meal (plus bowls of fluffy rice) that could serve a family of three or four.[18]

Prior to the publication of *New Chinese Recipes*, there existed only a few Chinese cookbooks in English, ranging from Jessie Louise Nolton's *Chinese Cookery in the Home Kitchen*, published in 1911, to Henry Low's *Cook at Home in Chinese* in 1938. No doubt the paucity of such cookbooks reflected a distinct prejudice against Chinese cooking, as if it was a slum food, a staple for lowly immigrants. And even these two cookbooks introduced either stereotypical items such as chop suey and egg foo yang or highly exotic ones such as shark fin soup and sea slugs. It was not until the publication of *How to Cook and Eat in Chinese* by Chao Yang Buwei in 1945—a book that introduced terms such as *stir-fry* into the English-language culinary lexicon—that America would have a more comprehensive encounter with Chinese food. But by then, as Mayukh Sen points out in *Taste Makers: Seven Immigrant Women Who Revolutionized Food in America* (2022), there was a wave of ethnic cookbooks that looked beyond America's borders in the post–World War II era.[19] Even Anna May's old friend Pinkie, after retiring from his service in China as a brigadier general, would publish a cookbook that included Chinese recipes.[20] Notably, *New Chinese Recipes*—or, more important, Anna May's trailblazing effort to take Chinese food mainstream—predated the postwar fad by several years.

Curiously, by adding gastronomic advocacy to her résumé, Anna May now embodied two of the most distinctively Chinese motifs in American popular culture: the Chinese laundry and Chinese food. If we recall how the early Chinese immigrants—drawn to America by the promise of gold but then driven off by racial discrimination—had turned to running hand laundries and chop-suey joints, we might say that laundry and food represented the uniquely Chinese experience in America. While Madame Chiang Kai-shek, with her eloquence, guile, and connections to the top echelons of American society, made the cover of *Time* magazine three times, it was Anna May Wong who worked so tirelessly to undo stereotypes and was, in a way, the real Lady from Chungking. Her singular achievement was what Madame Chiang, aided by the clout of two governments and the mythmaking magic of Hollywood, could only aspire to but never attain.

39

THE BIG NOWHERE

Portrait of Anna May Wong holding a porcelain cat *(Courtesy of Library of Congress, Prints and Photographs Division, Carl Van Vechten Collection, Reproduction Number LC-USZ62-135267)*

W HILE JAMES ELLROY—a childhood witness to the darkest side of his native city when his mother was raped and murdered—dubs Los Angeles "the Big Nowhere" in an eponymous novel, Kevin Starr, the most celebrated chronicler of California dreams, aptly captures the malaise plaguing the postwar city in *Embattled Dreams*. With a historian's keen eye, Starr describes that, in the years after the defeat of Hitler and the dropping of atomic bombs, Los Angeles became "a city of cops, crooks, and defense lawyers; a demimonde of rackets, screaming headlines, and politicians on the take; a town of gamblers, guys and dolls, booze and sex; a place for schemers, also-rans, suckers and those who deceived them: the kind of city in which a private detective such as Philip Marlowe might make his way down mean streets in search of the ever-elusive truth and get sapped with a blackjack for his effort by parties unknown."[1] Los Angeles was fast becoming the new Rome, cursed by all the wealth, sins, and decay that had once defined that ancient imperial city.

As for the nation, postwar America has usually been characterized as a period of unprecedented boom. Thanks to defense spending and hard-won victories in the war, the United States now commanded the world's strongest military power. The return of veterans benefiting from the munificent GI bills, the construction of interstate highways and public schools, and the manufacture of new cars, track houses, and military weapons, all contributed to a lasting economic growth. With the suburban sprawl, seventy-seven million baby boomers were born into a time capsule featuring white picket fences and postage-stamp lawns—that is, if you were largely Caucasian.

Under the veneer of affluence and stability, however, there lay an underbelly of tension and paranoia. The Cold War would cast a long shadow on the American psyche, and the Korean War opened another festering wound. Haunted by McCarthyism and the lingering legacy of institutionalized racism, America experienced major social unrest and changes, starting with the civil rights movement. Symptomatically, while the Golden Age of Television painted whitewashed images of America with family-friendly shows such as *Father Knows Best* and *I Love Lucy*, noir fiction and films suggested that there are always dead bodies hidden somewhere. On the silver screen alone, *The Big Sleep* (1946), *The Postman Always Rings Twice* (1946), *The Lady from Shanghai* (1947), *The Third Man* (1949), *Strangers on a Train* (1951), *Rear Window* (1954), and *Dial M for Murder* (1954) were all made during this postwar period. Simi-

larly, the popularity of Confessional poets and the Beats, such as Robert Low-
ell, Sylvia Plath, and Allen Ginsberg, also showcased America's addiction to
dark matters like suicide, depression, and dysfunctional relationships, reflecting a spiritual exhaustion from the increasingly commercialized, militarized,
and technocratic world.

For Anna May, the end of World War II portended a period that began in
euphoria but quickly turned into depression and decline. Celebrating the victory like everyone else in the country, she was especially happy to see Richard
return safely from the war. Unlike his older brother, James, whose education
at the University of Southern California Anna May supported, Richard would
attend the same institution and study photography courtesy of Uncle Sam.
The overnight mushrooming of aerodynamics and defense plants in Southern
California brought workers from all over the country, creating acute housing
needs in the area. Consequently, Anna May's apartment complex was fully
occupied, providing her with a steady income. No fan of housekeeping, she
decided to put the property on the market to cash in on the real estate boom.
After the for-sale sign was up for a month, she had several prospective buyers, but she did not like any of the philistines. Then one day a windstorm blew
down the sign. Superstitious like her film characters, she took it as an omen
not to sell and decided to continue to live contentedly as a landlady.[2]

As someone who had debuted on Hollywood's social scene at those wild
soirees at Alla Nazimova's 8080 Club, Anna May, in her forties, was essentially
all partied out. Even before the war, when her film career had begun to plateau
and the phone got quiet, she had done a little soul-searching. "I know that
when I used to go to many big parties, I found that I was talking too much,"
she once confessed to a journalist. "There is an atmosphere at many big affairs
that is almost malicious. Light, gay but malicious gossip is the spice of the evening. . . . You think of something smart, something witty, something not quite
kind about a figure in the public eye or a mutual acquaintance or someone
connected with pictures, if you are in pictures. At the moment, you are amusing, gay; you make people laugh and they look at you admiringly for the time
being, or they seem to do so. I have done things like that, and afterward I have
suffered terribly because of what I had said. I've wished the words unsaid, but I
couldn't unsay them. So, I do not go to many big parties now."[3]

The lull in Anna May's social life, resulting from her growing unease with
Tinseltown gossip and gabble, was in fact symptomatic of a far more pervasive
issue in Hollywood: ageism. Hollywood has never been kind to aging actors;

actresses, in particular, bear the brunt of age discrimination. "The camera was a cruel observer," writes Jeanine Basinger in her canonical work, *The Star Machine*, "and it saw *age*: wrinkles, thickness, the loss of that glistening shine of the first blush of ripe sexuality."[4] In a culture obsessed with youth, women are subject to even stricter standards of beauty than men, giving credence to Meryl Streep's outcry that "once women passed childbearing age they could only be seen as grotesque on some level."[5]

In fact, female stars often face "double jeopardy," a sociological concept originally introduced to describe the combined effects of sexism and racism on the experiences of minority women. Scholars have argued that the joint effects of gender and racial biases tend to be "more deleterious than the sum of their separate effects." Applied to Hollywood, double jeopardy means that the combination of ageism and sexism has made aging female stars far more susceptible to neglect and downright erasure than their male counterparts.[6] According to studies based on data available from silent Hollywood to the present day, there is a persistent age gap between female and male stars. One study shows that the average age of female stars in 1917 was 24.6, as opposed to 33.9 for males. A century later, in 2021, the average age for lead females increased to 35, while it rose to 42 for males. In the 1950s, the decade in which Anna May saw her career grinding to a halt, the median age for female stars was 32 or 33 years, with a quarter of the top roles going to actresses under the age of 27. According to Robert K. Fleck and F. Andrew Hanssen, not only do female stars tend to be younger than their male counterparts, they also start *and* finish their careers at substantially earlier ages: "At the beginning of their careers women in their early 20s received 80% of the leading film roles; by age 30 it was 40%; but past age 30, women only had 20% of the leading roles while men had 80%." The controversy over the Academy Award nominations in 2020 was particularly illuminating: For the nominees in the Best Actor and Best Supporting Actor categories, there was a 21.6-year gender age gap—61.3 years in median age for men and 39.8 for women. Every study, every iteration of facts, reveals that there is a specter of ageism that continues to haunt Hollywood's women, creating a revolving door of youth churning endlessly through the movie grist mill.[7]

Even the biggest stars are not immune to the impact of double jeopardy. The handful of actresses able to defy Hollywood's time machine have become true legends: Bette Davis, Myrna Loy, Barbara Stanwyck, Rosalind Russell, Katharine Hepburn, Joan Crawford, and, more recently, Meryl Streep.[8] Most of the other so-called yesterday's glamour queens were not so lucky. Although

Marlene Dietrich, after turning fifty, did appear in a few unforgettable movies, such as Alfred Hitchcock's *Stage Fright* (1950) and Billy Wilder's *Witness for the Prosecution* (1957), the Blonde Venus became mostly a cabaret artist from the 1950s to the 1970s, charming the crowds with her musical talents and vaudeville skits. The same situation occurred for Mae West, the so-called sex goddess of the 1930s, who in her middle years tried to maintain her Aphroditic image by performing on stage in Las Vegas and on Broadway, peddling naughty jokes and barroom humor amid a squad of scantily clad musclemen in various states of adoring repose. Greta Garbo, born in the same year as Anna May, virtually disappeared from the screen after *Two-Faced Woman* in 1941, when she was only thirty-six—although, in her case, much of this was self-imposed. Lana Turner did beat the rap, if you will, and enjoyed a miraculously long career. But after a yearlong scandal in 1958, her triumphant comeback in *Imitation of Life* (1959) was riddled with the age question. In this Douglas Sirk satire of the racial complexities of American life, thirty-eight-year-old Turner, no longer the fresh-faced "sweater girl" discovered at fifteen while playing hooky from Hollywood High, inhabited the role of Lora Meredith, a late-blooming stage actress on Broadway. As Steve, the leading man, bluntly says to Lora, "Time isn't on your side." It was a brutal reminder more for Lana than for Lora—by then, as Sam Kashner and Jennifer MacNair point out in their study of Hollywood in the 1950s, "the bombshell baton was being passed to younger stars like Marilyn Monroe."[9]

Hollywood's most poignant portrayal of its own chronic ageism is Billy Wilder's *Sunset Boulevard* (1950). Starring Gloria Swanson, the now-classic film tells the story of Norma Desmond, once a screen celebrity in the silent era and now an aging recluse hiding out in a decrepit mansion, attended to by a butler named Max, who is, in fact, her ex-husband and a failed director. Childless, her only other companion is a pet monkey, which has just died. Forgotten by the world, Norma whiles away her lonely hours by relishing old memories, rewatching her old films, playing cards with over-the-hill "waxworks," and daydreaming about her glorious return to the big screen. Into this crumbling palazzo of delusions enters Joe Gillis (William Holden), a young and struggling screenwriter on the run from repo men, intent on reclaiming his car. In Joe, Norma thinks she has found the perfect man who can not only rekindle her love life but also reboot her film career. But Joe finds Norma's romantic-turned-obsessional attraction creepy and her desire for a cinematic comeback delusional. "You're a woman of 50," he yells at Norma. "Now grow up!" Echoing Steve's snide remark to Lora/Lana, Joe's words actually reveal his own hypocrisy: Over thirty, he is not really a budding young thing himself, yet he is infatuated with twenty-two-year-old Betty Schaefer. Here the ugly truth about Hollywood's age bias against women is laid as bare as the face of the dead monkey on the table: While it is common to see grizzled men consorting with barely legal-age girls on screen (Humphrey Bogart romancing Audrey Hepburn in *Sabrina*, for example), mature women of Norma's age are not only *not* depicted as romantic, but rather as histrionic and pathetic.[10] As Joe, reflecting the biases of the time, quips again, "There's nothing tragic about being 50, not unless you try to be 25." Predictably, the story of *Sunset Boulevard* begins and ends tragically. Consumed with jealousy and desperation, Norma shoots Joe dead near the pool. Then she descends her grand staircase, ready for her "close-up," accompanied by the swirling music adapted for the score from the mad scene of the Richard Strauss opera *Salome*.

Notably, it was an outsider such as Wilder, a German émigré, who was able to shed light on the darker side of the world's grandest Dream Factory. An insider like Louis B. Mayer, for instance, was furious at Wilder for making the exposé. The MGM mogul allegedly threatened to run the former Berlin taxi dancer out of Hollywood in tar and feathers. If we look closely, it is not hard to see why the Tinseltown elders felt so scandalized by *Sunset Boulevard*—it cut too close to the truth. In fact, several of the actors play themselves in the film, as if this were in part a thinly veiled documentary, or a wax museum display of Old Hollywood: The comedic genius Buster Keaton, for example, appears as himself, with his facial features ravaged by time and alcoholism. The same with Cecil B. DeMille, a little stooped in the shoulders, while still dominating as the big boss. Erich von Stroheim, playing Max, is also reprising a version of himself as the director who had made some of the earliest Swanson flicks. Even Hedda Hopper, the imperious gossip columnist, cameos as herself, calling her paper's copy desk from Norma's bedside phone to dictate her predictably sensationalized lines.[11]

The ultimate verisimilitude in *Sunset Boulevard* is, of course, the extent to which Norma Desmond's story resembles Gloria Swanson's life. Not only did many props used in the film come from Swanson's private collection—including publicity photos, film stills, decorations, and artworks—but key facts were also borrowed from the career of the silent-film star. Born in the penultimate year of the nineteenth century, Swanson debuted on screen at the tender age of fifteen and worked at the Essanay Studio alongside Charlie Chaplin in Chicago before arriving in Hollywood. After several slapstick roles in Mack Sennett Studio productions, she moved on to Famous Players–Lasky and began her long professional relationship with Cecil B. DeMille, who helped turn her into a silent-screen star. One of the most bankable stars of her epoch, she had the audacity to turn down a million-dollar-a-year contract with Paramount to join United Artists in 1925. Her performance in *Sadie Thompson* (1928), which garnered her a Best Actress nomination for the first Academy Award, represented her crowning achievement in the silent era. However, the combination of Hollywood's transition to sound, her repeated failures in marriage, and her physical aging left a shining star of the previous decade struggling to find film jobs in the 1930s.[12] Not yet forty, she became, in Ross Macdonald's hard-boiled, sexist lingo of the time, "a woman on her way out."[13] Like Norma Desmond, Swanson also dreamed of a comeback. After a fifteen-year hiatus, her opportunity finally arrived when Wilder was getting ready to make what would be widely interpreted as a cinematic indictment of the company town for its disgraceful treatment of the distaff population, who had always, as the Chinese would say, "held up half the sky."

Like Swanson, and her doppelgänger, Desmond, Anna May was seen as having passed her prime by conventional Hollywood standards. Not exactly trying to be twenty-five again, she was nonetheless eager for imaginative and rewarding work in the postwar era. To seek relief from the doldrums in her career and life, she studied drawing and costume design with Hugo Ballin, a famous artist and muralist who lived across the canyon from her in Pacific Palisades. She learned to draw facsimiles of the female form. Increasingly interested in the subject, she even considered enrolling at one of LA's art institutes but decided against it due to the number of courses required to get through the program.

Like fishing out of season, sometimes a movie gig, albeit not the expected kind, would nibble at the line. In 1948, Anna May was tapped by the director Arthur Lubin to cameo in *Impact* (1949). Starring Brian Donlevy and Helen Walker, the film was a noirish story of infidelity, murder, and courtroom drama that purported to be in the tradition of *The Postman Always Rings Twice* or *The Lady from Shanghai*, but it had little of their artistry. Set in San Francisco with an interlude in small-town Idaho, the film cast Anna May once again in a subservient role, as Su Lin, a timid Chinese maid struggling with the English language, while Philip Ahn played her uncle. Coincidentally, Su Lin, as noted earlier, also happened to be the name of the first panda cub brought to the

United States from China in 1936. It was a humiliating role for a global star who was now regarded as a washup. In fact, the part originally called for a Swedish maid, but the character's nationality was altered to take advantage of the setting of San Francisco's Chinatown—a favorite locale for film noir, as it had been for early movies, to evoke a mysterious, sinister ambience. In the story, the detective has to comb through the rabbit warrens in Chinatown in order to locate the missing key witness named after a panda. Sensing the irony, Anna May quipped that as much as she was happy to see the director letting a Chinese play a Chinese part for a change, she would not have minded impersonating a Swede and returning the favor after Warner Oland had played so many Chinese roles.[14] Despite the impressive lineup, *Impact* was, as *Harrison's Reports* put it, "hampered by a long drawn-out story." The *New York Times* considered the leading man as having "all the animation and charm of an automaton" and the female lead as convincing as Idaho's most famous crop. Passing over the Chinese maid in its review, the paper labeled the film "a dull thud."[15]

Philip Ahn and Anna May Wong in *Impact*, 1949 *(Courtesy of Everett Collection)*

Unsurprisingly, getting a bit part did little to boost Anna May's confidence. In some ways, she came to share Norma Desmond's situation: There was always talk of a new scheme, something stewing, a magic pill to get one's mojo back, making a triumphant return to the big screen. But then nothing would pan out; everything fizzled like foaming bubbles in a surging sea, after the mermaid disappeared. One recurrent thread was the promise of a television series. As an actor who had made a successful transition from silent films to talkies two decades earlier, Anna May now lived through another seismic shift in the film industry: Television was drastically changing the cultural landscape of America. After attaining the highest rate of theater attendance in 1946, Hollywood was dismayed to see shrinking box-office returns in the following years, realizing that movies were losing patronage for the first time since the Great Depression.[16] Television programs began to cut into the lion's share of the entertainment business that had been enjoyed by Hollywood moguls for decades. As Samuel Goldwyn admitted begrudgingly in 1949, "It is a certainty that people will be unwilling to pay to see poor pictures when they can stay home and see something which is, at least, no worse."[17] Always alert to any new streak in the cinematic Klondike, many studios began to produce programs exclusively for television.

Unlike Norma, who frowned upon the new medium by quipping, "I am big. It's the pictures that got small," Anna May saw the future in television. She understood that whether one liked it or not, television was here to stay. Compared to live theater, which uses crude lighting and thus exposes signs of aging (a major concern for her now), she thought the filming of television programs could give an actor an opportunity to correct any fluffs.[18] Her first television work was in the fall of 1951, when the Dumont Network offered her a thirteen-week series. According to Conrad Doerr, who was renting the room above her garage (sort of reprising a scene in *Sunset Boulevard*, where Joe lives in a room above Norma's garage), Anna May had some friends over at her place on the night before leaving for the East to do the series. In the middle of the dinner, she fell apart, "terrified not only over returning to work but over doing so in a new medium."[19] The series that eventually was produced —*The Gallery of Mme. Liu-Tsong*—had twelve episodes. Using Anna May's Chinese name directly in its title, the show featured her as the owner of an art gallery who gets dragged into an international intrigue of crime and mystery. A pioneer in the early days of live television, Dumont broadcast programs in New York City and Washington, DC. The first episode of *The Gallery of Mme. Liu-Tsong* aired on September 3, and the last on November 21, 1951. Unfortunately, when the Dumont Network folded in 1956, its kinescope archives were dumped into New York's East River, depriving us of any opportunity to assess the series.[20] If a contemporary review was any indication, though, Anna May's first venture into TV-land was not too successful. As *Variety* opined, the show was "strictly out of the pulp mill. . . . Neither the acting nor the direction contributed toward its enhancement as a major TV contender."[21]

At the same time that the television series failed to provide Anna May with a comeback, she hit menopause at the age of forty-seven. As she confided to Fania Marinoff, it was a very strange experience. She did not know how she was going to feel from one day to another, as the physical changes in her body affected her mentally and worsened her depression.[22] Consequently, she turned to the bottle. According to Doerr, his Chinese landlady "was often tipsy during the day, frequently buying bottles of vodka."[23] In the amphetamine-ridden, pill-popping milieu of Hollywood, where some were overworked under pressure and others became dejected for lack of work, Anna May was certainly not alone in seeking the consolation of Bacchus. As Josef von Sternberg, by no means a teetotaler himself, observed in his memoir, "A clear record of the trail left by those who formed the tradition of the theater today favors the impression that there was a constant leaning toward inebriety."[24] Warner Oland was under the influence of alcohol most of the time when he was impersonating the amiable Chinese detective. In fact, his slurred diction resulting from drinking became in essence part of the character. As success and stress continued to build, his drinking problem had gotten worse till he walked off the set one day and died of alcoholism at age fifty-eight. Even more famously, Judy Garland struggled with alcoholism and drug addiction throughout her career and would perish at the age of forty-seven. In fact, on the set of *The Wizard of Oz* (1939), Garland's fellow actors portraying the Munchkins were a wild, booze-guzzling bunch. In other words, F. Scott Fitzgerald's *Pat Hobby Stories* were as much a self-mocking portrait of a down-and-out alcoholic hack as a composite profile of Hollywood down-and-outers.

Daily inebriety, compounded by depression and stress, finally sent Anna May to the hospital on December 10, 1953. The diagnosis was a serious liver disease called Laennec's cirrhosis, and her doctor at Santa Monica Hospital had to transfuse eight pints of blood into her. Upon release, and on the doctor's recommendation, she checked herself into Sierra Madre Lodge, a sanitorium in Pasadena. Located at the foot of mountains on Barhite Street and surrounded by picturesque trees, the convalescent home was run by a Dr. Pearson, who sounded like a character out of a Raymond Chandler novel. Keeping a regular office in the valley, the doctor would check on his lodgers on Mondays and Wednesdays, and sometimes on Saturdays if a new quarry arrived. The capacity of the lodge was kept tidily at nineteen, so that the patients would feel neither crowded nor neglected. Some of them would even go to work during the day while taking their meals and treatments at the lodge, as well as sleeping there at night. With no work to go to, Anna May spent her days sleeping in, lazing under a palm tree, writing letters to friends, and eating plenty of nutritious food professionally prepared by the doctor and his staff.[25] Of course, Anna May was not alone among artists of her generation who resorted to substance abuse and were consequently institutionalized at mental asylums or rehab centers.

Sierra Madre provided Anna May a much-needed respite from the fruitless rush and mental wear and tear. But the expenses for the hospital and the sanitorium were shockingly steep. To cover the bills, she was forced to part with a few pieces of fine jewelry. She discreetly asked friends for help, hoping that the forthcoming Valentine's Day would make it easier to dispose of the rings and watches, which would make ideal gifts for young women. Eventually, an old acquaintance running a jewelry shop at the Beverly Hills Hotel came to her rescue by accepting her prized items on consignment. But the jewelry sale failed to relieve her other financial burdens, such as keeping a sizable house on two lots in a prime location and paying skyrocketing property taxes. Richard had been working the swing shift at the Douglas Aircraft plant in Santa Monica to save money for a Chinese gift shop. The siblings talked over the situation and decided to sell the empty lot to developers, while retaining the apartment complex.

With the real estate boom still going strong, the sale was quick and lucrative, but it greatly upset Anna May to see her own hacienda torn apart. The new owners immediately went into action, bringing in roaring bulldozers and chopping down majestic old trees. Even worse, the workers left the uprooted trees lying in the yard for days. The dead limbs flapping in the wind haunted Anna May, delivering a dreadful reminder of her evaporating fame and faded glamour.

40

READY FOR CLOSE-UP

Dragon's Den, Los Angeles restaurant/tavern *(Courtesy of Harry Quillen Collection / Los Angeles Public Library)*

CAREENING THROUGH the final years of her life with a drink in one hand and a cigarette in the other, Anna May acquired yet a new addiction: television. From 1946 to 1951, the number of television sets in use exploded from six thousand to twelve million. By 1955, half of all American homes had at least one black-and-white TV.[1] Anna May acquired hers in the summer of 1953 and became glued to the little tube, suffering from "televisionitis," a cultural malady that would one day be famously parodied on yet another television show, *The Brady Bunch*.

Anna May liked watching old movie reruns on TV, but, unlike Norma Desmond, she would avoid any of her own films—that is, if they were even featured. Perhaps the memories of her movie-star days were too painful. One time when Conrad Doerr offered to take Anna May to a revival of her greatest silent hit, *Piccadilly*, she emphatically refused, claiming that "she had been in too great an emotional state when that film was made to risk the memories."[2] Like ghost towns dotting the Old West, dead mines lie deep in human souls.

On New Year's Day 1955, right before she turned fifty, Anna May stayed home and watched the Tournament of Roses Parade on TV, followed by the Rose Bowl. A rare rainstorm doused Pasadena all day, putting a damper on the festivities. The parade featured a preview of Disneyland, soon to open its door in Anaheim, with floats that included replicas of the castle, Mickey Mouse, and the Dumbo Flying Elephant ride.[3] At the afternoon football match, top-ranked Ohio State fought a muddy battle with USC. In driving rain, slimy muck, and a foggy blur, the Buckeyes trounced the Trojans 20 to 7. Watching the parade and the game from the comfort of her home, Anna May felt lucky that she did not have to go out and get soaked at the stadium.

To cheer herself up, she read *The Power of Positive Thinking* (1952), by Norman Vincent Peale. Combining the old American dogma of self-reliance and Methodist spiritualism with a dash of Freudian psychiatry, the popular self-help book outsold every nonfiction book except the Bible in midcentury. Anna May read the book several times, finding it to be a great help in ridding herself of nervous tensions and in adopting the right attitude toward life's infinite problems.

However, no amount of positive thinking could alleviate the annoyance caused by the commotion next door. Having chopped down the trees, the developer who had bought the lot began erecting an eighteen-unit apartment building. Besides the dust and noise, she was also irritated by such seemingly trivial matters as the builder trying to borrow her electricity or placing the workmen's portable potty alongside her property line.

To escape the hectic daily tempo, Anna May traveled to London in September 1955. Returning to her favorite city for the first time since 1937 re-created some thrills, as well as nostalgia for the bygone years. Staying at a new hotel, The Westbury, near Berkeley Square, she found that postwar London had a new look—familiar streets were still there but far more congested, and many buildings had changed. Her old flame, Eric Maschwitz, who had served in secret intelligence during the war, was now married to his second wife and continued to make a name for himself as a songwriter. Besides meeting old friends, Anna May also attended the theatre, including a British musical and an Agatha Christie mystery. A highlight of the trip was her lunch with Somerset Maugham at the Dorchester Hotel, a rendezvous that would soon pay off. She had also planned to visit Paris and possibly Munich, but four weeks in London had burned a hole in her pocket, and she had to curtail her trip and return to America in October. This would be her last journey abroad.

The sad reality of her inability to travel freely made her next action seem like a reasonable step to take. Upon her return from England, she received a generous offer for her house. As much as she cherished the place she had owned for nineteen years, overhead expenses and rising taxes had become too much for her. Besides, the building was in a sad state and needed repairs of all types. In her unenviable financial situation, the offer was too good to pass up. So, she sold the house and bought a much smaller one at 308 Twenty-first Place, just off San Vicente Boulevard. Richard undertook the herculean task of moving everything, with the help of a brawny boy hired for a couple of Sundays. They also needed to remove the furnishings and appliances in her rental units. As a longtime tenant and friend, Conrad Doerr got the desk that used to belong to Judith Anderson, the star of such noir classics as *Rebecca* (1940) and *Laura* (1944). Ever frugal, Anna May traded in four refrigerators and four stoves for a pair of new ones. Richard also brought over many of their rare plants from their old place and wallpapered the new rooms with Japanese grass cloth, providing a nice background for their Chinese paintings and furnishings. To take a break from the frenzy of relocation, Anna May binged on going to the movies and saw three newly released films: *Picnic*, *Court Jester*, and *The King and I*.

As Americans were mesmerized by the film adaptation of the Broadway musical by Rodgers and Hammerstein, in which Russian-born Yul Brynner impersonated a half-naked, barefooted Siamese king romancing a British governess known simply as "Anna," Anna May also had a chance that year to titillate TV viewers' Oriental imagination. Thanks in part to her London lunch date with Somerset Maugham, she landed a gig to play a Chinese mistress in the NBC-TV film *The Letter*, based on the British writer's short story and directed by William Wyler. In fact, when Wyler made an earlier version of the film in 1940, starring Bette Davis with the able assistance of Otto Yamaoka, Anna May had been considered for the same secondary role, but she was rejected by Wyler because he thought she was "kind of a sex kitten and too young."[4] That film ended up casting the first recipient of the Oscar for Best Supporting Actress, Gale Sondergaard, in yellowface.

Getting redemption sixteen years later, Anna May gave a memorable performance that cemented her legacy as an actress who became known for her prowess in playing powerful, mysterious Oriental roles. The story was set in Singapore—or, as the title card says, "a teeming Oriental city"—where Anglo-European colonialists get rich from "liquid white gold," i.e., rubber. In a rage of jealousy, Leslie Crosbie (Siobhan McKenna) kills her lover, Geoff Hammond, and then claims that Hammond tried to rape her. Leslie is tried for murder and is about to walk free when a copy of a letter appears that reveals the truth. It is Leslie's note to Hammond that somehow has fallen into the hands of his mistress, a Chinese woman. In order to suppress the incriminating evidence, Leslie and her lawyer have to bribe the woman with a large sum of money. After her acquittal, Leslie confesses to her husband not only her undying love for the man she has killed, but also the inconvenient truth that her husband's entire rubber fortune has been spent on the purchase of that letter.

As in *Impact*, where Anna May's character as a meek maid holds the key to a mystery, her role of "the other woman" in *The Letter* is also the linchpin of the entire plot. In the two scenes where she appears, the Chinese woman speaks only two lines in barely comprehensible Malay Chinese, but her expressive eyes and grief-stricken face are as meaningful as theatrical gestures in a Chinese opera. Her dramatic entrance into the back room of a Chinese shop is highly stylized like a noir mystery, her shadow on the floor preceding her figure behind a beaded curtain. "As in the old days," exclaimed a reviewer for the *New York World-Telegram*, using stereotypical language to describe an Asian femme fatale, "Miss Wong was beautiful—and savage! Her eyes were dagger points and her silken shoulders quivered with hate." Assuming a role that was marginal and yet impactful, Anna May continued to radiate her vintage allure.[5]

Following the release of *The Letter*, Anna May finally fulfilled her longtime wish of presenting the film of her China trip to a national audience. Featured as an episode of the television series *Bold Journey*, "Native Land" aired on ABC on February 14, 1957. Earlier, during her war relief work, she had screened the footage at fundraisers as *Where the Wind Rocks the Bamboo*. The new label worked just as well. Displaying scenes of her visits to a tailor shop in Shanghai, a drama school in Peking, and her ancestral village in Canton, the episode was introduced and narrated by Anna May herself.[6] Sounding rather like Meryl

Streep's magnetic voiceover in the opening scene of *Out of Africa* ("I had a farm in Africa . . ."), Anna May's *sotto voce* mid-Atlantic accent evoked a sense of nostalgia and affection for a distant land. For many Americans still mourning "the loss of China" to Communism and still reeling from the frenzy of McCarthyism, the country revealed by Anna May on television in 1957 represented an old China a galaxy of light-years away.

Anna May's excitement over the television show did not last. The tedium of the daily routine soon set in. "Why not, buy a goddamn big car," as Robert Creeley suggested in a 1955 poem that captured the materialistic gestalt of postwar America.[7] Indeed, why not? Anna May bought an Oldsmobile in gray and red, the same colors as her house. Richard had begun earnestly pursuing his dream of a gift shop. After a trial period at a local farmers' market, he finally opened his store, Kim Wong Oriental Specialties, at Barrington Walk in Brentwood. On the day of the grand opening in July 1958, Anna May arrived in her Oldsmobile as the first customer and pretended to make a deal on a brass lotus lamp.[8] Later on, whenever Richard was away, she would help him by holding down the fort. It is almost too ironic—indeed, outrageous—that a global icon who would be admired by the likes of Andy Warhol and Susan Sontag was now reduced, in effect, to being an old maid running around a small shop with a Chinese feather duster.

In her final years, Chinatown remained Anna May's most frequent destination, as it had been since the day she had learned to walk. When he was still her tenant, Conrad Doerr remembered seeing his landlady return from Chinatown with bags of groceries and cook a feast in the kitchen, her big pots filled with bits and pieces of things. "Most of it tasted wonderful," he recalled, "and I soon learned not to ask what I was eating."[9]

Idle evenings often found the former Daughter of the Dragon relaxing, coincidentally, at a place called the Dragon's Den. A restaurant and tavern run by Eddy and Sissee, both scions of the See family, the Den was a brick building sloping down a hill, with the sign painted in Chinese and English on the outside wall. Sporting dragon murals and funky music inside, the place, according to Lisa See, had become a haven for gays and lesbians.[10] There Anna May, now a lonely celibate who had once liaised with countless men and occasionally women, could meet old friends like Keye Luke, Charlie Chan's Number One Son; or James Howe and his Caucasian wife—the interracial couple still hiding their "illegal" union from the authorities in the years before *Loving v. Virginia*, the 1967 Supreme Court case that would legalize interracial marriage. In casual sweaters-and-slacks, or occasionally a flashy silk gown, she would eat, drink, smoke, play poker with the boys—all while cracking corny jokes. A veteran of vaudeville, she would blow a smoke ring, let it sashay in the air, and then mutter, "You know, fifty million Chinamen can't be Wong." Her favorite joke was about a fisherman catching a beautiful mermaid. After reeling her in, he took a good look at the gorgeous thing and then tossed her back into the sea. A fellow fisherman was surprised, asking, "Why?" He replied, "How?"[11]

Besides the bottle and these friendships, Anna May found consolation in religion. Attending classes at the Unity School of Christianity in Santa Monica, she felt inspired by the calming and wise words of the minister and teacher Sue Sikking. In 1944, after surviving a near-fatal automobile accident, Sikking had turned to God and founded the Unity by the Sea Church. Since then, she had been an influential evangelist not only to her congregation but also on radio and television, in addition to lecturing all over the world and writing books.[12] To Anna May, Reverend Sikking spoke a simple, sensible, and inspirational language against a madly chaotic world that worshipped Moloch, the demon condemned by Allen Ginsberg in his famous 1956 poem "Howl." The teachings of Reverend Sikking gave Anna May a happy and joyful outlook on life when she was down and not yet out, depressed by the passing of youth and fame, the flagging of her career, and her deteriorating health.

Perhaps her prayer was answered. Like a flaming sunset, Anna May's prospects suddenly brightened with a flurry of television and film jobs in the final year of her life. In November 1959, she appeared on the new ABC series *Adventures in Paradise*, adapted from the popular South Seas stories by James Michener. In two sixty-minute episodes, starring Gardner McKay and veteran actress Paulette Goddard, Anna May played Madame Lu Yang, a moneychanger who operates across the entire Pacific region. Her adept portrayal of a dragon lady with a heart convinced ABC to put her in the long-running Western series *The Life and Legend of Wyatt Earp*. In the "China Mary" episode, while Hugh O'Brian impersonated the legendary rough-and-tumble lawman in Tombstone, Anna May starred as a leader of the Chinese community in the crime-ridden mining town, sort of an older-and-wiser daughter of Fu Manchu trafficking on both sides of the law. The thirty-minute installment—the only episode she was in—gave her ample airtime, and she received excellent reviews.

Anna May's last film role was in *Portrait in Black* (1960), directed by Michael Gordon and starring Lana Turner and Anthony Quinn. A noirish melodrama of infidelity, murder, and superficial suspense, the film cast Anna May as a silent housekeeper who has little to do with the story. Appearing in nine scenes, she always hovered in the background, like an extra hired from the street. We may recall that Anna May's film debut was as an uncredited Chinese lantern carrier in *The Red Lantern*, a proverbial face-in-the-crowd where she could not even identify herself. Now, after four decades in global cinema, she ended up the same way she had started: *Portrait in Black* was a portrait of Anna May in absentia. She loomed in the background like those faceless characters with stereotypical Chinese names who populate the hard-boiled world of midcentury film noir and detective fiction, figures who are there for no other reason than to provide an eerie atmosphere or comic relief. Even the most finicky critics felt scandalized by the indignity, with the *Variety* reviewer, among others, believing that Anna May had "chosen a thankless vehicle."[13]

Before sailing into the gloaming, Anna May repeated her subsidiary role one more time. In the *Barbara Stanwyck Theatre* on NBC, she appeared in an episode titled "Josephine Little: Dragon by the Tail." The story was set in Hong Kong, where Jo Little (Stanwyck), an adventuress born in China of a missionary mother and a newspaperman father, commits petty crimes ranging from cheating at cards to fencing stolen goods. Anna May played Jo's faithful amah, Ah Sing, who tries hard to keep her impetuous mistress out of trouble. Every time Jo falls victim to a honey-tongued crook, Ah Sing helps her see through the ruse. Impersonating such a woman of wisdom and pragmatism, Anna May, now fifty-five years old, wore long braids and a shapeless servant's blouse, with crow's feet clearly stamped around the edges of her haggard face. Such would be our last glimpse of her on the screen during her lifetime. Serendipitously, the woman born at the tail end of the Year of the Dragon would conclude her acting career with a television episode called "Dragon by the Tail."

In January 1961, when the taped episode was ready to air on NBC, Anna May was spotted by Conrad Doerr at a bank in Santa Monica. According to her former tenant, she looked ill. Sessue Hayakawa, who had regained his corona with the Oscar-nominated film *The Bridge on the River Kwai* (1957), in which he takes on the role of a ruthless Japanese general, visited his former costar and described Anna May as being "very thin and pale."[14] In fact, she had come down with a virus before Christmas and had just gotten back on her feet around the New Year. Because of her work in *Portrait in Black*, she had built a rapport with the producer, Ross Hunter, who had just purchased the rights to *Flower Drum Song* in order to adapt to the screen the Rodgers and Hammerstein musical set in San Francisco's Chinatown. Hunter had offered Anna May one of the lead roles, as Madame Liang, with the production to begin in February. It was an ideal job for Anna May, to display her consummate skills on both the stage and the screen. Having missed out on *The Good Earth*, she would now get another shot at starring in a blockbuster Chinese-themed production.

This was not to be. Two weeks after the inauguration of John F. Kennedy as the first Catholic president of the United States, on the afternoon of February 3, 1961, while she was taking a nap in her Santa Monica home, Anna May unexpectedly died of a heart attack, caused possibly by her chronic liver disease. She was only fifty-six.

The obituaries repeated most of the ethnic tropes that had immured Anna May throughout her career. *Time* magazine labeled her "the screen's foremost Oriental villainess," while the *New York Times* dubbed her "one of the most unforgettable figures of Hollywood's great days" and "a movie symbol of 'the mysterious East.'" The *Los Angeles Times* was the most appreciative of the hometown star, calling her "one of the first to bring the charm of the Orient to the American screen," "a symbol of Oriental mystery," and "a beauty of poise and culture." These major publications poured much ink to describe Anna May's "exotic" looks in a vernacular typical of the era, dripping in stereotypes. As usual, the *New York Times* spearheaded the charge, portraying her as "tall, slim and sloe-eyed," with a complexion of "rose blushing through old ivory," which "shone on the screen like the texture of an old Ming vase."[15]

None of the eulogies drew attention to the troubling fact that, charming and talented as they said she was, she had been unable to get a meaningful part in any film since 1942. Conveniently consigning her to a bygone era, America had by then moved on with other, obviously younger, female icons or symbols of "the mysterious East." Two phenomenally successful films, *The World of Suzie Wong* (1960) and *Flower Drum Song* (1961), marked 1960–61 as the banner year of Hollywood's Orientalism and led to the meteoric rise of Nancy Kwan and Miyoshi Umeki. While relishing the Oriental flavors from these Suzie Wongs, Mei Lings, or Linda Lows, America also spiced things up with its own favorite sauce—yellowface. Produced in the same epic year of 1961, Paramount's *Breakfast at Tiffany's*, starring Audrey Hepburn, scandalously cast Mickey Rooney as a buck-toothed Japanese man named Mr. Yunioshi. Racial humor has always been America's tonic or opiate.

In the "real East," the going was tough, to say the least. Under the Great Helmsman, red China was reeling from the aftermath of the "Great Leap Forward," a three-year utopian campaign that had commenced in 1958 and

Anna May Wong in *Portrait in Black*, 1960 *(Courtesy of Everett Collection)*

ended with millions of people starved to death. In Taiwan, where the defeated Nationalists had taken refuge under the protection of the Pacific fleets of the US Navy, Generalissimo Chiang Kai-shek ruled the island under martial law, suppressing political opposition with military tribunals and "White Terror," while plotting to reclaim his lost domain. Mainland and island newspapers were too preoccupied with domestic woes to notice the passing of an aging star in faraway Hollywood. Only newspapers in Hong Kong, still a British colony, reprinted bits of the obituaries pulled off the English-language newswire.[16]

Reportedly, when Anna May died, lying next to her was a copy of the *Flower Drum Song* film script. In her final hours, she was still assiduously preparing for her big comeback in Hollywood's Dream Factory. Or, as Norma Desmond says in the climactic scene of *Sunset Boulevard*, "All right, Mr. DeMille, I'm ready for my close-up."

EPILOGUE:
ANNA MAY WONG ON THE MONEY

Anna May Wong, image on US quarter
(Photograph by Yunte Huang)

O**N A FINE SPRING DAY** in 2022, I drove from Santa Barbara to a dinner party at a friend's house in Pacific Palisades. As it was a Saturday, the often execrable Los Angeles traffic turned out to be as smooth as a babbling brook. So, with some extra time on my hands, I decided to make a field trip to the Angelus Rosedale Cemetery, the final resting place of Anna May Wong.

There is a saying in Hollywood that one's fame is measured by the distance one lies from the stars. Take a walk in Glendale's Forest Lawn Cemetery and look at the great vaults and crypts with multicolored marbles, and you'll know the truth of that saying. In fact, after Jean Harlow's early death and grand burial ceremonies in 1937, there was a rushed land grab in the vicinity of her mausoleum. Driving her paramour Eric Maschwitz and his friend Val Gielgud to Pasadena one day that summer, Anna May stopped by Forest Lawn and showed her British visitors a prime example of what Evelyn Waugh would call "an Anglo-American Tragedy"—that is, America's eschatological obsession that became a real estate craze. In his novel *The Loved One* (1948), inspired by his own visit to Forest Lawn, Waugh satirized how death was wrapped up and sold American-style like a package trip. In his diary from that tour, Gielgud wrote about "passing the Forest Lawn Cemetery, where trustification has been applied to the limit to the whole apparatus of death and burial." Impressed by Irving Thalberg's $3,500 vault, Gielgud repeated the Hollywood cliché he had just heard from Anna May: "The nearer to dead 'stars' you wish to lie, the more you must pay—the late Miss Harlow being, I gather, the summit of this grisly pyramid."[1]

Angelus Rosedale, however, is no Forest Lawn. Lying quietly off Highway 10 and bordering on South Central Los Angeles, it is one of the oldest cemeteries west of the Rockies. Founded in 1884 as Rosedale, it was the first Los Angeles cemetery open to all races and creeds. Hemmed in by Washington Boulevard, Normandie Avenue, and Venice Boulevard, the cemetery now occupies sixty-five acres. Even though it has a fair share of Hollywood stardust, including the gravesites of Todd Browning and Marshall Neilan, both of whom romanced Anna May, Rosedale was better known as a burial ground for politicians and leading community members, with notable internments including several former mayors and David Burbank, after whom the city of Burbank was named.[2]

After her passing in 1961, Anna May was remembered in a service at the Unity by the Sea Church, officiated by Reverend Sue Sikking, whose teachings had brought much consolation to her desolate final years on Earth. Afterward, Anna May's body was cremated and her ashes were entombed next to the graves of her mother and her sister Margaretta, who had died in infancy.

Having seen pictures of the trio's shared gravestone, and having memorized the plot number found online, I thought I could find the site without difficulty by relying on my sixth sense. Wandering around the old cemetery full of wildflowers, brambles, and ancient engravings dating back more than a century, I was soon lost. Following a path lined with tall palms, I went back to the office near the cast-iron front gate. Because of the COVID-19 pandemic, which had by then killed about one million Americans, the office was closed to visitors without an appointment. But I rang the doorbell anyway, thinking they could at least answer a simple question. A young man in a polo shirt opened the door but held it to keep me from entering. After I told him I was looking for Anna May Wong's grave, he raised his thick eyebrows: "Who?" I repeated her name, spelling out "Wong" and adding that she was a famous actress who had died long ago. He told me to wait and then shut the door.

Standing under the small white portico, I gazed at the eternal blue sky of Southern California that looked like the background of a play the stage manager had been too lazy to change. The giant palms soaring over the grassy ground looked parched; some of them had even turned dark, like stone pillars blackened by fire or time.

After a long ten minutes, the clerk returned and handed me a photocopied map on which a spot had been marked with a blue pen.

Map in hand, I quickly located the grave in an older section of the cemetery. On a brown marble slab erected on a cement base, the horizontal English inscription on the top read: LEE TOY WONG, OUR BELOVED MOTHER. Beneath that were three Chinese names displayed vertically. Anna May's was on the right: DAUGHTER, LIU TSONG. In front of the headstone stood a metal tube holding an American flag, and behind it was a Dusty Miller with its yellow flowers and silvery tomentose leaves. Some people also call the plant Silver Dust. It reminded me of fairy dust, the glittery powder coming out of the magic

Anna May Wong grave, Angelus Rosedale Cemetery, Los Angeles
(Photograph by Yunte Huang)

wand of stardom that had touched young Anna May at the beginning of her long journey. I also recalled her mother's admonition at the time. Having ventured out against her mother's wishes, and having captivated the world with her charm and talent, Anna May was finally back in the maternal embrace, forever.

According to Chinese custom, one should bow before the grave, as Anna May had done at the burial ground of the Ming emperors outside Peking many years earlier. But perhaps instigated by the American flag, I placed a pebble on the cement base and said a silent prayer. Since Anna May was familiar with both Chinese and American traditions, I was sure she would understand my gesture.

Before going to my friend's, I had one more stop to make. A cemetery might be the final resting place of one's physical being, but for an actor there is another, in some ways more permanent, place for their legacy—the Hollywood Walk of Fame.

Driving down Washington, I passed streets with august names: Harvard, Cambridge, Oxford, Roosevelt. Turning north around a corner, I was soon on bustling Western Avenue, the aorta of Koreatown, lined with shops and restaurants displaying Korean signs. News on the car radio reminded me that it was actually the thirtieth anniversary of the 1992 Los Angeles Riots. In the wake of the Rodney King beating and the acquittal of LAPD officers, angry protests erupted in South Central, the Black neighborhood, and quickly turned into riots that spilled across the highway into Koreatown. For six days, the former frontier city that had seen plenty of race unrest in its long history—the Chinese Massacre in 1871, the Zoot Suit Riots in 1943, the Watts Riots in 1965, to name just a few—once again witnessed widespread looting, assault, and arson. By the time the joint forces of the California National Guard, US military, and federal agencies put an end to the carnage, sixty-three people had died, thousands had been injured, and Koreatown suffered disproportionate damage.

Coincidentally, during my first summer in America, I had taken a Greyhound bus from Tuscaloosa, Alabama, to San Francisco. On that three-day journey in early May of 1992, I was as excited as Jack Kerouac hitchhiking on LSD. In Los Angeles, as my bus rolled through the forlorn district, I saw astonishing remnants of the devastation—singed walls, broken storefronts, and boarded-up windows. Going up Western Avenue now, after visiting Anna May Wong's gravesite, I felt that I was driving through history and, more palpably, a forgotten lane of my own memory.

Even with the raging pandemic, Hollywood Boulevard was still packed with tourists on a Saturday afternoon. Open-top tour buses crowded with out-of-town folks wheeled around, making scheduled stops at celebrity houses. They reminded me of those rubberneck cars that took people slumming in Chinatown in the early days. As I have written in this book, the initial rise of Hollywood had something to do with American curiosity about China-town, which fortuitously also opened a door for Anna May. The inauguration of Grauman's Chinese Theatre on May 18, 1927, an event she had attended, marking the height of Hollywood's chinoiserie, also gave a huge boost to Tin-seltown tourism. Today, the Chinese Theatre, whose courtyard with celebri-ties' handprints and signatures inspired the Walk of Fame, remains a center of attraction for visitors.

A short distance from the Chi-nese Theatre, on the sidewalk near the corner of Hollywood and Vine, once described by Ross Macdon-ald as "where everything ends and a great many things begin," I found the terrazzo-and-brass star bearing the name of Anna May Wong.[3] For-tunately, she had received the honor in 1960, a year before her passing. Curiously, lying next to her star was that of the Chinese actress Lucy Liu. In fact, at her ceremony on May 1, 2019, Liu paid homage to Anna May for being a pioneer who had to endure racism, marginalization, and exclusion, blazing a trail for the future generation of Asian American artists. Pointing out the close prox-imity of their stars on the sidewalk,

Anna May Wong's star, Hollywood Walk of Fame
(Photograph by Yunte Huang)

Liu quipped, "We can actually start our own little Chinatown right here."[4] An affectionate expression, the remark also contained a dig at an industry still struggling with the racism that has plagued the entire nation. Actually, from Grauman's Chinese Theatre to the film set of *The Good Earth* to the manufac-tured China City, Hollywood has always had its Chinatown, except that it's usually been a town without Chinese.

Driving down Sunset Boulevard toward my evening rendezvous, I peered at the strip through the windshield tinted by a layer of golden twilight. Blue jacarandas dotted the sidewalks, disrupting the monotony of palms and lamp-posts. Night prowlers were not out yet, but I could feel the pulse of the strip quickening, as neon signs began to stir and valets stood ready in front of clubs and restaurants, showing a look of eagerness.

A few months earlier, I had heard the news that the United States Mint had planned to issue quarter coins commemorating, in the first year, five American women: African American poet Maya Angelou, Cherokee Chief Wilma Mankiller, astronaut Sally Ride, New Mexico suffragist Nina Otero-Warren, and Anna May Wong. Like Lucy Liu's poignant tribute to her a century after Anna May's film debut, I knew it would be a long-overdue honor for her image to appear on US currency. But as someone who had tracked her life and career in awe and admiration, I also knew that Anna May Wong had always been on the money.

ACKNOWLEDGMENTS

As the third and final installment of my trilogy, "Rendezvous with America," this book marks a milestone in my pursuit of the Asian American story in the making of American culture. Along this lengthy, at times difficult, journey, I have been fortunate to have Bob Weil as my editor and inspirational guide. I am surely no Dante, but Bob—with his vision, acumen, erudition, and genuine care for his authors—is truly a modern-day Virgil in this still-divine comedy called "literature."

I am also deeply grateful to Glenn Mott, my agent and best friend. It is not hyperbole to say that, without his help, these three books—*Charlie Chan*, *Inseparable*, and *Daughter of the Dragon*—would not have existed. As I turn a new page in my career, I am comforted by the thought that I can always count on his friendship and counsel.

I also wish to thank Haley Bracken at Liveright for her excellent editorial guidance; Cordelia Calvert for her enduring enthusiasm for the book; Hangping Xu and Chunmei Du for reading the manuscript and sharing their expertise; Annie Fu and Richard Song for research assistance; Wendy Sun for her help with German texts; Marjorie Perloff, Charles Bernstein, and Hank Lazer for their mentorship and emotional support; Graham Hodges for his pioneering work on Anna May Wong, as well as his generosity over the years; and Deidre Lynch for the Emily Dickinson gem.

The following people at various institutions have also most ably and generously assisted me in accessing precious images and research materials: John

Cahoon at Seaver Center for Western History Research; Daniel Keough at Hoover Institution Library and Archives, Stanford University; Sharon Yang at Harvard-Yenching Library, Harvard University; Melissa Barton at Beinecke Library, Yale University; Jia Junying at China Film Archives, Beijing; Michele Hadlow at Everett Collection; Terri Garst at Los Angeles Public Library; and Jamie Carstairs at Special Collections, University of Bristol, UK.

It is my good fortune to have again had Kathleen Brandes as a gatekeeper of my writing, a superb copyeditor who always goes beyond her call of duty to turn the manuscript into a much better book.

When COVID-19 first broke out in January 2020, I was only a few hundred miles away from Wuhan, the epicenter of the pandemic, visiting my family for the Chinese New Year. On that wintry day when I said good-bye to them—my mother in her seventies, my wife JZ, and our three-year-old son Henry—I had no idea that I would not be able to see them for a very long time. While interminable lockdowns, quarantines, closed borders, canceled flights, and invalidated visas have defined the past three years of our lives, and the day of reunion remains elusive, I wish to express my gratitude to JZ and Henry, still stuck in China, for the love and strength they send daily from afar. I am also grateful to Isabelle and Ira, two vivacious youngsters now pursuing their own dreams, who have always been part of whatever journey I have been taking.

NOTES

PREFACE

1. Anna May Wong, "Bamboo, or China's Conversion to Film," *Mein Film* (June 4, 1930).
2. Sylvia Plath, *Ariel: The Restored Edition* (New York: Harper Perennial, 2004), pp. 15–17.

PROLOGUE

1. Raymond Lou, "The Chinese American Community of Los Angeles, 1870–1900: A Case of Resistance, Organization, and Participation" (PhD dissertation, University of California, Irvine, 1982), p. 118.
2. Robert L. Wagner, "Two Chinese Girls," *Rob Wagner's Script* (November 21, 1936), p. 1. See also Graham Russell Gao Hodges, *Anna May Wong: From Laundryman's Daughter to Hollywood Legend* (New York: Palgrave Macmillan, 2004), p. 14; Shirley Jennifer Lim, *Anna May Wong: Performing the Modern* (Philadelphia: Temple University Press, 2019), p. 21.

CHAPTER 1. YEAR OF THE DRAGON

1. In the Chinese zodiac, each of the twelve animal signs is further divided into five types, corresponding to the five elements, forming a sixty-year cycle: Gold, Wood, Water, Fire, and Earth.
2. Hodges, pp. 2, 9.
3. "Brief Weather Report," *Los Angeles Times* (January 3, 1905), p. I1; "The Fall of Port Arthur," *Los Angeles Times* (January 3, 1905), p. II6.
4. "Glad Hand for People," *Los Angeles Times* (January 3, 1905), p. I4; "About Mediation," *Los Angeles Times* (January 4, 1905), p. I7.
5. "Japanese in High Feather," *Los Angeles Times* (January 3, 1905), p. II12; "Geisha Girls Sing," *Los Angeles Times* (January 4, 1905), p. II8.
6. "Railroads Break Records," *Los Angeles Herald* (January 3, 1905), p. 5.
7. "Rain Helped Tournament," *Los Angeles Times* (January 2, 1905), p. I15.
8. "Rose Festival Draws Thousands," *Los Angeles Herald* (January 3, 1905), p. 1.
9. "Flags and Flowers, Throngs and Glory," *Los Angeles Times* (January 3, 1905), p. II1; "Envoy Wong Comes to See," *Los Angeles Times* (January 4, 1905), p. II1.
10. "Bigger Ships and Bigger Guns," *Los Angeles Times* (January 4, 1905), p. II12.
11. "The Immigration Evil," *Los Angeles Times* (January 3, 1905), p. II6.

CHAPTER 2. CHINATOWN

1. Jacob A. Riis, *How the Other Half Lives: Studies Among the Tenements of New York*, ed. Sam Bass Warner Jr. (Cambridge: Harvard University Press, 2010), pp. 91, 100.

2. "Jacob A. Riis on Slum and Paradise," *Los Angeles Times* (January 4, 1905), p. II1.

3. David L. Ulin, ed., *Writing Los Angeles: A Literary Anthology* (New York: Library of America, 2002), p. 1; Kevin Starr, *Inventing the Dream: California Through the Progressive Era* (New York: Oxford University Press, 1985), p. 58.

4. Lou, pp. 20–21; Stan Steiner, *Fusang: The Chinese Who Built America* (New York: Harper and Row, 1979), pp. 79–81.

5. Yunte Huang, *Inseparable: The Original Siamese Twins and Their Rendezvous with American History* (New York: Liveright, 2018).

6. Lou, p. 20.

7. Ibid.; Scott Zesch, *The Chinatown War: Chinese Los Angeles and the Massacre of 1871* (New York: Oxford University Press, 2012), p. 14.

8. *Los Angeles Star* (July 13, 1861); Maurice H. Newmark and Marco R. Newmark, eds., *Sixty Years in Southern California, 1853–1913, Containing the Reminiscences of Harris Newmark* (New York: Knickerbocker Press, 1916), pp. 297–98.

9. Carey McWilliams, *Southern California: An Island on the Land* (Salt Lake City, UT: Peregrine Smith Books, 1973), p. 86.

10. Roger Daniels, *Asian America: Chinese and Japanese in the United States since 1850* (Seattle: University of Washington Press, 1988), p. 39; Lou, pp. 3–4.

11. Daniels, pp. 59–62.

12. Lou, pp. 33–34.

13. Zesch, p. 19.

14. Lou, p. 5.

15. Nora Sterry, "Housing Conditions in Chinatown Los Angeles," *Journal of Applied Sociology* (November–December 1922), pp. 71–73; Roberta S. Greenwood, *Down by the Station: Los Angeles Chinatown, 1880–1933* (Los Angeles: Cotsen Institute of Archaeology Press, 1996), pp. 16, 19.

16. Sterry, "Housing Conditions in Chinatown Los Angeles," p. 71.

17. Fae Myenne Ng, Foreword to Louis Chu, *Eat a Bowl of Tea* (Seattle: University of Washington Press, 2020), p. ix.

CHAPTER 3. THE LAUNDRYMAN

1. Wen Yiduo, *Selected Poems*, ed. Zhou Liangpei (Wuhan, China: Changjiang Art and Literature Press, 1988), p. 70; translation mine.

2. The word *Lee* on the sign of SAM LEE LAUNDRY or SING LEE LAUNDRY is actually the character for "profit" rather than the last name "Lee." See John Jung, *Chinese Laundries: Tickets to Survival on Gold Mountain* (Las Vegas, NV: Yin & Yang Press, 2007), p. 55.

3. Paul C. P. Siu, *The Chinese Laundryman: A Study of Social Isolation*, ed. John Kuo Wei Tchen (New York: New York University Press, 1987), p. 2.

4. *National Laundry Journal* (Chicago: Dowst Brothers Co., 1905), p. 41.

5. Zesch, p. 17.

6. Siu, pp. 46–47.

7. Hodges, p. 6.

8. Zesch, p. 18; Lou, pp. 125, 64–65.

9. Greenwood, p. 21.

10. Hodges, p. 2; Lisa See, *On Gold Mountain: The One-Hundred-Year Odyssey of My Chinese-American Family* (New York: Vintage Books, 1995), p. 64.

11. Hodges, p. 6; Karen J. Leong, *The China Mystique: Pearl S. Buck, Anna May Wong, Mayling*

Soong, and the Transformation of American Orientalism (Berkeley: University of California Press, 2005), pp. 59–60.

12. Hodges, p. 2.

CHAPTER 4. FUN IN A CHINESE LAUNDRY

1. Josef von Sternberg, *Fun in a Chinese Laundry: An Autobiography* (New York: Collier Books, 1965); John Baxter, *Von Sternberg* (Lexington: University Press of Kentucky, 2010), pp. 16, 37.

2. Lou, p. 121.

3. Siu, p. 60.

4. Ibid., pp. 61, 51.

5. Ibid., p. 62.

6. Ibid., p. 68.

7. Ibid., p. 52.

8. Lou, p. 122.

9. Robert Sklar, *Movie-Made America: A Cultural History of American Movies* (New York: Vintage, 1994), pp. 3, 21.

10. Sabine Haenni, "Filming 'Chinatown': Fake Visions, Bodily Transformations," in Peter X. Feng, ed., *Screening Asian Americans* (New Brunswick, NJ: Rutgers University Press, 2002), p. 21.

11. Ibid.; Erika Lee, *The Making of Asian America: A History* (New York: Simon & Schuster, 2015), p. 89.

12. Jung, *Chinese Laundries*, p. 99.

13. Stanley Cavell, *The World Viewed: Reflections on the Ontology of Film* (Cambridge: Harvard University Press, 1979), p. 101.

14. Paul McDonald, *The Star System: Hollywood's Production of Popular Identities* (London: Wallflower, 2000), pp. 20–21; Tom Gunning, "The Cinema of Attractions: Early Film, Its Spectator and the Avant-Garde," in T. Elsaesser, ed., *Early Cinema: Space Frame Narrative* (London: British Film Institute, 1990), pp. 56–62.

15. McDonald, p. 21; Kevin Brownlow, *The Parade's Gone By . . . .* (Berkeley: University of California Press, 1968), p. 2.

16. Siegfried Kracauer, *Theory of Film: The Redemption of Physical Reality* (Princeton, NJ: Princeton University Press, 1960), pp. 60, 72.

17. Baxter, p. 20.

CHAPTER 5. ANNA

1. Los Angeles Unified School District, *History of Schools: 1855–1972*, 3d ed. (Los Angeles: Education Housing Branch, 1973), p. 8. According to the same record, the California Street School was closed in 1939.

2. Victor Low, *The Unimpressible Race: A Century of Educational Struggle by the Chinese in San Francisco* (San Francisco: East/West Publishing Company, 1982), pp. 59–67.

3. James W. Loewen, *The Mississippi Chinese: Between Black and White* (Prospect Heights, IL: Waveland Press, 1988), pp. 66–68.

4. Harry Carr, "I Am Growing More Chinese—Each Passing Year!" *Los Angeles Times* (September 9, 1934), p. H3; Anna May Wong, "The True Life Story of a Chinese Girl," *Pictures* (August 1926), pp. 107–8.

5. Simon Winchester, *A Crack in the Edge of the World: America and the Great California Earthquake of 1906* (New York: HarperCollins, 2005), p. 214.

6. Wong, "The True Life Story," p. 108.

7. Ibid.

8. Ng Poon Chew, "The Chinese in Los Angeles," *Land of Sunshine* (October 1894), pp. 102–3.

9. Myra Paule, "Chinese Mission Thrives amid Squalor," *Los Angeles Times* (January 24, 1926), p. 20.

10. Nora Sterry, "Social Attitudes of Chinese Immigrants," *Journal of Applied Sociology* (July–August 1923), p. 326.

11. Wong, "The True Life Story," p. 108; Hodges, p. 15.

CHAPTER 6. CURIOUS CHINESE CHILD

1. McWilliams, p. 331.

2. Sklar, *Movie-Made America*, pp. 67–68; McDonald, p. 23.

3. Sklar, *Movie-Made America*, pp. 50–51.

4. McDonald, p. 33.

5. Sklar, *Movie-Made America*, p. 46.

6. Miriam Hansen, *Babel and Babylon: Spectatorship in American Silent Film* (Cambridge: Harvard University Press, 1991), p. 61; Anna May Wong, "Wode zishu" (An Autobiography), *Liangyou* 114 (1936), p. 24; Carr, p. H3.

7. Hodges, p. 19.

8. Wong, "The True Life Story," p. 108.

9. Nathanael West, *The Complete Works of Nathanael West* (New York: Farrar, Straus and Giroux, 1957), p. 316.

10. Sklar, *Movie-Made America*, p. 74.

11. Haenni, pp. 22–23.

12. Bonnie Tsui, *American Chinatown: A People's History of Five Neighborhoods* (New York: Free Press, 2009), pp. 114–16.

13. Wong, "The True Life Story," p. 108.

14. Kevin Brownlow, *Behind the Mask of Innocence* (Berkeley: University of California Press, 1990), p. 332; Timothy G. Turner, "Maid of Orient Unspoiled by Success Dips Her Ivory Hands in Suds," *Los Angeles Times* (July 24, 1921), p. 1.

CHAPTER 7. THE RED LANTERN

1. Anthony Chan, *Perpetually Cool: The Many Lives of Anna May Wong, 1905–1961* (Lanham, MD: Scarecrow Press, 2003), p. 30.

2. Sklar, *Movie-Made America*, p. 53.

3. Gina Marchetti, *Romance and the "Yellow Peril": Race, Sex, and Discourse Strategies in Hollywood Fiction* (Berkeley: University of California Press, 1993), p. 33; Brownlow, *Behind the Mask*, pp. 320, 325.

4. Brownlow, *Behind the Mask*, p. 332.

5. Gavin Lambert, *Nazimova: A Biography* (Lexington: University Press of Kentucky, 2021), p. 207.

6. *Moving Picture World* (May 1919), pp. 920–21; Brownlow, *Behind the Mask*, p. 327.

7. Carr, p. H3.

8. Ibid.

9. Ibid.

10. Brownlow, *Behind the Mask*, p. 330.

11. Lambert, p. 210; Axel Madsen, *The Sewing Circle: Hollywood's Greatest Secret—Female Stars Who Loved Other Women* (New York: Open Road, 1995), p. 100.

12. Lambert, p. 210; Madsen, p. 115.

CHAPTER 8. ANNA MAY

1. Herman Melville, *Moby-Dick, or, The Whale*, ed. Harrison Hayford et al. Northwestern-Newberry ed. (Evanston, IL: Northwestern University Press and Newberry Library, 1988), p. 3.

2. Carr, p. H3.

3. Ibid.

4. Turner, p. 1.

5. Jack Spears, *Hollywood: The Golden Era* (New York: Castle Books, 1971), pp. 293–94; Hodges, pp. 35–36.

6. Brownlow, *Behind the Mask*, p. 337.

7. *Photoplay* (December 1923), p. 114.

8. Hodges, p. 36.

9. Wong, "The True Life Story," p. 107.

CHAPTER 9. MADAME BUTTERFLY IN TECHNICOLOR

1. Andrea Most, "'You've Got to Be Carefully Taught': The Politics of Race in Rodgers and Hammerstein's *South Pacific*," *Theatre Journal* 52:3 (2000), pp. 306–7.

2. Cari Beauchamp, *Without Lying Down: Frances Marion and the Powerful Women of Early Hollywood* (New York: Scribner, 1997), p. 143.

3. Carr, p. H3.

4. *Film Daily* (December 3, 1922), p. 7; *Variety* (December 1, 1922), p. 35; *New York Times* (November 27, 1922), p. 18.

5. *New York Times* (November 27, 1922), p. 18; *Variety* (December 1, 1922), p. 35.

6. L. T. Troland, "Some Psychological Aspects of Natural Color Motion Pictures," *Transactions of the Society of Motion Picture Engineers* 11:32 (1927), pp. 687–88.

7. Kirsty Sinclair Dootson, "The Politics of Color," *Frames Cinema Journal* 17 (2020), https://framescinemajournal.com/article/the-politics-of-colour/.

8. Xin Peng, "Color-as-Hue and Color-as-Race: Early Technicolor, Ornamentalism and *The Toll of the Sea* (1922)," *Screen* 62:3 (Autumn 2021), pp. 299–300.

9. "Picture and People," *Motion Picture News* (December 9, 1922), p. 2900.

10. *New York Times* (November 29, 1922), p. 24.

11. *New York Times* (November 27, 1922), p. 18.

CHAPTER 10. HOLLYWOOD BABYLON

1. Starr, *Inventing the Dream*, p. 313.

2. Madsen, pp. 124–26.

3. Starr, *Inventing the Dream*, pp. 324–29.

4. Ibid., p. 334; David Robinson, *Hollywood in the Twenties* (New York: A. S. Barnes, 1968), pp. 9–14.

5. Sklar, *Movie-Made America*, p. 77; Starr, *Inventing the Dream*, p. 335.

6. Starr, *Inventing the Dream*, p. 337.

7. Turner, p. 1.

8. Anthony Slide, *Hollywood Unknowns: A History of Extras, Bit Players, and Stand-Ins* (Jackson: University Press of Mississippi, 2012), p. 82; Turner, p. 1.

9. A. Chan, p. 34.

CHAPTER 11. THE THIEF OF BAGDAD

1. James S. Peters, *Sadakichi Hartmann, Alien Son: A Biography* (Santa Fe, NM: Sunstone Press, 2017), p. 11.

2. Starr, *Inventing the Dream*, p. 338.

3. Hodges, p. 49.

4. "Troubles of a Bagdad Thief," *New York Times* (March 16, 1924), p. 5.

5. F. Scott Fitzgerald, *The Great Gatsby* (New York: Charles Scribner's Sons, 1925), p. 182.

6. *New York Times* (March 18, 1924).

7. Rob Edelman, *The Thief of Bagdad*, in *Magill's Survey of Cinema, Silent Films*, vol. 13, ed. Frank N. Magill (Englewood Cliffs, NJ: Salem Press, 1982), pp. 1109–10.

8. Peters, pp. 13, 107.

9. Ezra Pound, *The Pisan Cantos*, ed. Richard Sieburth (New York: New Directions, 2003), p. 73.

10. "Police Clear Jam at Movie Premiere," *New York Times* (March 19, 1924), p. 19.

11. A. Chan, p. 211.

12. "Fairbanks Wins Berlin," *New York Times* (January 23, 1926), p. 19.

CHAPTER 12. HER OWN COMPANY

1. John Higham, *Strangers in the Land: Patterns of American Nativism, 1860–1925* (New York: Atheneum, 1955), p. 330.

2. A. Chan, p. 37; Hodges, p. 53; "Re-Chinafying Herself: Ashamed No Longer," *South China Morning Post* (January 25, 1924), p. 6.

3. Hodges, p. 47.

4. A. Chan, p. 37.

5. Arthur Dong, *Hollywood Chinese: The Chinese in American Feature Films* (Santa Monica, CA: Angel City Press, 2019), pp. 223–25; Jenny Cho and the Chinese Historical Society of Southern California, *Chinese in Hollywood* (Charleston, SC: Arcadia Publishing, 2013), pp. 9–12.

6. Dong, pp. 228–29.

7. Emma-Lindsay Squier, "The Dragon Awakens," *Picture Play Magazine* (January 1922), pp. 84–86.

8. Brownlow, *Behind the Mask*, p. 330.

9. Yunte Huang, *Charlie Chan: The Untold Story of the Honorable Detective and His Rendezvous with American History* (New York: W. W. Norton, 2010), p. 193.

10. A. Chan, p. 37.

11. *Variety* (September 17, 1924).

12. Todd Rainsberger, *James Wong Howe: Cinematographer* (San Diego, CA: A. S. Barnes, 1981), pp. 11–20, 152–53.

13. Philip Leibfried and Chei Mi Lane, *Anna May Wong: A Complete Guide to Her Film, Stage, Radio, and Television Work* (Jefferson, NC: McFarland and Company, 2004), p. 39.

14. Ibid., pp. 39–40.

15. "Re-Chinafying Herself," p. 6.

16. Ibid.

17. Ibid.

CHAPTER 13. VAUDEVILLE

1. Kracauer, pp. l-li.

2. George C. Warren, "Anna May Is Pure Delight," *San Francisco Chronicle* (January 22, 1925), p. 11.

3. For the history and politics of casting Charlie Chan, see Huang, *Charlie Chan*.

4. Warren, p. 11.

5. V. I. Pudovkin, *Film Technique and Film Acting: The Cinema Writings of V. I. Pudovkin*, trans. Ivor Montagu (London: Vision, 1954), p. 109.

6. Warren, p. 11.

7. Ibid.

8. Moon Kwan, *An Anecdotal History of the Chinese Cinema (Zhongguo yintan waishi)* (Hong Kong: Guangjiaojing Press, 1976), pp. 61–62.

9. Hans J. Wollstein, *Vixens, Floozies and Molls: 28 Actresses of Late 1920s and 1930s Hollywood* (Jefferson, NC: McFarland and Company, 1999), p. 250; Leibfried and Lane, p. 12; A. Chan, p. 39.

10. Wollstein, p. 250.

11. "Picture Actors Jailed in Omaha Board Bill Dispute May Sue Hotel for $70,000," *San Francisco Chronicle* (March 6, 1925), p. 4; Wollstein, p. 250; A. Chan, pp. 39–41; Leibfried and Lane, pp. 12–13.

CHAPTER 14. 1927

1. James Ellroy, *The Big Nowhere* (New York: Mysterious Press, 1988), p. 115.
2. Alice Tildesley, "I Am Lucky That I Am Chinese," *San Francisco Chronicle* (June 3, 1928), p. 3.
3. Cho, p. 23.
4. Ironically, the TCL Corporation, a Chinese electronics manufacturer based in Canton, acquired the naming rights in 2013 and rebranded the historical landmark in Hollywood as TCL Chinese Theatre (Dong, p. 107).
5. Hodges, p. 60.
6. D. H. Lawrence, *Studies in Classic American Literature* (London: Martin Secker, 1924), p. 160; Philip J. Deloria, *Playing Indian* (New Haven, CT: Yale University Press, 1998), p. 3.
7. Michael Rogin, *Blackface, White Noise: Jewish Immigrants in the Hollywood Melting Pot* (Berkeley: University of California Press, 1996), pp. 12–13.
8. Leibfried and Lane, p. 48.
9. Brownlow, *Behind the Mask*, p. 341.
10. Carr, p. H3.
11. Ibid.
12. Grace Kingsley, "Anna May Wong Goes to Europe for UFA," *Los Angeles Times* (March 17, 1928), p. 1.

CHAPTER 15. WEIMAR BERLIN

1. Peter Gay, *Weimar Culture: The Outsider as Insider* (New York: W. W. Norton, 2001), p. xiv; David Clay Large, *Berlin: A Modern History* (New York: Basic Books, 2000), pp. 6, 157.
2. Quoted in Large, p. 211.
3. Detlev J. K. Peukert, *The Weimar Republic: The Crisis of Classical Modernity*, trans. Richard Deveson (New York: Hill and Wang, 1992), p. 178.
4. Christopher Isherwood, *Christopher and His Kind, 1929–1939* (New York: Farrar, Straus and Giroux, 2015), pp. 2, 3, 29.
5. Stefan Zweig, *The World of Yesterday*, trans. Anthea Bell (Lincoln: University of Nebraska Press, 2013), p. 338.
6. Stephen Spender, *The Temple* (New York: Grove Press, 1988), p. 185.
7. Walter Benjamin, "Gespräch mit Anne May Wong," *Die Literarische Welt* (July 6, 1928), p. 213. Unless otherwise indicated, all quotes from German texts were translated by Wendy Xiaoxue Sun specifically for this book. I also wish to thank Marjorie Perloff for her help with the translations from German.
8. Thomas Saunders, *Hollywood in Berlin: American Cinema and Weimar Germany* (Berkeley: University of California Press, 1994), p. 89.
9. Large, p. 197.
10. Tim Bergfelder, "Negotiating Exoticism: Hollywood, Film Europe and the Cultural Reception of Anna May Wong," in *"Film Europe" and "Film America": Cinema, Commerce and Cultural Exchange 1920–1939*, ed. Andrew Higson and Richard Maltby (Devon, UK: University of Exeter Press, 1999), pp. 307–8.
11. Erich Gutinger, "A Sketch of the Chinese Community in Germany: Past and Present," in *The Chinese in Europe*, ed. Gregor Benton and Frank Pieke (New York: St. Martin's Press, 1998), p. 201; Dagmar Yu-Dembski, "Cosmopolitan Lifestyles and 'Yellow Quarters': Traces of Chinese Life in Germany, 1921–1941," in *Chinatown in a Transnational World: Myths and Realities of an Urban Phenomenon*, ed. Vanessa Künnemann and Ruth Mayer (New York: Routledge, 2011), pp. 65–67.

12. For a humorous autobiographical account of Billy Wilder as a hired dancer at Hotel Eden, see Noah Isenberg, ed., *Billy Wilder on Assignment*, trans. Shelley Frisch (Princeton, NJ: Princeton University Press, 2021), pp. 23–42.

13. Large, p. 190.

14. Joseph Roth, *What I Saw: Reports from Berlin 1920–1933*, trans. Michael Hofmann (New York: W. W. Norton, 2003), p. 157.

15. Ibid., p. 86.

16. Gay, p. 128.

CHAPTER 16. "ORIENTALLY YOURS"

1. Anna May Wong, "I Am Very Happy," *Mein Film* 123 (1928), p. 6.

2. Gongzhen Ge, "Anna May Wong Missing Homeland," *Life Weekly* 4 (1928–1929), p. 258.

3. Bergfelder, "Negotiating Exoticism," pp. 308–9.

4. Cynthia Walk, "Anna May Wong and Weimar Cinema: Orientalism in Postcolonial Germany," in *Beyond Alterity: German Encounters with Modern East Asia*, ed. Qinna Shen and Martin Rosenstock (New York: Berghahn Books, 2014), p. 141.

5. Ibid., p. 143.

6. Lim, p. 37.

7. Ernst Jaeger, "FilmKritik," *Film-Kurier* (August 21, 1928). It may be worth noting that some scholars have made an interesting mistake transcribing/translating a key word in Jaeger's review. The original German sentence reads, "*Anna May Wong, die östliche hat lang genug in den exotischen Gärten Kaliforniens gefilmt.*" Unfortunately, the word *exotischen* (exotic) was rendered as "erotic" in some previous studies (see Hodges, p. 84; Lim, p. 50).

8. Quoted in Bergfelder, "Negotiating Exoticism," p. 310.

9. *The Bioscope* (September 19, 1928); *New York Times* (September 22, 1928); *Variety* (January 1, 1929).

10. Carr, p. H3.

11. *Close Up* 3:6 (December 1928), p. 9.

CHAPTER 17. CONVERSATION WITH AMW

1. Walter Benjamin, *Selected Writings*, vol. 3, 1935–1938, ed. Michael W. Jennings, trans. Edmund Jephcott et al. (Cambridge: Harvard University Press, 2002), pp. 104–5.

2. Benjamin, "Gespräch mit Anne May Wong"; John Scott, "European Bouquets Get Notice: Chinese Flapper Crashes Continent Before Finding Recognition Here," *Los Angeles Times* (August 23, 1931), p. 2.

3. Walter Benjamin, *One-Way Street*, trans. Edmund Jephcott (Cambridge: Harvard University, Press, 2016), p. 21.

4. Walter Benjamin, *Moscow Diary*, ed. Gary Smith, trans. Richard Sieburth (Cambridge: Harvard University Press, 1986), p. 34.

5. Benjamin, *One-Way Street*, pp. 447–48.

6. Benjamin, "Gespräch mit Anne May Wong"; Lim, p. 39.

7. Kakuzo Okakura, *The Book of Tea* (1906; Boston: Shambhala, 2001), p. 27.

8. Benjamin, "Gespräch mit Anne May Wong."

9. Benjamin, *One-Way Street*, p. 52.

10. Benjamin, "Gespräch mit Anne May Wong." For previous studies of this rare rendezvous between Walter Benjamin and Anna May Wong, as well as varying English renditions of the German text, see Hodges, pp. 77–79; Lim, pp. 39–50.

11. *Die Literarische Welt* (*The Literary World*) was one of the leading journals with a circulation of about thirty thousand among the cultural elites in Germany in the interwar years: Momme Brodersen, *Walter Benjamin: A Biography*, trans. Malcolm R. Green and Ingrida Ligers, ed. Martina

Dervis (New York: Verso, 1997), p. 159. It is worth noting that, in 2009, Chinese American artist Patty Chang made a two-channel video installation, titled *The Product of Love—Die Waren der Liebe*, about the meeting between Wong and Benjamin. The first video alternates among three people, each individually translating Benjamin's German essay into English, illuminating the ease with which mistranslation occurs in Benjamin's "reading" of Wong. "On the other screen, two Chinese actors portray Benjamin and Wong's meeting as an imaginary, intimate encounter. The installation restages and recontextualizes this meeting as a porno in China with Chinese television actors—a reversal of sorts, turning a Chinoiserie into a Western" (Exhibition Brochure, Mary Boone Gallery, New York, 2009).

12. Okakura, p. 14.

CHAPTER 18. THE VAMP

1. *Film-Kurier* (April 11, 1929), quoted in Bergfelder, "Negotiating Exoticism," p. 311.

2. *Sozialistische Bildung* (May 1929), quoted in Walk, p. 147.

3. *Variety* (May 8, 1929); *The Bioscope* (December 18, 1929).

4. Hodges, p. 79.

5. Charles Baudelaire, *The Parisian Prowler*, trans. Edward K. Kaplan (Athens: University of Georgia Press, 1997), back cover.

6. Peukert, p. 96; Anton Kaes et al., eds., *The Weimar Republic Sourcebook* (Berkeley: University of California Press, 1995), pp. 195, 206–7.

7. Peukert, p. 99.

8. Patrice Petro, ed., *Idols of Modernity: Movie Stars of the 1920s* (New Brunswick, NJ: Rutgers University Press, 2010), pp. 270–71.

9. Karin Wieland, *Dietrich and Riefenstahl: Hollywood, Berlin, and a Century in Two Lives*, trans. Shelley Frisch (New York: Liveright, 2015), p. 113.

10. Hodges, pp. 86–87.

CHAPTER 19. PICCADILLY

1. G. C. Lawrence, ed., *The British Empire Exhibition 1924 Official Guide* (London: Fleetway Press, 1924), p. 79.

2. Anne Witchard, *Lao She in London* (Hong Kong: Hong Kong University Press, 2012), pp. 60–61.

3. Mary De Rachewiltz et al., eds., *Ezra Pound to His Parents: Letters 1895–1929* (Oxford: Oxford University Press, 2011), p. 317.

4. Virginia Woolf, *To the Lighthouse* (New York: Harcourt Brace Jovanovich, 1989), p. 17.

5. *China Express and Telegraph* (January 15, 1925).

6. *China Express and Telegraph* (January 29, October 15, and October 29, 1925); Witchard, p. 107; Sarah Cheang, "Dragons in the Drawing Room: Chinese Embroideries in British Homes, 1860–1949," *Textile History* 39:2 (2008), pp. 223–49.

7. Witchard, p. 109; Xiao Qian, *Traveller without a Map* (London: Hutchinson, 1990), p. 75.

8. Ruth Vasey, *The World According to Hollywood, 1918–1939* (Madison: University of Wisconsin Press, 1997), pp. 40–42. According to the 1927 law, a minimum of 7.5 percent of all films distributed and 5 percent of all films exhibited in the year 1928 had to be made in the UK. These percentages were to rise by increments of 2.5 percent until they both reached 20 percent in 1936. See also Sklar, *Movie-Made America*, p. 220.

9. John McCrae, "In Flanders Fields," https://www.poetryfoundation.org/poems/47380/in-flanders-fields.

10. For an excellent analysis of the aesthetics and politics of Anna May Wong's wardrobe in *Piccadilly*, see Anne Anlin Cheng, *Ornamentalism* (New York: Oxford University Press, 2019), pp. 66–73. See also A. Chan, pp. 216–18.

11. Cheng, p. 67.

12. Witchard, p. 95.

13. Audrey Rivers, "Anna May Wong Sorry She Cannot Be Kissed," *Movie Classics* (November 1939): p. 39.

14. Edgar Morin, *The Stars*, trans. Richard Howard (New York: Grove Press, 1960), p. 179.

15. *The Bioscope* (February 6, 1929); *Close Up* 5:1 (July 1929); *Variety* (July 24, 1929); Marjory Collier, "The Chinese Girl: East Meets West in Anna May Wong," *The Picturegoer* (May 1930), p. 27.

CHAPTER 20. THE CIRCLE OF CHALK

1. In the Old Testament, there is a similar story about King Solomon's wisdom. Facing two women making claims on a child, Solomon ordered that the child be sliced into two parts, with each woman receiving half. The real mother begged the king for compassion: "O my lord, give her the living child, and by no means kill him!" But the other woman said, "Let him be neither mine nor yours, but divide him." So the king gave the first woman her child back (Kings 3:16–28).

2. Basil Dean, *Mind's Eye: An Autobiography, 1927–1972* (London: Hutchinson, 1973), p. 67.

3. Ibid., p. 65.

4. Ibid., p. 66.

5. James Laver, *The Circle of Chalk: A Play in Five Acts Adapted from the Chinese by Klabund* (London: William Heinemann, 1929), pp. 4, 6, 69, 103.

6. Bertrand Russell, *The Problem of China* (New York: Routledge, 2021), pp. 4–7.

7. Neil Okrent, "Right Place, Wong Time," *Los Angeles Magazine* (May 25, 1990), p. 84.

8. Victoria Sherrow, *Encyclopedia of Hair: A Cultural History* (Westport, CT: Greenwood Press, 2006), pp. 47–48.

9. A. Chan, p. 56.

10. Sydney W. Carroll, "A Star of Film and Drama: Anna May Wong," *South China Morning Post* (April 15, 1929), p. 9.

11. Thomas Kiernan, *Sir Larry: The Life of Laurence Olivier* (New York: Times Books, 1981), p. 61.

12. Quoted in Barrie Roberts, "Anna May Wong: Daughter of the Orient," *Classic Images* 270 (December 1997), p. 21.

13. Quoted in Anthony Holden, *Olivier* (London: Weidenfeld and Nicolson, 1998), p. 53.

14. Dean, pp. 67–68.

15. *Los Angeles Examiner* (August 12, 1934).

16. Roberts, p. 21.

CHAPTER 21. THE FIRST WORD

1. *Time* (October 1, 1934); Judy Chu, "Anna May Wong," in *Counterpoint: Perspectives on Asian America*, ed. Emma Gee (Los Angeles: Asian American Center, 1976), p. 286.

2. Henry James, *The Question of Our Speech* (Boston: Houghton Mifflin, 1905), p. 42.

3. Rose Eichenbaum, *The Directors Within: Storytellers of Stage and Screen* (Middletown, CT: Wesleyan University Press, 2014), p. 6.

4. Sternberg, p. 32.

5. Sklar, *Movie-Made America*, p. 154.

6. Wieland, p. 162.

7. Sklar, *Movie-Made America*, p. 176.

8. Anna May Wong, "Mein erstes Wort im Sprechfilm" (My First Word in a Sound Film), *Mein Film* (July 22, 1930).

9. Scott, p. 2.

10. *Lichtbildbühne* (February 28, 1930); *Film-Kurier* (February 27, 1930).

11. *The Bioscope* (March 12, 1930); *New York Times* (November 3, 1930); *Variety* (November 5, 1930).

12. *Hebdo-Cinéma* (October 4, 1930); *Cinémonde* (September 18, 1930); *New York Times* (April 12, 1931).

13. Hodges, p. 99.

14. *Screenplay Secrets* (October 1931); Hodges, pp. 108–9.

CHAPTER 22. ON THE SPOT

1. "Anna May Wong, Combination of East and West," *New York Herald Tribune* (November 9, 1930), p. G5.

2. J. P. O'Malley, "Edgar Wallace, Literary Mercenary," *The American Conservative* 15:1 (2016), p. 51.

3. Margaret Lane, *Edgar Wallace: The Biography of a Phenomenon* (London: Hamish Hamilton, 1938), pp. 269–70.

4. "Anna May Wong, Combination of East and West," p. G5.

5. "All for Mr. Wallace," *New York Times* (November 16, 1930), p. 3.

6. "Anna May Wong, Combination of East and West," p. G5.

7. Edgar Wallace, *On the Spot* (Middlesex, UK: Echo Library, 2006), p. 2.

8. In *On the Spot*, Edgar Wallace mistakenly described Minn Lee as a graduate of Columbia University, unaware that women in those years would graduate from Barnard College, not Columbia.

9. Brooks Atkinson, "Presenting Edgar Wallace," *New York Times* (October 30, 1930), p. 7.

10. "Anna May Wong, Combination of East and West," p. G5.

11. "Injuries Fatal to Mrs. Wong: Mother of Oriental Film Actress Dies Following Auto Accident," *Los Angeles Times* (November 12, 1930), p. 5; Steven J. Dubner, "The Perfect Crime," *Freakonomics Radio Podcast* (May 1, 2014), https://freakonomics.com/podcast/the-perfect-crime-2/.

CHAPTER 23. DAUGHTER OF THE DRAGON

1. Hodges, p. 113.

2. Sax Rohmer, *The Insidious Dr. Fu-Manchu* (San Jose, CA: New Millennium Library, 2001), p. 13.

3. Cay Van Ash and Elizabeth Sax Rohmer, *Master of Villainy: A Biography of Sax Rohmer* (Bowling Green, OH: Bowling Green University Press, 1972), pp. 72–73.

4. Huang, *Charlie Chan*, pp. 146–60.

5. Sax Rohmer, *The Daughter of Fu Manchu* (New York: Zebra Books, 1986), pp. 241, 148, 60, 143.

6. Richard Corliss, "That Old Feeling: Anna May Win," *Time* (February 3, 2005), http://content.time.com/time/arts/article/0,8599,1024222,00.html.

7. Hodges, p. 114.

8. *New York Times* (August 22, 1931); *Variety* (August 25, 1931).

9. "Dragon Lady," *Urban Dictionary*, https://www.urbandictionary.com/define.php?term=dragon%20lady.

10. Eugene Franklin Wong, *On Visual Media Racism: Asians in the American Motion Pictures* (New York: Arno Press, 1978), p. 15.

11. Louise Leung, "East Meets West," *Hollywood Magazine* (January 1938), p. 55.

12. Sheridan Prasso, *The Asian Mystique: Dragon Ladies, Geisha Girls, and Our Fantasies of the Exotic Orient* (New York: Public Affairs, 2005), p. 9.

13. Rudolf Arnheim, *Film as Art* (Berkeley: University of California Press, 1964), p. 11.

14. Miriam Hansen, introduction to Kracauer, *Theory of Film*, p. viii.

15. Yiman Wang, "The Art of Screen Passing: Anna May Wong's Yellow Yellowface Performance in the Art Deco Era," *Camera Obscura* 20:3 (2005), pp. 167–69.

16. Ibid., pp. 160–61.

17. Ken Hanke, *Charlie Chan at the Movies: History, Filmography, and Criticism* (Jefferson, NC: McFarland and Company, 1989), p. 45.

18. Donald Bogle, *Toms, Coons, Mulattoes, Mammies, and Bucks: An Interpretive History of Blacks in American Films* (New York: Continuum, 1996), pp. 35–36.

19. Wang, p. 176.

CHAPTER 24. SHANGHAI EXPRESS

1. Anna May Wong, "Manchuria," *Beverly Hills Script* 5:153 (January 16, 1932), pp. 6–7.

2. Sternberg, p. 49.

3. Gay, p. 102.

4. Joan Didion, *Slouching Towards Bethlehem: Essays* (New York: Farrar, Straus and Giroux, 1968), p. 3.

5. Sternberg, p. 262.

6. Maria Riva, *Marlene Dietrich* (New York: Ballantine Books, 1992), p. 125.

7. "Even Chinese Think Oland Is Oriental," *Seattle Post-Intelligencer* (February 10, 1932), p. 5.

8. "Carlton Theatre, Shanghai Express," *London Times* (March 18, 1932), p. 2.

9. Riva, p. 127.

10. Wollstein, p. 253.

11. Donald Spoto, *Blue Angel: The Life of Marlene Dietrich* (New York: Doubleday, 1992), p. 39.

12. Michael Blowen, "Hollywood Hotline," *Boston Globe* (September 28, 1990).

13. Riva, p. 127.

14. Ibid., p. 128.

15. Nora M. Alter, "The Legs of Marlene Dietrich," in *Dietrich Icon*, ed. Gerd Gemünden and Mary R. Desjardins (Durham, NC: Duke University Press, 2007), p. 60.

16. *Vanity Fair* (March 1932).

17. Sternberg, p. 263.

18. Ironically, in the recent Netflix miniseries *Hollywood* (2020), the self-aggrandizing Tinseltown rewrote history by having Anna May Wong, played by Taiwan-born Michelle Krusiec, win an Oscar for Best Supporting Actress.

CHAPTER 25. TO BE KISSED, OR NOT

1. Sklar, *Movie-Made America*, pp. 161–62.

2. Arthur Conan Doyle, *Sherlock Holmes: The Complete Novels and Stories* (New York: Bantam, 2003), p. 37.

3. A. Chan, p. 242.

4. Wong, "Bamboo, or China's Conversion to Film."

5. "Wong's Beauty Talk to Draw Record Crowd," *San Francisco Chronicle* (October 2, 1931), p. 13.

6. "Chinese Star Advises Care in Makeup," *San Francisco Chronicle* (October 13, 1931), p. 15; A. Chan, p. 74.

7. *New York Times* (September 22, 1934); *Film Daily* (September 22, 1934); *Motion Picture Exhibitor* (October 1, 1934); *The Times* (London) (August 20, 1934), p. 12.

8. "British Film Success in New York," *The Times* (London) (September 25, 1934), p. 4.

9. Hodges, p. 144.

CHAPTER 26. NOT SO GOOD EARTH

1. Sternberg, p. 62, 102.

2. A. Chan, p. 75; Hodges, p. 140.

3. "Music Hall Marks," *Liverpool Evening Echo* (January 30, 1934).

4. Tim Bergfelder et al., *Film Architecture and the Transnational Imagination: Set Design in 1930s European Cinema* (Amsterdam: Amsterdam University Press, 2007), p. 193.

5. Alan Schroeder and Heather Lehr Wagner, *Josephine Baker: Entertainer* (New York: Chelsea House Publications, 2006), pp. 51–52.

6. "China Rises Out of Hollywood," *Picturegoer Supplement* (December 18, 1937).

7. Quoted in Dong, p. 69.

8. Erich Schwartzel, *Red Carpet: Hollywood, China, and the Global Battle for Cultural Supremacy* (New York: Penguin, 2022), pp. xiii, 6.

9. *Beverly Hills Script* (July 13, 1935), p. 21.

10. Quoted in Dong, pp. 78–79.

11. See Anna May Wong, letter to Carl Van Vechten and Fania Marinoff, December 16, 1935, Beinecke Library, Yale University; cited hereafter as CVV.

12. Ray Coll, "Anna May Scorns Minor Role: Chinese Star Leaves Hollywood Flat," *Honolulu Advertiser* (January 30, 1936), p. 3.

13. Victor Jew, "Metro Goldwyn Mayer and Glorious Descendant" (paper presented to 2003 meeting of American Historical Association). Quoted in Hodges, p. 154.

14. Dong, p. 73.

15. "Wrecking Crews Begin Clearing Depot Site," *Los Angeles Times* (December 23, 1933), p. 2.

16. *Los Angeles Examiner* (March 8, 1936).

17. Carolyn Anspacher, "Star Goes 'Home': Anna May Wong Leaves for China," *San Francisco Chronicle* (January 24, 1936), p. 17.

Chapter 27. Transpacific Interlude

1. Anna May Wong, "Anna May Wong Tells of Voyage on 1st Trip to China," *New York Herald Tribune* (May 17, 1936), p. B1.

2. Ibid.

3. Anspacher, p. 17.

4. "Newsmen, Photographers Rush on Hoover to See Noted Film Star," *The China Press* (February 12, 1936), p. 5.

5. Wong, "Anna May Wong Tells of Voyage," p. B6.

6. Ibid.

7. Melville, p. 483.

8. Wong, "Anna May Wong Tells of Voyage," p. B6.

9. Anna May Wong, "Anna May Wong Relates Arrival in Japan, Her First Sight of the Orient," *New York Herald Tribune* (May 24, 1936), p. B1.

10. Ibid.

11. Ibid.

12. Ibid.

13. Ibid., pp. B1–B2.

14. Ibid., p. B2.

15. Ibid.

16. Ibid.; Anna May Wong, "Anna May Wong 'Amazed' at Chinese Appetite," *New York Herald Tribune* (June 7, 1936), p. B2.

17. Wong, "Anna May Wong Relates Arrival in Japan," p. B1.

18. Anna May Wong, "Anna May Wong Recalls Shanghai's Enthusiastic Reception," *New York Herald Tribune* (May 31, 1936), p. B2.

19. Ibid., pp. B2, B6.

Chapter 28. Shanghai

1. Louis L'Amour, *Yondering: Stories* (New York: Bantam Books, 2018), p. 111.

2. L'Amour, p. 115; Harriet Sergeant, *Shanghai* (London: Trafalgar Square, 2002), p. 9.

3. J. G. Ballard, *A User's Guide to the Millennium* (New York: HarperCollins, 1996), pp. 286–87.

Ballard, a famous British writer, was born in Shanghai in 1930 and lived there with his family till the end of World War II. For a detailed account of his childhood in Shanghai, a fascinating experience that might have molded the imagination of the future master of dystopian fiction, see Ballard's memoir, *Miracle of Life: Shanghai to Shepperton, an Autobiography* (New York: Liveright, 2008).

4. Edgar Snow, *Journey to the Beginning* (New York: Random House, 1958), p. 16.

5. W. H. Auden and Christopher Isherwood, *Journey to a War* (London: Faber and Faber, 1939), pp. 227–28.

6. Wong, "Anna May Wong Recalls Shanghai's Enthusiastic Reception," p. B6.

7. "Mob Meets Chinese Film Star at Shanghai," *South China Morning Post* (February 17, 1936), p. 11; "Many Friends Greet Anna May Wong," *The China Press* (February 12, 1936), pp. 1, 12.

8. "Many Friends Greet Anna May Wong," p. 1.

9. "Mob Meets Chinese Film Star at Shanghai," p. 11; "Many Friends Greet Anna May Wong," p. 1.

10. Wong, "Anna May Wong Recalls Shanghai's Enthusiastic Reception," p. B6.

11. Anna May Wong, CVV, February 22, 1936.

12. Hui-lan Koo, *An Autobiography as Told to Mary Van Rensselaer Thayer* (New York: Dial Press, 1943), p. 258.

13. Wong, "Anna May Wong Recalls Shanghai's Enthusiastic Reception," p. B6.

14. Ibid.

15. Ibid.

16. Koo, pp. 255–56.

17. Andrew David Field, "Freddy Kaufmann, Shanghai Club Impresario and Master of the Cathay Hotel Tower Club 1935–1938," http://shanghaisojourns.net/shanghais-dancing-world/2018/10/10/freddy-kaufmann-shanghai-club-impresario-and-master-of-the-cathay-hotel-tower-club-1935-1938.

18. Pat Patterson, "The Dawn Patrol," *The China Press* (March 30, 1936).

19. Ken Cuthbertson, *Nobody Said Not to Go: The Life, Loves, and Adventures of Emily Hahn* (Boston: Faber and Faber, 1998), p. 132.

20. Wong, "Anna May Wong Recalls Shanghai's Enthusiastic Reception," p. B6.

CHAPTER 29. CHINESE ALICE IN SHANGHAI'LAND

1. Wong, "Anna May Wong 'Amazed' at Chinese Appetite," p. B2.

2. Koo, p. 265.

3. Ibid., p. 266; Wong, "Anna May Wong 'Amazed' at Chinese Appetite," p. B2.

4. Koo, p. 260.

5. Yu Dafu, "Malady of Spring Nights," trans. Yunte Huang and Glenn Mott, in Yunte Huang, ed., *The Big Red Book of Modern Chinese Literature: Writings from the Mainland in the Long Twentieth Century* (New York: W. W. Norton, 2016), p. 60.

6. Koo, p. 263.

7. Wong, "Anna May Wong 'Amazed' at Chinese Appetite," p. B2.

8. Ibid.

9. Charles Dickens, *American Notes for General Circulation*, ed. John S. Whitley and Arnold Goldman (New York: Penguin, 1972), p. 145.

10. Wong, "Anna May Wong 'Amazed' at Chinese Appetite," p. B2.

11. Ibid.

12. Susan Blumberg-Kason, "Ballet in the City: Jewish Contributions to the Performing Arts in 1930s Shanghai," *Los Angeles Review of Books* (September 18, 2021), https://lareviewofbooks.org/article/ballet-in-the-city-jewish-contributions-to-the-performing-arts-in-1930s-shanghai; Cuthbertson, p. 134; Susan Blumberg-Kason, "The Movie Star and Madame Salon: The Friendship of Anna May Wong and Bernardine Szold Fritz," *Ms. Magazine* (March 3, 2022), https://msmagazine.com/2022/03/03/anna-may-wong-asian-women-history-bernardine-szold-fritz.

13. Ned Kelly, "Emily Hahn: The American Writer Who Shocked '30s Shanghai," *That's Mags* (January 28, 2020), https://www.thatsmags.com/shanghai/post/28822/emily-hahn-the-american-writer-who-shocked-30s-shanghai.

14. Emily Hahn, "The Big Smoke," *The New Yorker* (February 15, 1969), https://www.newyorker.com/magazine/1969/02/15/the-big-smoke.

15. Cuthbertson, pp. 147–49.

16. Emily Hahn, *China to Me: A Partial Autobiography* (New York: Doubleday, Doran and Company, 1944), p. 1.

17. Ibid., p. 37.

18. "Columbia Country Club," *Historic Shanghai*, https://www.historic-shanghai.com/columbia-country-club/.

19. James Carter, *Champions Day: The End of Old Shanghai* (New York: W. W. Norton, 2020), p. 133.

20. Hahn, *China to Me*, p. 37.

CHAPTER 30. FRAGRANT HARBOR

1. Kamiyama Sojin, *The Unpainted Faces of Hollywood* (Tokyo: Jitsugyo no Nihonsha, 1930), pp. 60–61; Hodges, p. 65.

2. "Anna May Wong: Expresses View on Modern Chinese Women," *South China Morning Post* (February 27, 1926), p. 7.

3. "Anna May Wong: Severely Criticized by the Chinese Press," *South China Morning Post* (February 28, 1936), p. 8.

4. "Anna May Wong: Expresses View on Modern Chinese Woman," p. 7; "Anna May Wong: Severely Criticized by the Chinese Press," p. 8.

5. "Styles of Actress Are Noted Here," *The China Press* (February 26, 1936), p. 11; "Among Anna May Wong's Dresses," *The China Press* (March 8, 1936), p. 11.

6. "Taishan Folks Refused to Let Anna May Wong Go Home," *Entertainment Weekly* (March 2, 1936), p. 218.

7. "Anna May to Be Entertained Tonight," *The Hong Kong Telegraph* (February 25, 1936); "Obituary," *Ta Kung Pao* (September 15, 1982).

8. Matthew Polly, *Bruce Lee: A Life* (New York: Simon and Schuster, 2018).

9. Hahn, *China to Me*, p. 37.

10. "Anna May Wong Visited Sir Robert Ho-tung Yesterday," *Tianguang Newspaper* (February 27, 1936).

11. Frank Welsh, *A History of Hong Kong* (London: HarperCollins, 1997), p. 385.

12. Chris Wood, "'Never Thought It Could Be as Cold as This in Hong Kong': Charlie Chaplin on 1936 Visit," *South China Morning Post* (March 8, 2018).

13. Anna May Wong, CVV, March 14, 1936.

14. "Anna May Wong Feted in South," *The China Press* (March 17, 1936), p. 1; "Miss Anna May Back," *North China Herald* (April 1, 1936), p. 9.

15. "Anna May Wong Passed through Hong Kong on Her Way to Canton Yesterday," *Hong Kong Industry and Commerce Daily* (March 10, 1936), p. 1.

16. Hodges, pp. 8–9.

17. Lim, p. 170; Hodges, p. 169.

18. Leung, p. 40.

19. Huang, *Charlie Chan*, p. 252.

20. "Anna May Wong and Charlie Chan (Warner Oland)," *Manhuajie* 2 (1936), p. 34; translation mine.

21. "Anna May Gives a Farewell Tea Party," *South China Morning Post* (March 24, 1936), p. 7.

CHAPTER 31. CHINESE GESTURES

1. "Anna May Wong Slipped into City" and "Japanese Forces Will Fire Blank Ammunition," *The China Press* (March 27, 1936), p. 1.

2. Barbara W. Tuchman, *Stilwell and the American Experience in China, 1911–1945* (New York: Macmillan, 1970), pp. 136–37.

3. *The China Press* (April 5, 1936), p. 4.

4. "Anna May Wong Will Study Mandarin Here," *The China Press* (March 28, 1936), p. 1.

5. "Actress Plans Production of Historical Play," *The China Press* (May 9, 1936), p. 1.

6. Bertolt Brecht, *Brecht on Theatre: The Development of an Aesthetic*, ed. and trans. John Willett (New York: Hill and Wang, 1964), pp. 91–95.

7. Ibid., p. 95.

8. Jay Leyda, *Dianying: An Account of Films and the Film Audience in China* (Cambridge: MIT Press, 1972), p. 1.

9. Mark Cousins, "The Asian Aesthetic," *Prospect Magazine* (November 21, 2004), https://www.prospectmagazine.co.uk/magazine/theasianaesthetic.

10. Lily Xiao Hong Lee et al., eds., *Biographical Dictionary of Chinese Women* (London: M. E. Sharpe, 2003), pp. 236–40.

11. Hu Die, *Recollections of Hu Die*, ed. Liu Huiqin (Taipei, Taiwan: Lianhe Press, 1987), p. 181; translation mine.

12. "Anna May Wong Visits Star Company," *Screen and Stage News* 2:17 (1936), p. 7; "Butterfly Wu Accompanying Anna May Wong on Tour of Star Film Company," *Tianguang Newspaper* (May 7, 1936), p. 2.

13. "Anna May Wong Quits Smoking," *Entertainment Biweekly* 2:11 (1936), p. 218; "Anna May Wong's Pet Peeves," *Linglong* 1:12 (1931), p. 424; "Should We Welcome Anna May Wong?" *Modern Films* 5 (1936), p. 2; "Shameless Anna May Wong Should Be Executed," *Camera* 53 (1932), p. 2.

14. "Anna May Wong Plans Sneak Departure to Avoid Crowds," *The China Press* (February 19, 1936), p. 1.

15. Leung, p. 55.

16. "Anna May Wong Was 'Resurrected,'" *Tianguang Newspaper* (May 22, 1936), p. 2.

CHAPTER 32. THE DUST OF THE EARTH

1. Sternberg, pp. 263–64; George N. Kates, *The Years That Were Fat: Peking, 1933–1940* (New York: Harper and Brothers, 1952), p. 1.

2. "Anna May Wong Given Big Peiping Welcome," *The China Press* (May 17, 1936), p. 1.

3. Lin Yutang, *Imperial Peking: Seven Centuries of China* (New York: Crown Publishers, 1961), pp. 12–13; Harold Acton, *Peonies and Ponies* (Hong Kong: Oxford University Press, 1983), p. 1.

4. Tuchman, pp. 148–49.

5. "$1,800,000 Lost in Six Days from Smuggling into Tientsin," *The China Press* (May 17, 1936), p. 1.

6. Tuchman, p. 149.

7. Ibid., p. 155.

8. Paul French, *Destination Peking* (Hong Kong: Blacksmith Books, 2021), pp. 22–23.

9. Ibid., p. 30.

10. Leung, p. 40.

11. Robert Sklar, "Mr. Smith Goes to Washington" (2002), https://www.loc.gov/static/programs/national-film-preservation-board/documents/mr_smith.pdf.

12. "Anna May Wong Bows Repeatedly," *Entertainment Biweekly* 2:21 (1936), p. 416.

13. Blumberg-Kason, "The Movie Star and Madame Salon."

14. French, *Destination Peking*, pp. 76, 79; Edmund Backhouse, *Décadence Mandchoue: The China Memoirs of Sir Edmund Trelawny Backhouse*, ed. Derek Sandhaus (Hong Kong: Earnshaw Books, 2011), back cover.

15. French, *Destination Peking*, p. 35. In July 1937, at the age of twenty-eight, Parsons died of Hodgkin's lymphoma in Switzerland.

16. Alfred Emile Cornebise, *Soldier Extraordinaire: The Life and Career of Brig. Gen. Frank "Pinkie" Dorn (1901–81)* (Fort Leavenworth, KS: Combat Studies Institute Press, 2019), p. 47.

17. Zheng Hanli, "Anna May Wong Returns to Shanghai from Peiping," *Wanying* 3 (1936), p. 24; Blumberg-Kason, "The Movie Star and Madame Salon."

18. Cornebise, p. 43.

19. L. C. Arlington and William Lewisohn, *In Search of Old Peking* (1935; New York: Paragon Book Reprint Corp., 1967), p. 141. See also French, *Destination Peking*, pp. 28–29.

20. Arlington and Lewisohn, p. 230; Cornebise, p. 46.

21. Cornebise, p. 47.

22. John P. Marquand, *Thank You, Mr. Moto* (1936; Boston: Little, Brown, 1985), pp. 136–37.

23. "An Interview with Anna May Wong Before Departure for England," *Entertainment Biweekly* 2:35 (1936), p. 696; Zheng, p. 24; "Anna May Sees Infinite Possibilities for China Movies," *The China Press* (September 17, 1936), p. 1.

CHAPTER 33. AT THE PALACE OF THE DRAGON LADY

1. "An Interview with Anna May Wong Before Departure for England," p. 696.

2. Zheng, p. 24; "An Interview with Anna May Wong Before Departure for England," p. 696; "Anna May Sees Infinite Possibilities for China Movies," p. 1.

3. "An Interview with Anna May Wong Before Departure for England," p. 696; "Anna May Wong Goes Chinese," *The Hong Kong Telegraph* (August 13, 1936), p. 3.

4. Lao She, *Rickshaw*, trans. Jean M. James (Honolulu: University of Hawaii Press, 1979), p. 173; "Updates on Anna May Wong"; Hodges, p. 173.

5. "Anna May Wong Drew Lots in Tientsin," *Entertainment Biweekly* 2:31 (1936), p. 618.

6. "Anna May Wong Goes Chinese," p. 3.

7. "Anna May Wong to Reflect on China Under U.S. Palm," *The China Press* (October 9, 1936), p. 3.

CHAPTER 34. THESE FOOLISH THINGS

1. Paramount Press Clippings, Academy of Motion Pictures, Arts, and Sciences, Los Angeles.

2. Madeline Yuan-yin Hsu, *Dreaming of Gold, Dreaming of Home: Transnationalism and Migration Between the United States and South China, 1882–1943* (Stanford, CA: Stanford University Press, 2000), p. 75.

3. Dhruti Bhagat, "How Long Have We Loved Pandas?" Boston Public Library Blogs, September 2, 2020, https://www.bpl.org/blogs/post/how-long-have-we-loved-pandas.

4. Hannah Pakula, *The Last Empress: Madame Chiang Kai-shek and the Birth of Modern China* (New York: Simon & Schuster, 2009), p. 22. Even though Angel Island did not officially become a detaining station until 1910, incarcerating Chinese immigrants in waterfront cell blocks started as soon as the Chinese Exclusion Act was passed in 1882.

5. Hodges, p. 176.

6. A. Chan, p. 76.

7. David Amoruso, "How the Chicago Outfit Made Its Hollywood Dreams Come True," *Gangsters Inc.* (November 30, 2010), https://gangstersinc.org/profiles/blogs/how-the-chicago-outfit-made.

8. "Police Guard Film Figures: Mutilation Threatened Anna May Wong," *Daily Boston Globe* (March 25, 1937), p. 32; "Chinese Film Star: Anna May Wong Threatened with Disfigurement," *South China Morning Post* (March 26, 1937), p. 15; "Threat Sent to Producer, Screen Star," *Hartford Courant* (March 25, 1937), p. 9.

9. "Anna May Wong Again Target of Threat Letter," *Los Angeles Times* (April 3, 1937); Hodges, pp. 179–80.

10. "Anna May Wong's 'Boy Friend' Is a 6-Foot 4-Inch Police Guard," *Hartford Courant* (April 18, 1937), p. A6.

11. Eric Maschwitz, *No Chip on My Shoulder* (London: Herbert Jenkins, 1957), pp. 59–60.

12. Ibid., pp. 87–88.

13. Anna May Wong, CVV, June 19, 1937.

14. Maschwitz, pp. 103–4.

15. Ibid., pp. 105, 112, 115; Val Gielgud, *Years of the Locust* (London: Nicholson and Watson, 1947), pp. 152–57.

16. Maschwitz, p. 117.

17. Maschwitz wrote the song under his pseudonym, Holt Marvell. Hermione Gingold, *How to Grow Old Disgracefully* (New York: St. Martin's Press, 1989), p. 54.

CHAPTER 35. DAUGHTER OF SHANGHAI

1. Tuchman, pp. 164–65.

2. Paul French, *Bloody Saturday: Shanghai's Darkest Day* (Beijing: Penguin, 2017), p. 37.

3. "Anna May Wong: Sister Remains at Work in Shanghai," *South China Morning Post* (September 12, 1937), p. 6.

4. Anna May Wong, CVV, January 3, 1938.

5. Mayme Peak, "Bombs Rain on Shanghai: Anna May Wong Plays On," *Daily Boston Globe* (October 10, 1937), p. B6.

6. *New York Times* (December 25, 1937); *Motion Picture Exhibitor* (January 1, 1938).

7. Hye Seung Chung, *Hollywood Asian: Philip Ahn and the Politics of Cross-Ethnic Performance* (Philadelphia: Temple University Press, 2006), pp. 76–77; Liu, p. 31; Hodges, p. 185.

8. Chung, p. 76.

9. Madsen, pp. x–xi.

10. Riva, pp. 433–34; Spoto, p. 142; Madsen, p. 25.

11. Patricia White, "Black and White: Mercedes de Acosta's Glorious Enthusiasms," *Camera Obscura* 45 (2001), pp. 228–29.

12. Edward White, *The Tastemaker: Carl Van Vechten and the Birth of Modern America* (New York: Farrar, Straus and Giroux, 2014), p. 261; James Smalls, "Van Vechten's Secret," *The Gay and Lesbian Review Worldwide* 13:3 (2006), p. 25.

13. "Anna May Wong's Sister Arrives Home from Shell-Torn Shanghai," *Los Angeles Times* (November 18, 1937), p. 1.

14. "Anna May Wong to Aid Fund," *New York Herald Tribune* (June 22, 1938), p. 8.

15. Tsui, p. 116.

16. Ibid., p. 117.

17. Cho, pp. 55–56, 63.

18. "Chinese Hold Moon Festival," *Los Angeles Times* (October 9, 1938), p. A16.

19. William Gow, "A Night in Old Chinatown: American Orientalism, China Relief Fundraising, and the 1938 Moon Festival in Los Angeles," *Pacific Historical Review* 87:3 (2018), pp. 439–72.

20. "Colorful Moon Festival," *Federation News* (November 1938).

21. Wong, "The True Life Story."

CHAPTER 36. YOUR NAME IN CHINESE

1. Emily Dickinson, letter to Abiah Root, September 8, 1846, in Emily Fragos, ed. *Emily Dickinson: Letters* (New York: Everyman's Library, 2011), p. 19.

2. Tuchman, pp. 214–15.

3. "Anna May Wong Aid Sale Sponsor," *Los Angeles Times* (January 21, 1940), p. 3; "America and China Called Last of World's Democracies," *Los Angeles Times* (May 25, 1940), p. 1; George Atcheson Jr., "The Chargé in China (Atcheson) to the Secretary of State," *Foreign Relations of the United States: Diplomatic Papers*, 893.20/792, No. 1583, September 17, 1943, https://history.state.gov/historicaldocuments/frus1943China/d101.

4. "China Relief Show Given: Anna May Wong Directs Oriental Talent on War Benefit," *Los Angeles Times* (June 28, 1941), p. 1.

5. See the correspondence between Anna May Wong and Richard Walsh, dated February 23 and March 2, 1938, now in the John Day Company Archive at the Princeton University Libraries.

6. Derham Groves, *Anna May Wong's Lucky Shoes: 1939 Australia Through the Eyes of an Art Deco Diva* (Ames, IA: Culicidae Press, 2011), pp. 11–15; "Gardening and Cooking: Chinese Star's Hobbies," *Sydney Morning Herald* (June 5, 1939), p. 4; Lim, p. 193.

7. Mae Ngai, *The Chinese Question: The Gold Rush and Global Politics* (New York: W. W. Norton, 2021).

8. Hodges, p. 193.

9. *New York Times* (March 12, 1938); *Motion Picture Exhibitor* (March 1, 1938).

10. *Variety* (March 22, 1939).

11. *New York Times* (August 17, 1939); *Variety* (August 23, 1939).

12. Lim, p. 184.

13. Groves, pp. 15–16; "Bright Show at Tivoli: Anna May Wong," *The Argus* (June 13, 1939), p. 12.

14. Groves, pp. 17–18.

15. "Chinese Film Star at Ball," *Sydney Morning Herald* (August 9, 1939), p. 6.

16. "Anna May Wong Returns from Tour," *Los Angeles Times* (September 5, 1939), p. 1.

CHAPTER 37. GODDESS OF MERCY

1. Tuchman, p. 203.

2. Franklin D. Roosevelt, "Fireside Chat," https://www.presidency.ucsb.edu/documents/fireside-chat-9.

3. Kevin Starr, *Embattled Dreams: California in War and Peace, 1940–1950* (New York: Oxford University Press, 2002), pp. 27–28, 34.

4. "Gardening and Cooking: Chinese Star's Hobbies," *Sydney Morning Herald* (June 5, 1939), p. 4; Wang Yun, "Anna May Wong in America," *Pacific Weekly* 1:46 (1942), p. 855.

5. Patti Gully, *Sisters of Heaven: China's Barnstorming Aviatrixes* (San Francisco: Long River Press, 2008), pp. 62–63.

6. Anna May Wong, CVV, May 9, 1940.

7. "Mary Wong Hangs Self: Sister of Anna May Wong Ends Life in California," *New York Times* (July 26, 1940), p. 36. The article listed her age as twenty-six, but, according to the 1940 US Census, Mary was thirty at the time of her death.

8. Mike Moffitt, "Tora! Tora! Tora! Over SF: When Imperial Japan 'Attacked' the City," *SFGate* (December 7, 2016), https://www.sfgate.com/bayarea/article/Tora-Tora-Tora-over-SF-When-Japanese-10652456.php.

9. Starr, *Embattled Dreams*, p. 63.

10. "Summary Removal of Japs Demanded," *Los Angeles Times* (February 25, 1942).

11. "How to Tell Japs from the Chinese," *Life* (December 22, 1941), pp. 81–82.

12. Jeremy Chan, "Chinese American Responses to the Japanese American Internment and Incarceration," *Hastings Race and Poverty Law Journal* 16:2 (2019), pp. 212–14; Gary T. Ono,

"Japanese American Fortune Cookie: A Taste of Fame or Fortune," *Discover Nikkei* (November 1, 2007), http://www.discovernikkei.org/en/journal/2007/11/1/fortune-cookie/.

13. Slide, p. 195; Greg Robinson, "Otto and Iris Yamaoka: Asian Actors in 1930s Hollywood," *Discover Nikkei* (April 17, 2022), http://www.discovernikkei.org/en/journal/2022/4/17/otto-and-iris-yamaoka-1/.

14. "Yuki Shimoda Does an Imitation," *Online Archive of California*, https://oac.cdlib.org/ark:/13030/ft2t1nb12j/.

15. Starr, *Embattled Dreams*, p. 162.

16. Paramount Press Clippings, Academy of Motion Pictures, Arts, and Sciences, Los Angeles; "Anna May Wong Reports First Runs Really Are, in Alaska," *Los Angeles Times* (July 25, 1944), p. 8.

17. Brian Taves, "Joseph H. Lewis, Anna May Wong, and *Bombs over Burma*," in Gary D. Rhodes, ed., *The Films of Joseph H. Lewis* (Detroit: Wayne State University Press, 2012), p. 120.

18. Rhodes, pp. 1–8.

19. Taves, p. 129.

20. "Thrillers Share Bill," *Los Angeles Times* (July 10, 1942), p. 17; *Variety* (August 19, 1942); *New York Times* (August 10, 1942).

21. *Harrison's Reports* (December 5, 1942); *Variety* (January 20, 1943); "Signs New Contract," *New York Times* (March 13, 1942), p. 22.

22. Nathan Masters, "The Shadow of War: Southern California's WWII Dimout Restrictions," USC Libraries, April 2, 2020, https://libraries.usc.edu/article/shadow-war-southern-californias-wwii-dimout-restrictions.

23. "Anna May Wong Adds Work of Air-Raid Warden to Duties," *Los Angeles Times* (December 8, 1942), p. 13.

CHAPTER 38. WILL THE REAL LADY FROM CHUNGKING PLEASE STAND UP?

1. Starr, *Embattled Dreams*, p. 162.

2. Pakula, p. 320; "Almond-Eyed Cleopatra Is 'Power Behind Power' in War-Time China," *Cincinnati Times-Star* (April 29, 1938); Theodore H. White and Annalee Jacoby, *In Search of History* (New York: Harper & Row, 1978), p. 143.

3. Gardner Cowles, *Mike Looks Back* (New York: Gardner Cowles, 1985), p. 89; Pakula, pp. 410–11.

4. Laura Tyson Li, *Madame Chiang Kai-shek: China's Eternal First Lady* (New York: Atlantic Monthly Press, 2006), pp. 194–95; Pakula, 415–16.

5. Grace Tully, *F.D.R., My Boss* (New York: Charles Scribner's Sons, 1949), p. 331; Pakula, pp. 425, 427.

6. Eleanor Roosevelt, *This I Remember* (New York: Harper & Brothers, 1949), p. 282.

7. Paluka, pp. 418–21; Li, pp. 201–2; Leong, p. 149; *New York Herald Tribune, Washington Post,* and *Los Angeles Examiner* (February 19, 1943).

8. John Jung, *Southern Fried Rice: Life in a Chinese Laundry in the Deep South* (Las Vegas, NV: Yin & Yang Press, 2016), pp. 33, 132–34, 240; *Macon [GA] Daily Telegraph* (September 22, 1910), p. 12; Leong, p. 110. "Heathen Chinee" had become a racial slur against the Chinese since the publication of the poem "The Heathen Chinee" by Bret Harte in 1870.

9. "Mme. Chiang Stirs Throng at Bowl," *Los Angeles Daily News* (April 5, 1943), pp. 2, 5, 7; Leong, pp. 141–42.

10. Hedda Hopper, "Miss Bergman Again!," *Washington Post* (April 28, 1943), p. 16.

11. Anna May Wong, CVV, March 17, 1944.

12. Anna May Wong, CVV, May 22, 1944.

13. *Milady's Style Parade and Recipe Book for 1935* (publisher unknown, 1935). See also "Anna May

Wong's Tea Cakes," *Hollywood Kitchen* (July 26, 2021), https://www.hollywoodkitchenshow
.com/post/anna-may-wong-s-tea-cakes.

14. Anna May Wong, "Foreword," in Fred Wing and Mabel Stegner, *New Chinese Recipes* (New York: Edelmuth Company, 1942), p. 1.

15. Hodges, p. 203.

16. Wong, "Foreword," pp. 1–2; "Gardening and Cooking: Chinese Star's Hobbies," p. 4.

17. Wong, "Foreword," p. 2.

18. Clementine Paddleford, "Chinese Suggest Recipes for Meat Economy," *New York Herald Tribune* (September 3, 1942), p. 10.

19. Mayukh Sen, *Taste Makers: Seven Immigrant Women Who Revolutionized Food in America* (New York: W. W. Norton, 2022), pp. 10–17.

20. Frank Dorn, *A General's Diary of Treasured Recipes* (Chicago: Henry Regnery Company, 1953).

CHAPTER 39. THE BIG NOWHERE

1. Starr, *Embattled Dreams*, p. 213.

2. Anna May Wong, CVV, January 6, 1945.

3. Alice Tildesley, "Why Waste Your Time?" *Seattle Daily Times* (April 9, 1939), p. 9.

4. Jeanine Basinger, *The Star Machine* (New York: Knopf, 2007), p. 320.

5. Vicki Woods, "Meryl Streep: Force of Nature," *Vogue* (December 12, 2011), https://www
.vogue.com/article/meryl-streep-force-of-nature.

6. Anne E. Lincoln and Michael Patrick Allen, "Double Jeopardy in Hollywood: Age and Gender in the Careers of Film Actors, 1926–1999," *Sociological Forum* 19:4 (2004), p. 614.

7. Robert K. Fleck and F. Andrew Hanssen, "Persistence and Change in Age-Specific Gender Gaps: Hollywood Actors from the Silent Era Onward," *SSRN* (January 22, 2020), https://
papers.ssrn.com/sol3/papers.cfm?abstract_id=2169573; Linda Outcalt, "Overview on Gender Bias and Age Discrimination in Hollywood," https://onlineacademiccommunity.uvic.ca/
outcaltl/statistics-overview-on-gender-bias-and-age-discrimination-in-hollywood/.

8. Basinger, p. 320.

9. Sam Kashner and Jennifer MacNair, *The Bad and the Beautiful: Hollywood in the Fifties* (New York: W. W. Norton, 2002), p. 256.

10. Abi Aherne, "'Sunset Boulevard' and the Ageing Woman: Sexism and Ageism in Hollywood," *Screen Queens* (June 4, 2020), https://screen-queens.com/2020/06/04/sunset-boulevard-and
-the-ageing-woman-sexism-and-ageism-in-hollywood.

11. Kashner and MacNair, pp. 15, 337–38.

12. Tricia Welsh, *Gloria Swanson: Ready for Her Close-Up* (Jackson: University Press of Mississippi, 2013), p. 299.

13. Ross Macdonald, *The Moving Target* (New York: Vintage Crime, 1998), p. 41.

14. Leibfried and Lane, p. 141.

15. *Harrison's Reports* (March 19, 1949); *New York Times* (March 21, 1949).

16. Sklar, *Movie-Made America*, pp. 269–79.

17. Samuel Goldwyn, "Hollywood in the Television Age," *Hollywood Quarterly* 4 (Winter 1949), p. 146.

18. Anna May Wong, CVV, December 31, 1951.

19. Conrad Doerr, "Anna May Wong," *Films in Review* (December 1968), p. 661.

20. Leibfried and Lane, p. 163.

21. *Variety* (August 29, 1951).

22. Anna May Wong, CVV, October 3, 1952.

23. Quoted in Hodges, p. 217.

24. Sternberg, p. 62.

25. Anna May Wong, CVV, December 28, 1953; "Anna May Wong in Hospital," *New York Times* (December 12, 1953).

CHAPTER 40. READY FOR CLOSE-UP

1. Mitchell Stephens, "History of Television," https://stephens.hosting.nyu.edu/History%20 of%20Television%20page.html#:~:text=The%20number%20of%20television%20 sets,all%20U.S.%20homes%20had%20one.
2. Doerr, p. 661.
3. Todd James Pierce, "Disney and the Rose Parade—1955," *Disney History Institute*, http:// www.disneyhistoryinstitute.com/2015/12/disney-and-the-rose-parade-1955.html.
4. Hodges, p. 221.
5. *The New York World-Telegram* (October 16, 1956).
6. Lim, p. 201.
7. Robert Creeley, *The Collected Poems of Robert Creeley, 1945–1975* (Berkeley: University of California Press, 1982), p. 132.
8. "Brentwood Living: Steve's Eye View," *The Brentwood Citizen* (July 31, 1958).
9. Doerr, p. 662.
10. See, p. 198.
11. Ibid., pp. 215, 284.
12. Myrna Oliver, "The Rev. Sue Sikking; Founder of Unity by the Sea Church," *Los Angeles Times* (June 22, 1992).
13. *Variety* (June 8, 1960).
14. Doerr, p. 662; Fred Watkins, "Sessue Hayakawa Today," *Films in Review* (June–July, 1966), p. 392.
15. *Time* (February 10, 1961); *New York Times* (February 4, 1961), p. 19; *Los Angeles Times* (February 4, 1961), p. 3.
16. *South China Sunday Post* (February 5, 1961), p. 9; *Dagongbao* (February 5, 1961), p. 1; *Industrial and Commerce Evening Post* (February 5, 1961), p. 1.

EPILOGUE: ANNA MAY WONG ON THE MONEY

1. Evelyn Waugh, *The Loved One: An Anglo-American Tragedy* (New York: Little, Brown, 1948); Gielgud, p. 154.
2. "Rosedale—The Opening of a New Cemetery in This City," *Los Angeles Times* (November 20, 1884); Allan R. Ellenberger, *Celebrities in Los Angeles Cemeteries: A Directory* (Jefferson, NC: McFarland and Company, 2001), p. 192.
3. Macdonald, p. 44.
4. https://walkoffame.com/lucy-liu.

SELECTED ANNA MAY WONG FILMOGRAPHY

The Red Lantern (Metro Pictures, 1919)

Outside the Law (Universal Pictures, 1920)

Dinty (Associated First National Pictures, 1920)

Bits of Life (Marshall Neilan Productions, 1921)

The Toll of the Sea (Metro Pictures, 1922)

Drifting (Universal, 1923)

The Thief of Bagdad (United Artists, 1924)

The Alaskan (Paramount, 1924)

Peter Pan (Paramount, 1924)

Forty Winks (Paramount, 1925)

Mr. Wu (MGM, 1927)

Old San Francisco (Warner Bros., 1927)

The Chinese Parrot (Universal, 1927)

Streets of Shanghai (Tiffany-Stahl, 1927)

Across to Singapore (MGM, 1928)

Song (aka *Show Life*; *Wasted Love*; German-British International, 1928)

Pavement Butterfly (aka *Großstadtschmetterling*; British International, 1929)

Piccadilly (British International, 1929)

Hai-Tang (British International, 1930)

Daughter of the Dragon (Paramount, 1931)

Shanghai Express (Paramount, 1932)

A Study in Scarlet (KBS Productions, 1933)

Tiger Bay (Wyndham, 1934)

Chu Chin Chow (Gaumont–British, 1934)

Java Head (ATP, 1934)

Daughter of Shanghai (Paramount, 1938)

Dangerous to Know (Paramount, 1938)

When Were You Born? (Warner Bros., 1938)

King of Chinatown (Paramount, 1939)

Island of Lost Men (Paramount, 1939)

Bombs over Burma (PRC, 1942)

Lady from Chungking (PRC, 1942)

Impact (United Artists, 1949)

Portrait in Black (Universal, 1960)

Selected Bibliography

ACTON, HAROLD. *Peonies and Ponies*. Hong Kong: Oxford University Press, 1983.

ARLINGTON, L. C., and William Lewisohn. *In Search of Old Peking*. New York: Paragon Book Reprint Corp., 1967.

ARNHEIM, RUDOLF. *Film as Art*. Berkeley: University of California Press, 1964.

AUDEN, W. H., and Christopher Isherwood. *Journey to a War*. London: Faber and Faber, 1939.

BACKHOUSE, EDMUND. *Décadence Mandchoue: The China Memoirs of Sir Edmund Trelawny Backhouse*, ed. Derek Sandhaus. Hong Kong: Earnshaw Books, 2011.

BALLARD, J. G. *A User's Guide to the Millennium*. New York: HarperCollins, 1996.

BAUDELAIRE, CHARLES. *The Parisian Prowler*, trans. Edward K. Kaplan. Athens: University of Georgia Press, 1997.

BAXTER, JOHN. *Von Sternberg*. Lexington: University Press of Kentucky, 2010.

BENJAMIN, WALTER. "Gespräch mit Anne May Wong," *Die Literarische Welt* (July 6, 1928).

——. *Moscow Diary*, ed. Gary Smith, trans. Richard Sieburth. Cambridge: Harvard University Press, 1986.

——. *One-Way Street*, trans. Edmund Jephcott. Cambridge: Harvard University Press, 2016.

——. *Selected Writings*, vol. 3, 1935–1938, ed. Michael W. Jennings, trans. Edmund Jephcott et al. Cambridge: Harvard University Press, 2002.

BERGFELDER, TIM. "Negotiating Exoticism: Hollywood, Film Europe and the Cultural Reception of Anna May Wong," in *"Film Europe" and "Film America": Cinema, Commerce and Cultural Exchange 1920–1939*, ed. Andrew Higson and Richard Maltby. Devon, UK: University of Exeter Press, 1999.

—— ET AL. *Film Architecture and the Transnational Imagination: Set Design in 1930s European Cinema*. Amsterdam: Amsterdam University Press, 2007.

BLUMBERG-KASON, SUSAN. "Ballet in the City: Jewish Contributions to the Performing Arts in 1930s Shanghai," *Los Angeles Review of Books* (September 18, 2021), https://lareviewofbooks.org/article/ballet-in-the-city-jewish -contributions-to-the-performing-arts-in-1930s-shanghai.

——. "The Movie Star and Madame Salon: The Friendship of Anna May Wong and Bernardine Szold Fritz," *Ms. Magazine* (March 3, 2022), https:// msmagazine.com/2022/03/03/anna-may-wong-asian-women-history -bernardine-szold-fritz.

Bogle, Donald. *Toms, Coons, Mulattoes, Mammies, and Bucks: An Interpretive History of Blacks in American Films*. New York: Continuum, 1996.

Brecht, Bertolt. *Brecht on Theatre: The Development of an Aesthetic*, ed. and trans. John Willett. New York: Hill and Wang, 1964.

Brodersen, Momme. *Walter Benjamin: A Biography*, trans. Malcolm R. Green and Ingrida Ligers, ed. Martina Dervis. New York: Verso, 1997.

Brownlow, Kevin. *Behind the Mask of Innocence*. Berkeley: University of California Press, 1990.

———. *The Parade's Gone By. . . .* Berkeley: University of California Press, 1968.

Carter, James. *Champions Day: The End of Old Shanghai*. New York: W. W. Norton, 2020.

Chan, Anthony. *Perpetually Cool: The Many Lives of Anna May Wong, 1905–1961*. Lanham, MD: Scarecrow Press, 2003.

Cheng, Anne Anlin. *Ornamentalism*. New York: Oxford University Press, 2019.

Cho, Jenny, and the Chinese Historical Society of Southern California. *Chinese in Hollywood*. Charleston, SC: Arcadia Publishing, 2013.

Chu, Judy. "Anna May Wong," in *Counterpoint: Perspectives on Asian America*, ed. Emma Gee. Los Angeles: Asian American Center, 1976.

Cornebise, Alfred Emile. *Soldier Extraordinaire: The Life and Career of Brig. Gen. Frank "Pinkie" Dorn (1901–81)*. Fort Leavenworth, KS: Combat Studies Institute Press, 2019.

Creeley, Robert. *The Collected Poems of Robert Creeley, 1945–1975*. Berkeley: University of California Press, 1982.

Cuthbertson, Ken. *Nobody Said Not to Go: The Life, Loves, and Adventures of Emily Hahn*. Boston: Faber and Faber, 1998.

Daniels, Roger. *Asian America: Chinese and Japanese in the United States since 1850*. Seattle: University of Washington Press, 1988.

Dean, Basil. *Mind's Eye: An Autobiography, 1927–1972*. London: Hutchinson, 1973.

Deloria, Philip J. *Playing Indian*. New Haven, CT: Yale University Press, 1998.

Dickens, Charles. *American Notes for General Circulation*, ed. John S. Whitley and Arnold Goldman. New York: Penguin, 1972.

Didion, Joan. *Slouching Towards Bethlehem: Essays*. New York: Farrar, Straus and Giroux, 1968.

Doerr, Conrad. "Anna May Wong," *Films in Review* (December 1968).

Dong, Arthur. *Hollywood Chinese: The Chinese in American Feature Films*. Santa Monica, CA: Angel City Press, 2019.

Dorn, Frank. *A General's Diary of Treasured Recipes*. Chicago: Henry Regnery Company, 1953.

Ellroy, James. *The Big Nowhere*. New York: Mysterious Press, 1988.

Fitzgerald, F. Scott. *The Great Gatsby*. New York: Charles Scribner's Sons, 1925.

FRAGOS, EMILY, ed. *Emily Dickinson: Letters*. New York: Everyman's Library, 2011.

FRENCH, PAUL. *Bloody Saturday: Shanghai's Darkest Day*. Beijing: Penguin, 2017.

———. *Destination Peking*. Hong Kong: Blacksmith Books, 2021.

GAY, PETER. *Weimar Culture: The Outsider as Insider*. New York: W. W. Norton, 2001.

GIELGUD, VAL. *Years of the Locust*. London: Nicholson and Watson, 1947.

GINGOLD, HERMIONE. *How to Grow Old Disgracefully*. New York: St. Martin's Press, 1989.

GOW, WILLIAM. "A Night in Old Chinatown: American Orientalism, China Relief Fundraising, and the 1938 Moon Festival in Los Angeles," *Pacific Historical Review* 87:3 (2018), pp. 439–72.

GREENWOOD, ROBERTA S. *Down by the Station: Los Angeles Chinatown, 1880–1933*. Los Angeles: Cotsen Institute of Archaeology Press, 1996.

GROVES, DERHAM. *Anna May Wong's Lucky Shoes: 1939 Australia Through the Eyes of an Art Deco Diva*. Ames, IA: Culicidae Press, 2011.

GUTINGER, ERICH. "A Sketch of the Chinese Community in Germany: Past and Present," in *The Chinese in Europe*, ed. Gregor Benton and Frank Pieke. New York: St. Martin's Press, 1998.

HAENNI, SABINE. "Filming 'Chinatown': Fake Visions, Bodily Transformations," in *Screening Asian Americans*, ed. Peter X. Feng. New Brunswick, NJ: Rutgers University Press, 2002.

HAHN, EMILY. *China to Me: A Partial Autobiography*. New York: Doubleday, Doran and Company, 1944.

HANKE, KEN. *Charlie Chan at the Movies: History, Filmography, and Criticism*. Jefferson, NC: McFarland and Company, 1989.

HANSEN, MIRIAM. *Babel and Babylon: Spectatorship in American Silent Film*. Cambridge: Harvard University Press, 1991.

HIGHAM, JOHN. *Strangers in the Land: Patterns of American Nativism, 1860–1925*. New York: Atheneum, 1955.

HODGES, GRAHAM RUSSELL GAO. *Anna May Wong: From Laundryman's Daughter to Hollywood Legend*. New York: Palgrave Macmillan, 2004.

HU, DIE. *Recollections of Hu Die*, ed. Liu Huiqin. Taipei, Taiwan: Lianhe Press, 1987.

HUANG, YUNTE. *Charlie Chan: The Untold Story of the Honorable Detective and His Rendezvous with American History*. New York: W. W. Norton, 2010.

———. *Inseparable: The Original Siamese Twins and Their Rendezvous with American History*. New York: Liveright, 2018.

———, ed. *The Big Red Book of Modern Chinese Literature: Writings from the Mainland in the Long Twentieth Century*. New York: W. W. Norton, 2016.

ISENBERG, NOAH. *Billy Wilder on Assignment*, trans. Shelley Frisch. Princeton, NJ: Princeton University Press, 2021.

ISHERWOOD, CHRISTOPHER. *Christopher and His Kind, 1929–1939*. New York: Farrar, Straus and Giroux, 2015.

JUNG, JOHN. *Chinese Laundries: Tickets to Survival on Gold Mountain*. Las Vegas, NV: Yin & Yang Press, 2007.

———. *Southern Fried Rice: Life in a Chinese Laundry in the Deep South*. Las Vegas, NV: Yin & Yang Press, 2016.

KAES, ANTON, et al., eds. *The Weimar Republic Sourcebook*. Berkeley: University of California Press, 1995.

KATES, GEORGE N. *The Years That Were Fat: Peking, 1933–1940*. New York: Harper and Brothers, 1952.

KOO, HUI-LAN. *An Autobiography as Told to Mary Van Rensselaer Thayer*. New York: Dial Press, 1943.

KRACAUER, SIEGFRIED. *Theory of Film: The Redemption of Physical Reality*. Princeton, NJ: Princeton University Press, 1960.

KWAN, MOON. *An Anecdotal History of the Chinese Cinema (Zhongguo yintan waishi)*. Hong Kong: Guangjiaojing Press, 1976.

L'AMOUR, LOUIS. *Yondering: Stories*. New York: Bantam Books, 2018.

LAMBERT, GAVIN. *Nazimova: A Biography*. Lexington: University Press of Kentucky, 2021.

LANE, MARGARET. *Edgar Wallace: The Biography of a Phenomenon*. London: Hamish Hamilton, 1938.

LAO, SHE. *Rickshaw*, trans. Jean M. James. Honolulu: University of Hawaii Press, 1979.

LARGE, DAVID CLAY. *Berlin: A Modern History*. New York: Basic Books, 2000.

LAVER, JAMES. *The Circle of Chalk: A Play in Five Acts Adapted from the Chinese by Klabund*. London: William Heinemann, 1929.

LAWRENCE, D. H. *Studies in Classic American Literature*. London: Martin Secker, 1924.

LEE, ERIKA. *The Making of Asian America: A History*. New York: Simon & Schuster, 2015.

LEIBFRIED, PHILIP, AND CHEI MI LANE. *Anna May Wong: A Complete Guide to Her Film, Stage, Radio, and Television Work*. Jefferson, NC: McFarland and Company, 2004.

LEONG, KAREN J. *The China Mystique: Pearl S. Buck, Anna May Wong, Mayling Soong, and the Transformation of American Orientalism*. Berkeley: University of California Press, 2005.

LEYDA, JAY. *Dianying: An Account of Films and the Film Audience in China*. Cambridge: MIT Press, 1972.

LIM, SHIRLEY JENNIFER. *Anna May Wong: Performing the Modern*. Philadelphia: Temple University Press, 2019.

LIN, YUTANG. *Imperial Peking: Seven Centuries of China*. New York: Crown Publishers, 1961.

LOEWEN, JAMES W. *The Mississippi Chinese: Between Black and White*. Prospect Heights, IL: Waveland Press, 1988.

LOU, RAYMOND. "The Chinese American Community of Los Angeles, 1870–1900: A Case of Resistance, Organization, and Participation." PhD dissertation, University of California, Irvine, 1982.

LOW, VICTOR. *The Unimpressible Race: A Century of Educational Struggle by the Chinese in San Francisco*. San Francisco: East/West Publishing Company, 1982.

MACDONALD, ROSS. *The Moving Target*. New York: Vintage Crime, 1998.

MADSEN, AXEL. *The Sewing Circle: Hollywood's Greatest Secret—Female Stars Who Loved Other Women*. New York: Open Road, 1995.

MARCHETTI, GINA. *Romance and the "Yellow Peril": Race, Sex, and Discourse Strategies in Hollywood Fiction*. Berkeley: University of California Press, 1993.

MARQUAND, JOHN P. *Thank You, Mr. Moto*. Boston: Little, Brown, 1985.

MASCHWITZ, ERIC. *No Chip on My Shoulder*. London: Herbert Jenkins, 1957.

MCDONALD, PAUL. *The Star System: Hollywood's Production of Popular Identities*. London: Wallflower Press, 2000.

MCWILLIAMS, CAREY. *Southern California: An Island on the Land*. Salt Lake City, UT: Peregrine Smith Books, 1973.

MELVILLE, HERMAN. *Moby-Dick, or, The Whale*, ed. Harrison Hayford et al. Northwestern-Newberry ed. Evanston, IL: Northwestern University Press and Newberry Library, 1988.

MORIN, EDGAR. *The Stars*, trans. Richard Howard. New York: Grove Press, 1960.

NG, FAE MYENNE. Foreword to Louis Chu, *Eat a Bowl of Tea*. Seattle: University of Washington Press, 2020.

NGAI, MAE. *The Chinese Question: The Gold Rush and Global Politics*. New York: W. W. Norton, 2021.

OKAKURA, KAKUZO. *The Book of Tea*. Boston: Shambhala, 2001.

PENG, XIN. "Color-as-Hue and Color-as-Race: Early Technicolor, Ornamentalism and *The Toll of the Sea* (1922)," *Screen* 62:3 (Autumn 2021).

PETERS, JAMES S. *Sadakichi Hartmann, Alien Son: A Biography*. Santa Fe, NM: Sunstone Press, 2017.

PETRO, PATRICE, ed. *Idols of Modernity: Movie Stars of the 1920s*. New Brunswick, NJ: Rutgers University Press, 2010.

PEUKERT, DETLEV J. K. *The Weimar Republic: The Crisis of Classical Modernity*, trans. Richard Deveson. New York: Hill and Wang, 1992.

PLATH, SYLVIA. *Ariel: The Restored Edition*. New York: Harper Perennial, 2004.

POLLY, MATTHEW. *Bruce Lee: A Life*. New York: Simon and Schuster, 2018.

POUND, EZRA. *The Pisan Cantos*, ed. Richard Sieburth. New York: New Directions, 2003.

PRASSO, SHERIDAN. *The Asian Mystique: Dragon Ladies, Geisha Girls, and Our Fantasies of the Exotic Orient*. New York: Public Affairs, 2005.

PUDOVKIN, V. I. *Film Technique and Film Acting: The Cinema Writings of V. I. Pudovkin*, trans. Ivor Montagu. London: Vision, 1954.

RAINSBERGER, TODD. *James Wong Howe: Cinematographer*. San Diego, CA: A. S. Barnes, 1981.

RIIS, JACOB A. *How the Other Half Lives: Studies Among the Tenements of New York*, ed. Sam Bass Warner Jr. Cambridge: Harvard University Press, 2010.

RIVA, MARIA. *Marlene Dietrich*. New York: Ballantine Books, 1992.

ROBINSON, DAVID. *Hollywood in the Twenties*. New York: A. S. Barnes, 1968.

ROGIN, MICHAEL. *Blackface, White Noise: Jewish Immigrants in the Hollywood Melting Pot*. Berkeley: University of California Press, 1996.

ROHMER, SAX. *The Daughter of Fu Manchu*. New York: Zebra Books, 1986.

——. *The Insidious Dr. Fu-Manchu*. San Jose, CA: New Millennium Library, 2001.

ROTH, JOSEPH. *What I Saw: Reports from Berlin 1920–1933*, trans. Michael Hofmann. New York: W. W. Norton, 2003.

RUSSELL, BERTRAND. *The Problem of China*. New York: Routledge, 2021.

SAUNDERS, THOMAS J. *Hollywood in Berlin: American Cinema and Weimar Germany*. Berkeley: University of California Press, 1994.

SCHWARTZEL, ERICH. *Red Carpet: Hollywood, China, and the Global Battle for Cultural Supremacy*. New York: Penguin Press, 2022.

SEE, LISA. *On Gold Mountain: The One-Hundred-Year Odyssey of My Chinese-American Family*. New York: Vintage Books, 1995.

SEN, MAYUKH. *Taste Makers: Seven Immigrant Women Who Revolutionized Food in America*. New York: W. W. Norton, 2022.

SHERROW, VICTORIA. *Encyclopedia of Hair: A Cultural History*. Westport, CT: Greenwood Press, 2006.

SIU, PAUL C. P. *The Chinese Laundryman: A Study of Social Isolation*, ed. John Kuo Wei Tchen. New York: New York University Press, 1987.

SKLAR, ROBERT. *Movie-Made America: A Cultural History of American Movies*. New York: Vintage, 1994.

SNOW, EDGAR. *Journey to the Beginning*. New York: Random House, 1958.

SOJIN, KAMIYAMA. *The Unpainted Faces of Hollywood*. Tokyo: Jitsugyo no Nihon-sha, 1930.

SPEARS, JACK. *Hollywood: The Golden Era*. New York: Castle Books, 1971.

SPENDER, STEPHEN. *The Temple*. New York: Grove Press, 1988.

SPOTO, DONALD. *Blue Angel: The Life of Marlene Dietrich*. New York: Doubleday, 1992.

STARR, KEVIN. *Embattled Dreams: California in War and Peace, 1940–1950*. New York: Oxford University Press, 2002.

——. *Inventing the Dream: California Through the Progressive Era*. New York: Oxford University Press, 1985.

STEINER, STAN. *Fusang: The Chinese Who Built America*. New York: Harper and Row, 1979.

STERNBERG, JOSEF VON. *Fun in a Chinese Laundry: An Autobiography*. New York: Collier Books, 1965.

TAVES, BRIAN. "Joseph H. Lewis, Anna May Wong, and *Bombs over Burma*," in *The Films of Joseph H. Lewis*, ed. Gary D. Rhodes. Detroit: Wayne State University Press, 2012.

TSUI, BONNIE. *American Chinatown: A People's History of Five Neighborhoods*. New York: Free Press, 2009.

TUCHMAN, BARBARA W. *Stilwell and the American Experience in China, 1911–1945*. New York: Macmillan, 1970.

ULIN, DAVID L., ed. *Writing Los Angeles: A Literary Anthology*. New York: Library of America, 2002.

VASEY, RUTH. *The World According to Hollywood, 1918–1939*. Madison: University of Wisconsin Press, 1997.

WALK, CYNTHIA. "Anna May Wong and Weimar Cinema: Orientalism in Postcolonial Germany," in *Beyond Alterity: German Encounters with Modern East Asia*, ed. Qinna Shen and Martin Rosenstock. New York: Berghahn Books, 2014.

WALLACE, EDGAR. *On the Spot*. Middlesex, UK: Echo Library, 2006.

WANG, YIMAN. "The Art of Screen Passing: Anna May Wong's Yellow Yellowface Performance in the Art Deco Era," *Camera Obscura* 20:3 (2005).

WAUGH, EVELYN. *The Loved One: An Anglo-American Tragedy*. New York: Little, Brown and Company, 1948.

WELSH, FRANK. *A History of Hong Kong*. London: HarperCollins, 1997.

WEST, NATHANAEL. *The Complete Works of Nathanael West*. New York: Farrar, Straus and Giroux, 1957.

WIELAND, KARIN. *Dietrich and Riefenstahl: Hollywood, Berlin, and a Century in Two Lives*, trans. Shelley Frisch. New York: Liveright, 2015.

WINCHESTER, SIMON. *A Crack in the Edge of the World: America and the Great California Earthquake of 1906*. New York: HarperCollins, 2005.

WITCHARD, ANNE. *Lao She in London*. Hong Kong: Hong Kong University Press, 2012.

WOLLSTEIN, HANS J. *Vixens, Floozies and Molls: 28 Actresses of Late 1920s and 1930s Hollywood*. Jefferson, NC: McFarland and Company, 1999.

WONG, ANNA MAY. "Anna May Wong 'Amazed' at Chinese Appetite," *New York Herald Tribune* (June 7, 1936).

———. "Anna May Wong Finds Shanghai Life Glamorous," *New York Herald Tribune* (June 14, 1936).

———. "Anna May Wong Recalls Shanghai's Enthusiastic Reception," *New York Herald Tribune* (May 31, 1936).

———. "Anna May Wong Relates Arrival in Japan, Her First Sight of the Orient," *New York Herald Tribune* (May 24, 1936).

———. "Anna May Wong Tells of Voyage on 1st Trip to China," *New York Herald Tribune* (May 17, 1936).

——. "Bamboo, or China's Conversion to Film," *Mein Film* (June 4, 1930).

——. "Foreword," in Fred Wing and Mabel Stegner, *New Chinese Recipes*. New York: Edelmuth Company, 1942.

——. "I Am Very Happy," *Mein Film* 123 (1928).

——. "Manchuria," *Beverly Hills Script* (January 16, 1932).

——. "Mein erstes Wort im Sprechfilm" (My First Word in a Sound Film), *Mein Film* (July 22, 1930).

——. "The True Life Story of a Chinese Girl," *Pictures* (August 1926).

——. "Wode zishu" (An Autobiography), *Liangyou* 114 (1936).

WONG, EUGENE FRANKLIN. *On Visual Media Racism: Asians in the American Motion Pictures*. New York: Arno Press, 1978.

WOOLF, VIRGINIA. *To the Lighthouse*. New York: Harcourt Brace Jovanovich, 1989.

XIAO, QIAN. *Traveller without a Map*. London: Hutchinson, 1990.

YU, DAFU, "Malady of Spring Nights," in *The Big Red Book of Modern Chinese Literature: Writings from the Mainland in the Long Twentieth Century*, ed. Yunte Huang. New York: Norton, 2016.

YU-DEMBSKI, DAGMAR. "Cosmopolitan Lifestyles and 'Yellow Quarters': Traces of Chinese Life in Germany, 1921–1941," in *Chinatown in a Transnational World: Myths and Realities of an Urban Phenomenon*, ed. Vanessa Künnemann and Ruth Mayer. New York: Routledge, 2011.

ZESCH, SCOTT. *The Chinatown War: Chinese Los Angeles and the Massacre of 1871*. New York: Oxford University Press, 2012.

ZWEIG, STEFAN. *The World of Yesterday*, trans. Anthea Bell. Lincoln: University of Nebraska Press, 2013.

INDEX

Page numbers after 318 refer to endnotes.